HOMOSEXUALITY

For John De Cecco, Noretta Koertge, Fred Suppe

HOMOSEXUALITY

A Philosophical Inquiry

MICHAEL RUSE

Basil Blackwell

Copyright © Michael Ruse 1988

First published 1988

Reprinted 1988

Basil Blackwell Ltd
108 Cowley Road, Oxford OX4 1JF, UK

Basil Blackwell Inc.
432 Park Avenue South, Suite 1503
New York, NY 10016, USA

British Library Cataloguing in Publication Data

Ruse, Michael
    Homosexuality : a philosophical inquiry.
    1. Homosexuality
    I. Title
    306.7'66   HQ76.25

    ISBN 0-631-15275-X

Library of Congress Cataloging in Publication Data

Ruse, Michael.
    Homosexuality : a philosophical inquiry.

    Bibliography: p.
    Includes index.
    1. Homosexuality – Psychological aspects.   I. Title.
HQ76.25.R87   1988   306.7'66   87 – 30924
ISBN 0-631-15275-X

Typeset in 10 on 12 pt Baskerline
by Pioneer Associates, Perthshire
Printed in the USA

Contents

Acknowledgements

In 1979, I participated in a symposium at the annual meeting of the American Association of the Advancement of Science (in Houston, Texas) on the topic of 'Homosexuality and Philosophy'. My fellow symposiasts are the three people to whom I dedicate this book. I doubt they will agree with all I have to say, but I acknowledge them both personally and as symbols of my respect for, and indebtedness to, all who believe that important and sensitive issues must be approached with reason, not emotion. Many other people have given advice and encouragement. These include: Robert Baker, John Bishop, Christopher Boorse, Colin Brewer, Arthur Caplan, Stephan Chambers, Gunter Dörner, Fred Elliston, H. Tristram Engelhardt Jr, David Hull, Alan Miller, Richard Pillard, Lawrence Splitter and Jim Weinrich. I hardly need say that I alone. am responsible for the book's inadequacies.

I am grateful to the following for permission to reproduce figures and tables: *British Journal of Psychiatry* (figure 3.3); Sir Kenneth Dover and Duckworth (figures 8.1, 8.2); Elsevier Science Publishers (figures 5.10, 5.11, 5.12, 7.1, reprinted by permission of the publisher from A. A. Ehrhardt (1977). Prenatal androgenization and human psychosexual behaviour. In J. Money and H. Mustaph (eds), *Handbook of Sociology*, pp. 249, 250, 251. Copyright 1977 by Elsevier Science Publishing Co., Inc. Also for figure 3.4, reprinted by permission of the publisher from K. W. Freund (1974). Male homosexuality: an analysis of the pattern. In J. A. Lorrain (ed.), *Understanding Homosexuality*, p. 48. Copyright 1974 by Elsevier Science Publishing Co., Inc.); Elsevier Science Publishers and Professor Gunter Dörner (figures 5.14, 5.15, 5.16, 5.17, 5.18); The Johns Hopkins University Press (figures 5.7, 5.8, 5.9); The Kinsey Institute (figures 1.1, 1.2, 1.3, from A. Kinsey et al. (1948). *Sexual Behaviour in the*

viii ACKNOWLEDGEMENTS

Human Male, A. Kinsey et al. (1953). *Sexual Behaviour in the Human Female*. Reproduced by permission of the Kinsey Institute for Research in Sex, Gender and Reproduction, Inc.); Little, Brown & Co. Ltd (figures 3.1, 3.2, from W. H. Masters and V. E. Johnson (1966). *Human Sexual Response*. Boston: Little, Brown.); Plenum Publishing Corporation (table 9.3); D. Reidel Publishing Company (figure 7.4 copyright © 1979 by D. Reidel Publishing Company, Dordrecht, Holland); W. B. Saunders Publishing Co. (figure 5.4, from C. D. Turner and J. T. Bagnara (1971). *General Endocrinology*.); *Science* and Dr Brian A. Gladue (figure 5.19 copyright © 1984 by the AAAS); Simon and Schuster Inc. (tables 6.1, 6.2, 9.1, 9.2, from *Homosexualities* copyright © 1978 by Alan P. Bell, Ph.D. and Martin S. Weinberg Ph.D., reprinted by permission of Simon and Schuster, Inc.); Stanford University Press (figure 4.1, reprinted from L. Kohlberg (1966). A cognitive developmental analysis of children's sex-role and attitudes. In Eleanor E. Maccoby (ed.), *The Development of Sex Differences*, with the permission of the publishers, Stanford University Press. © 1966 by the Board of Trustees of the Leland Stanford Junior University); University of Colorado, Boulder (figures 5.1, 5.2, 5.3, from R. Le Baron (1972). *Hormones: A Delicate Balance*); University of Minnesota Press (figure 9.1); John Wiley and Sons Ltd (figures 5.5, 5.6, 5.13, from J. Money and M. Schwartz (1978). Biosocial determinants of gender identity differentiation and development. In J. Hutchinson (ed.), *Biological Determinants of Sexual Behaviour* copyright © 1978 John Wiley and Sons Ltd. Reprinted by permission of John Wiley and Sons Ltd); Williams and Wilkins Co. (table 1.1 copyright © 1973, the Williams and Wilkins Co., Baltimore).

Prologue

Homosexuality — same-gender sex — needs no introduction. From pre-Christian times, it has troubled, terrified — and inspired — the western mind and culture. Sodom and Gomorrah, the Cities of the Plain, were supposedly destroyed because of it; Paul warned the early Christians against it; leading scholars of the Church wrote eloquently opposing it; English kings were assassinated on suspicion of it; and countless common people have been victimized, blackmailed, and persecuted because of it. Yet at the same time it has been the channel for some of humankind's most moving stories of love and affection, and the spark for poetry, painting and sculpture — a fountain of that which we would most readily call good and worthwhile. Some of our greatest civilizations have allowed, even encouraged, an overt homosexual component. One thinks, most obviously, of Ancient Greece.

For various reasons, however, homosexuality seems particularly an obsession of our own age. In major part this is no doubt due to the ideas and influence of Sigmund Freud, which have forced on people's minds both the phenomenon of homosexuality and the possibility (if not need) of interpreting it in terms fundamentally different from those which have been handed down through the ages. But there is more to it than this. Recently the question of homosexuality and of homosexuals has been kept in high profile by homosexuals themselves, as with a new-found confidence they battle for what they believe to be their rights, both to respect as people and to the opportunity to live and work as freely and openly as any other members of society. It hardly needs saying that these moves by homosexuals have met with a strong and sometimes hysterical opposition, amplified in the past few years by dread of a new affliction, AIDS, which strikes right at the heart of the male homosexual segment of society. All suggests that the issue of homosexuality is yet far from resolution.

The time is therefore surely ripe for a detailed *philosophical* analysis — an analysis which tries to go beneath the rhetoric and emotion and to uncover the foundational suppositions which lead people to such different conclusions. This, at least, is the aim of this book. Because one cannot make judgements without knowing the facts, my empirical treatment is comprehensive. Yet I do not aim to write a general survey of the topic of homosexuality — a sort of 'Everything you wanted to know about homosex but were afraid to ask'. Rather, I want to see why it is that people think (and act) as they do on and about the topic.

I believe my inquiry has a special urgency. This is not a book on AIDS. There will be (I trust) an adequate discussion of that topic. But this is a book about human beings, not about microbes. Nevertheless, the spread of AIDS makes urgent a rethinking of homosexuality — indeed, a rethinking of sexuality generally. Some diseases do more than make people sick: they permeate the very roots of a culture. I fear a backlash against homosexuals because of AIDS — because male homosexuals engage sexually in ways that put them especially at risk, and because AIDS is now starting to make its way into the heterosexual segment of the western population. There is a dreadful human propensity for seeking out and persecuting scapegoats, often from conspicuous groups, for our own worries and follies. Before the troubles of this century — defeat in war, inflation, economic depression — it was in Germany that Jews had achieved their highest status.

I hope I exaggerate and that my analogy proves ill-founded. Towards precisely such an end, and before the climate becomes too heated for reason to apply at all, I offer this extended discussion — trying deliberately to be as comprehensive as possible and taking no conclusion as definitive until proven so. But what form should a philosophical analysis take? Roughly speaking (*very* roughly speaking) philosophical inquiry seems to fall into two camps. On the one hand, there are what one might call *epistemological* concerns. People disagree about the nature of, and what they know about, the world, broadly conceived. There are questions about what constitutes good evidence for certain knowledge claims, how far knowledge can go, whether all real existence is of the same nature, and so forth. On the other hand, there are what one might call *ethical* concerns. These involve questions about what we ought and ought not to do. They get us into normative matters, that is, matters to do with human conduct. These two categories are of course not absolutely watertight, but if we use them rather than let them use us, they can be helpful.

I want to suggest that we find both epistemological and ethical questions surrounding the subject of homosexuality. I shall therefore structure this book accordingly, working from the epistemological towards the ethical. First, however, it will be necessary to have some grist for our mill. Therefore, the first chapter of this book will contain a brief exposition of some of the main recent claims about homosexuality — although even here, it will be necessary to go beyond the purely phenomenological towards the theoretical. Next, moving well into the epistemological part of my discussion, I shall consider the various kinds of causal explanation that have been offered for homosexuality. There seem to be three main kinds: psychological (most particularly, the so-called 'psychoanalytic'), biochemical, and genetic. For clarity, with the introduction of each kind of explanation I shall raise pertinent philosophical questions. In concluding this part of the book there will be an attempt to see how the various explanatory models relate to each other.

Where appropriate, either during or at the conclusion of my philosophical analyses, I shall make scientific evaluations of the various putative claims about homosexuality. I hope to present enough material to let the reader make up his/her own mind, but I shall not conceal my own opinions. If it be objected that only a scientist can properly draw conclusions about empirical or causal claims, I would reply that because of the distinctive problems we shall encounter, one is unqualified to draw such conclusions unless one is a philosopher. I would prefer, however, not to see a rigid and competitive distinction between philosopher and scientist, believing instead that each can usefully contribute to the whole. The same holds true when I come to consider claims made by other professionals, like physicians or lawyers.

Following discussion of homosexuality and its variously suggested explanations, I shall start to move towards the side of philosophy more concerned with questions of value. Referring to work both of the past and of the present I shall ask whether, in any proper sense at all, homosexuality can be said to be a morally or otherwise pernicious form of sexual orientation and behaviour. Also, I shall raise and analyse a much discussed question, namely whether in some sense homosexuality can be said to be a sickness or disease. Finally, I shall ask questions about what position society ought to take towards homosexuality. Ought homosexuality be repressed, or ought it be tolerated? And if the latter, ought the rights of homosexuals be enshrined in law, as one might feel ought to be the case for blacks and women?

The programme is before us. Let us turn at once to the task at hand.

1

Words and Facts

My aim in this chapter is to present, in as disinterested a way as possible, some of the basic facts about homosexuality. More precisely, recognizing that there is no such thing as a 'fact' on its own isolated from theory and value, and so appreciating that all may stand in need of revision from later theory, I shall offer information which is about as basic as possible.[1] But before we do get to the facts (or 'facts') there is the matter of language. Philosophers, particularly modern Anglo-Saxon philosophers, sometimes seem obsessed (unhealthily obsessed some would say) with language. And there is some justification for this impression. Yet language is important: needless, time-wasting disputes can occur if one is not careful with it. Hence, I shall open this chapter by introducing and defining some basic terms. (Weinrich 1976 has a useful discussion about language. See also Silverstein and White 1977, and De Cecco and Shively 1984.)

1.1 A working vocabulary

I take it that a *homosexual* is someone, male or female, who is erotically attracted to members of his/her own sex. By 'erotic attraction' I mean (at the very minimum) fantasizing about sexual encounters; one might well feel an attraction towards someone without its being erotic. A *heterosexual* is someone erotically attracted to someone of the sex opposite to his/her own. In biology, a *bisexual* is someone (or something) with functioning sex organs of both sexes; but here unless qualified I shall use the term in the sense common to sexologists, namely as referring to a person erotically attracted (not necessarily simultaneously) to members of both sexes.

Masters and Johnson (1979) prefer to use the term *ambisexual* to refer to such a person, but I rather think of ambisexuality as involving overlap between the sexes. Male and female are ambisexual in having lips as erogenous zones in common. Broader senses of bisexuality which we shall encounter (and distinguish) — either physiological or psychological — simply involve males having 'female' characteristics (of whatever sort), and vice versa. If nipples are distinctively 'female', for example, then in this respect all males are bisexual. Obviously, the conventional biological and sexological senses of 'bisexual' are special cases of these broader notions, if we assume that erotic attractions towards a male are 'female', and vice versa. This is an assumption which will be analysed and evaluated at a later point. .

Strictly speaking one ought to distinguish between a person with homosexual inclinations, or whose *sexual orientation* is homosexual, and a person who participates in homosexual acts. It hardly anticipates the coming discussion too much to allow that a person might be homosexual by inclination but yet behave heterosexually; conversely, a heterosexual person might, for various reasons, behave homosexually. In what follows, however, I shall assume in speaking of a 'homosexual' (or a 'heterosexual') that these are people in whom inclinations and practices coincide. Of course, if necessary I shall separate the two out. A term much favoured by recent writers on homosexuality is that of 'homosexual identity'. I shall defer discussion of this notion until later in the chapter.

Homosexuality, like other aspects of sexuality, attracts a lot of slang — some of it vulgar, much of it demeaning. Two terms which have almost completely passed from slang to regular usage and which are much favoured by homosexuals themselves (particularly males) are *gay* and *straight* to refer to homosexual and heterosexual respectively. There seems no regular term (in English) exclusively denoting male homosexuals, but *lesbian* refers exclusively to female homosexuals. *Homophobia* is a term used to denote hostility towards homosexuals. The converse would seem to be *homophilia*, a kind of attraction towards homosexuality. More commonly seen is the term *homophile*, which is usually used to refer to organizations campaigning for homosexual rights and for the reduction of penalties and prejudice.

Two words which cause frequent misunderstanding are *transvestite* and *transsexual*. A transvestite is someone who dresses in the clothing their culture considers proper to a member of the opposite sex in order to achieve some kind of erotic arousal. The last qualification is most important — if no erotic arousal is intended, the person is better known as a *cross-dresser*. It should be noted that being a transvestite does not have any implications about one's sexual orientation. A man who puts on a bra before he has sex with his wife is a transvestite. Indeed, the evidence is that most transvestites are heterosexual — if anything, to a more extreme degree than usual (Kinsey et al. 1953; Pomeroy 1975; Stoller 1975).

In order to introduce the notion of transsexualism, it is necessary to distinguish the concepts of *sex* and *gender* (Stoller 1968; Green 1974; De Cecco and Shively 1978). Sex refers to whether one is male or female. Most people (indeed all people for most purposes) distinguish sex on the basis of morphological features — physical characteristics of form and structure. Those people with sexual characteristics which are a mixture of male and female are hermaphrodites. Biologists now know that the ultimate causes of sexual characteristics are the genes, to be found on the chromosomes in the nuclei of cells. Males have different sex chromosomes, X and Y, whereas females have similar sex chromosomes, XX. This gives us another criterion for maleness and femaleness. Qualifications and exceptions will be discussed later.

If sex can be regarded as the objective phenomenon, then gender or gender identity can be regarded as more the subjective phenomenon. A person's gender refers to the sex with which one identifies, and to a certain extent the degree to which one wants to carry this through in action. To say that someone has a male or masculine gender is to say that they identify themselves with males, and conversely a female gender involves identification with females. A *transsexual* is someone whose sex and gender are not the same: they have the body of a male, but inwardly identify with females, or vice versa. It may be thought that transsexuality is an extreme form of homosexuality. Transsexuals themselves, however, (and most homosexuals) would deny this strongly. A transsexual male, for instance, would not regard his attraction towards other males as homosexual — rather he regards himself as a woman, attracted towards members of the opposite sex. Conversely a homosexual male might well feel quite satisfied with his own masculinity, and have no desire to change into a woman — 'It's just that I like to go to bed with guys.' Of course, this general statement about the desirability of not confusing homosexuality with transsexuality does not preclude the possibility that on average homosexuals might show more cross-gender characteristics than heterosexuals. (Nor does it preclude the possibility of *our* deciding later to see transsexuality as an extreme form of homosexuality.)

1.2 Basic statistics

Just how prevalent is homosexuality? Nearly forty years since they first appeared, the foundational reports on human sexuality pioneered and directed by Alfred Kinsey are still the authoritative sources (Kinsey et al. 1948; Kinsey et al. 1953). The figures for the human male staggered the 1948 audience when first published. Undoubtedly, they were a major source of the distrust many people felt towards Kinsey's work, although the figures have been confirmed by several surveys since (Ramsay et al. 1974; Whitam 1983).

Drawing on a pool of some 6000 (male) Americans, Kinsey and his co-workers estimated that of the total number of orgasms achieved, 24 per cent came from masturbation and wet dreams, 69.4 per cent from heterosexual contacts, and 6.3 per cent from homosexual contacts. Looking at matters another way, and remembering here that homo-sexuality is being defined as homosexual experience to the point of orgasm, Kinsey found that 37 per cent of the male population after adolescence had had some homosexual contact, that 13 per cent had been more homosexual than heterosexual for at least three years between adolescence and 55, and 4 per cent were exclusively homosexual after adolescence. All told, 50 per cent had had some homosexual dealings, if one includes yearnings (which might not have led to orgasmic activity).

What about women? The most significant finding of the Kinsey study (of 6000 females) was that female homosexuality (homosexual experience, that is, to the point of orgasm) is a lot less common than male homosexuality.

Among the females, the accumulative incidences of homosexual responses had ultimately reached 28 per cent; they had reached 50 per cent in the males. The accumulative incidences of overt contacts to the point of orgasm among the females had reached 13 per cent . . . among the males they had reached 37 per cent. This means that homosexual responses had occurred in about half as many females as males, and contacts which had proceeded to orgasm had occurred in about a third as many females as males. Moreover, compared with the males, there were only about a half to a third as many of the females who were, in any age period, primarily or exclusively homosexual. (Kinsey et al. 1953: 475)

We must forbear detailed theoretical speculation at this point, but no doubt some will argue that this difference between males and females is primarily a function of male oppression — women three decades ago were not given as much choice about sex as men, and hence potential lesbians were herded into heterosexuality. Today, it will be argued, the figures will be more even, as women become more free (and lesbianism will increase even further in the future). Perhaps there is some truth in this rejoinder; however, underlining the difference in rates between male and female homosexuality, we find that an eminent English researcher (working more recently) puts the figure for lesbianism at about the same rate as the Kinsey survey (Kenyon 1974). If nothing else, one obviously must not uncritically run together male and female homosexuality, assuming that they are necessarily of the same kind and have exactly the same causes. Similarities must be proven, not just taken for granted.

It is not enough to talk simply of male and female homosexuality. Some people tend not to be exclusively homosexual or exclusively heterosexual in interests and activity — they are rather what we are calling 'bisexual', in the unqualified sense: the sense of the sexologists (Klein and Wolf 1985). It is to the Kinsey researchers that we owe the now classic scale of degrees of homosexual orientation and commitment. This scale runs evenly from 0 to 6, where 0 is defined as exclusively heterosexual both in action and in thought, and 6 is defined as exclusively homosexual. One suspects that the Kinsey researchers would not have felt the need to set up such a scale were it not for the fact that many people fall between its end points, a fact which their findings strongly confirmed. Indeed, we have seen already that although only about 4 per cent of the male population is exclusively homosexual in thought and deed, up to 37 per cent of males have had some homosexual experience to the point of orgasm. (See figure 1.1.)

Of course, one might with reason object that a claim like this is more striking than informative. It lumps together in the bisexual category adults who oscillate constantly and indiscriminately between hetero and homosexual contacts, adults who have been exclusively heterosexual except for an isolated incidence of mutual masturbation at 14, and adults who have been lifelong homosexuals but once played 'doctor' with their sisters' friends. Fortunately, the Kinsey survey was sensitive to this objection, and the authors could show that persistent bisexuality in males, certainly with respect to activity, is a very real phenomenon. As figure 1.2 well illustrates, there is a substantial percentage of men in the population who have had some (but not exclusive) ongoing homosexual experience for at least part of their lives. Furthermore, with the qualification that the overall rates are lower, the Kinsey survey tells a very similar story for women. A substantial proportion of the female population have been or are in the category of bisexual — part hetero and part homosexual. (See figure 1.3.)

When we come to discuss the putative causal explanations of homosexuality, we shall see that the notion of bisexuality (its nature and its existence) is crucial. For this reason, it is worth stating simply that surveys subsequent to the original Kinsey reports completely back the findings of widespread bisexual activity (and, indeed, orientation). This,

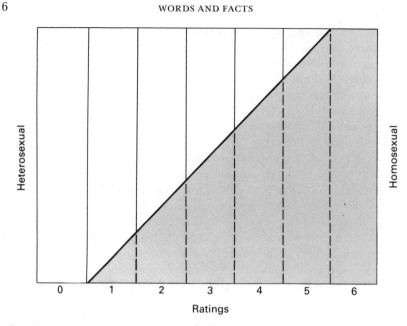

Based on both psychological reactions and overt experience, individuals
rate as follows:
  0 Exclusively heterosexual with no homosexual
  1 Predominantly heterosexual, only incidentally homosexual
  2 Predominantly heterosexual, but more than incidentally homosexual
  3 Equally heterosexual and homosexual
  4 Predominantly homosexual, but more than incidentally heterosexual
  5 Predominantly homosexual, but incidentally heterosexual
  6 Exclusively homosexual

FIGURE 1.1   *Heterosexual — homosexual rating scale*
(Kinsey et al. 1948: 638, fig. 161)

for instance, was the conclusion of another Kinsey survey reported in the
late 1970s. Apparently, for many people there is no sharp gap between
heterosexuality and homosexuality (Bell and Weinberg 1978).

1.3 Behaviour and life styles

So far we have been talking about the incidences, rates and degrees of
homosexual acts and feelings. But what exactly is it that homosexuals do?
How exactly is it that homosexuals live and behave? Let us start with
physical questions and then turn to broader, more social issues.
    Basically there seem to be three major kinds of sexual activity between

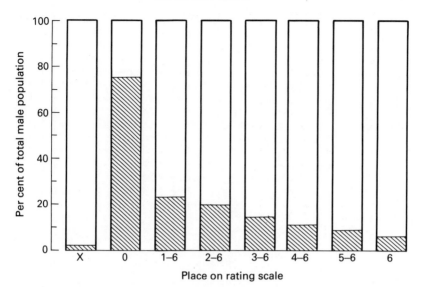

Passing experiences eliminated from data by showing only ratings which have involved a period of at least 3 years after the males turned 16. Percentage shown as 'X' have no socio-sexual contacts or reactions.

FIGURE 1.2   Heterosexual—homosexual ratings in total male population
(single and married) in any single year
(Kinsey et al. 1948: 656, fig. 169)

males which lead to orgasm: mutual masturbation, oral-genital (fellatio), and anal intercourse (sodomy or buggery) (Silverstein and White 1977). Heterosexuals, and indeed many who have commented professionally on homosexuality, have tended to assume that male homosexuals can be sharply categorized into active or passive, dominant or non-dominant, ejaculating or non-ejaculating (in a homosexual encounter). There is, however, growing evidence that the supposition of such a sharp dichotomy is mistaken. The recent (American based) Kinsey study for instance, found that male homosexuals generally employ a wide range of sexual techniques, sometimes being the active partner and sometimes being the passive partner. Oral-genital sex is a favoured form of activity. In England and Mexico male homosexuals are reputedly more anally oriented. Likewise, apparently, in parts of the mid-East, where fellatio is looked upon with the utmost disgust (Carrier 1971). In Ancient Greece, as I shall explain later, a sophisticated form of mutual masturbation was the norm (Dover 1978).

Female homosexuals also employ a variety of techniques. One fairly

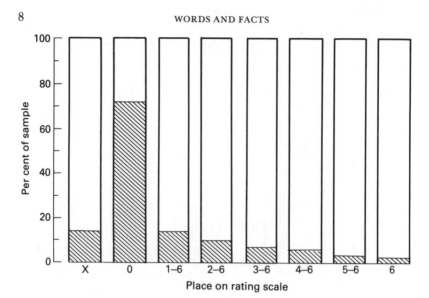

FIGURE 1.3 Active incidence: heterosexual — homosexual ratings, single females, age twenty-five. (This figure is not entirely comparable to figure 1.2, since it tells only of single females, age twenty-five. However, looking at all the data only confirms the fact that there are far fewer women than men involved in homosexual activities)
(Kinsey et al. 1953: 473, fig. 94)

explicit work, written by lesbians for lesbians, lists five: mutual masturbation; oral-genital (cunnilingus); mutual stimulation of the clitorises through two women rhythmically pressing against each other's genitalia (tribadism); stimulation through penis substitutes or dildos; and finally stimulation of the anus with the tongue or possibly finger (analingus) (Martin and Lyon 1972). Heterosexual males seem obsessed with the idea of dildos and other penis substitutes — no doubt they find it difficult to imagine that women could find sexual satisfaction without their own presence, at least by proxy. However, although dildos do have a role in lesbian love-making, they seem not to figure as large as popular imagination would have it. If anything, they find more of a role in self-masturbation.

As in the case of homosexual males, there is a growing realization that between lesbians the active—passive dichotomy is nowhere like as rigid as once thought. A common phenomenon not long ago was for lesbian couples to adopt a facsimile of a heterosexual relationship, with one woman, the 'butch', playing the male role, and the other, the 'femme', the female role. However, this role playing often did not extend to the bedroom, and indeed the whole butch—femme scenario is starting to die down as lesbians increasingly reject the need to pattern their behaviour on heterosexual models.

Moving now from intimate physical behaviour to the more social aspects of life: what do homosexuals do in society and how do they live? The answer is simple. In an important sense, probably *the* most important sense, homosexuals do what heterosexuals do and live how heterosexuals live. There really is no such thing as a 'typical' homosexual, male or female; any more than there is any such thing as a 'typical' heterosexual, male or female. There are heterosexual nurses, and there are homosexual ones; there are heterosexual philosophy professors, and there are homosexual ones. Of course, none of this is to deny that certain professions or trades have a far higher proportion of homosexuals than others. It is well known that there is a high number of male homosexuals on the stage. Some fairly obvious reasons for the clustering of homosexuals in certain professions do spring at once to mind. If one is a homosexual, there is going to be a natural attraction to areas where one knows that one will find similarly oriented people — one will find friends, sexual partners, and more tolerance than otherwise (Tripp 1975).

What about the home lives of homosexuals? Again the question defies a simple retort, just as would be the case for a similar question about heterosexuals. Most informative on this area — although already probably badly dated (for fairly obvious reasons, to be discussed in a moment) — is the Second Kinsey study referred to above (Bell and Weinberg 1978). Its authors proposed a five-fold classification, which they maintained represented natural groupings of homosexual life styles. The groupings were thought appropriate for both males and females, although the relative series did reveal quite dramatic differences between the life styles of male homosexuals and lesbians — differences which, it is hardly too rash to say, tell us as much about gender as they do about sexual orientation (Symons 1979). Summarizing, the Kinsey classification ran from those people who live in exclusively monogamous relationships ('close coupled') through those living in more or less open situations ('open coupled' and 'functional') to those who really are not that happy with or interested in sex anyway ('dysfunctional' and 'asexual'). About 10—15 per cent of males fell at the exclusive (monogamous) end of the spectrum; a good half or more were in the middle, often (at least by self-report) comfortable and satisfied; and the other males (say 25 per cent) were at the unhappy, lonely, non-functioning end of the spectrum.

In considering females, the researchers found a radical shift towards the exclusive life style. At least a third of the surveyed lesbians were monogamous, fewer were open in any sense, and the rest fell towards the other end of the spectrum. And emphasizing this shift is the fact that when one peers more deeply into individual categories, differences between males and females become yet more stark. Not only are most homosexual males not monogamous, not only do those who live with partners tend to have sexual encounters with others anyway, but the numbers of actual contacts a male will have is very high — staggeringly high by heterosexual standards. The Kinsey researchers found that nearly half of the males surveyed had had over 500 different sexual partners, another third had had between 100 and 500, and over 90 per cent had had at least twenty-five sexual partners. Much of this sex had taken place between comparative or absolute strangers, met in baths or bars or the like.

Lesbians, on the contrary, were found to be much more like heterosexual women than like homosexual men in this respect. Very few lesbians go out 'cruising' (that is, looking for casual contacts), most lesbians have had fewer than ten female sexual partners through their homosexual careers, and there is comparatively little sex which takes place between absolute strangers — certainly it is rare to let a relationship drop after a one-night stand.

All surveys have problems — a theme I shall return to more than once in this book. The most obvious problem with the Second Kinsey survey is that it was conducted in San Francisco. This is a city where, more than anywhere, homosexuals can live openly, satisfying whatever sexual needs or whims they might feel. If one is going to find promiscuity anywhere, one will find it in San Francisco, especially among the patrons of baths, bars and clubs catering to homosexuals (the loci from which the Kinsey researchers tended to draw their subjects). However, the highly promiscuous behaviour of many (if not most) male homosexuals is a phenomenon confirmed by many other studies. And the male/female differences are, if anything, made more dramatic by the locale, rather than less. If lesbians are not promiscuous in San Francisco, one doubts they will be that promiscuous elsewhere, either.

But, of course, this discussion is taking place in a vacuum, or at least in a time-warp. Frequent encounters with different sexual partners, especially with total strangers, lay open the way for disease, most particularly venereal or sexually transmitted diseases (STDs). Even in 1978, the threat was there, and (for males) it was serious: gonorrhea, syphilis, parasites, certain forms of hepatitis. Unfortunately, all of these pale beside the latest scourge: AIDS. Strictly speaking, Acquired Immune Deficiency Syndrome is not itself a disease. It is the name given to a range of symptoms brought on from infection by a virus, HTLV-III/LAV (human T-cell lymphotropic virus type III/lymphadenopathy-associated virus). However, by whatever name, these symptoms — cancers, pneumonia, dementia, and more — kill. The body's defence mechanisms go haywire, and previously healthy and fit people can collapse and die — if not within weeks, then within months or a year or two (Institute of Medicine 1986).

AIDS is not an affliction exclusively threatening male homosexuals: in parts of Africa it is widespread through populations affecting hetero as well as homosexuals. However, in western countries it is no accident that AIDS is usually linked with (male) homosexuals. Intercourse, of whatever variety, is the sure-fire way to spread the virus — and frequent intercourse, with many partners, pours fuel on the fire. As of September 1987, in the US there had been 42,000 reported cases of AIDS. Nearly three-quarters of these were male homosexuals, with many of the others being haemophiliacs and IV (intravenous) drug abusers. Few AIDS cases came from purely heterosexual contacts, even though these are now starting to become more common. Figures from Europe are comparable. Putting matters in perspective, one might respond that 42,000 is but a small fraction of the US male homosexual population (if the original Kinsey figures are to be believed). But against this, the 42,000 are but the tip of an iceberg of an estimated at least one million homosexuals who carry the virus. How many of these will develop full-blown AIDS is unknown; but figures suggest that at least 10 per cent are thus fated in the next five years, and the proportion may be as high as 50 per cent (Institute of Medicine 1986).

AIDS is cutting through the homosexual communities of North America and Europe like an Egyptian plague — an analogy which has not escaped certain Protestant evangelicals. Here, I will simply draw attention to the fact that, whatever else AIDS may have done, it has changed male homosexual life styles. People are much more aware of the need for restraint and for 'safe sex', in which no bodily fluids are exchanged. However, although behaviour may be curtailed, the potential remains. The differences between males and females continue to exist, for lesbians did not need the fear of disease to rein in their appetites for sexual variety. Were some fairly sound way of arresting the spread or effects of AIDS to be found, then who would doubt that the Kinsey findings will escape from their encapsulated past and become again relevant? And male/female differences do remain. The quest for safe sex has led to the formation of clubs promoting 'a meeting of men who wish their primary sexual outlet to be masturbation in the company of other like-minded men' (Altman 1986: 157). It is hard to imagine several hundred women gathering together in a disused New York warehouse towards such an

end. Moreover: 'My own observations . . . suggested that . . . surprising
numbers of people continue to use the baths in the same way as before
the epidemic' (p. 155).[2]

1.4 Heterosexual—homosexual differences

I have been talking of differences between male and female homosexuals.
What of the differences, real and apparent, between homosexuals (of
either sex) and heterosexuals (of the respective corresponding sex)? I ask
this question with a particular eye towards some of the putative causal
explanations I shall be discussing, although for now I shall continue the
fiction that my inquiry is purely factual.

First, let us ask whether in some sense homosexuals look different from
heterosexuals — are they built differently, or something? Now, I am sure
we all know somebody, a heterosexual male, who claims to be able to
'spot a faggot a mile off' (or, alternatively, at close quarters 'because of
the eyes'). And it is indeed true that some homosexuals dress and behave
in such a way as to leave little doubt as to their sexual orientation. But of
course, deliberately parading one's homosexuality is one thing: being a
recognizably homosexual 'type' is another. And the general consensus by
researchers is that there really is no such thing. At least, one can put
matters this way: those people who make it their business to enquire into
other people's sexual orientations find that they cannot very accurately
guess what the orientations will be before they ask (Braaten and Darling
1965). On the other hand, this is not to deny that careful measurement
might find some significant physical differences between homosexuals
and heterosexuals — almost certainly not between *all* homosexuals and
all heterosexuals, but perhaps some average differences might exist. And
indeed, there have been studies which have concluded that homo and
heterosexuals are not quite the same, even though other studies have led
to rather different results.

One surveyor, having measured the body builds of some 44 homosexual
men and 111 heterosexual men, concluded that there were indeed physical
differences. In particular, Evans (1972) found that although homosexuals
and heterosexuals were about the same height, the heterosexuals were
very significantly heavier than the homosexuals — there was an average
difference of 6.25 kilograms. Also very significant was the heterosexuals'
muscle strength as opposed to that of the homosexuals (measured by
using a 'dynamometer', a hand-grip device). Faced with results like
these, the sceptic immediately wonders if there were any significant bias
in the sample groups. However, whilst there were certainly some

differences — for instance, the heterosexuals were older than the homosexuals: 38.3 mean as opposed to 33.9 — these were not such as to make one suspect that the causes of the physical differences would probably be something unconnected with sexual orientation.

With respect to women, although some slight differences have been found between lesbians and heterosexuals, the overall conclusion is hardly that there is a distinctively 'lesbian type'. Indeed, in some respects the findings about lesbians cancelled each other out. One study by F. E. Kenyon (1968) found (in a survey of 123 lesbians and a similar number of controls) that: 'The three measurements which significantly distinguish lesbians from controls are weight, waist, and bust. Lesbians are heavier, with bigger busts and waists. They are less tall than controls (although the difference is not significant, it nearly reaches the 5 per cent level), but have slightly but not significantly bigger hips' (p. 487). Qualifying these findings, a slightly more recent study of forty-two lesbians by a group of British researchers found that lesbians are taller rather than shorter, although if anything again the evidence was that lesbians tend to be more 'solid' than heterosexuals. 'The only striking finding was the visual impression that the Lesbian subjects mostly looked older than their age, and sometimes strikingly so' (Griffiths et al. 1974: 550). Even more recent studies do little to overthrow these non-results and to establish a definitive lesbian body-type.

A question which is often asked about homosexuals is whether or not there were any childhood indicators of their adult sexual orientation. The whole question of the early years of homosexuals is one which has been discussed at very great length and is a matter which will much occupy us in the next few chapters. Here, I can simply record that study after study designed to elicit homosexuals' recollections of themselves as children has found that (on average) there are striking differences between the memories of homosexuals of themselves as children and the comparable memories of heterosexuals. In particular, many more male homosexuals remember themselves as having been 'sissies' as children, that is to say, as much happier playing with girls and doing girl-like things (such as playing with dolls) rather than playing with boys and joining in their activities. Conversely, many more lesbians remember themselves as having been 'tomboys'. One often-cited study produced pertinent figures, reproduced in table 1.1. Other studies (including cross-cultural studies) reporting on many more subjects have produced very similar results (Whitam 1977; Grellert et al. 1982; Whitam and Zent 1984). The Second Kinsey study (on 979 homosexual men and women and 477 heterosexual men and women) stressed gender-nonconformity in childhood as just about the most significant finding distinguishing

TABLE 1.1   *Homosexuals' and heterosexuals' memories of themselves as children*

	Homosexual			Heterosexual		
	N	f	%	N	f	%
Male						
Considered a sissy as a child	72	48	67	35	1	3
Female						
Considered a tomboy as a child	56	39	70	43	7	16

N = total number of subjects
f = number responding positively
Source: Saghir and Robins 1973: 19, 193

homosexuals from heterosexuals. As can be seen from table 1.1, however, there is a substantial minority of homosexuals who do not remember themselves as atypical. The Kinsey Study confirmed this.

Finally, let me mention studies on another set of putative characteristics of homosexuals, namely suspected significant differences between homo and heterosexual birth orders, family sizes, and parental ages (at birth time of the future homosexual). Put simply, the studies are very confusing! It is quickest and easiest to quote an encyclopaedia account on these matters.

With respect to family size, two studies report no differences in the number of brothers of male homosexuals and heterosexuals, two report no differences in the number of sisters, and one reports no difference in whether the subject has an older brother or sister. Similar results are found for female homosexuals: two studies report no differences in the number of siblings, three studies report no differences in the number of sisters, while one study reports that the homosexuals had more sisters, one study reports no differences in the number of younger brothers and sisters, and one final study reports that homosexuals have fewer older brothers and sisters . . .

With respect to birth order, five studies report no differences between male homosexuals and heterosexuals in sibling position, five report that homosexuals are more likely to be the youngest child, one that they are more likely to be an only child. For females, one study found no differences, three report that female homosexuals are more likely to be only children, one that they are more likely to be the youngest, one that they are more likely to be the youngest or the oldest, and one that in small families they are more likely to be the oldest whereas in large families they are more likely to be the youngest. (Lester 1975: 57—8. See also Siegelman 1973)

Yet still the reports and studies pour forth. One more recent study, for instance, found that lesbians are more likely to be only children (Hogan et al. 1977). Other studies have confirmed the absence of hetero/homo family differences (for instance, the Second Kinsey survey). No doubt some will soon tell us something else again. It would be a daring person, indeed, who would claim that there is much order in the welter of facts and figures.

1.5 The homosexual — reality or artefact?

We are getting to the point where the mere listing of facts and findings without reference to theory — without reference to possible causes — is yielding diminishing returns. Simply asking questions about (say) childhood behaviour and recollections, or family birth order, is all rather pointless unless one has some theory (however speculative) in mind. Otherwise, why not ask how often homosexuals cut their toenails? But before we can plunge right into expositions and analyses of putative aetiologies, there is one major query that must be addressed. Have we not been rather assuming something that presupposes a positive answer even before we begin? Have we not been assuming that there is such a thing as 'homosexuality' and such people as 'homosexuals', that are open to description (as in this chapter) and that stand in need of explanation (as in following chapters)?

Well, of course, we have. That there is something to be described and people to be categorized has been assumed. However, there is today an articulate group, whose most eloquent spokesman was probably the late French philosopher/historian Michel Foucault (1978), that argues that this traditional approach (accepted by me) is fundamentally flawed. (See also McIntosh 1968 for a seminal discussion.) Its members argue that homosexuality, or more particularly, the 'homosexual', is not something waiting out there in the real world, ready to be described and explained — much, for instance, as one might describe and explain Nelson's column. Nor is the homosexual something with an 'essence', rather like a right-angled triangle or even a particular natural species (like the house sparrow, *Passer domesticus*).

According to this school, the homosexual does not exist in reality at all. The homosexual is rather an artefact, a 'social construction'. It was an idea invented in the late eighteenth and nineteenth centuries, primarily by the medical community, so that physicians and associate workers could assume control over a particular segment of society, previously controlled by the Church and the courts. But, of course, for this move to be effective, the notion of the homosexual had to be projected as if it were a facet of reality, something which could be described and explained. Hence, the confusion and misunderstanding today.

Thus Foucault writes:

As defined by the ancient civil or canonical codes, sodomy was a category of forbidden acts; their perpetrator was nothing more than the juridical subject of them. The nineteenth-century homosexual became a personage, a past, a case history, and a childhood, in addition to being a type of life, a life form, and a morphology, an indiscreet anatomy and possibly a mysterious physiology. Homosexuality appeared as one of the forms of sexuality when it was transposed from the practice of sodomy onto a kind of interior androgyny, a hermaphrodism of the soul. The sodomite had been a temporary aberration; the homosexual was now a species. (Foucault 1978: 43)

In a like fashion, the English social historian Jeffrey Weeks (1977, 1981) argues that the notion of the homosexual is something made rather than found.

This is a theme now taken up by many, including those actively involved in the field of health care and counselling. What we learn is that we should speak no longer of homosexuality or of someone being a homosexual. More appropriate is the notion of someone having adopted a 'homosexual identity' (or 'heterosexual identity') — of the person having accepted a certain behavioural pattern and role in society (or, more drastically, having had such a role thrust upon him/her). For this reason, whatever else may be the case, it is inappropriate to look for causes, since these lie outside the individual, or at most (at best) involve an act of free will or choice: 'A homosexual identity in this sense is not assumed to be an inborn and permanent characteristic, although it may be construed by the individual in this way. Rather, sexual identity is considered to be socially constructed and maintained through the process of social interaction' (Richardson 1981: 35). (See also Plummer 1981.)

In response, and defence of the approach I am taking, I will later explore questions to do with causation and free will; noting here parenthetically that even if homosexuality be a cultural artefact, there remain questions of historical and social causation (that Foucault and Weeks quite brilliantly attack). Moreover, because something is an artefact it does not mean that it is either totally unreal or totally unimportant. Would one want to say either of these things about the US Constitution? However, there is much in what the social constructivists have to say.

The notion of the 'homosexual' as we understand it, in our society, is obviously theory-laden (that is, impregnated with beliefs) and owes much to societal attitudes and the role thrust upon or adopted by people who are so categorized. There is still something about the homosexual, a person apart, that one cannot imagine would have existed in Ancient Greece, a society where homosexual behaviour was much more open and tolerated. (How open and how tolerated homosexual behaviour and orientations were in Ancient Greece will be discussed in some detail in a later chapter.)

For this reason, I cannot too strongly endorse the social constructivist's thrust: that attempts to explain every last facet of contemporary homosexuality in terms of maternal influences or vital bodily fluids or whatever, assuming that such explanations are external verities like Pythagoras' theorem, are doomed to failure. Such attempts are conceptually crazy and show an insensitivity to the historical process. But, having said this much, let us sort out the reality from the rhetoric of the social constructivist's case. The physicist's notion of mass has changed drastically from the nineteenth-century Newtonian concept to the twentieth-century Einsteinian concept; yet there is a continuity, and we can now see that both the nineteenth- and twentieth-century scientists were talking about the same thing. The same, I suggest, is true of homosexuality, or more particularly, the homosexual.

Let me make three supporting and clarifying points, starting with the most obvious and non-controversial. First, no one is denying the existence of homosexual activity per se or that it is transtemporal and transspatial. The very essence of the social constructivist's case is that people engage in homosexual acts in all societies. What the constructivist argues (truly) is that different peoples tend to put different interpretations on the acts. But the sex goes on, is real, and is not an epiphenomenon of history — 'feelings, needs and desires, and experiences are different from identity' (Weeks 1985: 303).

Second, no one denies the existence of homosexual inclinations or that these can and do lead (though not invariably) to homosexual activity. Nor does anyone deny that these too are transtemporal and transspatial. Again, we have what is, if anything, a plank of the social constructivist case and again we have more than social construction. Third (and here we do start to get more controversial, but not that much more), it is surely the case that in all societies (across time and space) there are some individuals with more or less exclusively homosexual inclinations. These are people who can truly be described as having what I have earlier categorized as a 'homosexual orientation'. No doubt some of these people have been fairly exclusively (or in large part) active homosexually —

what I have been describing, without qualification, as 'homosexual'. Of course, others (perhaps many in some societies) may not have been homosexually active at all.

This third point is intended as a factual claim and thus needs evidence. This can be found, and it is worth noting (in passing) that the social constructivists offer no counter evidence (which they must do, if they are to deny the claim). The leading historian of the relationship between homosexuality and Christianity, John Boswell (1980, 1982), shows in full detail that, right through the ages from Ancient Greek times to the Renaissance, there were men and women who were recognizable (and frequently acknowledged) as having a more or less exclusively homosexual orientation. The Ancient Greeks again and again show awareness of the homosexually oriented individual. Sometimes they even offer a kind of proto-Kinsey classification: homosexual, bisexual, heterosexual. To quote a poem from the *Greek Anthology*: 'Zeus came as an eagle to god-like Ganymede, as a swan came he to the fair-haired mother of Helen. So there is no comparison between the two things: one person likes one, another likes the other; I like both' (Paton 1918: 1.16, quoted in Boswell 1982: 99). The Arabs of the Middle Ages likewise recognized the homosexual (qua orientation and qua activity). There are frequent references to such a type of person, as in Night 419 of the classic *Thousand and One Nights*: 'I perceive that you are among those who prefer men to women' (Boswell 1982: 102). And the same is true of western medieval society. Chaucer's pardoner (a cleric) was clearly homosexual in orientation.

Examples could be multiplied, including accounts from more recent times. But the point is made. The homosexual, in the sense being discussed in this chapter (and to be theorized about in succeeding chapters) — the person whose erotic yearnings and fantasies are directed towards his/her own sex and whose activities are influenced by such yearnings and fantasies — is not merely an artefact. (See also Whitam 1983 for transcultural evidence of the persistence of homosexual individuals.)

1.6 Should this inquiry be made?

History and culture are vitally important in the understanding of human beings, but it is as dangerous to assume that they are all-important as to assume that they are non-important. People with homosexual orientations, leading more or less to homosexual activity, are a fact of nature. Trying to describe them is not pointless, and trying to explain and understand their nature is not an enterprise doomed to conceptual failure before we begin.

But should we — attempt an explanation of homosexual orientation, that is? The issue of homosexuality very much focuses the kinds of doubts one might have about the virtues of unrestrained inquiry. I will take as already answered the objection of the social constructivist, that there is nothing to explain, and (as noted) I will defer until later questions to do with free will and how they impinge on attempts to provide causal explanations. Rather, I will home in here on the *moral* desirability of putative explanations of homosexuality. Is it a good thing to try to understand sexual orientation (and behaviour) directed towards members of the same sex?

The traditionalist will object at this point that morality, as such, is irrelevant to the issue of scientific inquiry. The latter is about the way the world *is*, and the former is about the way the world *ought* to be. Never the twain shall meet — at least, not without committing all sorts of well-known fallacies (Nagel 1961). But this is surely too quick a response (McMullin 1983). The very act of inquiring into a subject can show value commitments, perhaps even outright prejudice. Were I to apply for huge sums of grant money to study (say) Jewish nose sizes, you would with reason (you should with reason) wonder about my private programme. Obviously, prejudice and (rather nasty) values are involved here.

However, the traditionalist can with reason object that the study of homosexuality is hardly on a par with the study of what are almost certainly mythical questions, and highly value-loaded myths at that. In looking at homosexual orientation alone, we are here dealing with 5 or 10 per cent of the population — hardly a pseudo-phenomenon by anybody's count. Moreover, likewise defending the legitimacy of this study, the inquiry into the nature of homosexuality is certainly not confined just to those most directly concerned. As we learn about — a necessary condition and consequence of learning about — so many of our fellows (perhaps including ourselves), we thereby throw light on the nature of us all. Fully to understand the homosexual demands and implies that you understand the heterosexual, also. Given the importance to us all of sexuality — and of the way that this influences almost every facet of life — the worth of the enterprise in which we are now engaged needs no defence.

Yet the critic may persist. The very act of picking out the homosexual for explanation both demeans and puts such a person in jeopardy.

As long as society has not made its own peace with the homosexuals, research into the possible causes are potentially a public danger for them. Seen in this light it is good that we know so little about what causes heterosexuality and homosexuality. And I notice with much respect and sympathy that the homosexuals, by refusing to take part in and boycotting etiological research are increasingly doing their best to keep matters that way. (Schmidt 1984: 137)

With more respect, this is surely to put the cart before the horse. It is precisely because we are not beginning with a *tabula rasa*, because society is not supportive of (or even indifferent to) someone with a homosexual orientation, that causal inquiry is demanded, and that this is indeed so very much a moral issue. Of course information, including causal information, can always be used for ill. But it can be used for good, and I am not such a pessimist about the human spirit as to deny that it is often used for good. Furthermore, I trust none of us are such cowards as to pretend that it is better to bumble along in the darkness, hoping through ignorance to avoid evil, than to try to do good through knowledge.

But even this option is not really open. Whatever may be the causes of homosexuality, what cannot be denied is that such an orientation today can and often does make people unhappy — even if it be agreed (what has not yet been proven) that society is responsible for most of the unhappiness. Finding explanations will not bring instant relief. They may, as I hope to show in this book, help in the slow process of making this a better world for us all, whatever our sexual orientation.

2

The Freudian Analysis

We come now to causes, or at least, to putative causes. I begin with the 'psychoanalytic' approach of (or influenced by) Sigmund Freud. In this chapter, I take the ideas of Freud himself. Then, in the next two chapters, I look at those related or subsequent suggestions which follow the Master in thinking that the key to sexual orientation lies primarily in causal inputs to a person's environment, particularly the early environment. I shall introduce critical analysis as I go along. Because this is something which is rather forced upon me, my focus at first will be exclusively on male homosexuality.

2.1 Freud's explanations of (male) homosexuality

Freud's fullest exposition of his views on sexuality in general, with all the implications for homosexuality in particular, are to be found in his *Three Essays on the Theory of Sexuality*, first published in 1905 but much augmented over the years, in which was presented his 'libido' theory. It is on this work that I shall concentrate here, although I shall feel free to supplement where necessary. (Fisher and Greenberg 1977 contains a good overview of pertinent parts of Freud's thinking. See also Fenichel 1945; Jones 1955; and Sulloway 1979.)

Towards an understanding of Freud's view of human development, including human sexual development, we must start with two things he sees as crucial: humans' basic heredity, including their inherited 'instincts', and the effects of the environment, the 'accidental' occurrences to which the human is subjected when growing. (As noted, I am talking here of males; although, as we shall learn, nearly every general statement is intended to apply to females also.) It was Freud's position that 'normal' development, including 'normal' (that is, conventional heterosexual) sexual development, requires a combination of 'normal' heredity and 'normal' environment. A person could go off the track simply because of his heredity; similarly, if a person's environment were in some sense peculiar his growth could get deflected from what it would otherwise have been. Freud believed that it is the impinging of environmental factors on the very young that has the greatest effects on the attitudes and behaviour of the adult, even though consciously the adult himself might be quite unaware of what causally motivates him.

How does human development occur? Two key notions need to be grasped. First, Freud believed that every human is *bisexual*, where this is to be understood in the broader sense as incorporating general attributes of both sexes. Freud believed this to be the case anatomically, and by direct analogy he believed it to be also the case mentally or psychically. He certainly believed that in men, for example, the masculine side could and (normally) would become dominant; but he believed that in development we all go through phases appropriate to different sexes, and that as adults, all of us still have bisexual elements. Second, Freud posited the concept of the *libido*. This is a kind of psychic or sexual energy that we all have, that motivates us sexually (and in other ways), and which in some manner fixes on objects as the centre of its attention. It desires them in order to discharge itself and to achieve gratification through obtaining them. Thus, when I (an adult) get excited by the thought of a female breast or a male penis, it is my libido at work, exciting me and motivating me to do something to relieve my emotions. (See also Knapp 1966.)

What makes Freud such an innovative (and exciting) thinker is that he wanted to take the notion of the libido to the earliest point in childhood, to illustrate and to give causal flesh to the stages through which he believed we all develop. So first there is the *oral* stage (Abraham 1927). The young infant is dependent on the mother for sustenance and all other bodily needs. Sexually, therefore, the infant is directed towards the mother, particularly as she is symbolized through the life-giving breast. The libido directs the child this way to achieve gratification. Next at about eighteen months (perhaps a little earlier, depending on circumstances like the age of weaning) the child gets directed by the libido towards its own body as it enters the *anal* stage (Freud 1959). The child becomes aware of and stimulated by its own ability to produce faeces. The child itself has an ability to control its own bodily functions. At this point, it is the homosexual (that is, female-within-the-male) side of the child's bisexual nature which becomes predominant, as the child narcissistically becomes attracted to its own body.

Then around the age of three or four we get a shift to the third stage, as the child's attention moves from anus to genitals. In boys this is the *phallic* stage (Fenichel 1945). The boy becomes aware of his penis as a penis, and of girls as not having them. Once again the libido causes a shift in interest, as (in boys) the sexual direction is switched back to the most significant non-penis possessor in a boy's life, namely his mother. From homosexuality we are now back to heterosexuality, and we have arrived at the time where the boy must begin to work through the most famous, or notorious, concept in the whole Freudian corpus, his *Oedipus complex*. (See Freud 1953, 1961c, d.)

The child next enters a latent period as other aspects of his growth take place. This lasts until puberty, at which point the final phase of psychosexual development occurs. Coming into adolescence a boy senses that there is something wrong with his love for his mother. He is barred from consummating his relationship with her fully by the universal taboo against incest. Hence, for a totally successful resolution of his Oedipus complex, a boy must transfer his heterosexual libidic attraction from his mother onto other mature females. This done, normal sexual development is completed.

So, let us turn now to the ways in which things might go wrong with 'normal' sexual development. (By putting 'normal' in quotation marks, I intend the reader to realize that I mean 'average' as opposed to 'morally desirable'. I intend no value ascriptions at all at this point.) As pointed out earlier, there seem to be two basic ways. On the one hand, there might be something unusual with one's constitution. One's libido might be stronger than normal, or atypically directed in some way, or some such thing. On the other hand, the growing child's environment might cause things to go out of regular paths. In this latter case there again seem to be two basic possibilities: there are things causing *neuroses* and there are things causing *perversions* (Freud 1953: 165; Fenichel 1945).

As one is growing up, going through the various stages, one has got to change — or rather put down — various aspects of one's psychic make-up, and let other aspects come to the fore. In other words, normal growth requires the repression of certain basic urges. If a repression is too great, or wrongly directed, then this is liable to lead to neurosis. What happens is that with undue repression one gets a build-up of psychic energy, which would normally be discharged (for example, by suckling at the breast). The energy must go somewhere; therefore, its normal path of flow being blocked, it finds some other, anomalous paths. Unfortunately, although tension is thus relieved, the new ways of discharging energy might well make the individual involved unhappy — such an individual is neurotic.

Perhaps the classic illustrative case of this is the anal retentive (Freud 1959). Suppose the child in its anal phase is over-rigorously toilet trained, being taught that everything to do with its faeces is bad, disgusting, smelly, wrong. Unable to discharge its libido in the proper way, the child develops habits of compulsion about keeping things in, and under control — but he overdoes these habits. He becomes habitually constipated, inordinately tidy and obedient to rule and time, distrustful of anything creative or out of the ordinary, touchy, and so forth. In short, as this carries on into adulthood, we have a thoroughly neurotic human being: unhappy with himself, unhappy with others, at best pitied, at worst disliked.

A perversion is the opposite of a neurosis — 'neuroses are, so to say, the negative of perversions' (Freud 1953: 165). In the case of perversions, the problem is not that childhood impulses have been overly repressed, but rather that they have not been properly controlled at all. What we have then are adults who are in some sense still under the control of their childhood urges. And this obviously brings us to the subject of homosexuality, because as we have seen it is part of Freud's picture of normal childhood growth that every boy should go through a homosexual phase — a phase in which the primary focus of his libido's attention is a being with male genitals (initially, his own). In a sense, therefore, homosexuality is a perversion rather than a neurosis, where by this is meant a kind of state of arrested development. The way in which the homosexual is caught by his libido's fascination with his own genitals, and then by transference with the genitals of like beings, is well brought out when (later) Freud expands on the notion of narcissism.

There comes a time in the development of the individual at which he unifies his sexual instincts (which have hitherto been engaged in auto-erotic activities) in order to obtain a love-object; and he begins by taking himself, his own body, as his love-object, and only subsequently proceeds from this to the choice of some person other than himself as his object. This half-way phase between auto-erotism and object-love may perhaps be indispensable to the normal course of life; but it appears that many people linger unusually long in this condition, and that many of its features are carried over by them into the later stages of their development. The point of central interest in the self which is thus chosen as a love-object may already be the genitals. The line of development then leads on to the choice of an outer object with similar genitals — that is, to homosexual object-choice — and thence to heterosexuality. Persons who are manifest homosexuals in later life have, it may be presumed, never emancipated themselves from the binding condition that the object of their choice must possess genitals like their own . . . (Freud 1958: 466)

A passage like this emphasizes how crucial is the concept of bisexuality to Freud's understanding of homosexuality (that is, of bisexuality both in the broad psychological sense, and in the special case, the conventional sexologists' sense — a mixing of erotic urges). We are all homosexual to a greater or lesser degree (that is, we possess cross-sex desires), and indeed at some early stage in our lives we are all homosexual to a greater degree — this is a result of our libido's attraction to our own genitals. Adults predominantly homosexual have been stuck with a childhood phase. Part of the male's female aspects have more force in the adult than is usual. (Note that, erotically speaking, what is really important for Freud is a kind of serial bisexuality. During development we swing to and fro between the male and female ends of our erotic desires. As adults we may — probably do still — have elements of both kinds of desires, but Freud does not want to claim that all adults are tugged both ways, equally.)

What environmental factors might cause one's development to be arrested with the homosexual inclinations uppermost? Freud did not want to claim that any single factor was the invariable cause of homosexuality. However, there were three key periods in development, where a future pattern of homosexuality might be started. First, as might be expected from what has just been said above, future homosexuality might be caused by something happening during the auto-erotic phase, the time when the child is turned in upon himself and by transference to beings with genitals like himself. In an important sense, therefore, the future homosexual is a narcissist. Of course, precisely what might cause a child to stay at this stage can vary. Freud did speculate briefly that the use of male slaves in rearing boys in Ancient Greece might have caused the prevalence of homosexuality there (Freud 1953: 230). Perhaps something like this would fit the pattern being suggested: at a crucial stage one just gets so used to regarding male genitals as the norm, that they remain the norm for the rest of one's life.

Second, we have the crucial point where the child is starting to come out of the exclusively homosexual phase, back to heterosexuality (and mother). We are now entering the phallic phase, where the penis is the prime focus and organ for the discharge of the libido. The boy discovers that females do not have penises and this scares him. He looks upon females as castrated males, and because he has himself experienced deprivations earlier (for instance, when he has not been allowed to play with his faeces), he too fears castration. This fear of the loss of the prized organ Freud labelled the 'castration complex'. All of us seem to start with a castration complex; for some, however, a successful resolution is not possible, perhaps because the fear of loss caused by earlier experiences is too great. Hence, future homosexuality is ensured (Freud 1953, 1961c). Females, particularly their genitals, are feared because they trigger feelings of castration anxiety, and concomitantly and not altogether consistently they are despised as mutilated males.

Third, we get the best known of Freud's explanations of homosexuality — unsuccessful resolution of the Oedipus complex. Coming into adolescence, the boy has a kind of truncated heterosexuality. He is in love with his mother, cautious or fearful about his father as rival. What he has got to do, coming up against the incest taboo, is transfer his libidic attractions to other females. Suppose, however, that he cannot do this: his ties with his mother are just too strong, or his fears of his father as rival preclude his forming a heterosexual relationship with another woman. The incest taboo forbids his consummating his relationship with his mother, so the boy-becoming-adult turns to the only 'safe' outlet: other males. He lets the homosexual side of his nature come to the fore — loving men does not violate the incest taboo, nor does it cause a castration anxiety for the adolescent boy no longer strives in rivalry with his father (Freud 1955a).

We see therefore that there are several ways in which future homo- sexuality can be triggered. As can be imagined, one can add various details to the Freudian scheme, although we need not go into these in any depth. There are, however, two points to be mentioned in bringing this section to an end. First, there is the question of 'latent homosexuality'. Freud saw us as all being bisexual (generally and specifically with respect to desires). Some of us keep our homosexual side well hidden, even from ourselves — but it is somewhere there, deep down inside. Others, although ostensibly heterosexual, have their homosexual nature closer to the surface. They have fairly explicit homosexual dreams. They fantasize homosexually occasionally. They sometimes give way to homosexual impulses, particularly under the influence of alcohol. Often, most significantly, they feel threatened by homosexuals and homosexuality — they are the people who want to geld all 'queers'. And so forth. These people merit the label 'latent homosexuals'. (Freud did argue that problems with repressing homosexual impulses can lead to paranoia. But while all paranoids of this kind are struggling with their homo- sexuality, not all who are struggling with homosexuality are paranoid. (See Freud 1958; Lester 1975.))

Second, there is the matter of cure. For Freud, the hope of 'curing' homosexuals was not great, and indeed was basically ruled out by his theory. (I mean 'cure' here simply in a non-evaluative sense of turning homosexuals into heterosexuals.) As is well known, Freud invented the method of probing into our subconscious by allowing a free flow of ideas, paying attention to such things as verbal slips ('Freudian slips'), and above all by analysing dreams — taking dream events as symbolic of things important to us but also things not necessarily fully recognized at a conscious level. By bringing into the light of day repressions, Freud aimed to undo the damage caused by them, and to allow the libido to flow into normal channels. Neuroses are thus relieved. However, as we have seen, homosexuality is not a neurosis, it is not caused by repression (the opposite rather), and thus analysis is nothing like as appropriate.

In a famous 'Letter to an American mother', he wrote

By asking me if I can help, you mean, I suppose, if I can abolish homosexuality and make normal heterosexuality take its place. The answer is, in a general way, we cannot promise to achieve it. In a certain number of cases we succeed in developing the blighted germs of heterosexual tendencies which are present in every homosexual, in the majority of cases it is no more possible. (Jones 1955: 208–9, dated 9 April 1935)

What analysis might do, Freud added, is to bring some peace and acceptance to the wretch who is filled with self-hatred at his sexual orientation. This is where therapy can make a real and lasting contribution.

2.2 Science or pseudo-science?

Freud stirs people's emotions. For every avid defender — and there are many — there is a rabid critic. How are we to decide on and evaluate his ideas? A natural first inclination is to plunge right in, asking whether Freud's views on homosexuality — call them speculations, hypotheses, fantasies, if you so wish — are true or false. Or are they somewhere in the limbo of the non-proven? The earth goes round the sun. Humans evolved from blobs. DNA is the key to life. Are men homosexual because they had trouble with father? Unfortunately, simply rushing in, looking for and assessing empirical evidence, would be premature. We must ask first whether the kinds of ideas we have just seen presented are the kinds of things which could, even in principle, however good the evidence, be genuine science. Is Freudianism in general, and Freud on (male) homosexuality in particular, the sort of thing which (now or in the future) could be a body of achievement akin to Newtonian physics or Darwinian biology? Or is it a pseudo-science, merely playing with the evidence, like astrology or Creationism?

In the opinion of most (at least, many) philosophers, and not a few of their scientific fellow travellers, Freud's work is bogus through and through. Thus, the well-known conservative philosopher Roger Scruton has written recently of Freud's 'ability to proclaim speculative nonsense in the tone of voice appropriate to meticulous science' (Scruton 1986: 208). And in like vein, the winner of the Nobel prize in medicine, Sir Peter Medawar, writes that psychoanalytic theory is 'akin to a dinosaur or a zeppelin in the history of ideas, a vast structure of radically unsound design and with no posterity' (Medawar 1975: 17). It is tempting to point out that if something lasts for one hundred and fifty million years, the span of the dinosaurs, its design cannot be all *that* bad. But I will leave such retorts to the debating school.

What then of the critiques of Freud? Most strike me as being without substance, telling more (in good Freudian fashion) of their proposers than their targets. Only too typical is Scruton's main complaint, which seems to rest exclusively on Freud's great use of metaphor. The libido, as a kind of energy, is supposed to be something akin to a fluid, passing through bodily passages. But, objects Scruton, this has to be a metaphor, and hence cannot be genuine science. 'In this [Freud's theory] differs from all genuine scientific theories, which contain a core of meaning that tells us literally *how things are* (even though models and metaphors are often required if we are to grasp them)' (Scruton 1986: 201).

I need hardly say that this is an incredibly anachronistic view of science. If one thing has become clear in the past few years, from detailed studies by philosophers, historians and others on actual science, it is that metaphor runs rampant through science, from physics to sociology (Hesse 1980; Lakoff and Johnson 1980). Is the electron really a wave? Is it really a particle? Does natural selection really select? Is it a genuine code that molecular biologists set out to crack? Did the fins on the back of the stegosaurus have a real function? The answer to all of these questions, and many, many more of the same sort, is 'No!' — that is, if we take a literal approach. Waves and particles and selectors and codes and functions are all metaphors. But if you were to deny them, to insist on their elimination in the name of literalist purity, you simply could not do science. Never to inquire into the 'function' of a palaeontological object would bring that study to a stop — at once. The metaphor is vital. Hence, for the mere use of such in his field, Freud should not be faulted.

Freud should not be faulted (a priori) for many other things philosophers find offensive — for instance, the very use of 'unconscious' desires (Pap 1958). Why should Freud not move, analogically, from that which we know to that which he believed has to be postulated in order to make sense of much that we think and do? We may decide that Freud's whole enterprise is worthless or misleading because it leads to no interesting predictions. It would be unfair to bar the attempt on philosophical grounds. If a man does many of the things that one would normally associate with lust, why should we not say that he is 'subconsciously' or 'unconsciously' in love with his mother, even if consciously the thought would appal them both? But let me not linger on these side issues. I must go right to the heart of things. As many readers may know, the man who has fair claim to being the world's best known philosopher of science has decreed against the scientific nature of Freud's work, and in this he has been extremely influential. I refer, of course, to Sir Karl Popper and to his critique of classical psychoanalytic thought. I shall, therefore, put my main effort into a discussion of Popper's views, taking his position as a paradigm for all such critiques of the scientific nature itself of Freud's work.

To Popper, the mark of genuine science is the crucial element of risk taking. A real science — unlike astrology or (perhaps in a different vein) Christianity — exposes itself against the empirical world, and if it fails in this respect it must be revised or rejected. Real science is not false science. It may be true. But it is *falsifiable* science. And before this requirement, psychoanalytic theory collapses entirely.

I may illustrate this by two very different examples of human behaviour: that of a man who pushes a child into the water with the intention of drowning it; and that of a man who sacrifices his life in an attempt to save the child. Each of these two cases can be explained with equal ease in Freudian and in Adlerian terms. According to Freud the first man suffered from repression (say, of some component of his Oedipus complex), while the second man had achieved sublimation. According to Adler the first man suffered from feelings of inferiority (producing perhaps the need to prove to himself that he dared to commit some crime), and so did the second man (whose need was to prove to himself that he dared to rescue the child). I could not think of any human behaviour which could not be interpreted in terms of either theory. It was precisely this fact — that they always fitted, that they were always confirmed — which in the eyes of their admirers constituted the strongest argument in favour of these theories. It began to dawn on me that this apparent strength was in fact their weakness. (Popper 1962: 35)

What then have we got in psychoanalytic theories, including those about the origins of homosexuality? Fascinating things undoubtedly, but things with all of the scientific status of Homer's stories about Mount Olympus. 'These theories describe some facts, but in the manner of myths. They contain most interesting psychological suggestions, but not in a testable form' (Popper 1962: 38).

There is much one might say in response to this claim. Not a few critics would fault Popper's 'criterion of demarcation'. They would object that Popper's case against Freud fails because falsifiability is not the mark of genuine science. There is much that we would and do want to call 'science' — good science, even — that is not obviously falsifiable (Kitcher 1983). But we need not attack Popper's tools to criticize his handiwork. It is singularly clear that his case against Freud fails, however highly we may rate falsifiability. The reason is simple. Popper talks not of psychoanalytic theory at all, but at most of a crude caricature. Where does Freud say that pushing a child into water is a result of repression, of an inadequately resolved Oedipus complex? Where does Freud say that saving a child occurs to achieve sublimation? What has any of this to do with neurosis, psychosis, paranoia, homosexuality, heterosexuality, mothers, fathers, children, or whatever?

The answer, obviously, is 'Nothing'. Popper tells us nothing bad about Freud, for he tells us nothing at all about Freud. We hardly even get a crude caricature, for then at least there would have to be some likeness to the original — and Popper offers not even this.

Yet what of Freud on the specific subject of homosexuality? Is it true science? Does Freud tell us why some boys become homosexual? Does he tell us why others do not? Perhaps I am a bit too hasty in dismissing Popper. Freud rather suggests that if fathers display too intense a love for their sons, these sons are liable to be turned into homosexuals. Conversely, Freud suggests that if fathers are hostile, indifferent, and threatening, homosexuality may possibly ensue (Freud 1905, 1922). This seems to be a case of damned if you do, damned if you don't: apparently homosexuality may or may not come about, whatever the father's actions. Falsification is impossible. The spectre of pseudo-science still looms.

This is too quick a conclusion. Freud's point is that any kind of *undue* paternal (or, more generally, parental) giving or withholding of love may cause homosexuality — not any kind of behaviour whatsoever. Moreover, the effect of the behaviour depends crucially on the stage of the child's psychosexual development. A child in the pre-Oedipal years (until four or so) ought to be close to mother — hence, strong or abnormal affection by father at this stage could have effects. Later, when the child is in the Oedipal phase and reacting against father, undue hostility could have effects that cause homosexuality. We have here unequivocally empirical, testable claims. The suggestion is that, on average, we are going to find significant differences between the family backgrounds of homosexuals and heterosexuals. For reasons to be explained shortly, simply finding differences will not give us all of the answers; but if the Freudian position be true, such differences there must surely be. Conversely, if there are no differences at all, then the Freudian position is either false or in need of some pretty desperate ad hoc hypotheses to rescue it. I would go so far as to say that the difference in

family background is as pertinent to the Freudian position as is the truth
of Kepler's laws to the Newtonian position.

I conclude, therefore, that Popper and his much-quoted critique of
Freud fails. Granting — especially granting — that falsifiability is a mark
of genuine science, what Freud has to say about human nature is
genuinely scientific. In particular, what he has to say about the origins of
male homosexual orientation belongs to the realm of empirical inquiry
— unlike astrology, Creationism, and other pretenders. (I am much
indebted in my critique of Popper to the definitive discussion in
Grünbaum, 1985. Wollheim and Hopkins 1982 is a good collection of
philosophical discussions of Freud.)

2.3 A question of evidence

Freud on homosexuality is (potentially) genuine science. But is it good
science? Does it tell us about the real world? What tests have been
performed that are designed to probe Freudian claims about the aetiology
of homosexuality, and with what results?

Freud's views on homosexuality are very much part of his overall
position on human nature. Hence, before we even get to questions about
family background, something ought first to be said about his doctrine of
bisexuality, given its central and fundamental importance. In particular,
something ought to be said about general psychological bisexuality, for
if, as Freud claimed, homosexuals land on atypical points of the male/
female erotic scale, one would expect (Freud certainly expected) hints of
a similar atypicality for the general scale. Moreover, Freud here would
seem to be on solid ground, for surely there is strong evidence that
homosexuals show atypical gender traits. Male homosexuals are more
feminine than male heterosexuals, and conversely for women. Freud
(1953) certainly thought so, identifying activity as a masculine feature
and passivity as a feminine feature. Sex researchers, bank managers and
landlords apparently think so. Bell and Weinberg write that: 'Homosexual
men's reputation for skillfully and imaginatively renovating [old
Victorian] houses — an avocation that invariably enhanced neighborhood
property values — was so well-known among realtors and banks that
they seldom had trouble acquiring mortgages . . .' (1978: 234). Conversely,
landlords 'believed that homosexual women were careless about rent
payments, poor at housekeeping, contentious about repairs, and
disturbingly noisy tenants' (p. 235). And such a belief is certainly part of

the general stereotype. (Quick: Which of *The Odd Couple* do you think
was gay? Now, suppose it were an all-female cast?)

Backing this is a large number of reports of psychological tests,
apparently showing that male homosexuals score more strongly towards
the feminine ends of scales than do male heterosexuals, and conversely
lesbians score more towards masculine ends than do heterosexual women
(Aaronson and Grumpelt 1961; Dean and Richardson 1966; Siegelman
1972a, b; Thompson et al. 1973, are the tip of the iceberg). However, at
this point, without wanting to be unfair to Freud, I shall counsel a certain
caution. My own feelings are towards belief in a certain amount of
gender exchange. Yet there are some fairly serious queries about these
psychological tests and the groups to which they are given. I shall detail
some of these problems in chapter 9, when I take a direct look at all such
testing.[1] Also there are some important conceptual questions, which will
have to be discussed, about the propriety of using such terms as
'masculine' and 'feminine', especially of females and males respectively.
Here, let me simply note that Freud himself soon realized that matters
are not simple. In 1915 he added a lengthy footnote to *Three Essays on
Sexuality*, significantly modifying his previously stark stand. Males are
not exclusively active nor are females exclusively passive.

At this point, therefore, I shall rather play down questions about
general (adult) psychological bisexuality and move on to questions
directly aimed at the supposed psychodynamics of the process that
produces homosexuals. What about parental influences, and so forth? As
it happens, most of the studies have involved the giving of questionnaires
to homosexuals, and to comparable heterosexuals, in order to probe
perceptions and memories of family backgrounds. I shall report
uncritically on some of these to give a flavour, and then comment on
them.

The best known of all the studies, one which seems to have been the
impetus for much of the subsequent work and which seems still in some
circles to be considered authoritative (Moberly 1982), is a study reported
in 1962 by a group of practising analysts (Bieber et al. 1962). Essentially
what the group did was to work at second hand. It devised a questionnaire
intended to probe family background, and then asked some seventy-
seven members of the Society of Medical Psychoanalysts to report on
patients whom they had in therapy. In other words, it was not the
patients themselves who filled out the questionnaire, but their analysts,
reporting on what they had been told. In all, some 206 men were
reported on, 106 homosexual (that is, considered by their therapists in
some degree homosexual) and 100 heterosexual.

The results were, to say the least, very striking. Prima facie, they provide very strong confirmation for the Freudian viewpoint, especially with regard to homosexuality caused through fear of father.[2] (No one seems much impressed by or interested in homosexuality caused by overly warm fathers.) Time and again among homosexuals the Bieber group found a 'classic triangle', a pattern virtually absent among even the sickest heterosexuals. The mother is close-binding and intimate with her son, protecting him, smothering him with love, and in various ways showing her preference for him rather than for her husband. The father is cold, detached, regarding the son as a bit of a sissy. The son is attached to mother, hating and fearing the father, and as like as not a rather 'delicate' child, avoiding games and the rough and tumble of normal boyhood — the kind of child that maiden aunts (of both sexes) adore.

In the years since this study (not to mention the years before), there have been many similar studies, differing primarily in using questionnaires which have been given directly to the subjects themselves without the intermediary of a therapist, and indeed usually involving subjects who are not in therapy at all (that is, who are not already identified as people who are sufficiently troubled emotionally to seek professional help). In many, many cases, these studies have underscored the validity of the Bieber findings (for example, Bene 1965a, b; Snortum et al. 1969; Thompson et al. 1973).

The Second Kinsey study also reported differences (slanted in the way a Freudian would expect) between heterosexual and homosexual parental backgrounds. 'More homosexual than heterosexual men described their mothers as relatively strong individuals, i.e., as dominant, active, strong, and independent (57 per cent to 39 per cent)' (Bell et al. 1981: 47). Additionally, during upbringing, mothers were considered stronger than fathers (53 per cent to 30 per cent). 'The homosexual males . . . reported less-favourable childhood and adolescent relationships with their fathers than did their heterosexual counterparts' (23 per cent to 52 per cent) (p. 54). And so forth. Admittedly, these statistics are for white males; but the Kinsey researchers record analogous findings for blacks. And, more generally, there are many other studies pointing to very similar conclusions. (See Fisher and Greenberg 1977.)

On the other hand, I must acknowledge that the Kinsey researchers themselves felt that parental backgrounds and homo/hetero differences are not as significant as one might think. There could well be other causal factors affecting — perhaps even more important in — sexual orientation development. And there are some studies which are even less supportive of the Freudian picture (for instance: West 1959—60; Braaten and Darling 1965; Gigi 1970; Freund et al. 1974b). One very careful study by Marvin Siegelman (1974b) compared 307 homosexuals with 138 heterosexuals. Although Siegelman found that on average homosexuals felt their fathers had been cold and distant (though mothers did not fit the classic triangle), after he controlled for neuroticism (that is, considered subsamples of those scoring low on a neuroticism test) he found that differences between homosexuals and heterosexuals with respect to parental background vanished.

Nevertheless, taking an outsider's view of all the studies, the Freud supporters do have a strong edge. It seems fair to state that if one asks homosexuals about their backgrounds, the chances are that a significantly higher proportion than of heterosexuals will describe their fathers as cold, rejecting, hostile, fear-inducing. And although there is not quite the same degree of evidence, homosexuals more often than heterosexuals will describe their mothers as strong, intimate, binding, over-protective. With the son, delicate and timorous, turned towards mother rather than father, we have the classic triangle.

But what are all of these studies and their results worth? I must confess that the Bieber study strikes me as being scientifically on a par with reports of faith healing or psychic surgery, and for much the same reasons. Moreover, although some of the later studies avoid a number of the more outstanding problems vitiating the Bieber study, I rather suspect that methodologically most are so crippled as to be of primary value in reinforcing the prejudices of True Believers, rather than providing solid objective evidence in favour of the Freudian position. (I direct these remarks primarily against those — the majority — who think they have strong evidence for the Freudian triangle and that is the end of the matter. In respects, my comments do apply also to more careful studies, like the Kinsey survey, but they are tempered in ways that I trust will be obvious. I am not about to fault people for things they do not accept.)

Starting with the Bieber study, two glaring sources of error or distortion are very obvious. First, there is the way in which the information was obtained. The subjects (homosexual and heterosexual) did not answer the questionnaire directly: rather, they did so through the medium of their analysts who answered for them. Admittedly the analysts would have spent a long time listening to tales about their patients' childhood, but the possibilities for distortion are enormous. Test after test has shown that when one believes something, one is liable to find evidence in its favour (for example, Rosenthal 1966); and there are specific studies showing that therapists are particularly prone to reading into the data the precise things they expect to find (for example, Chapman and Chapman 1967).

The other glaring methodological weakness in the Bieber study concerns the biased sample of the homosexual population which was considered. Disturbed homosexuals in analysis in the New York city areas are not typical. For a start, people in analysis are not typical. They tend to be middle class (how else could they afford the fees?), with an occupation which gives them freedom (for a minimum of three hours a week on the couch), Jewish (with respect to the overall Jewish population numbers), and as like as not they are either themselves in the health care business or related to someone in the business (Aronson and Weintraub 1968; Kadushin 1969; Siegel 1962).

Moreover, people in analysis tend to be troubled — why else would they invest the time and money, not to mention emotional trauma, that analysis demands? Admittedly, Bieber and his associates compared their homosexuals with other disturbed (heterosexual) people, but this does not eliminate the possibility of bias — disturbed homosexuals might still be in a class separate from well-balanced homosexuals. (By speaking of 'well-balanced homosexuals' I do not mean to take a stand on a matter to be discussed later, namely whether in some ultimate sense any homosexual can be considered 'well-balanced'. What I mean is homosexuals who would consider themselves sufficiently well-balanced not to seek therapy.) All in all, the findings of the Bieber study about parental attitudes are methodologically worthless. A group of people, with a vested interest in a hypothesis, chose their own subject-data and found their hypothesis confirmed. The situation is, as I have said, on a par with faith healers' reports of their successes — they too have a vested interest in their hypothesis. I do not imply that either the participating analysts or the faith healers are deliberately dishonest. Just rather naive, in a self-serving way.

Now, it must in fairness be admitted that many of the investigators since the Bieber study have tried hard to fill the methodological lacunae I have been discussing. For a start, as mentioned above, more recent studies have eliminated the analyst intermediaries and given the questionnaires directly to the subjects. Second, great efforts have been made to eliminate the biases from the sample as studied by Bieber. Homosexuals and heterosexuals who do not have overt psychological problems have been sought, and the aim has also been to study people from different social classes — not just the well-to-do middle class of the Bieber study. (For instance: Braaten and Darling 1965; R. B. Evans 1969; Snortum et al. 1969; Thompson et al. 1973; Gigi 1970.)

Nevertheless, I remain unconvinced that the validity of the classic triangle (where the parents are taken to be a causal influence) has been demonstrated. First, I suspect that there are still problems with some if not all of the samples chosen. For instance, one of the studies mentioned above considered men in trouble with the military (Snortum et al. 1969). Yet there is good evidence to suggest that those homosexual soldiers who do get into trouble with the authorities are very atypical (Williams and Weinberg 1971). This almost has to be so, since the number caught is so much smaller than the number practising. In certain respects the number caught are bound to be more reckless, more 'suicidal'. This could be a reflection of other character differences from the average homosexual.

More generally, there is fairly clear evidence that people who fill out questionnaires tend to differ significantly from those who do not. The answerers tend to be brighter, more educated, more successful, more in need of approval, more friendly, more unconventional, more often first born, younger (Rosenthal 1966). How will factors like these affect one's answers? For instance, although Gigi (1970) was working with homosexuals not in psychiatric treatment, his sample was the 887 men who filled in and returned his questionnaire out of 2400 men to whom he sent it in the first place. What about the other 1513 men? In the specific cases of surveys of homosexuality, one thing which does worry me is that — naturally enough — the homosexual subjects are often drawn from homophile organizations. It would be interesting to know how typical of homosexuals are members of homosexual societies, particularly given that in the western world there is such a pressure to conceal one's homosexuality entirely (Gonsiorek 1977).

My second point of concern is connected to the point just made, but is much more serious. All of the studies we have considered devolve eventually on people's memories and perceptions of their childhood, and particularly of parental attitudes and how they as children were affected and responded. It is an extremely large and unjustified assumption that the actual happenings of our childhoods and our memories of our childhoods are identical. I do not suggest that people are systematically dishonest, although of course that is always possible in some cases, but simply that people cannot remember their childhoods that clearly or objectively. Apart from anything else, there is very good evidence to suggest that children's perceptions of their parents are not that accurate. Children tend to perceive their parents in light of the way that they think they ought to perceive them — the way that peers, and films, and so forth, suggest (Kagan 1956; Kagan and Lemkin 1960; Kagan and Moss 1962). This means that in a society where fathers are supposed to be stronger and more distant and mothers weaker and more tender (that is, a society like ours which has this kind of ideology), children will be inclined to see their parents this way, even though the parents may not be like this.

But this difficulty of childrens' perceptions of parents pales beside the fact that our memories of the past are going to be coloured by our beliefs and attitudes of the present. In the case of homosexuality, I suspect that this fact causes tremendous difficulties. Present attitudes towards parents are bound to affect the way one remembers one's childhood. If, as an adult, one is fond of mother, could one possibly think back to her as difficult when one was a child, even if she was? Moreover, how does one handle the fact that the Freudian story about the classic triangle is not a very well kept secret? The basic outline — dominant mother and weak father — is as well known as $E = mc^2$. Such an outline is surely known to most homosexuals. Such an outline is certainly known to most members of homophile organizations, who are, as we have seen, the people who tend to be the subjects of homosexual studies. In all of this undoubtedly we have a potentially seriously disruptive factor. People are being asked questions, about a matter on which they are liable to be inaccurate, in order to confirm or contradict a hypothesis which they most probably already know about — and which, after they have answered a whole set of questions about their mothers and fathers, they probably realize is the topic under investigation at that time.

To be honest, the situation is really not very promising. There are very few of us who do not have in our backgrounds some items which would allow us to embroider a picture either way, and so depending on how one responds to the Freudian hypothesis, one might subtly influence the tenor of one's answers. The person who is happy in his homosexuality might well overstate the case. The unhappy homosexual, guilty about his orientation, and not wishing to lay blame on his one great comfort in life — his mother — might understate the case. The point is that the reports are simply not that reliable. It is not that people are deliberate liars. It is just that they cannot always tell the truth — particularly about matters of great emotional concern to them. (See Gonsiorek 1977 for an excellent discussion of the limitations of most tests of Freud on male homosexuality.)

2.4 More on the triangle

I have argued that Freudian psychoanalytic theory qua homosexual orientation is not a pseudo-theory. Therefore, I do not want to be misunderstood here. I am not arguing that the classic triangle hypothesis is in principle untestable. What I am arguing is that the way people have gone about testing it so far is fairly unimpressive. But the hypothesis could be tested, in a more or less satisfactory way. Ideally, what one would like would be some sort of long-term longitudinal study, where parents and children could be examined, both when the children are infants and then as they grow up. Does one in fact find that families that fall into certain patterns (assessed on self-reports, reports of friends and relatives, and other tests) tend to produce children of a certain type — and does anyone remember in later life what the patterns really were?

Failing major studies of this kind, a start might be made by asking a few questions of people other than the homosexuals themselves. What do the parents think, for instance? How do they rate their marriage relationship? How do they rate their relationship with their various children, including but not exclusively with the homosexual child? How do they think their spouse feels towards their various children? And how do siblings, and perhaps other family members and friends, rate the various family dynamics?

I am painfully aware that many of the objections I have used against the already existing studies might be made against my suggestions — how readily will a man admit that he is dominated by his wife and dislikes his son? However, some sort of consilience in results might be taken as a sign that we are taking a few steps towards the truth. If all in the family agree that mother favoured one son rather than any other and that father consequently rather neglected him, then our confidence in the claim is surely increased. One point worthy of note is that the parents and perhaps some of the older siblings would not be relying exclusively on childhood memories.

In fairness to Bieber, about whom I have been so critical, I must note that (subsequent to his original study) he has in fact reported, not merely the observation of many more homosexuals who fit the classic triangle, but the observation of some fifty pairs of parents of homosexuals, most of whom make up their expected corners of the triangle — dominant, smothering mother and distant hostile father (Bieber 1976). Unfortunately, beyond this bare claim, Bieber offers no elaborating detail. Who knows, therefore, how reliable his report really is? One can only go on the past, and approach his new claim with caution and perhaps scepticism.

Suppose, however, some reliable positive evidence for the hypothesis about the classic triangle were obtained. We are not yet out of the woods; at least, we cannot at once conclude that dominant mothers and cold fathers are the causes of homosexual behaviour. In particular, we might be committing the fallacy of confusing cause and effect, or perhaps failing to identify a common cause (Salmon 1973). The case might be as follows: some male children have certain characteristics (perhaps inherited) and these particular children grow up to be homosexual. Moreover, the childhood characteristics of the (future) adult homosexuals are such as to elicit in the parents certain behaviours and attitudes, specifically the behaviours and attitudes of the classic triangle. In this case, the parents' behaviour, although it does really obtain and conform to the Freudian hypothesis, is in fact not the cause of the adult homosexuality. It is something which is caused incidentally on the way to such homosexuality.

Of course, we know already that this little picture is more than a purely speculative hypothesis. The evidence for the classic triangle is indeed equalled by the evidence suggesting that homosexual men have tended to have had atypical childhoods when compared to heterosexual men. Not every homosexual has differed from the (heterosexual) norm, any more than every homosexual has (reported) a dominant mother. But homosexual men, when children, have tended to have been out of phase with their contemporaries. They disliked playing boys' games. They were more into dolls and dressing up. They were much more likely to be perceived as sissies than were boys who later grew into heterosexuals. In behaviour and attitude, they were more pitched towards the female gender end of the spectrum.

All of this suggests that (at least in respects) the Freudians may have got things back to front. There is indeed evidence that children influence parents' behaviour, as well as vice versa (Chess et al. 1960). But, with respect, who needs a social scientist to tell you that? Perhaps it is the delicate 'mother's boy' who alienates the potentially friendly father. The coldness and distance does then exist, and later the adult homosexual is reporting truly. Yet what he is reporting is an effect, not a cause. How could he (the homosexual) know that it was his own childhood nature that made his father what that father undoubtedly became?

It is a causal link going in this direction that is (primarily) favoured by the second set of Kinsey researchers (Bell et al. 1981), and clearly, given what has been presented, there is much to commend it. But, without wanting to appear awkward for the sake of being awkward, and ignoring the fact that if the causal link does go this way then we are now left with no explanation of homosexual orientation (merely with a description of its effects), even this option is not entirely problem free. The biggest worry is the most obvious. We have faulted the Freudian for going too quickly from reports of parental natures to claims that parental natures were indeed as reported. Likewise, we may find fault now for going too quickly from reports of childhood natures to claims that childhood natures were indeed as reported.

How do we know that male homosexuals really were sissies as children? How do we know that they really wanted to play with dolls rather than with bat and ball? Could not adult distortions (subconscious, non-malicious) be giving the researchers answers that, by now, they are expecting to hear? Apart from anything else, one suspects that the questionnaire-answering homosexual is as aware that his childhood was supposed to be atypical as that his mother was supposed to be dominant. Moreover, I can well imagine many people (hetero and homosexual) suppressing the rather uncomfortable memories of having been sissy-like. Even if this does not happen, one thing which does seem fairly certain is that memories of childhood will be influenced by the society within which one lives, no less than will memories of parental attitudes. Choosing Sweden and Australia as the extremes of sexual sensitivity and crude male chauvinism, M. W. Ross (1980) had little trouble in showing that homosexuals reported themselves a great deal more gender-atypical (as children) in the latter society than the former.

Fortunately, however, matters are not quite as black as all this. There is now information starting to come in from long-term studies showing that boys judged more effeminate or gender-atypical than usual do in fact have a much greater probability of growing up into adult homosexual orientation. Richard Green (1985) reports on sixty-six boys who were referred to his gender-disorder clinic, who 'showed extensive interest in cross-dressing, preferentially role played as females, frequently played with female-type dress-up dolls, had a primarily female peer group, expressed the wish to be girls, and avoided rough-and-tumble play and sports' (p. 340). These boys, of average age seven and a half, were matched against fifty-six volunteers, controlling for 'age, gender, and sibling sequence of the child and race, religion, educational level, and marital status of the parents' (p. 339). Today, these children are late teenagers/young adults, and of forty-four previously referred boys, 68 per cent have bisexual to homosexual erotic fantasies and of those 80 per cent have bisexual to homosexual behaviour. None of the thirty-four controls still remaining in the study is other than heterosexual in either behaviour or fantasy.

There are still questions. Most homosexuals, whatever their childhood behaviour, did not end up being referred to a gender-disorder clinic; and by the age of seven and a half, parents can have had a great deal of influence on a child's behaviour. Nevertheless, given that this study avoided the pitfalls of retrospection, given that childhood behaviour could be (and was) assessed independently, given the strongly significant result, it does start to seem that there really are crucial childhood indicators pointing towards adult sexual orientation. It should be noted that there is not an invariable sequence: Green has subjects highly atypical as children, wholly heterosexual as adults. Yet one is left with the suspicion that, while Freudians may well have the phenomena right, they may also in respects have the aetiology backwards. (See also Lebovits 1972; Zuger 1978.) (It should also be noted that we are talking here of *childhood* indicators. The evidence does not refer to adult gender attributes and feelings. My own feeling is that, in our society at least, children tend to be more gender-stereotyped than adults. A boy of ten who likes dolls is a sissy. A man of thirty who loves cooking is not.)

2.5 Can we test indirectly?

Must we then reject Freud? This is surely premature. The points made thus far hardly destroy the Freudian framework. What they do rather is suggest that some of the most-prized evidence which is paraded in Freud's favour is probably less supportive than enthusiasts insist. We are dampening the Freudian's hopes. They are hardly being washed away in a downpour. As I have just said, by seven and a half years of age, a great deal might have happened. Can the spirits of the Freudian be revived, somewhat? Before bringing this discussion to an end, let us try casting our net somewhat more widely. Suppose you want to hold, not merely to the Freudian facts, but also to a strict Freudian aetiology. What can you do?

Thus far, I have been looking only at direct tests (or attempted tests) of Freud's position. I have been looking only at work which tackles the classic triangle head on. However, this is, of course, not the only way to test hypotheses — indeed, in most branches of science this is not the usual way to test hypotheses. You cannot look directly at the hydrogen atom, to check that it is one proton and one electron. Nor can you go back in time to map the exact size and location of Gondwanaland. What you must do, rather, is test *indirectly*. From your hypothesis you try to tease out observable consequences, and then you test these, thus providing (at second hand) proof for or against your position (E. Nagel 1961; Hempel 1966). You come up with chemical reactions that would be true, were hydrogen made from one proton and one electron. You predict present land formations, were Gondwanaland a reality in the past. And then you go and check (Ruse 1981d). The obvious move for the Freudian at this point, therefore, is to see if his/her theoretical structure can be examined indirectly, through expected consequences, rather than simply through direct reports.

There is one note of caution that must be struck before we scamper happily up the path of indirect testing. The opportunities it offers you are bought at a price. The difficulty with indirect tests is that the further one gets from the central hypotheses one is trying to evaluate, the greater the chance that other factors might intrude, thereby reducing the relevance of one's tests to the hypotheses under study. Of course this is a problem in any science, and this is certainly not an argument against indirect tests per se. But it is a worry, especially when one is dealing — as even Freud (1955b) admitted — with a body of claims like psychoanalytic theory, which is loose and not always tightly tied together. In such a case, the possibility of extraneous disturbing factors does rather get manifested.

Underlining this point, but showing also that Freud's claims on homosexuality can be (and have been) tested indirectly, let me refer to one ingenious set of experiments attempting to test psychoanalytic thinking about homosexuality through the 'subliminal exposure of drive related stimuli' (Silverman et al. 1973: 178). It was argued (surely correctly) that one of the key features of the psychoanalytic position on homosexuality is that the male homosexual will be caught up in incestuous conflicts about his relationship with his mother. On the one hand, the homosexual loves mother; on the other hand, he realizes he cannot have mother fully without violating the incest taboo. Male heterosexuals have no such incestuous conflicts. The homosexual fears women because he is liable to get castrated if he is caught, and because (being penis-less) women are a nasty reminder of what does happen if one does get caught.

Ingeniously, Silverman and his associates therefore argued that if one can trigger or intensify incestuous wishes in a homosexual, then as a consequence one ought to get an intensification of homosexual urges. The urges come about as a defence against the wishes. In line with this reasoning, a picture was flashed on a screen viewed by homosexuals. The flash, which was far too brief to be picked up consciously (four milliseconds), showed a nude male and nude female in a sexually suggestive position, and was accompanied by the message (in heavy letters one inch high) FUCK MOMMY. As the Freudian would expect, after being exposed to such flashes, homosexuals (thirty-six non-neurotic volunteers) showed a significant increase in homosexual urges. A control group of thirty-six heterosexuals showed no increase in sexual urge at all. The conclusion was therefore drawn that supporting evidence had been found for the psychoanalytic theory about the genesis of male homosexuality. At least, somewhat more cautiously: 'These findings lend support to the psychoanalytic hypothesis that a homosexual orientation in males is linked to conflict over incestuous wishes' (1973: 185).

Obviously this experiment does rather illustrate some of the already mentioned problems with indirect tests. In order to conclude that the experiment really tests the core of psychoanalytic theory, one has to accept a number of subsidiary assumptions, particularly that subliminal presentation of a picture of a sexually suggestive nude pair with FUCK MOMMY will in fact trigger incestuous urges. Even if we accept that subliminal messages can trigger urges in the rather straightforward way being assumed, one still might wonder why the urges of the viewing homosexuals should be incestuous. Perhaps they were simply acting defensively against *any* heterosexual liaison. But if this is so, support for anything Freudian or neo-Freudian drops drastically.

Also, some of the rather familiar objections apply. The subjects were volunteers, recruited by an advertisement in the *Village Voice*, a weekly Greenwich Village tabloid. How typical were they? But, to its credit, the experiment does get round some of the worst objections to direct testing (at least, direct testing as it has generally been done). Most significantly, there was no need to rely on dubious self-reports of childhood. Moreover, in defence of Silverman and his co-workers one must point out that this experiment was but one of a series of similar tests of psychoanalytic theory (Silverman et al. 1972).

One wishes that one could report on many more forays into the indirect testing of Freudian claims about homosexuality. Unfortunately, this seems not to be possible. Researchers in this field are obsessed with questionnaires and surveys. They show not even the experimental ingenuity of a first-year physics student. All one can therefore conclude is that, for all its problems, indirect testing remains a plausible line of inquiry — one which might indeed throw some useful light on some of the queries about causal connections raised in previous sections. Freudians certainly have nothing to lose, and given even the mild encouragement of Silverman's findings, they might have much to gain. (See also Kline 1981.)

2.6 Conclusion

Freud's theories are not pseudo-science. At least, the critics have given us no reason to conclude this. It seems fair to say also that Freud's views on homosexuality may well draw our attention to some interesting facts about the early lives of (male) homosexuals — although the numbers of exceptions are almost as interesting as the numbers of confirmations. However, almost all of the studies on Freud's work — especially almost all of the direct studies — raise as many questions as they purport to solve. If nothing else, we are left with major questions about which are causes and which effects. Do parents trigger sons' future sexual orientations, or do sons' childhood behaviours trigger parental attitudes? There is probably some fire behind all of the Freudian smoke. How much, is another question.

One alternative, thus far unmentioned, does present itself. Perhaps matters are more complex either than that homosexuality is a direct function of parental behaviour or that parental behaviour is simply an epiphenomenon of the life of a child who is going to be homosexual anyway. It could be that a child of a certain kind triggers parental behaviour, which then in turn plays a crucial role in the child's future sexual orientation and behaviour. In short, both a child of a certain kind and parents of a certain kind are needed. Obviously in order to see if a hypothesis like this has any worth, we are going to have to try to dissect and separate the genetic and environmental components in human ontogeny. I am loathe to start here what must necessarily be a premature discussion before we have introduced any ideas about genetics. For the moment, then, I shall let things rest, but shall return to the issue in subsequent chapters.

3

The Adaptational Analysis

Freud is the seminal thinker in psychoanalytic theory. Everything since him has been done either in continuation or reaction. For instance, Melanie Klein (1932) and Edmund Bergler (1956) adopt a fairly thoroughly Freudian standpoint, but argue that the key triggering point for adult homosexuality lies right back at the oral phase. Other thinkers, however, have reacted more strongly against Freud, and I want in this chapter to discuss what I sense is the main rival position with respect to homosexuality — one which is nevertheless very much indebted to Freud. I shall refer to it as the 'adaptational' position, or alternatively (for reasons that will be obvious) as the 'phobic' position (Rado 1940, 1949; Ovesey 1954, 1955a, b, 1956, 1965; Kardiner et al. 1959a, b, c, d; Ovesey and Person 1973; Salzman 1965; and, at least in respects, Socarides 1968, 1978 and Person 1980). As in the last chapter, I speak now only of males.

3.1 Problems and revisions

We start with the denial of two cornerstones to Freud's own position: universal bisexuality and the existence of the libido. The criticism of universal bisexuality dates to an article by Sandor Rado, first published in 1940. Although Rado admits that humans, like other animals, may have in them at the beginning certain potentials for development either one way or another, he denies absolutely that it is very meaningful to talk of humans (particularly adult humans) as being 'bisexual' in the sense of having mixed up in them in various proportions elements of both sexes, where it is appropriate to speak of some such element as 'male' (or 'female'). Freud, points out Rado, argued for some sort of psychological bisexuality on the basis of a supposed biological (particularly anatomical) bisexuality. However, in the biological realm

it is not permissible to single out any one element, no matter how conspicuous, such as the gonad, and make it the sole criterion of sex. To attempt to determine 'maleness' or 'femaleness' by the relative percentage of male and female hormones in blood or urine is obviously to carry this error to an extreme. Sex can be determined only by the character of the reproductive action system *as a whole.* (Rado 1940: 180)

Furthermore, because something at one stage of its development may have certain characteristics, or potentialities for taking either of two paths, it does not follow that at a later stage of development (including full growth) one can automatically read in these characteristics or potentialities. 'In humans the complicated embryological past of the reproductive system has no detectable influence on the efficient reproductive functioning of the normal individual' (p. 181). To make an ascription of bisexuality, to the adult human in particular, we must evaluate the concept in its own proper terms — whether the adult human can reproduce both as a male and as a female, which is the sense in which we use 'bisexual' of things like oysters. And the answer is obvious: 'Using the term bisexuality in the only sense in which it is biologically legitimate, there is no such thing as bisexuality either in man or in any other of the higher vertebrates' (p. 182). In other words, Rado denies what I am terming the broader sense of biological bisexuality — that some features like nipples show that males possess essentially female parts (and conversely for other features).

Freud's critical analogy is thus destroyed, and when we turn to human psychology we see that there is no more justification for speaking of someone as being psychically bisexual than as being anatomically bisexual (psychically bisexual in the broad sense, with the sexologists' sense as a special case). First of all, as in the biological realm, there is the near impossibility of deciding which psychic phenomena are to be taken as male (or masculine) or female (or feminine) considered out of the overall context. Certainly, this is impossible as soon as we get away from direct reference or imagery of genitalia or reproductive acts. Freud's own suggestion that active/passive symbolizes masculine/feminine is riddled with obvious problems (and indeed, had to be abandoned by Freud himself). Second, we just cannot argue from adults to children, and vice versa. Because we might consider some idea characteristic of adult females, we cannot assume that a male child who has such an idea is bisexual. 'A fantasy whose content is unquestionably male or female in an adult, might in a child reflect nothing but complete ignorance or deliberate misinformation' (Rado 1940: 185). And third, because someone exhibits homosexual behaviour, this does not mean that they are thereby showing behaviour appropriate to the opposite sex, and are revealing their bisexuality. Such behaviour might be evidence of dominance, submission, cooperation, or whatever, rather than an act of sex-role reversal. In short, the vague notion of bisexuality in any sense has as little validity in the psychic realm as it has in the anatomical realm.

The libido fares little better at the hands of the critics. It is argued that the concept is at best tautological and at worst meaningless and confusing. The notion of psychic energy, of which the libido is a form, finds no support in the study of the nature of neural activity. Under the most charitable interpretation the notion of psychic energy is only a metaphor. But Freud treats it as a concrete entity, and this gets him into impressive sounding, but tautological, redescriptions of everyday phenomena.

For example, suppose we observe an infant's relation to its mother. We can say from this clinical observation: The infant is intensely interested in the mother, who is the source of all his gratifications. This is an inference based on observation with which we can all agree, and it tells us something about the mother—child relationship. Suppose now we make use of the energic hypothesis and say: The infant intensely cathects the mother with libidinal energy. This statement does not add anything to our knowledge about the relationship between the mother and the child. We have merely restated the original observation in hypothetical energic terms. Hence, the tautology. (Kardiner et al. 1959b: 137)

All of this talk about the libido is just not 'operational', and moreover leads one mistakenly to think that instinct is at least as important as the environment in forming character traits. One believes that the libido is going to go through certain evolutionarily fixed patterns as the child develops, and that this lies outside of the scope of the environment and of education. Thus, for instance, Freud described the creation of an anal retentive in terms of an anal phase through which the child is innately predestined to go. But what is needed, rather, is an explanation of the way a child behaves and develops which is not done in terms of hypothetical concepts and which instead shows how the child can respond to the exigencies of the external environment (Kardiner et al. 1959b).

With bisexuality and the libido gone, what have we got left? Well, obviously we have a child who is born, and who develops to adulthood. The essential assumption of the position we are considering here is that normally such a child will develop into a heterosexual adult. However, to use a well-known phrase, life is a struggle for existence (Darwin 1859), and if something untoward occurs, the child must respond — he must 'adapt' to survive. And this can be the starting point for adult homosexual behaviour, for now the adaptational position starts to run on familiar lines, that is to say (despite all the criticisms) Freudian lines. What is argued is that at various points in childhood development there might be set up a fear of women, of their genitals in particular, and of heterosexual relationships. There is thus an adaptive switch to homosexuality.

The sort of thing which might set up such a fear will vary. It could be an early childhood experience. More likely, and most commonly, it will be an unsuccessful resolution of the Oedipus complex. Simply speaking, one fears women because one is in intense rivalry with one's castration-anxiety-inducing father; one is caught in a guiltily and incestuously binding love for one's mother, which feeling gets transferred to other females; and also probably mother is doing her best to make sure that 'other girls' do not seem very attractive.

It should be noted that there is going to be one major difference here between the full Freudian position and the adaptational position. For Freud, because we are all bisexual (in the broad sense), the causing of homosexuality can be seen as both a push and pull affair, or as either a push or a pull affair (Cooper 1974). We might become homosexual because we fear women; but it might also be because we like men. It might just be that we get locked into our narcissistic phase and never want to get out. For the adaptational theorist, however, this kind of preference explanation is ruled out. We never do go naturally through a homosexual phase. We have to be deflected into it. And fear will be the key. 'A homosexual adaptation is a result of "hidden but incapacitating fears of the opposite sex"' (Bieber et al. 1962, p. 303).

Two points remain to be made. The first is that the adaptation theorists are somewhat distrustful of the concept of 'latent homosexuality'. One would perhaps expect this. The concept of latent homosexuality grew out of Freud's belief in ubiquitous bisexuality, in just about all senses. We all have homosexual elements in us, and that these should lie fairly close to the surface in some overt heterosexuals is clearly going to be the case. However, having rejected ubiquitous bisexuality, adaptation theorists want to play down latent homosexuality. 'It is obvious that, although this concept may have served a useful purpose in the initial development of the psychology of sex behaviour, its continued use is detrimental in a scientific and humanistic sense' (Salzman 1965: 244). It is probably not too paradoxical to say that adaptation theorists are happier with a notion of latent heterosexuality in homosexuals, than with latent homosexuality in heterosexuals! Such theorists believe that homosexuals have been diverted from their true path, and in partial evidence of this they report how many homosexuals have fleeting heterosexual urges and fantasies.

But there still remains a problem. What about the fact that many essentially heterosexual men occasionally have homosexual urges and fantasies? If these are not evidence of bisexuality, how then can we explain them? One adaptation theorist has introduced the notion of 'pseudohomosexuality'. Lionel Ovesey argues that many men develop homosexual urges, not because they are really homosexual (which would involve fear of women), but because of crises or failures in their lives — their work, or their social or sexual lives. These men then set up unconsciously an equation which leads them to a form of homosexuality. 'I am a failure as a man = I am castrated = I am a woman = I am a homosexual' (Ovesey 1965: 212). This kind of homosexuality, however, is bogus, or 'pseudo'.

In what sense is pseudohomosexuality an adaptive manoeuvre? Ovesey argues that as children we are all dependent, particularly on the mother's breast for milk. Therefore adult failure brings up again these dependency feelings — we feel in some sense the need for support. In some way the penis becomes the symbol for the maternal breast, and hence homosexual behaviour comes about. For instance, in sucking the semen from a penis one is symbolically taking milk from the breast. Alternatively, taking the penis either orally or anally one is taking over the 'masculine' strength of the donor, undoing one's own castration, and fitting oneself to fight the world's battles again. Or perhaps one might try to deny one's weakness by taking a dominant role sexually with other men. The crucial point is that what one is trying to do is conquer perceived failures, and one's ultimate motives are not really sexual at all. Hence the term 'pseudohomosexuality'.

The second point is that, starting from their basic position, the adaptation theorists take a different position from Freud on the question of 'cure' (that is, change from homosexuality to heterosexuality). For Freud, as we have seen, adult homosexuality is a case of arrested development, and is not a sickness as such. For this reason it is, technically speaking, a perversion rather than a neurosis. Consequently, the whole question of 'cure' is very problematical. Analysis is not much help, because analysis aims to lift undue repressions, and the very problem with a perversion is that there is no repression. For the adaptation theorists, on the other hand, homosexuality is a neurosis — one is twisting away from the normal heterosexual path. It is therefore a sickness. 'Homosexuality . . . is a symptom of a neurosis, a defence against castration anxiety by the phobic avoidance of the female genitals' (Ovesey 1965: 221). It is a 'personality disorder' brought about by 'parental psychopathology' (Bieber et al. 1962: 42).

Fortunately, however, because homosexuality is an illness — a neurosis — the possibility of cure is open. By bringing to the light of day their fears, homosexuals can be brought over to heterosexuality. It is certainly not the case that adaptation analysts believe that all homosexuals can be made heterosexual; but they do believe that a significant proportion can be. The Bieber study, based on 106 men initially homosexual, claimed that twenty-nine men had become exclusively heterosexual as the result of treatment (Bieber et al. 1962: 276). Certain obvious factors make for a favourable prognosis: the initial desire to become heterosexual; being fairly young (and thus not too firmly entrenched in the homosexual pattern); being ambisexual in the sense of having some heterosexual urges in with one's homosexual urges, and thus clearly not being that frightened of women as sex objects; and so forth. (Although there is a denial of universal bisexuality, it is not denied that some people do have both hetero and homosexual urges. What is denied is that the homosexual urges are at all akin to the heterosexual urges of the people of the opposite sex. If one can stand yet another term, perhaps one could invent the term 'omnisexual' to express this notion.)

So much for the adaptational alternative to classical Freudianism. The revision obviously owes much to the model, even though it breaks from it in certain key respects. Let us turn now to critical philosophical discussion.

3.2 Bisexuality

A key issue, probably *the* key issue, is that of bisexuality. Freud wants to argue that we are all bisexual in some broad sense — biologically and psychologically — and that this is shown as we go through the homo and heterosexual phases of childhood, even though most of us eventually end up as heterosexuals. The revisionists, on the contrary, deny that we are bisexual in any sense, but most particularly in a psychological sense. Rado's attack centres on the point that the psychological or psychoanalytic bisexuality that is so crucial to Freud's position was derived by direct analogy from a concept of bisexuality in straight biology, where this is understood as a bisexuality involving crossover of male and female characteristics, and not simply possession of fully functioning organs of both sexes. Rado denies the thesis of ubiquitous biological bisexuality. And then he carries his attack over to the psychoanalytic realm. The key initial question, therefore, is just how successful Rado's attack on biological bisexuality really is. I would suggest that there are major problems with it.

All would agree that at the moment of conception there is not much difference between the zygotes of males and zygotes of females, especially in higher organisms like humans. (The difference is a matter of one chromosome. See Levitan and Montagu 1977.) Furthermore, as the embryo starts to develop, male and female go along the same path for a while, even with respect to their sexual organs. It is only as the embryo gets older that we start to get a real difference in the sexual features of male and female. It will also be agreed that even in the adult we get features pertaining to sex that *seem* to be similar or analogous — the obvious examples are the nipples of the male apparently corresponding to the functional nipples of the female. And moreover, it seems clear that under certain circumstances there can be a major switch in sexual development. Hormone treatment and so forth (not to mention certain natural events) can cause a child to grow up with the body of a member of the opposite sex. A child with male chromosomes can appear physically (phenotypically) female, and vice versa. (Much more on this in chapter 5.)

This much seems to be granted by all, including adaptationists. The question at issue, therefore, is whether (speaking purely biologically now) on the basis of these facts one can speak of a person as being in some sense 'bisexual'. I take it that such a claim could have two parts, which can to a certain extent be considered independently, but which taken together would make the fullest case. First, on the basis of development one might want to say that each person goes through a bisexual phase, one which will normally go on towards one sex but which could be switched towards the other (the serial notion). Second, one might want to say, on the basis of such things as male nipples (and perhaps the female clitoris), that in some sense the adult human is bisexual — meaning that (all) adult humans share sexual characteristics, even though they are much more developed and perhaps only fully functioning in one sex rather than the other.

Rado's argument, which seems to be directed indifferently against either of these notions of bisexuality, is singularly unconvincing. He writes as follows:

we see that sex in its entirety refers to the differentiation in the individuals as regards their contrarelated action systems of reproduction. Taking these considerations now in reverse order, we start from the fact that, insofar as concerns their reproductive action systems, individuals are of two contrarelated types. It is precisely this differentiation that constitutes the character of the sexes. Each of the two systems may be dissected into a multitude of structures, substances

and functions, of which it is composed. The sex aspect of every one of these
constituent parts is derived from the fact of its participation in the system as
a whole. (Rado 1940: 180)

He then goes on to draw the conclusion quoted above (p. 46) about the
impossibility of speaking of any particular feature as 'male' or 'female'.

This argument fails. Inasmuch as Rado makes a case, it presupposes
extreme holism or anti-reductionism. (See Polanyi 1968; Causey 1969;
and chapter 7.) Everything must be considered in relationship to fertilizing
ability — one cannot abstract or break things down into components. In
other words, what Rado is basing his position on is the philosophical
assumption that a part of the functioning whole is by definition or
stipulation understandable and definable *only* with respect to the entire
functioning whole. But this position is ridiculous, or at least it is far too
extreme. One might want to concede that, at the biological level,
fertilization is the key factor in sex, and one might also concede that
when one puts parts together one gets new properties emerging in the
whole; but those concessions do not imply that one cannot isolate out the
parts — in sex in particular. Nor do they mean that two things (especially
two sexual things) with different functions could not have been made
from the same sorts of parts or share the same parts when fully functioning,
or have a crossover of parts.

To consider an illustrative example: a petrol motor, a diesel motor,
and an electric motor are all different — they work on different principles.
On the other hand, it clearly makes good sense to say that the petrol and
diesel motors are a lot more similar to each other than is either to the
electric motor. And the reason is obvious. Although the principles of
ignition are different, the petrol and diesel motors share many features
in common, features not shared by the electric motor. Both, for example,
have cylinders. But if we take Rado's position seriously, we cannot really
say this. We should have to say that the cylinder-for-the-petrol-motor
and the cylinder-for-the-diesel-motor are two radically different things,
because the way the fuel is ignited in the two motors is different.
Obviously we do not want to say this, nor (considering development)
would we want to say that the petrol motor and the diesel motor could
not have been made from similar sorts of things, or even have been quite
alike until carburettor, spark plugs, and so forth, were added to the
petrol motor. Nor would we even want to deny that usually some parts
are found only in motors of one kind, but occasionally they are transferred
to motors of another kind.

Going back to human beings, we now see that Rado is being altogether
too restrictive by withholding the term 'bisexual' by fiat from anything

which is not a totally intermediate, fully fertile hermaphrodite. We can isolate parts and we can speak of them as being shared by different sexes, even though they may be far more developed in one than the other, or only fully functioning in one sex rather than the other. Of course, this is not to say that one thereby thinks that grown humans show many common sexual features. Even if one agrees that male nipples in some way correspond to female nipples, one might, for example, want to question just how far the clitoris can in any meaningful sense be considered analogous to the penis. Moreover, accepting a common origin is not to say that all humans go through a male phase and then a female phase and so on. I shall pick up later on these points.

Let us move on now to the psychological dimension. Having argued that human beings are entirely unisexual (that is, of one of two sexes) biologically, Rado has little trouble in arguing that they are entirely unisexual psychologically also. The orgasm is taken to be the crucial factor in the psychosexual dimension, and this can be tied to fertilization in the biological dimension.

It is man's practice to engage in genital activity regardless of reproductive intent. He may even abandon any possibility of reproduction by evading in this pursuit the genital organ of the opposite sex. But how then is the pleasure yield of genital activity obtained? What is its nature? It is, of course, orgasm, a reflex effect of the reproductive action system. Having so identified genital pleasure, we see that it is precisely the orgasmic element of the reproductive system that forms the basis of the genital pleasure function. Orgasm is a pivotal point, being also the point of insemination. (Rado 1940: 183)

Having made this connection, Rado can conclude immediately that since male physiological sex activity is entirely male, so also therefore is male psychological sex activity. And the same is true for females. 'Physiologically, genital activity in an individual with male organs is always male, and the same applies to the female. Whatever man does or fancies, it is just as impossible for him to get out of the confines of his biological sex as to get out of his skin' (p. 183).

In short, Rado is able to argue that homosexual inclinations and behaviour are not — cannot be — signs that we have been trapped with the 'wrong' side of our bisexual psychological natures: homosexuality cannot be a case of landing towards one end of the biological male/female spectrum and towards the other end of the psychological male/female spectrum. A person with a male body being attracted to other men cannot be being attracted to men in the way that a woman is attracted to men. Sexually speaking, there is no overlap between males and females. Virtually by definition, only females can be attracted to men as females are attracted to men. Homosexuality therefore has to be something else. It cannot be a function of our (psychological) bisexual natures, either as we all might possess such natures as adults or as some of us might be caught during development when all of us are far more overtly bisexual (or in the opposite sex phase) than when we become adults.

In response: much the same argument holds against this stage of Rado's argument as against the earlier state. Virtually by definition Rado is claiming that sex in a male, whether it be at the physiological level of ejaculation or the psychological level of attraction, cannot in any way be separated from the fact that it is occurring in a man. By definition, because it occurs in a man, what a man feels, even for another man, cannot be what a woman feels. But this is virtually to make one's case by stipulation. A priori, there is no reason why what a woman feels for a man should not also be what a man feels. No argument has been given against the possibility of bisexuality in this sense — a possibility on which the Freudian position crucially depends.

In fact, empirical studies since Rado have suggested that he could not have made a worse choice for staking his case on the absolute psychological difference between male and female than by concentrating on the orgasm. Once one drops the arbitrary stipulation that orgasm-in-male and orgasm-in-female necessarily are absolutely different, empirical investigation suggests strongly that the physiological/psychological differences between male and female are far, far less than the similarities. Masters and Johnson (1966, 1979), deservedly renowned pioneers in this area, find exactly the same four-part cycle (excitement, plateau, orgasm, and resolution) in male and female (see figures 3.1 and 3.2). And other investigators have noted the difficulty of distinguishing male and female orgasms: 'it would appear that individuals are unable to distinguish the sex of a person from that person's written description of his or her orgasm. Neither psychologists, medical students, nor obstetrician/gynecologists had significant success in this task' (Vance and Wagner 1976).

To re-emphasize my main point: what I am saying is that one simply cannot rule out by definition the possibility of psychological bisexuality in general (the broad sense) or of erotic bisexuality in particular — or even some serial variant as favoured by Freud. Much that the orthodox Freudian says may be true. Even if it is not, what one cannot do is to argue as Rado does, virtually claiming that the notion of bisexuality in any sense is contradictory and that Freud's position therefore must be mistaken. (For a defence of Freud's position on bisexuality see C. Thompson 1963.)[1]

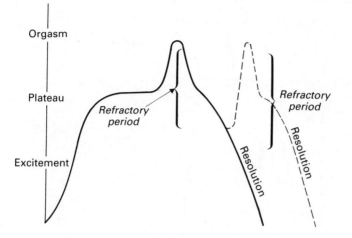

FIGURE 3.1   *The male sexual response cycle (the broken line represents*
possible variations on the main theme)
(Masters and Johnson 1966: 5)

3.3 The libido

The other main criticism of the adaptationists centres on the Freudian
libido, that key sexual force or energy which is hypothesized as the
driving mechanism putting the developing child through his various
psychosexual stages. This is criticized as redundant, as 'tautological', as
not 'operational'.

It is not my wish to defend Freud's libido concept unreservedly. Apart
from anything else, there seems to have been ambiguity in Freud's own
mind about what precisely the concept was supposed to mean or refer to.
Sometimes it is portrayed as a purely mental phenomenon, a kind of
psychic energy, and at other times as something with a rather direct
physiological base (Jones 1955; see also Sulloway 1979). One thing which
does seem fairly certain is that, in the light of the development of
physiological knowledge since Freud first developed his ideas, there is
no corresponding physical evidence for the kind of way that Freud
envisioned the libido; that is, as a sort of fluid which flowed in certain
channels, perhaps being redirected (as in neurosis — the libido must go
somewhere) or not being properly dammed (as in perversion). This has
been referred to as Freud's 'hydraulic model'. (See Knapp 1966 for an

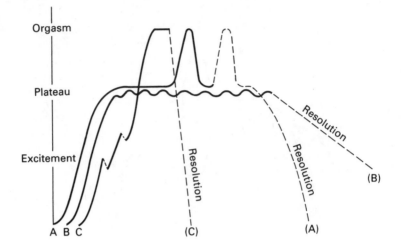

FIGURE 3.2   The female sexual response cycle
(Masters and Johnson 1966: 5)

informative discussion of physiological developments since Freud and
an attempt to reinterpret Freud in the light of these developments.)

However, it would be wrong to leave matters simply at this point —
particularly if it were thought that Freudian failure implies phobic
plausibility. I sense something radically flawed in the adaptationist
critique, and I suspect that terms like 'operational' give the clue. This
latter was a notion introduced by the physicist/philosopher Percy
Bridgman (1959), who hoped to do away with (or, at least, give full
account of) all of the strange and threatening concepts of early twentieth-
century physics. He hoped to show that notions like 'mass' and 'velocity'
could be translated into 'operations', namely the things we do with pencil
and paper and ruler and the like. He hoped, that is to say, to convert
physics to an extreme empiricism.

Of course, as people rapidly realized, both in theory and in practice
this is not possible — nor is it particularly desirable. Science, especially
good science, transcends the directly observable and measurable.
Recognizing (as we had to recognize in the first chapter) that there is no
absolute distinction, at one level we have the phenomena and at another
level we have the causal theory, introduced to explain the phenomena.
We have rays of light and we have undulations in the ether. We have tall
and short pea plants and we have independently assorting genes. We
have people falling sick and we have the HTLV-III virus. Moreover,

there is no way of eliminating waves or genes or viruses in terms of that which we can sense. The unobservable or theoretical notions have lives and roles of their own. (This is not to say that they are divorced from the real world. You get at them through indirect tests.)

It is obvious that in introducing the libido, Freud is doing no more (and no less) than any other empirical scientist. He is introducing an unobserved, perhaps unobservable, theoretical notion, in order to explain the physical phenomena — like anal retentives and homosexual sons. The libido is on a par with gene or molecule, and thus simply to fault it because it is not operational or is 'tautological' (whatever that might mean) is fundamentally to mistake the nature of science. Let me go further and point out that if the adaptationist objections were well made at this point, they would then have done only half of their self-appointed task. If Freud's causal hypotheses break down, what then is one to put in their place? The adaptationists, no less than Freud (in respects, identically to Freud), have the growing boy crucially influenced by parents in ways which are (to say the least of it) prima facie odd. Why should a strong mother turn a boy into an adult homosexual? Why not turn him into a philosopher or preacher? To answer questions like these it is incumbent upon the adaptationists to introduce their own theoretical causal concepts, tying together and explaining all that happens at the phenomenal level. They must not simply destroy the libido. They must put something in its place. And this they singularly fail to do.

There is no need to dwell or linger. The libido as presented by Freud probably needs modification, to put matters mildly. Yet if one is to offer a full account of psychosexual development, explaining why emotions and erotic attractions swing one way or another, some sort of underlying, causal hypothesis will be needed. And almost certainly this hypothesis will refer to unknown and unseen entities or substances, of one sort or another. Freud's sense was right, even if his execution was flawed. Perhaps, after we have looked at other approaches, we shall have some more idea of how an adequate causal backing might be supplied. What we can now say is that the negativism of the adaptationists is ill-founded.

3.4 Latent homosexuality

I have dealt now with the two major points of criticism that the revisionists bring against classical Freudianism. But we have also the possibility of indirect tests, for Freud and the adaptationists differ quite starkly on various of the implications of their positions. Let us therefore now open up the discussion by looking at the consequences of the two psychoanalytic approaches.

First, we have the matter of 'latent homosexuality'. We know that this notion is intimately connected with the concept of bisexuality — indeed, the former is almost a natural outgrowth of the latter. There is, therefore, some slight ambiguity. Given the possibility of (adult) bisexuality, at the erotic psychological level, one might argue that some people stand closer to the centre of the spectrum of bisexuality than others, and that as a consequence although some, if not most, adult humans are entirely heterosexual, others show homosexual urges — urges that might come out in the form of dreams and the like, or (being repressed) are expressed in terms of violent and extreme loathing of homosexuality. Or one might argue that all people stand somewhere within the bisexuality spectrum, and that as a consequence all of us (however overtly heterosexual) have some homosexual inclinations — homosexuals are at the other end of the spectrum. Likewise, all of us (however overtly homosexual) have some heterosexual inclinations — heterosexuals are at the other end of the spectrum.

Both of these options have found favour with Freudians, and frequently they are run together indifferently, either being known as latent homosexuality. (My feeling is that Freud's own position rather pushes him towards a belief in a ubiquitous latent homosexuality; however, as medical people concerned with helping unhappy people, the Freudians have tended in practice to concentrate on the more extreme kind of latent homosexual.) The ambiguity will not trouble us, however, for the revisionist attack is intended to apply indifferently against all senses. And indeed, given their argument against bisexuality (in any sense), the revisionists have of course already provided half their argument against (any kind of) latent homosexuality. If adult humans are unisexual there is certainly no immediate presupposition that most or all of us will have homosexual inclinations. One would surely expect the opposite, in fact. But what of the main theoretical argument against latent homosexuality, one directed against either a limited or ubiquitous latent homosexuality? It seems to me suspiciously like the argument against bisexuality — and about as strong. Essentially, the case seems to be that just as it is logically impermissible to speak of a male person having female attitudes, so also is it logically impermissible to speak of a heterosexual person having homosexual attributes. If one is heterosexual then that is it; homosexuality is logically barred.

'Latent homosexuality' is a meaningless term in any new conception of homosexual behavior, for it always characterizes a possibility for behaviour when heterosexual intimacy is interfered with — whether in early years by parental injunction of threats or in later years in prisons or under circumstances in which heterosexual behavior is impossible. (Salzman 1965: 245)

I will not dwell on the reasons why I find this position implausible. Because of the kinds of arguments sketched above in my discussion of bisexuality, I see no logical reason why an essentially heterosexual person should not have genuine homosexual urges. The fact that one is (rightly) to be judged heterosexual in an overall context or sense does not in itself imply that certain aspects of one's psychic nature cannot be homosexual in some genuine sense. It is an empirical matter whether a man who is generally heterosexual in desire and action can have some homosexual urges. But if he does have such urges, why deny that these urges are genuine, unless one can give some very good empirical reasons to think otherwise? It also seems to mean that people conventionally known as 'bisexual' (that is, as having erotic feelings towards both sexes) do not have urges akin to either homosexuals or heterosexuals, and that 'pseudohomosexuals' do not have genuine homosexual urges, and so on and so forth — which is counter-intuitive.[2]

3.5 The effects of therapy

What about the other major implication separating Freudians and adaptationists, namely that centring on hopes of treatment and 'cure' (that is, the changing of sexual orientation)? Freud did not think that homosexuality involves repression. Consequently, he was not very sanguine about the possibility of switching someone from homosexual to heterosexual orientation — analysis is certainly not the key. The adaptation theorists, however, see homosexuality as an adaptive manoeuvre against an inadequate family environment. For this reason, because we are all 'essentially' heterosexual, a bringing of homosexuals to heterosexuality is a real possibility.

The claim has been made that the adaptationist position is vindicated by the fact that many homosexuals have, through therapy, been brought over to successful heterosexuality. In particular, this is the conclusion of Bieber and his co-workers. In their study (1962), they claimed that the analysts on whom they were reporting had a 27 per cent success rate in achieving exclusive heterosexuality. Unfortunately, given the fact that Bieber's claim is presented with as little methodological delicacy as the rest of the study, it has with some reason been questioned (Freund et al.

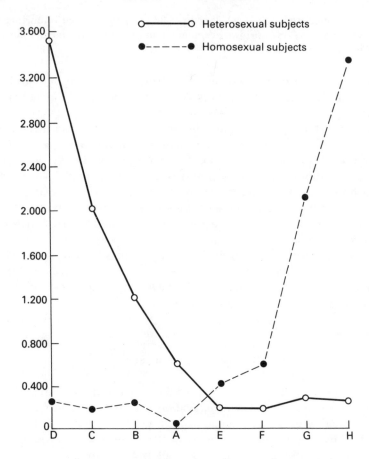

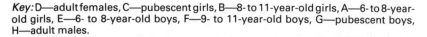

Key: D—adult females, C—pubescent girls, B—8- to 11-year-old girls, A—6- to 8-year-old girls, E—6- to 8-year-old boys, F—9- to 11-year-old boys, G—pubescent boys, H—adult males.

FIGURE 3.3   Penile responses of homosexual and heterosexual males to pictures
of females and males of various ages
(Freund 1974: 35)

1974a). In particular, there is no real discussion by Bieber of how completely the homosexuals have been switched to heterosexuality, nor is there any attempt at a long-term follow-up to see how permanent the change really is. All one gets are the analysts' subjective impressions.

Of course, one might argue that the ultimate truth of a psychoanalytic theory as such does not depend on the success rate of a therapy based on

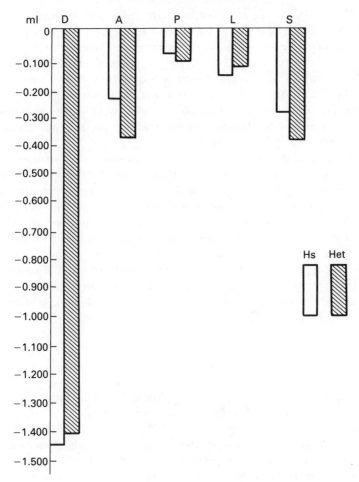

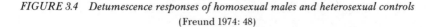

Key: ml—millilitres, D—dermatological pictures, A—pictures of adult persons of the non-preferred sex, P—pictures of pubescent persons of the non-preferred sex, L—pictures of landscapes, S—white drawings on black background, Hs—homosexual males, Het—heterosexual controls.

FIGURE 3.4   Detumescence responses of homosexual males and heterosexual controls
(Freund 1974: 48)

it. And this is true, although clearly a theory and its therapy are not entirely separate. If a therapy based on a theory is very successful, then this gives at least some presumption of the theory's truth. What we can surely say is that despite the enthusiastic claims of some of its supporters, as yet the hard evidence of successful change of sexual orientation is not sufficient to make one put aside other qualms about the truth of the phobic theory. Even if homosexuals are repressed heterosexuals, no one as yet seems very successful at lifting the repressions, at least in any significant way. At this point, Freud seems to have been ahead of his time. (The whole question of 'cure' as a result of psychoanalytic therapy is extremely controversial. A persistent critic is H. J. Eysenck (1952, 1966). An overview of the topic, together with many references, can be found in Fisher and Greenberg 1977.)

Similar doubts bedevil other optimistic claims of 'cure' (whether these be made by adaptationists, or not). Masters and Johnson (1979) made some dramatic claims about their abilities to alter sexual orientation, but their 'success stories' raise more questions than they answer — potential heterosexuals begin as people wanting to become heterosexual, having (at least some) heterosexual fantasies, being in heterosexual relationships (most were married), and so forth. More generally, there are few therapists prepared even to be as optimistic as Bieber and Masters and Johnson. General consensus is that the changes from homo to heterosexuality are few and far between. Most counselling now is directed towards making people accept their sexual orientation.

3.6 Conclusion

The adaptationist position has been highly influential, and its views on sickness undoubtedly still colour many people's thinking about homosexuality. I shall have more to say on this point in a later chapter. For now, it is enough to say simply that its critique of other positions — specifically traditional Freudianism — is badly flawed, and it offers little by way of alternative. It was truly more of a movement than a fruitful scientific option.

4

Freud:
Extensions and Replacements

Over all work on the origins of homosexuality, especially over work making central the influence of parents and others, falls the shadow of Freud — of Freud's theorizing about men, that is. Completing my discussion of approaches which locate the chief causes of homosexual orientation primarily in the forces which impinge on the growing child, I want now to extend out from the Freudian core (referring here chiefly to the orthodox, truly Freudian position). In particular, I shall look first at the major extension by Freud himself to his analysis of homosexuality — his extension from men to women. Then, second, I shall look quickly at the ideas of some who have tried to move on, beyond Freud.

4.1 Freud on women

To recap: the little boy, newly born, has his erotic attentions naturally directed towards his mother. After he has gone through the oral and anal phases, however, he reaches the phallic stage (three to four years old). The boy discovers his genitals, his penis particularly, and this becomes a source of great pleasure when he fondles it. But then the boy makes an alarming discovery. Half the human race do not possess penises — they are castrated, with nothing but gaping wounds to remind them (and the rest of us) of their loss. This sets up a great fear in the boy, his 'castration complex', and this fear is compounded on learning that his beloved mother is penis-less. Now, entering the Oedipal phase, the boy senses that his father is his rival, and that the father has the power to bring about the ultimate mutilating deprivation in the boy. There is therefore a massive repression of sexuality, until, on entering adolescence, overt erotic desires surface again. At this point, if the youth has learnt successfully to master the universal incest taboo, the result is hetero-sexuality; otherwise homosexuality (Freud 1953, 1955a).

Turning now to the girl, we again find a bisexual creature, bound to go through certain phases, and with the potential for different sexual orientations of different intensities (Freud 1933, 1955b, 1961a, b; Abraham 1954). It is not too much of an exaggeration to say that for Freud, if one could dress up a girl in a boy's 'surface' anatomy, she would develop like a boy psychologically — there is not some innate difference between the psychology of boys and girls. However, 'anatomy is destiny' — girls have no penis, and thereby hangs a story. Until they reach the corresponding phallic phase, girls are like boys: they have a primary erotic fixation on their mother. Moreover, they do not feel a sense of deprivation, because inasmuch as they want to fondle their genitals, they have a clitoris with which to masturbate. Then, girls make a shocking discovery — they have no penis, they are castrated. Furthermore, so also is the beloved mother castrated.

At this point a terrific sense of envy begins to be set up — girls want a penis, envying those who have them, and putting down those who do not. The girl starts to turn against her mother: 'The situation as a whole is not very clear, but it can be seen that in the end the girl's mother, who sent her into the world so insufficiently equipped, is almost always held responsible for her lack of a penis' (Freud 1925: 254). On the other hand, the girl starts to turn towards her father, as the other side to *her* Oedipus complex. (An Oedipus complex or phase involves attachment to the opposite-sexed parent and hostility to the same-sexed parent. Jung invented 'Electra complex' for girls, but Freud preferred the same term for both sexes.) Father has the much-desired penis, and moreover, magically, he has the power to give a girl a penis-substitute in the form of a child:

the girl's libido slips into a new position along the line — there is no other way of putting it — of the equation 'penis = child'. She gives up her wish for a penis and puts in place of it a wish for a child: and *with that purpose in view* she takes her father as a love-object. Her mother becomes the object of her jealousy. The girl has turned into a little woman. (Freud 1961b: 256)

As Freud put it, in boys the castration complex (fear of losing the penis) helps destroy the Oedipal triangle; in girls, the castration complex (regret at losing the penis) helps build the Oedipal triangle.

Along with a girl's switch from her mother to her father, there is a repression and cessation of clitoral masturbation. A girl realizes how inadequate is her clitoris against a real penis, and hence she comes to hold it in contempt. This relative ceasing of sexual activity continues right through the latent phase until puberty. At this point, the 'normal' girl will learn somehow to generalize her sexual feelings from her father to other men. At the same time, her primary erogenous zone will have moved from the immature site of the clitoris to the mature site of the vagina — this now becomes the prime focus of a woman's sex life, as she aims through intercourse to produce that substitute for her missing penis, a baby (preferably a male baby).

But what brings about a homosexual orientation? Freud always held open the option that the crucial causal factor in anyone's sexual orientation could be constitutional — what we today might consider a function of the genes. Above this, however, Freud believed that homosexuality in men could be a function of parents playing 'abnormal' roles, and although he really says very little directly about lesbianism, it is clear that Freud thought that causes somewhat along these lines might be the case for women also. The one pertinent case that Freud did discuss in some detail (and this by his own admission involved an incomplete analysis) was of a girl with lesbian tendencies, which Freud thought were a direct result of what the girl perceived as rejection by her father. In particular, when the girl was sixteen, the girl's mother gave birth to a baby boy. The girl's father has betrayed her, showing that he loved the mother more than his daughter: 'Furiously resentful and embittered, she turned away from her father and from men altogether. After this first great reverse she forswore her womanhood and sought another goal for her libido' (Freud 1955b: 157). Neither here, nor elsewhere, did Freud say much about the role of mothers in causing an adult lesbian orientation.

Freud also thought that fear of female genitals might play a significant causal role in homosexual orientation in men: women remind men of the possibility of castration, and indeed to put the penis into the vagina is to run the risk of having it bitten off. Similarly, Freud also thought that women might be frightened by male genitals. They set up uncomfortable feelings of envy, and threaten, both through the damage that they themselves might do and through the ensuing damage of childbirth. In other words, lesbians might simply dread penises. The adaptationists, incidentally, have taken up this idea, and they offer an analysis of lesbianism parallel to their analysis of male homosexuality (Ovesey 1956).

4.2 Testing Freud on women

A major criticism of Freudian psychoanalytic theory in general is that it is unfalsifiable, that there is no way in which it could be put to empirical test. Just such a criticism has been levelled against the Freudian analysis of female sexuality in particular. For instance, in her well-known book, *The Female Eunuch*, Germaine Greer wrote: 'Basically the argument is a tautology which cannot proceed beyond its own terms, so that it is neither demonstrable nor refutable' (Greer 1970: 91). But this is not true. There are a number of empirical, testable claims in Freud's analysis of female sexuality, including homosexuality. Most importantly, Freud claims that women suffer from penis envy. Associated with this idea, of course, is the idea that men tend to suffer from a castration complex. (Men have a penis and are scared of losing it; women do not have a penis and wish they had one.) We all know what envy is. We all know what penises are. I should have thought that a claim about penis envy is straightforwardly meaningful and empirical. After all, if someone said 'Students at redbrick universities envy Oxbridge students', no one would be in any doubt about meaning or testability. In this respect, why are penises in principle different from Oxbridge students?

Probably, many of the most effective tests would have to be somewhat indirect. However, as I have already pointed out, there is nothing wrong with an indirect test per se. In fact, almost all of the tests in science are indirect. I expect if you asked students at redbrick universities about Oxford and Cambridge, you would be met with scorn and contempt, rather than explicit envy. To get the full answer, you would have to go about matters indirectly, checking on prior entrance applications and so forth. Likewise with Freud on female sexuality.

Yet, having said this, I cannot pretend to great enthusiasm for much work which has actually been done on the question of penis envy/castration anxiety. Freudians have themselves to blame, as much as anyone, for the charges which are brought against them. Consider one typical study (Levin 1966). Two sets of women were tested, one group of twenty-six career women (unmarried and in high status 'masculine' positions) and the other group of twenty-five 'homemakers' (married, with children, and with no outside employment). The prediction was that the career women would be more envious of men than the homemakers, and would therefore have greater penis envy — they would react more strongly to male genitals, envying them or perhaps feeling hostile to what they could not have. And this was indeed judged to be so. But judgements were based on the different groups' members' reactions to Rorschach inkblots — responses to genital configurations and so forth. The highly subjective element here hardly needs labouring. It is true indeed that a great deal of subjective interpretation goes on in the rest of science: anyone who thinks it is unique to Freudians has never been inside a physics laboratory. However, more effort should have been made to devise repeatable, independently verifiable experiments and results. (See also Pitcher and Prelinger 1963.)

More promising, perhaps, for meaningful tests is another theme central to the Freudian analysis of women, namely his claims about the main focus of female sexual stimulation and orgasm. Freud argued that the young girl's masturbation centres on her clitoris. If she is to achieve full psychosexual maturity, her centre of orgasm must change from the clitoris — an inadequate penis substitute — to the vagina. The balanced grown woman no longer wants or needs to imitate boys — rather she responds sexually through the fully female organs, specifically the vagina. Here, we have not only the potential for test, but the potential for fairly direct test.

As it happens, the whole thesis about the vaginal orgasm has been heavily attacked in recent years, particularly because of the studies of the sexologists Masters and Johnson (1966). They have pointed out that the clitoris of a grown woman is very sensitive, whereas the vagina has very few nerve endings. On the basis of these and like studies, it has become generally believed that not only is Freudian psychoanalytic theory testable at this point, but that it has been tested and found false. Actually, however, matters are perhaps a little more complex than this. Nerve endings notwithstanding, more recent studies have suggested that some women do report experiencing orgasm as being more centred on the vagina than on the clitoris (Fisher 1973) — and one would imagine that logically speaking (and lying apart), if people report on experiencing something this way, then this is in fact how they experience it, even if there is no known physiological reason for it.

It does remain true that most women probably have orgasms centring on the clitoris, not the vagina. Hence, at the least one suspects that orthodox Freudianism will require revisions, perhaps substantial revisions. There may or may not remain much untouched. Of course, one could reply on behalf of the Freudian that this ongoing need of revision is the fate of all theories, especially the very best. However, general defences (or attacks) lead us from our main concerns. We ourselves can more profitably criticize/salvage/revise Freud on women from the perspective of our own interests. Now, it is enough to have established the overall background conclusion: there is no good reason to reject Freud (on women) simply on the theoretical grounds that his views are unfalsifiable.

4.3 Testing Freud on lesbianism

So, what of the specific question of female homosexuality? I argue that the pattern with male homosexuality repeats itself. There certainly are testable claims in the Freudian position; unfortunately, as in the case of male homosexuality, there are serious questions about the methodological adequacy of many tests that have in fact been performed. One major empirical claim in the Freudian analysis of lesbianism stands out, namely that the developing girl will have a difficult or inadequate relationship with her father. When, as part of her Oedipal development, the future lesbian turns from mother to father, she finds someone to whom she is unable to relate, so she is driven back (regresses) to an attachment to mother and to women generally. As noted, Freud does not say much about the mothers of lesbians; although his supporters have rushed to fill the vacuum. Apparently unlike the Freudian pre-homosexual boy, the Freudian pre-lesbian girl has no one to turn to — to cherish and be cherished. Mothers, supposedly, also reject their daughters, who, in turn, still smarting from the loss of a penis, refuse to identify with the (like-castrated) female parent. Thus, lesbianism is reinforced, and the testable hypothesis that lesbians have unsatisfactory relationships with their mothers is produced (Bell et al. 1981).

A number of studies have been aimed at testing these hypotheses. Invariably they have involved questionnaires designed to probe women's attitudes towards and perceptions of their fathers and mothers, together with their recollections of childhood. And usually, the findings have been significant — lesbian women feel their relationship with (especially) father was less satisfactory than do non-lesbian women. (See, for example, Bene 1965; Kaye et al. 1967; Kremer and Rifkin 1967.) In the Second Kinsey report, for instance, 58 per cent of white homosexual women reported their fathers in a negative fashion, as opposed to only 30 per cent of white heterosexual women. Although the absolute numbers studied were smaller, similar findings were obtained for blacks (Bell et al. 1981). Recollections and perceptions of lesbians' mothers were less consistently negative (for example, Gundlach and Riess 1968). However, the Kinsey researchers confirmed neo-Freudian speculations. Some 49 per cent of white lesbians had unfavourable memories of mothers, as opposed to a mere 21 per cent of heterosexuals. Analogously for blacks.

I have discussed at some length my reactions to studies of this kind on male homosexuals, and I see no reason to modify substantially my conclusions for these studies of women. Undoubtedly lesbians, like male homosexuals, tend to report feelings and memories of fathers significantly different from the feelings and memories of heterosexual women of their fathers. Moreover, there is no reason to believe these reports were anything other than genuinely intended. Nevertheless, this is far from saying that the fathers of lesbians really were so very hostile or abnormal in their relationships with (future lesbian) daughters, or from saying that the fathers rather than the daughters were the prime causal factors in the parent/offspring relationships. Similar caveats apply to those significant findings about the mothers of lesbians. As pointed out before, reports of childhood are notoriously unreliable, particularly when filtered through the consciousness of an intelligent person who knows what the answers ought to be ('ought to be', that is, if Freud is right). In addition, even if the reports are reliable, this is not to say that the disappointing father/daughter or mother/daughter relationships were in any significant sense caused by the fathers or mothers. The daughters might have been hostile and rejecting, to the extent that somewhat naturally the fathers or mothers withdrew from the attempt to maintain friendly bridges. Anyone who thinks that a father or mother makes all the running in the relationship with his/her daughter is naive indeed.

Relevant to this suggestion are findings of the Second Kinsey researchers (who, as in the case of male homosexuality, suspect that the Freudians may have the crucial causal links reversed). Most of the lesbians they surveyed reported that (as girls) they did not much enjoy typical girls' activities (like playing house). Most of the heterosexuals did enjoy such activities. About half of the lesbians really liked dressing up in boys' clothes. Hardly any of the heterosexuals did this. Most of the lesbians liked playing football and baseball and so forth. Few of the heterosexuals had felt this way as girls. And so on and so forth. All in all: 'These comparisons . . . corroborate the findings of other investigators that prehomosexual girls are much more likely than preheterosexual girls to display gender nonconformity in their play activities' (Bell et al. 1981: 147). (See also Siegelman 1974a.)

Finally, what about the question of fear? Freud in part and the adaptationists in whole have argued that lesbians fear male genitals — such organs set up all sorts of feelings of envy, not to mention the fear of being damaged by the thrusting phallus (Freud 1955b; Ovesey 1956). Again, this position seems testable in principle — are lesbians as opposed to heterosexual women more scared or threatened by men's penises? Unfortunately, however, other than the anecdotal reports that the adaptationist theorists seem to think are adequate substitutes for objective studies, the empirical evidence for or against this claim seems slight indeed. Only two direct studies exist, and although both of these report positively, their limitations outweigh their enthusiasm. One study was of ten women only and these were heterosexual women judged latent homosexuals (Goldberg and Milstein 1965), and the other study of twenty-four lesbians was conducted along the Bieber pattern, with analysts asked to report on the feelings of patients they were treating (Kaye et al. 1967).

So, what may we conclude thus far? Certainly, blanket charges about unfalsifiability are too harsh. Indeed, in respects it is clear that some revisions to Freudian theory are absolutely essential — this applies particularly to those unsubstantiated aspects of his thought implying that women are lying back, anticipating (but somewhat dreading) the thrusting male member. Yet we should not be too negative — at least, not at first. Not only is Freud (on women) testable in principle, but when it comes to lesbianism he may well have glimpsed something important. Certainly, self-reports of lesbians (as opposed to heterosexuals) suggest that their childhoods may have been different (specifically, their habits may have been switched towards more male-type roles), and their relations with parents less happy.

But, having said this much, all the qualifications and caveats of the last two chapters must be reasserted. The studies (usually based on the giving of questionnaires) tend to be distorted — if they do not suffer from the fallacy of insufficient statistics (and many do), then they suffer from the fallacy of biased statistics. There are all of the problems of retrospective reporting — there are no long-term studies, or indirect tests designed to get around the failures in self-perception. And, perhaps most crucially of all, in their rush to prove Freud right, Freudians ignore elementary warnings about properly distinguishing cause and effect. Even supposing that lesbians do, as a whole, have bad relationships with their parents, even supposing that lesbians do, as a whole, have less than usually friendly parents, does this show that the parents — one or the other or both — crucially influence future sexual orientation? Or does the causal connection go the other way? Or does it go both ways?[1]

Freud may have glimpsed something. Neither he nor his followers have seen very clearly what that might be.

4.4 Is Freud's position sexist?

This is hardly a very happy conclusion. Yet, in the case of men, matters could be left at this point; for women, there is more which must be said. I take the Freudian approach towards homosexuality in women seriously. This is not to say that I want to endorse it unreservedly; obviously I do not. But it is something which qualifies as real science (at least it is a proper candidate for real science), and does have the potential to advance our understanding. There are few if any exciting new theories in science which have not had to be modified, often drastically, as the years go by. I suspect, however, that some readers, particularly feminists, will be unhappy with my attitude. They will argue that Freud's 'perverted point of view', as one commentator has put it (Bardwick 1971: 9), is so biased and slanted against women that virtually anything he has to say about women, hetero or homosexual, is worthless. What is necessary is a whole new approach to female sexuality — one which does not start with the biases of a nineteenth-century Viennese male chauvinist.

To this criticism, let me make three responses. First, I think one would have to be very naive or insensitive to fail or refuse to admit there is some substance to the charges. Science, particularly good science, requires a commitment, an orientation of one's interests and energies, which goes beyond the reporting of bare facts. Values enter in. Moreover, the values are not necessarily very nice, as psychoanalytic theory itself shows. Prima facie it is a paradigm of a sexist science, in that its founder worked from men, showing through models, ideas, and language that in respects he considered females as inferior to males. We have seen how, although Freud himself became aware of and admitted to difficulties with such a dichotomy, men and things male do get referred to as active, as things positive. Females and things female are referred to as passive, as things negative. Even when the female has something active like her libido, it is labelled as masculine (Freud 1953). And consider some of the language. Lacking a penis, women suffer the 'anatomical tragedy' of a being who is a 'castrated', 'maimed', 'mutilated creature' (Freud 1953). Without 'the only proper genital organ', woman must come to face the 'fact of her own castration [and] the consequent superiority of the male and her own inferiority', even though she 'rebels against these unpleasant facts' (Freud 1932).

Science can be sexist. Freud is sexist. So much for my first point. My second point starts with the obvious (but not for that reason invalid) reminder that one must remember the context and culture within which Freud was writing. Turn-of-the-century Europe looked upon males as in important respects superior to females. That Freud himself should reflect these prejudices is hardly surprising. Being a genius is not incompatible with being a bigot. Of course one might agree with this, but still question what relevance Freud has for us. But then surely the point can properly be made that our own society is hardly free from bias in favour of things male and against things female; so perhaps what Freud has to say about women (including lesbianism) is not so unreasonable — at least, it ought not to be ruled out from possible study on a priori grounds.

Without necessarily accepting everything that Freud has to say, it might be worth considering the nature of the inferiority that a female faces *and often accepts* in our society. I do not see that one actually has to accept that male values are good in order to consider the hypothesis of penis envy (or related hypotheses) as worthy of serious study. Perhaps human beings do not necessarily have to develop as Freud thought they did, but perhaps also they frequently do develop in this way. One does not have to accept Freud's values to take this possibility seriously. Or to take seriously the idea (which may or may not have been Freud's own) that penis envy is more properly understood as a *symbol* of woman's place in society, than anything strictly literal. One pair of lesbian-feminist writers (Sisley and Harris 1977) have suggested that Freud knew as little about women as did God. Perhaps so. But assuming that God is the cause of women's lowly predicament, might one not suggest that a fellow-thinker would be our best guide to God's work? It takes one to know one. (See Mitchell 1972, 1974 and Janeway 1974 for articulate feminist defences of Freud, starting with the supposed *symbolic* nature of penis envy.)

My third point is the most important, although it grows out of the second point. Let us agree that Freud uses sexist language and concepts, even though (as I have just been arguing) in a society like ours this might give him relevance. Irrespective of whether this is so or not, the really important question seems to be whether there is something salvageable in Freud — whether Freud's basic premises are irrevocably value-laden (value-laden against women, that is) or whether there is the potential for a purified Freudianism which does not have a built-in bias against women. Must one simply throw out everything and simply start again?

In fact, there probably is a core to Freud's thought which could be used as the basis of an unbiased picture of human development, assuming that it succeeds qua evidence, and so forth. Freud's picture of humans is based on their bisexuality, in the various senses in which this term is used. This, it seems to me, is to treat males and females in a very similar way — in an identical way, in fact. There is no question of males being wholly male, and females being partly female and partly male. Admittedly, inasmuch as Freud identified active elements in all humans as male and passive elements as female — and failed to extricate himself with qualifications — bias started to come in. But to say, for instance, that males sometimes have urges for males and that these are essentially female reactions, and vice versa, is not inherently sexist — although, of course, it may be false.

Consider next the use to which Freud puts his thesis of ubiquitous bisexuality. He argues that, after we are born, we are going to go through a somewhat complex period of development, reacting with and against our parents, finding out about sex and sexual differences, and that all of these childhood experiences will have a profound effect on adult behaviour and feelings. Of course, at this point differences start to emerge between males and females — girls are portrayed as having a more complex and perhaps more difficult path to complete than boys, because they must switch from loving their mother to loving a member of the opposite sex. But pointing to differences, or even suggesting that girls have a more complex development than boys, is not sexist. There are differences. What is sexist is to suggest that because there are differences, one sex is better — to say, for instance, that because girls mature more rapidly than boys, they are better than boys, or worse.

What can one say of the persistent critic who faults some of the consequences of Freud's theorizing — for instance, what he has to say about penis envy? Probably, little needs to be said. Freud's claims (taken literally) are meaningful and testable. How well they have been confirmed is another matter. Until better quality tests are performed, it would be foolish to make firm commitments. In any case, here (if anywhere) a symbolic interpretation seems required and useful. In a totally non-sexist society, perhaps even symbolic penis envy will drop away: just a reminder of the past.

By this stage, either Freud has been defended, or he is beyond defence. There are questions one might raise about whether the Freudian is specifically prejudiced against women who are homosexuals, as opposed to women who are heterosexuals. But analogous points will be raised in the context of other theories, and they will be tackled there. The time has now come to move on to the post-Freudians.

4.5 The significance of transsexuals

Building on what has gone before, I shall assume now that (from here on) we are probably dealing with ideas/theories/speculations which have the potential to be genuinely scientific. Choosing very selectively, I turn first to recent careful studies by psychoanalysts on transsexuals, people of one anatomical sex who really believe themselves to be of the other sex (that is, people whose anatomical sex does not correspond to their sexual or gender identity). These investigators come from a Freudian background and accept many of the basic parameters, but they are trying to move our understanding forward. Referring specifically to the work of two of the leading thinkers, Robert J. Stoller (1968, 1975, 1976) and Richard Green (1974, 1975, 1976), we find that they propose both a pattern and an aetiology for male-to-female transsexualism. (These researchers consider also female-to-male transsexualism, thinking it probably essentially a reverse of the male-to-female pattern. However, relatively there are far fewer female-to-male transsexuals, and absolutely very few.) The key to such male-to-female transsexualism is thought to lie in early childhood (before two years). The males involved tend to be very beautiful ('as pretty as girls'), the mothers are lonely, wanting a being closely dependent upon them, the boy is permitted (if not encouraged) to dress up as a girl, the father is indifferent towards his son and makes no attempt to bring the son over to a masculine role, and even at this early age (and more so later) the available and encouraged playmates are girls rather than boys.

In the classic Freudian position, the boy must separate himself off from his mother, so that he can fall in love with her. Homosexuality results from difficulty in resolving this incestuous love. However, according to Stoller (1968, 1976) particularly, the key to male-to-female transsexualism lies in the fact that *the boy never separates himself off from mother*. He identifies with mother, because she and she alone is so all-enveloping initially, and she in turn encourages this dependence because it meets needs of her own. Consequently, the boy grows up just like mother, namely thinking of himself as female. And because there is no discouragement, rather because there is encouragement, the feminine gender identity is fixed. In the Freudian view, homosexuality results from an inadequately resolved Oedipal struggle: what is suggested here is that the child never even gets into the Oedipal phase.

After the hysterical and strident approach taken by some neo-Freudians, the writings of Stoller and Green come as a breath of fresh air. As these researchers themselves admit, however, one can still question just how far acceptance of the thesis that (male-to-female) transsexualism is caused by too great an identification with mother (and encouragement in a female role) provides a general causal explanation of male homosexuality, and conversely for females. For a start, the absolute numbers that these sex researchers are working with are really small. Who could possibly dare to generalize to all lesbians from thirteen female-to-male transsexuals (the number Stoller reports on), other than a great many of the people referenced in previous chapters? More importantly, no real attempt is made to study a representative, unbiased cross section. Suppose we grant that the boys Stoller studies really are rather beautiful, really do have lonely mothers, and really do have indifferent fathers. Are we to understand that any boy who has all three of these factors operating will be transsexual? There is no way of telling.

If indeed there are many men walking around who fitted all or most parts of the hypothesized pattern, but who have firm masculine gender identities, then clearly other factors must be involved. But unfortunately (from a methodological viewpoint) people with firm gender identities are rather like successful murderers. Just as really successful murderers never come to the attention of the police, so people with firm gender identities never come as clients to gender-identity clinics. Hence, if some people do have the hypothesized background and yet also have a firm gender identity, they will never be found. And furthermore, if factors other than those listed above are involved in making transsexuals, then just how vital are all the factors actually hypothesized? It is recognized by the sex researchers that not all of the transsexuals fit all of the features of the pattern exactly. How often is the fitting of the pattern a function of the researcher's expectations? A lot of little boys look very pretty — what is to count as exceptional beauty?

Perhaps the most crucial point standing in the way of a ready explanation of *all* homosexuality (and one which is recognized) is that there is a difference — a big difference — between the average homosexual and a full-blown transsexual. The average homosexual, male or female, is really quite happy to be the anatomical sex that he/she is. Homosexuals take pleasure in their biological sexuality in general, and in their genitals in particular. The last thing that most male homosexuals want, for instance, is to have their penises cut off. According to the phobic theorists, that is part of the problem! Transsexuals, however, are people who think themselves of the opposite sex, and who (as often as not) actively seek out sex-change surgery. Analogously, transsexuals want intercourse with heterosexuals, not homosexuals. (I except here those people who think of themselves as transsexual homosexuals.)

I do not see that there is necessarily a *logical* difference between (say) a male homosexual and a male-to-female transsexual (Meyer-Bahlburg 1984a). But even if one argues that transsexualism is a form of homosexuality taken to an extreme — that is, where behavioural and psychological aspects of the sex different from that of the anatomical sex are magnified and multiplied — this does not mean that there are no real differences, in fact, between transsexuals and homosexuals (that is to say most homosexuals). White is not dove-grey, even though there is a continuum between them. Consequently, even if one thinks the difference between transsexuals and homosexuals is one of degree rather than one of kind, the special causes of transsexualism are not necessarily the causes of homosexuality, certainly not all homosexuality.

Of course, if the difference is one of degree (not one of logical type), one could agree that the work on the aetiology of transsexualism is at least suggestive for (some) homosexuality.[2] The findings about the extent to which (male) transsexuals feel and show feminine characteristics remind one of the much-referred-to findings (provided in part by Green himself) about male homosexuals' recollections of being sissies — not to mention the findings about cross-gender features of average adult homosexuals. This at least suggests (hardly proves) that modelling oneself on others might be a crucial factor in homosexual orientation. There, one is starting to turn one's back on Freud's central thesis, where the essence of psychosexual development is that the growing child has a dynamic, determined course, moving through various phases: sexuality coming as a result of this movement, and homosexuality coming as a reaction. Now one is starting to pick up on Freud's side-hypothesis, about copying. (Remember his speculations about the effects of male slaves as role models for young boys in Ancient Greece.) The central Freudian thesis about the genesis of homosexuality is that the child's psyche bounces a little too violently off the environment (that is, the parents). Now the thesis, suggested by the work of the transsexual researchers, is that the environment proves a little too seductive, and one models oneself on it, atypically.

This whole notion of modelling, or *social learning*, has been embraced by a number of sexologists, who see in it the vital clue to the unravelling of the aetiology of homosexuality. Let us therefore turn directly to this.

4.6 Social learning and homosexuality

It is true that some sexologists, basically sympathetic to social learning theory approaches, still think that there is a place for an orthodox Freudian analysis in some cases of homosexuality. But these people, as do many other researchers, find the causes of most homosexuality in the way that growing children model themselves on the adults and peers around them. Thus, D. J. West (1967) writes that: 'The need for a growing boy to have a certain freedom of expression, and an adequately masculine father upon whom to model himself if he is to assume his expected social role, provides a plausible reason for the observed fact that fathers as well as mothers have a decisive influence upon their sons' sexual orientation' (p. 190). In line with this strand of thought, West emphasizes that we should be chary of assuming that sexual orientation is always fixed absolutely in early childhood. Indeed, he suggests that just one bad heterosexual experience in adolescence may be enough to tip into homosexuality a child who is already disposed to it. (See also West 1977.) Wainwright Churchill (1967) thinks likewise. Adolescent sexual encounters can have a very powerful effect on adult sexual orientation. Citing Kinsey in his support, Churchill suggests that one 'good' experience, either homosexual or heterosexual, can be sufficient to fix a person's entire sexual future (p. 119).

Others who embrace this kind of causal perspective include J. H. Gagnon and W. Simon (1973). And at a more general and theoretical level one should mention the work of Albert Bandura (1969). He emphasizes that although learning involves modelling on another in some way, one should avoid simplistic connections. A boy, for instance, does not learn to be a male simply from father (and hence homosexual males are not homosexuals simply because they did not get a strong heterosexual message from father). Teachers, peers, film stars, and others are models. Perhaps most important is mother (that is, someone *not* of the same sex).

In view of the extensive discrimination training, peer modeling, and frequent maternal demonstrations of masculine activities at times when the father is absent, it seems highly improbable that a three-year-old child looks and behaves like a boy primarily as a result of identifying with a 35-year-old man whom he can observe for relatively brief periods mainly during leisure-time activities if the commuting schedule happens to be favorable. (Bandura 1969: 215)

There is little point in simply providing a list of social learning theorists, and of those who might reject such labelling but who nevertheless make similar sounds. (See Acosta 1975, for a general review.) The general perspective on homosexuality of the social learning theorists is clear. Of course, there are differences within the school, if one may so term it. Some — for instance, Green (1974) and Stoller (1968, 1975) (if we include them here), and Bandura (1969) — emphasize the importance of learning at an early age, while others — for instance, West (1967) and Churchill (1967), and Gagnon and Simon (1973) — argue that adolescent experiences can be crucial. Again some, such as Churchill (1967), seem to think that one experience alone is enough, while others, such as Feldman and MacCulloch (1971) rather imply that an ongoing situation is required. And some, among them Churchill (1967), incline towards the belief that a positive homosexual experience affects adult orientation, while others, among them West (1967) and Feldman and MacCulloch (1971), emphasize negative heterosexual experiences.

Nevertheless, for all of the differences, general philosophical conclusions can be drawn — and as you might by now expect these are not much different from those already drawn. On the one hand, there really seems no reason at all to conclude that these approaches are non-scientific because they fail to satisfy criteria of falsifiability and the like. If one could show that a boy never ever had a heterosexual experience and that he was an adult homosexual, bad heterosexual experiences could not be the only cause of homosexuality. On the other hand, even if one irons out all of the differences between learning theorists (and I really see no reason why one person should not simultaneously hold parts of more than one approach), it is very clear that, taken together, the supporters of a learning theory position on homosexuality have not provided anything resembling a well-confirmed theory. Many of the problems and deficiencies that appeared in more orthodox Freudian circles resurface. There are altogether too many flat statements, with little or no evidence. For instance, Churchill (1967) gives no particular instances (that is, actually studied individual cases) to back up his claims. And when instances are given, as they are by others, they tend to rely on hearsay and have not been compared with other possibilities. West (1967) cites specific putatively confirmatory clinical examples, but they suffer from all of the faults of the Bieber study (they involve troubled homosexuals, they rely on memories, and so forth).

Furthermore, when the analyses are taken slightly deeper, large gaps still remain. For instance, R. J. McGuire and others (1965) argue that the reason why one initial homosexual encounter can fix a male in lifelong homosexuality is because, having had the encounter, he then reinforces its erotic impact through masturbation. Every time the adolescent boy works up to an orgasm (and this tends to be a fairly frequent occurrence in adolescent boys) he is reinforcing the homosexual encounter as a desirable phenomenon — and thus he gets turned towards homosexuality (see also D. R. Evans 1968). However, like Bieber et al. (1962) and West (1967), McGuire seems to think that reference to a few patients who fit his pattern is a substitute for genuine scientific test. There is no controlled study of the hypothesis — one does not learn, for example, how it is that some boys begin with homosexual encounters, even having masturbatory fantasies about them, and yet grow up entirely heterosexual, in thought and deed.

Even when the theorists make predictions from their hypotheses, serious questions remain. For instance, Feldman and MacCulloch (1971) argue that since (in many homosexuals) the homosexuality is learned, it ought to be possible to unlearn it (by getting the thought of such activity associated with unpleasant experiences). But although they report a high rate of success in their aversion therapy (57 per cent of forty-three homosexuals showed some decline in homosexuality), there have been serious questions raised about how effective their treatment really was. A replication of Feldman and MacCulloch's study by Birk (1974) found that although many homosexuals did indeed switch from their homosexual behaviour very rapidly and dramatically following shock treatment, after a year most had slipped right back to old patterns. In other words, one questions the effectiveness of the unlearning, which leads one to question the actuality of the learning in the first place. (Bancroft 1974a has been very critical of Feldman and MacCulloch. However, one perhaps ought to mention that he too is an aversion therapist with his own particular methods to promote. See Bancroft 1974b.)

Let me not be misunderstood. It is not my intention to leave the reader with a totally negative impression of social learning theory approaches to homosexuality, any more than I wanted to give a totally negative impression of more orthodox psychoanalytic approaches. Admittedly, even if the general perspective is relevant, it does seem fairly clear that no one single approach could fit all homosexuals which, no doubt, no social learning theorist would want to claim. However, whatever reservations one may have, the cross-cultural argument does seem strong. It is difficult to accept that societies (like that of the Ancient Greeks) which contain or contained widespread homosexual attitudes and behaviour are (were) so simply because the mothers are (were) more dominant. In a later chapter, we shall be looking in more detail at the specific example of Ancient Greece. I shall show then that its homosexuality (behaviour and feeling) was far from as open and universal as myth would have it. Yet the strong impression does remain that cultural norms, and the consequent social learning, were important.

4.7 Cognitive developmental theory

Concluding this second half of the chapter, and with it our survey of putative environmental/psychological causes of adult sexual orientation, let me make passing reference to an approach to the development of sex roles and gender identities which stems from the ideas of the influential child psychologist Jean Piaget, but which has been elaborated most fully by the American psychologist Lawrence Kohlberg (1966, 1969). 'Cognitive developmental theory' is certainly not entirely different from a social learning theory approach, but is distinctive in that it gives the developing child's conceptual ability — its power of organization of experience — a much more crucial role in the acquirement of a sense of gender and sexuality generally.

[In the view of the social learning theorists] sex-typed behaviour and attitudes are acquired through social rewards that follow sex-appropriate responses made by the child or by a relevant model. The social-learning syllogism is: 'I want rewards, I am rewarded for doing boy things, therefore I want to be a boy'. In contrast, a cognitive theory assumes this sequence: 'I am a boy, therefore I want to do boy things, therefore the opportunity to do boy things (and to gain approval for doing them) is rewarding'. (Kohlberg 1966: 89. For 'boy' read 'boy or girl'.)

According to Kohlberg, therefore, what we find is that by an early age (three or so), children have an idea of themselves as a boy or girl. There is no modelling here, although in an extension of Kohlberg's theory it has been suggested that social stereotypes may influence the child's conceptualization of 'boy/girl', 'male/female' (Frieze et al. 1978). But, however the recognition of oneself as boy/girl occurs, next comes the crucial step. One wants to belong — if one is a boy one wants to be in with the fellows and do what they do, and if one is a girl one wants to be in with the girls and do what they do. Belonging to the group (like Dad's or Mum's) is in itself the reward, rather than the reward coming because one joins up with Dad's or Mum's group. (If we look at Kohlberg's pictorial representation (figure 4.1), we can easily grasp not only his own position but also his differences with that of the classical Freudian and with that of the social learning theorist.)

The jury is not yet in, either on social learning theory, or on Kohlberg's cognitive development theory, or on the differences between the two. Like social learning theory, there is certainly some empirical evidence to support Kohlberg's position. Unfortunately, however, when we jump to our specific area of interest, namely the development of a homosexual orientation, there is virtually no evidence, if only because there is virtually no theory. Certainly there seems no reason why a theory or hypothesis for homosexual orientation should not be fashioned out of (or fitted into) cognitive developmental theory. Siegelman (1974a, b) favours some such approach as this. Presumably one would have to say that the adult homosexual as a boy/girl did not identify with males/females in quite the same way that (future) adult heterosexuals did, or perhaps one might say that having made the identification the rewards were not all that they might have been.

This, of course, all rather implies that adult sexual orientation is bound up with one's sense of gender identity. Reports like the Second Kinsey study (also Saghir and Robins 1973, as well as Stoller (1968, 1975)

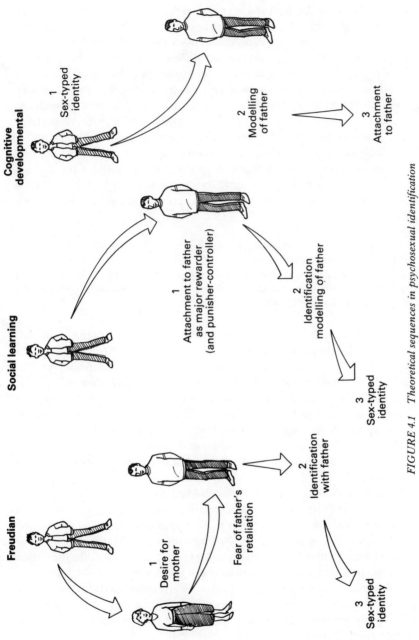

FIGURE 4.1 *Theoretical sequences in psychosexual identification*
(Kohlberg 1966: 128)

and Green (1974, 1985), especially if one considers transsexualism an extreme form of homosexuality) do suggest that childhood gender identities and gender roles may be connected to adult sexual orientation. But this rather opens up gaps than closes them. Whether or not one accepts a social learning claim that an adolescent homosexual experience can tip one into homosexuality, the connection being suggested is straightforward. It is somewhat less obvious why (for the cognitive development theorist) a boy who is a sissy should be attracted to males as an adult — is there a cause and effect relationship or is there perhaps mere constant contiguity brought about by a separate common cause?

In fact, as we know, there are studies suggesting that homosexuals show more cross-gender features than do heterosexuals. Nevertheless, Kohlberg himself rather discounts these. Interestingly, he hints that a full explanation of homosexual orientation may possibly take us back to Freud:

A consideration of theories of psychopathological identification requires the kind of developmental and longitudinal data on psychopathology not now available. The analysis of such data may provide more of an integration of psychoanalytic and cognitive-developmental concepts than this [discussion] has suggested. (Kohlberg 1969: 472).

With Freud's central ideas reappearing we have perhaps come full circle, which seems an appropriate place to end this discussion. I have two final comments. First, although Kohlberg uses the term 'psycho-pathology' about homosexuality, which presumably means that the homosexual is 'sick' in some sense, I suspect that this is a notion he is reading into homosexuality, rather than a conclusion to be drawn automatically from cognitive development theory. The alleged sickness of homosexuals under any environmental theory, including Freud's, is something to be discussed later. It is certainly not conceded as a true conclusion here.

Second, possible alliances with Freud's ideas apart, one can see easily why (as has indeed happened), many feminists have eagerly embraced either a version of social learning theory or of cognitive developmental theory. (See Frieze et al. 1978; Brooks-Gunn and Matthews 1979.) At some level, one may be able to defend Freud. I am inclined to think that one can and that the effort is worthwhile. But a social learning theory or cognitive developmental theory obviously sits more easily, at least at the face level. This is a sexist society that we are living in, and both theories readily go some or all the way to explaining why sexist notions are perpetuated. People learn them or (as children) make their categories influenced by them — simply because sexism surrounds us all. However, neither of these approaches in any way implies approval of sexism, and both offer hope of eliminating sexism. If we, as adults, deliberately stop our children from absorbing social sexism, they themselves will grow up without such a perverted ideology and the chain will be broken.

I am sure there is much truth in all of this. But let me counsel caution. Grant that a social learning or a cognitive developmental approach does indeed allow a non-sexist analysis of woman, including lesbian woman; but because one may find this fact ideologically comfortable, it does not necessarily follow that it is closer to the truth, if one excludes any other viewpoint. And in this enthusiasm for theories which suggest that society can be moulded according to one's ideals, one should beware of uncritically opening the way for all and sundry to suggest that society should be moulded according to their ideals — ideals which may exclude all variants of sexual orientation other than standard heterosexuality. It was not I who used the term 'psychopathology'.

5

Hormones and Homosexuality

We come now to the second of the three putative kinds of causal explanation for human homosexuality. This is the kind of explanation which makes reference in some way to hormones. I shall begin with a brief background treatment of hormones generally and of sex hormones in particular. Then I shall move on to discuss the way or ways in which study of hormones might be thought to throw light on human homosexuality. With this done, I shall turn to philosophical questions which are raised by the discussion: specifically, whether or not the proffered explanations are methodologically sound, and whether or not they contain implicit or explicit moral biases against homosexuals, in effect rendering them worthless as objective analyses.

5.1 The body's hormonal system

Some of the glands of the body have their own special passages, *ducts*, through which their products can be conveyed to the ultimate places of destination. The salivary glands, for instance, have ducts to take the saliva from the glands to the mouth. Scattered about the body, however, are a number of glands or gland areas (eleven in all) which pour their products directly into the blood stream, thus ensuring that these products are carried rapidly around the whole body. These ductless glands are known as *endocrine* glands (see figure 5.1), and their products are *hormones*. (There are many good introductions to endocrinology. A readable and reliable standard work is Turner and Bagnara (1971). Readers, like myself, who are not biologists will find that Le Baron (1972) gives a first-class, non-technical presentation.)

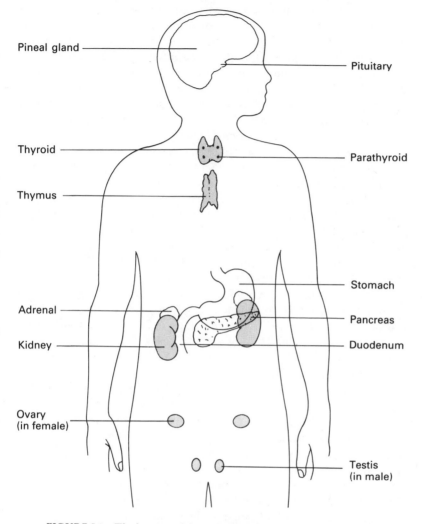

Pineal gland

Pituitary

Thyroid

Parathyroid

Thymus

Stomach

Adrenal

Pancreas

Kidney

Duodenum

Ovary
(in female)

Testis
(in male)

FIGURE 5.1   The location of the endocrine glands in the human body
(Le Baron 1972: 13)

It is not too much to say that without hormones, animals would neither develop nor would they function as infants or adults. Thus, for instance, the pituitary gland produces the so-called *growth hormone*, which controls the rate and extent of growth development in animals; conversely, the thyroid hormones are concerned primarily with general control of rates of metabolism. Endocrine glands, however, tend to produce many products, and growth and maintenance overlap. Thyroid hormones, for example, also affect growth rate. Some endocrine glands work fairly directly, being regulated in their rate of production by a kind of negative feedback system — the higher the concentration of hormone in the blood, the less active the gland is. Other glands work more indirectly, however, producing substances which then act on other glands, which are in turn stimulated into action or inaction. Hormones which act exclusively or primarily on other endocrine glands, regulating their action, are known as *tropic hormones*. These tropic hormones are crucial in human sexuality, for sexual attitudes, behaviour, and abilities depend not only on the direct sex glands themselves, but also on other glands, particularly the pituitary.

To illustrate the action of tropic hormones, let us look briefly at the mature human female. As everyone knows, sexually she goes through a cycle, marked every twenty-eight days or so by vaginal bleeding (menstruation), and is fertile for only a short while, somewhere in the middle of the cycle. It is the pituitary gland which controls the cycle. At the start, it begins by producing a substance known as the *follicle-stimulating hormone* (FSH). This then acts on the female sex organ, the ovary. There are two effects. The immature female egg (the *oocyte*) gathers around it a layer of cells (follicle cells), and at the same time the ovary itself releases into the blood stream one of the two crucial kinds of female sex hormones, *oestrogens*. These cause the wall of the uterus to build up, so that if the egg becomes fertilized, the uterus can receive and hold it.

Oestrogen concentration in the blood reaching a peak causes a switch in pituitary functioning, from the production of FSH to that of *luteinizing hormone* (LH). This releases the ovum from the follicle, and in turn causes (at the ovarian level) the production and release of another sex hormone from the *corpus luteum*, the name given to the transformed ruptured follicle. This new ovarian hormone, *progesterone*, causes further build-up of the wall of the uterus, until (if fertilization does not occur) all collapses in a flush of blood and the cycle starts again. (See figure 5.2.)

The picture for the adult human male is somewhat simpler, obviously, because he does not have a menstrual cycle. However, in the male's case, as in the female's, the pituitary tropic hormones stimulate the sex glands into action. In particular, FSH acts on the glands, the testes, to promote sperm production, and LH acts on the glands to cause production of male sex hormones. These male hormones are called *androgens*, the principle one being *testosterone*. Parenthetically, an empirical point which must be raised here and which will require further discussion later is that it is not entirely accurate to speak of testosterone as being a 'male' hormone and oestrogen as being a 'female' hormone, if by this one means

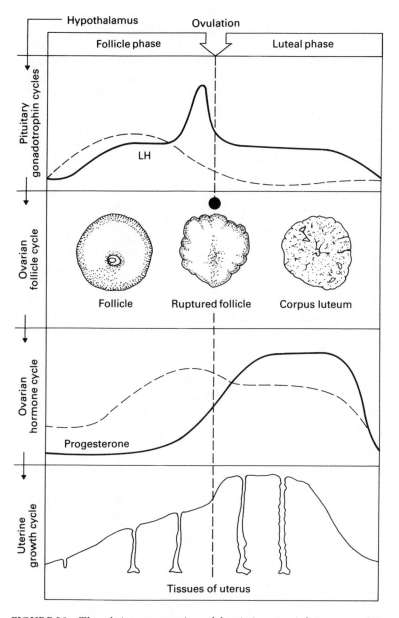

FIGURE 5.2   The relative concentrations of the pituitary tropic hormones and the ovarian hormones as they relate to stages in the development of the ovum and the corpus luteum and to the growth cycle of the uterine wall
(Le Baron 1972: 115)

that they are the *exclusive* possession of males and females respectively. Male glands produce a certain amount of oestrogen and female glands a certain amount of androgen. This fact is hardly surprising because there are close biochemical connections between androgen, oestrogen, and progesterone molecules. They all fall into the category of organic compounds known as *steroids*, and indeed are manufactured in the body sequentially: progesterone leading to testosterone and thence to oestrogens. (See figures 5.3 and 5.4.)

But, in a sense, we are ahead of ourselves. Let us go back to the birth of a human and follow through the growth, seeing the importance of hormones in the development of human sexuality. We begin by covering in detail some things just touched on in an earlier chapter. Humans (normally) have forty-six chromosomes — twenty-three pairs. One of the pairs constitute the sex chromosomes, and it is these that are crucial in making a boy or a girl (Levitan and Montagu 1977). Each parent contributes one (sex) chromosome to the *zygote*, the conjunction of sperm and ovum. Mothers always contribute so-called X chromosomes. Fathers contribute either an X chromosome or a Y chromosome. Normally, if the zygote contains two X chromosomes then the child is unambiguously a girl, and if the zygote contains an X and a Y chromosome, the child is unambiguously a boy.

At first, that is to say, in the second and third month of pregnancy, whatever the chromosomes the baby is hermaphroditic, in the sense that all are the same: all have the same rudimentary male and female organs, the *Wolffian* and *Mullerian* ducts respectively. (See figures 5.5 and 5.6.) Then differences start to appear, and as can be seen from the figures, in males the male organs develop and the female potentials shrink and disappear, and in females the reverse happens. Normally, by birth the

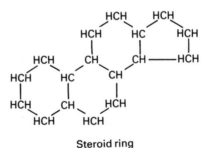

Steroid ring

FIGURE 5.3   The basic ring structure typical of steroid hormones
(Le Baron 1972: 20)

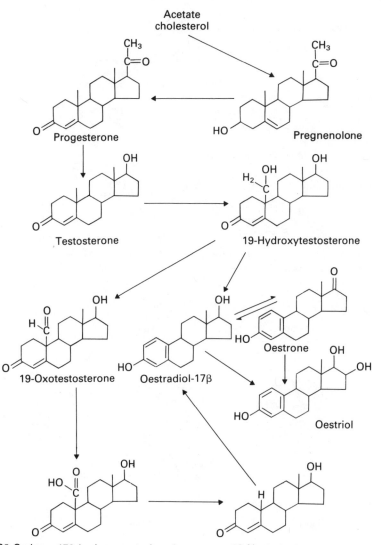

The predominant natural oestrogens in the human are oestradiol-17β, oestrone, and oestriol. One can see how minor are the differences between progesterone, testosterone, and (say) oestrone.

FIGURE 5.4   Probable pathways in the biosynthesis and metabolism of oestrogens
(Turner and Bagnara 1971: 499)

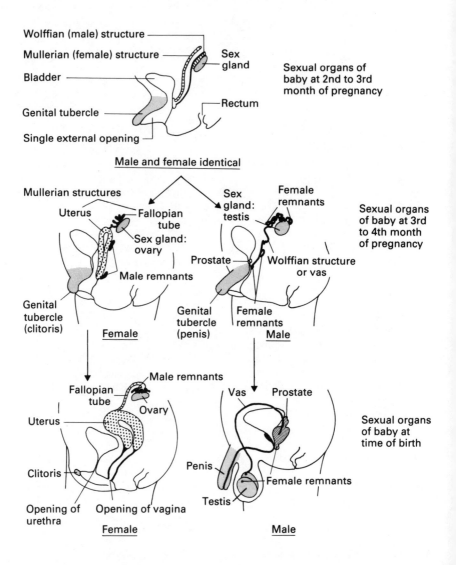

Wolffian (male) structure

Mullerian (female) structure

Bladder

Genital tubercle

Single external opening

Sex gland

Rectum

Sexual organs of baby at 2nd to 3rd month of pregnancy

Male and female identical

Mullerian structures

Uterus

Fallopian tube

Sex gland: ovary

Male remnants

Genital tubercle (clitoris)

Female

Sex gland: testis

Female remnants

Prostate

Wolffian structure or vas

Genital tubercle (penis)

Female remnants

Male

Sexual organs of baby at 3rd to 4th month of pregnancy

Male remnants

Fallopian tube

Ovary

Uterus

Clitoris

Opening of urethra

Opening of vagina

Female

Vas   Prostate

Penis

Female remnants

Testis

Male

Sexual organs of baby at time of birth

The internal reproductive anlagen (early stages of the organs) are at the outset dually represented. The male and female organs have the same beginnings and are homologous with one another.

FIGURE 5.5   Sexual differentiation in the human fetus
(Money and Schwartz 1978: 768)

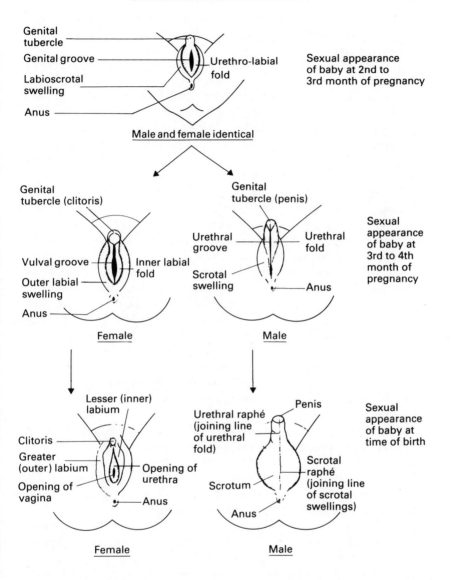

The external sex organs of male and female differentiate from the same anlagen and cannot be distinguished if a baby is born with differentiation unfinished.

FIGURE 5.6   External genital differentiation in the human fetus
(Money and Schwartz 1978: 768)

male has a developed penis, scrotum and testicles, and no vaginal opening, whereas the female has a vagina, ovaries, and (compared to the penis) relatively small clitoris.

The key causal factors in this differentiation are *male* sex hormones. Possession of a Y chromosome as such does not make a male almost by definition, as it were. Somehow the Y chromosome (about the sixth week of gestation) triggers the production in the fetal testes of two hormones, androgen and *Mullerian-inhibiting substance*. Fairly obviously, the Mullerian-inhibiting substance acts on the potentially female organs, causing the Mullerian ducts to regress and (comparatively) shrink, rather than developing into a uterus and Fallopian tubes. Androgen, on the other hand, acts positively, causing the Wolffian ducts to develop into male internal organs and the external *anlagen* (early stages of the organs) of the fetus to turn into penis, scrotum, and so forth.

The situation for male and female appears to be asymmetric. Fetal ovaries do not secrete hormones prenatally. Thus, we have an 'Adam Principle' at work here. Something must be added to make a male, and that something is androgen. It does not matter what the chromosomes are: if no androgen is produced or if androgen cannot be effective, then a person develops who is morphologically female (Money and Ehrhardt 1972; Money and Schwartz 1978). Illustrating this point dramatically is a group of people, genetically male (having XY chromosomes), who have a disorder known as the androgen-insensitivity syndrome. Their bodies can produce androgen, but their body cells are for some reason insensitive to the hormone. As a consequence, they develop phenotypically (morphologically) as females. Indeed, as figures 5.7 and 5.8 show dramatically, because (as mentioned above) in males there is also some production of oestrogen, when puberty is reached such chromosomal males develop fully as mature women. They cannot have children, however, because the early action of their Mullerian-inhibiting hormone has destroyed the effectiveness of their female organs (Money and Ehrhardt 1972; Lev-Ran 1977; Diamond 1968).

From birth to the time of puberty, the sex hormones take somewhat of a back seat, but then they come back into full play again. At the beginning of puberty the brain (in particular, the hypothalamus) triggers the pituitary to start producing tropic hormones, which as we have seen then go to work on the sex glands. In the case of males, androgens are produced by the testes, and these cause such sexual characteristics as the growth of pubic hair, the deepening of the voice, the enlargement of the penis, and the growth spurt in height. Also, obviously, there is the ability to produce sperm. In the case of females, oestrogens are produced, leading to such sexual characteristics as breasts and broad hips.

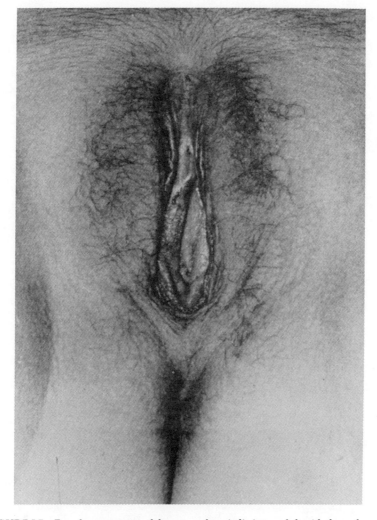

FIGURE 5.7   Female appearance of the external genitalia in an adult with the androgen-insensitivity syndrome. The sexual life is that of a female, in conformity with assigned sex, hormonal sex and gender identity
(Money and Ehrhardt 1972: 116)

The evidence of the effects of the sex hormones is unequivocal. Deliberate, natural, and inadvertent experiments on animals and humans make the central claims about as certain and well-established as they can be. As every choirmaster to the end of the eighteenth century knew full well, if one castrates a male child before puberty, then adult sexual

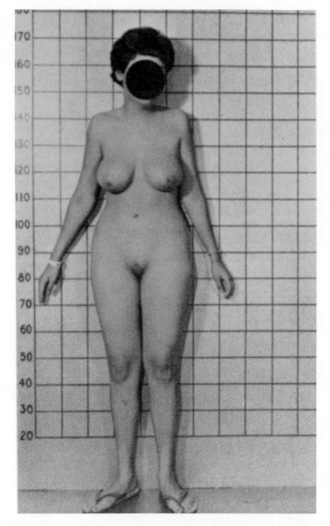

FIGURE 5.8   Body morphology in an adult with the androgen-insensitivity syndrome.
Feminizing puberty occurs with no hormonal treatment needed, under the influence of
oestrogens normally secreted by the testes in males, since the body is unresponsive to the
competitive effect of testicular androgen
(Money and Ehrhardt 1972: 116)

development will not occur. Conversely, females with missing or non-
functioning gonads also fail to develop as sexually mature women.
People with Turner's Syndrome have a missing sex chromosome — they
have but a single X chromosome (Levitan and Montagu 1977). This is

sufficient to let the embryo develop, which it does as a female. (Obviously no androgen is being produced.) But the ovaries do not develop properly. And at the time of adolescence, girls with Turner's Syndrome fail to mature sexually. However, when males and females with missing or non-functioning sex glands are treated with appropriate sex hormones, they mature in a normal sexual pattern. (See figure 5.9.)

What is the effect of missing or inappropriate sex hormones on the mature person? In males:

The visible effects are enlargement of breasts; a tendency to feminine deposition of subcutaneous fat; reduced oiliness of the skin; reduced facial acne, if present; and an arrest of masculine balding, if it has begun. Beard and body hair do not disappear, but the hairs tend to be less wiry, and more slow growing. (Money and Ehrhardt 1972: 208)

Penis and testicles shrink somewhat, ability to get and maintain an erection is lost, and production of sperm and seminal fluid ceases. In the case of women, dosage with androgen has the effect of switching them more towards male characteristics: more bodily hair, more oily skin, deepening of the voice, and perhaps also an element of balding. There is suppression of menstruation, and the clitoris may enlarge. There is, however, absolutely no question of its turning into a penis. Anatomically speaking, hormones in adulthood cannot undo the effects of hormones in early life (Gardner 1975).

Brief though this survey has been, it has shown clearly how crucial are the sex hormones in the development and maintenance of human sexuality, speaking at the physiological and morphological levels. There is nothing mysterious about being a male or being a female. It is all a question of the right hormones, in the right concentrations. But what relevance does all of this have to human sexual attitudes and behaviours, specifically human homosexual attitudes and behaviours? Let us now try and see.

5.2 Is homosexuality a function of hormones?

Although one can certainly separate off physiology and morphology from attitudes and behaviour, obviously in a sense the division is going to be somewhat artificial. One does not have to be much of a biologist to realize that if those humans born with male sexual apparatus do not normally have (at least a fair helping of) those attitudes and inclinations associated with male heterosexuality and if those humans born with female sexual apparatus do not normally have (at least a fair helping of)

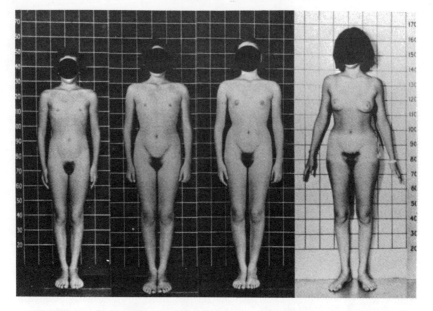

*FIGURE 5.9   Pubertal feminization of a genetic male hermaphrodite by means of
oestrogen therapy, photographs taken at 11, 12, 13 and 19 years*
(Money and Ehrhardt 1972: 214)

those attitudes and inclinations associated with female heterosexuality,
then the species *Homo sapiens* is going to grind to a fairly rapid halt. (I
am not saying that what is 'normal' is what is 'good'. Einstein was not
normal.)

But no extended argument is needed here. There is much empirical
evidence to suggest that physiology and morphology are closely
connected to attitudes and behaviour, and that moreover the hormones
are vitally important causal agents. Just as the hormones contribute to a
man's physiological ability to function sexually as a male, so also they
contribute to his inclination to function as a male. (No stand is being
taken here on what functioning as a male involves — whether it be hetero
or homosexual.) In the past, boys were castrated not only to preserve
beautiful soprano voices, but also to provide suitable attendants for the
harem. A eunuch, that is, one castrated before puberty, has little or no
sexual desire. On the other hand, if a male castrate (or the equivalent,
like someone born with non-functioning testicles) is given testosterone at
the normal time of puberty (and the dosage is maintained), then not only
does the normal physiological sexual maturing occur, but also sexual
drives and desires appear (Money and Ehrhardt 1972). Analogous points
apply to women.

This all seems relatively straightforward, and given the basics of hormonal theory rather what one might have expected. This being so, a fairly obvious explanation of homosexual inclination (mainly and most importantly attitudes, but also behaviour) immediately springs to mind. It starts with the assumption that the homosexual is (by definition) showing inclination (and probably behaviour) appropriate to her or his opposite sex: that when a male homosexual feels sexual attraction for another male, he is showing 'female' emotions, and that when he has intercourse with another male, he is showing 'female' behaviour. Similarly, a lesbian shows 'male' emotions and 'male' behaviour. What more obvious conclusion is there to draw, therefore, than that this is all caused by an imbalance of hormones? We know that both males and females have both male and female hormones, androgens and oestrogens. Clearly, therefore, male homosexuals must be tilted too far towards the oestrogen end of the scale, compared with male heterosexuals. Conversely, lesbians must be tilted too far towards the androgen end of the scale, compared with female heterosexuals.

I think it is true to say that all hormonal explanations of human homosexuality have some variant on this conclusion at their core — after all, it is difficult to see how they could avoid it. However, intensive studies on humans and animals have shown that whatever else may be the case, the relationship between hormones and homosexuality is not a simple one of cause and effect. It is just not true that in any straightforward crude sense male homosexuals have an excess of female hormones and lesbians have an excess of male hormones. If this were so, then correcting the imbalance ought to be a relatively simple matter, and ought to be followed by clear-cut, not to say dramatic, results. In particular, dosing homosexuals with the appropriate (or perhaps inappropriate!) hormones ought to produce heterosexuals, and (as a kind of control) dosing heterosexuals with appropriate hormones ought to produce homosexuals. But none of these results obtain. If male homosexuals are given androgens, their sexual drive if anything goes up; but it is just as fixedly or even more directly homosexual. Conversely, if heterosexuals are given oestrogen (as is sometimes done in the treatment of certain forms of cancer, particularly that of the prostate), they do not become homosexual. It is true that the drive and the ability of such heterosexuals is reduced, but this is a fact that they regret bitterly, for their heterosexual orientation is just as fixed as ever. And there are similar sorts of findings for women (Meyer-Bahlburg 1979).

A simple answer will not do. But this has not stopped investigators from probing more deeply or in more sophisticated fashions. First, what might be crucial is some long-term effect, say from puberty on. Whilst massive doses of hormones when one is already set in one's orientation may have little effect, an (adult) lifetime's experience of hormonal imbalance might affect orientation. Second, although not necessarily separately from the first way, imbalance of hormones at an early age, particularly prenatally, might be crucial. These might programme one for future sexual orientation, even though as an adult one might show a perfectly normal hormonal balance (that is, the same balance whether one be hetero or homosexual).

Both of these possibilities or suggestions have been explored, and I shall now review the evidence.

5.3 Hormones and adult homosexuals

Early attempts to find significant differences between the pertinent hormonal levels of adult heterosexuals and homosexuals met with little or no success. However, in recent years more sophisticated and accurate methods of hormone concentration measurement have been developed, and there have been renewed interests in comparing adult hetero and homosexuals hormonally (Meyer-Bahlburg 1977, 1979, 1984; Sanders et al. 1984). Unfortunately, the flood of studies has come up with entirely contradictory results. Some few studies have produced results suggesting that male homosexuals have depressed testosterone levels. Other studies found absolutely no significant differences between testosterone levels of homosexuals and heterosexual controls, nor (as was suggested by Loraine et al. 1971) did they find any connection between testosterone level and intensity of homosexual orientation (as measured by the Kinsey scale). And there are yet other studies suggesting that male homosexuals may have testosterone levels above those of heterosexuals! Furthermore, to add to the muddled picture, studies on free testosterone (assumed to be the actual biologically active hormone in the blood) are contradictory, and no connection can be found between testosterone levels and particular preferred modes of homosexual practice. The findings for women also fail to establish any direct connection between lesbianism and high adult androgen levels. And similar sorts of conflicting results have been obtained for other pertinent hormones (like the gonadotropins, LH and FSH). (See Meyer-Bahlburg 1984a, b; Erhardt and Meyer-Bahlburg 1981 for reviews of evidence.)

Obviously, there is something wrong or inadequate about many of these studies, and indeed not-too-close scrutiny does readily show that many suffer from methodological shortcomings. At least part of the difficulty is that most of the studies relied on only one reading of testosterone level per subject. However, this can be distorting, particularly given the fact that most of the studies were based on fairly small sample numbers (fewer than fifty — often *much* fewer than fifty). There is good evidence to suggest that in all people testosterone levels fluctuate, not only during the day, but also from day to day. Indeed, studies have shown fluctuations occurring naturally at least as great as differences which have been considered significant between hetero and homosexuals (Parks et al. 1974; Doering et al. 1975). This, of course, does not mean that there cannot be hormonal differences between people of different sexual orientation, but it does mean that repeated samplings are required to determine if there are any differences on average.

Another major difficulty with the studies is that most did not take too much care with matching homosexuals and heterosexual controls. It simply is not enough to compare a homosexual with a heterosexual, even if one tries to match for age, occupation, and so forth (and this sort of matching was not always done). For instance, it is fairly well documented that drug-taking can affect hormone levels — for instance, marijuana use can depress testosterone levels. Controls in this respect were usually absent. Likewise, it is known that stress can affect hormone levels — in particular, testosterone levels can get depressed (Dörner 1976). And again, one would like some control for this fact. Given our society's prejudice against homosexuals, there is at least a presumption that many are living under more stress than are average heterosexuals (Meyer-Bahlburg 1977).

The conclusion to be drawn from all of this is surely not that there are absolutely no hormonal differences between homosexuals and hetero-sexuals. What is clear, however, is that today one would be naive, not to say presumptuous, to claim definitively that there are such differences. This being so, let us therefore turn to studies performed and information gleaned about the effects of hormones and hormonal differences on the growing child, as they affect adult sexual orientation. Two researchers and their associates stand out particularly in this context: John Money in America and Gunter Dörner in East Germany. Since they represent different approaches to the problem, I shall deal with each separately.

5.4 John Money on prenatal hormones

Money's research centres on humans who, for various reasons, have experienced hormone deficiencies or excesses at some stage in their lives, primarily those who have experienced such imbalances before birth (in fetal development). Let us run briefly through the spectrum of his findings, beginning with people with no sex hormones at all during fetal development. These are people with non-functioning gonads, as occurs in Turner's Syndrome (mentioned earlier). Such people are born looking female and are raised as girls. Reintroducing the valuable term 'gender', and distinguishing between gender identity for the sense of belonging to one sex rather than the other, and gender role for the acting out of the typical activity of the sex of one's gender identity (Stoller 1968; Money and Ehrhardt 1972), all the evidence is that girls with Turner's Syndrome have a gender identity which is unequivocally female and a strong desire to play a full female role. Indeed, the evidence is that, if anything, girls with Turner's Syndrome have a stronger desire for heterosexual romance, marriage, babies, and so forth, than do most women. This could perhaps be due to their total lack of androgen, something which we know that normal girls produce in small amounts (Money and Ehrhardt 1972: 105—8) — although, even without critical discussion, I hope we would be wary of blanket claims that whole life styles could be simple functions of added (or subtracted) amounts of material substances.

Next on the spectrum are people who produce no functioning androgen at all, but some (perhaps small) amounts of oestrogen. Included here are people who produce androgen but are insensitive to it. One has trouble spotting genetic females fitting this category, but some genetic males in this position do come to notice (because, their bodies having produced Mullerian-inhibiting substance, they fail to develop full female internal organs). These latter people, although they have male chromosomes and lack female internal organs, are born looking unambiguously female. (See figures 5.7 and 5.8.) They are therefore raised as females, and since (unlike people with Turner's Syndrome) their bodies do produce some oestrogens, they mature as females. Again, as might be expected, these people tend to develop a strong female gender identity and to be heterosexual (that is, erotically attracted to males).

We now come to the cases of particular interest to us. First there are genetic males who are partially insensitive to androgen.

This syndrome, also known as Reifenstein's Syndrome, resembles complete androgen insensitivity, except that in fetal life there is partial masculinization of the external genitalia. In consequence, the baby may be assigned as a boy or a girl, dependent on local medical or midwife traditions concerning hermaphroditism in the newborn. (Money 1977: 262)

In a group of some ten such people studied by Money and Ogunro (1974) eight were brought up male and two female. There were some quite marked differences between those in the study treated as males and normal (that is, fully androgenized) boys. In particular, the subjects tended to be less aggressive, less competitive in sports, less socially assertive, and so forth. However, apart from one case of a female brought up in an atmosphere of ambiguity about her sex, all of the subjects felt themselves to be unequivocally members of the sex to which they had been assigned. The eight men and one woman felt themselves to be male and female respectively. Moreover, all were heterosexually oriented, both in attitudes (daydreams, imagery, etc.) and, insofar as their sexual organs allowed, behaviour.

Next we have the converse situation, that is, girls who got exposed to more androgen than normal fetuses. Some cases involved girls artificially androgenized (as a side-effect of treatment to prevent the mothers miscarrying), but most were girls with a genetic defect causing too much androgen, the adrenogenital syndrome (AGS). Consistently, the findings have been that girls exposed to more androgen than normal are tomboys and show more male attitudes and behaviour than normal, even though they have been reared unequivocally as females, have had any physical problems surgically corrected, and have had treatment (where appropriate) to suppress excess androgen. One study on seventeen females considered attitudes and behaviour with respect to three themes: activity and aggression; marriage and maternalism; and gender role, appearance, and adolescent dating behaviour (Ehrhardt 1977). Figures 5.10, 5.11 and 5.12 tell much if not all.

What about the crucial question of adult sexual orientation? Reading between the lines of the reports one detects a change of attitude by the researchers. The early reports (about fifteen years or more ago) seem fairly confident that although excess androgen may cause tomboyism, and that this can extend to adult life (that is, showing more interest in a career than in traditional female roles, and although excess androgen may retard sexual, psychological maturity, nevertheless, androgenized women are just as likely to turn out heterosexual as non-androgenized women. In other words, too much androgen cannot be a key factor in lesbian orientation. Or, at the very least, assignment to a female gender role can overcome the effect of prenatal androgenization (Money 1961; Ehrhardt, 1977).

More recent reports on the girls as they grow older, however, is that in fact homosexuality, and bisexuality, both in attitudes and behaviour, are more common than might be expected in a randomly chosen group. It is not suggested that all prenatally and androgenized girls are turned homosexual or bisexual as adults, as a result of their early hormonal experiences. On the other hand, there is now some evidence that higher than usual levels of androgen at the fetal stage can make it more likely

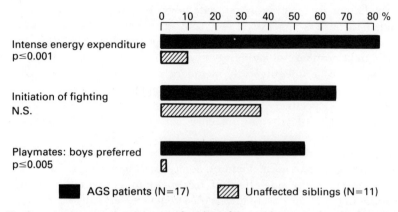

The bars represent the percentage of subjects from each group who were reported to exhibit the behaviour specified by the category.

For those with little knowledge of mathematics, the information given in such a term as 'p≤0.001' is that the probabilities of getting such a result purely by chance are very unlikely, in this case less than 1 time in 1,000. N.S. means that such a result is 'not significant', meaning that chance cannot be ruled out.

FIGURE 5.10   Comparison of female AGS patients versus female siblings on activity and aggression
(Ehrhardt 1977: 249)

that the adult woman will move towards a lesbian orientation (Money and Schwartz 1978; Money et al. 1984; Money and Mathews 1982).

Boys with more than normal prenatal androgen tend to be excessively aggressive and competitive, but not in any way distinctive in sexual orientation (Ehrhardt 1977: 251; Ehrhardt and Baker 1974). This leaves, as the remaining potentially interesting group, boys who received more than normal doses of oestrogen and/or progesterone before birth. One study (on twenty six-year-olds and twenty sixteen-year-olds) suggested that all of the children were less assertive and less athletic than other children (Ehrhardt 1977: 252; Yalom et al. 1973). Nothing, however, was reported on their sexual orientation. Also, a complicating factor was that the mothers of the subjects suffered severely from diabetes (this was the reason for the hormone shots). Mothers who are themselves ill or delicate tend to be overly protective of their children, and this in turn could affect the mannerisms and behaviour of their children.

Summing up the results of his (and like) studies, Money therefore sees a picture where prenatal hormones can play an important role in future gender identity (including presumably sexual orientation), but where the environment in the form of the child's upbringing can play just as

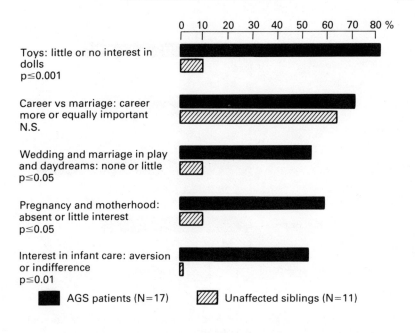

The bars represent the percentage of subjects from each group who were reported to exhibit the behaviour specified by the category.

*FIGURE 5.11   Comparison of female AGS patients versus female siblings
on marriage and maternalism*
(Ehrhardt 1977: 250)

important a role — indeed, probably more important. (See figure 5.13.) In his own words, development 'can be interpreted metaphorically as a relay race, each entry being the equivalent of a runner who carries the programme for gender-identity differentiation and passes it on to a successor' (Money and Schwartz 1978: 767). Adult sexual orientation can therefore be influenced by prenatal hormones, although there is certainly no absolute link of cause and effect.

5.5 Gunter Dörner on prenatal hormones

Without stopping here to comment on Money's findings and position, let us go straight on to discuss the work of the other major modern researcher on possible prenatal hormonal effects on adult sexual orientation, Gunter Dörner. Essentially Dörner's work falls into two parts: that on animals,

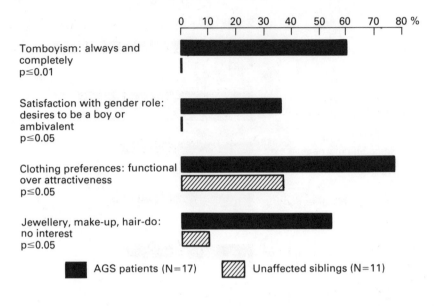

The bars represent the percentage of subjects from each group who were reported to exhibit the behaviour specified by the category.

*FIGURE 5.12   Comparison of female AGS patients versus female siblings on
gender role and clothing preference*
(Ehrhardt 1977: 251)

specifically rats, and that on humans. We will take them in turn (Dörner 1969, 1970, 1972, 1976, 1977; Dörner and Staudt 1968; Dörner and Hinz 1975; Dörner et al. 1975, 1980, 1983a, b).

Male and female rats show very distinctive sexual (copulatory) behaviour. The male rat mounts on the back of the female, grasping her with his front paws, thrusting his pelvis (and penis) forwards and backwards. The female in heat shows the *lordosis* response: she lets the male mount her, hollowing her back to aid this, and pushing her tail to one side to allow her vagina to be entered. (See figure 5.14.) Dörner (1976) defines a male 'heterosexual' rat as one that normally shows male behaviour and a male 'homosexual' rat as one that normally shows female behaviour; and vice versa for females.

The initial task that Dörner and his co-workers set themselves was seeing if, through hormonal manipulation, they could bring about homosexuality in rats. Essentially, what they found was that the crucial point in adult sexuality was just before and just after birth. By the time a

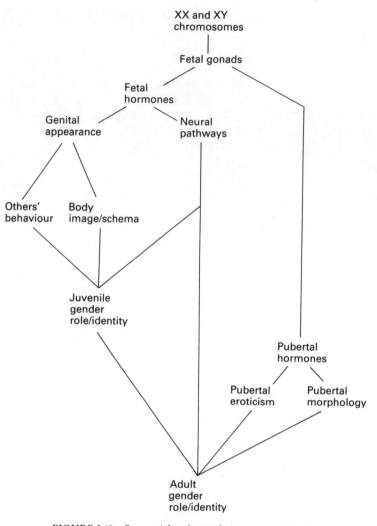

FIGURE 5.13 *Sequential and cumulative components of*
gender-role/identity differentiation
(Money and Schwartz 1978: 766)

rat reaches adulthood its sexual orientation, or rather its sexual
orientation potential, is fixed. For the adult, either male or female, homo
or heterosexual, the key activating hormone appears to be androgen, but
this can only bring out what is potentially already there. The crucial
causal factor in directing adult sexual orientation and behaviour appears

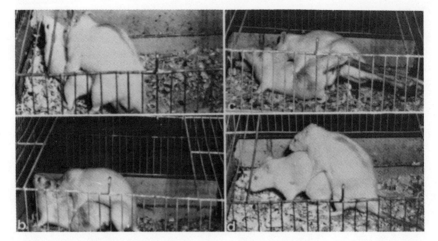

FIGURE 5.14   Sexual behavioural patterns of female and male rats: (a) oestrous female
showing lordosis response when mounted by a normal heterosexual male; (b) homosexual
male (orchidectomized on the first day of life and substituted with androgen in adulthood)
displaying lordosis response when mounted by a normal heterosexual male; (c) homosexual
male (orchidectomized on the first day of life and substituted with androgen in adulthood)
displaying lordosis response when mounted by a bisexual male (orchidectomy plus low
androgen dosis in newborn life and androgen replacement in adult life); (d) normal
heterosexual male showing no lordosis response when mounted by another vigorous
heterosexual male
(Dörner 1976: 134)

to be the way in which the part of the brain known as the hypothalamus
differentiates, and this has occurred at the latest by the end of the first
few days of life (Dörner 1976, chapter 4).

Moreover, the finding was that the way in which the hypothalamus
differentiates is dependent on the androgen levels at the time of
differentiation (in females, oestrogen can have the same positive effect as
androgen at this point). If the androgen levels at the time of birth of a rat
are high, no matter what the genetic, gonadal, or morphological sex of
the animal may be, if primed with androgen when adult the sexual
behaviour will tend to be male-like. On the other hand, if the androgen
(and oestrogen) levels at the time of the birth of a rat are low, no matter
what the genetic, gonadal, or morphological sex of the animal may be, if
primed with androgen when adult the sexual behaviour will tend to be
female-like. Figure 5.15 demonstrates Dörner's claims graphically.

Because it seems to be the hypothalamus and the way in which it
develops which is so crucial to adult sexual orientation, Dörner and his
associates concentrated their specific attention on this. They found that

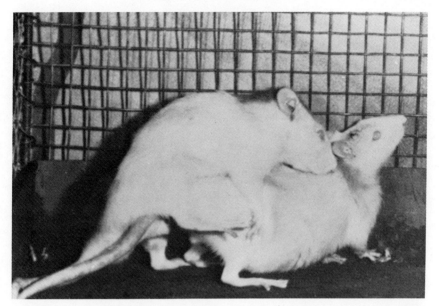

FIGURE 5.15   Female rat mounting a male rat that is showing lordosis. The female was perinatally and postpubertally treated with testosterone propionate and the male was castrated neonatally and substituted with androgen during adulthood. A total sex hormone-dependent inversion of sexual behaviour is demonstrated

(Dörner 1976: 170)

mechanical tampering (by electrolytic lesions) with this part of the brain could bring about an alteration in adult sexual drive, perhaps bearing out the importance of the nature of the hypothalamus in sexual orientation (Dörner 1969). They found also that there were cellular differences between the hypothalami of animals (male or female) with male-differentiated brains and animals (male or female) with female-differentiated brains (Dörner 1972; Dörner and Staudt 1968; Staudt and Dörner 1968). And, most interestingly, they found that those animals that had been exposed to high androgen at hypothalamus-differentiation time (that is, which had male-type brains) reacted differently to oestrogen priming from those which had not been so exposed (that is, which had female-type brains) (Dörner et al. 1975; Dörner 1976). (See figure 5.16.)

In order to understand these different reactions, one must begin by recollecting that, as we saw earlier in the chapter (figure 5.2), the female hormonal cycle is a rather complicated feedback system. The follicle-stimulating hormone (FSH) spurs the production of oestrogen, which in turn spurs the production of luteinizing hormone (LH), which in its turn

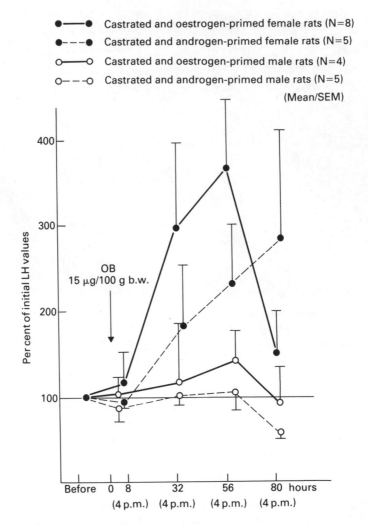

Serum LH response to a subcutaneous injection of oestradiol benzoate (15 μg/100 gms of body weight) expressed as per cent of the mean initial LH values in postpubertally castrated and oestrogen- or androgen-primed female and male rats (means and SEM (standard error around the mean)).

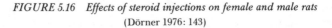

FIGURE 5.16   Effects of steroid injections on female and male rats
(Dörner 1976: 143)

spurs the production of progesterone. This rather leads one to expect, therefore, that in the normal female a sizable dose of oestrogen would bring about a reaction from the hypothalamus, namely a triggering of the pituitary into the production of LH. On the other hand, in the normal male there is no reason to believe that an oestrogen priming would lead to a production of LH — his hormonal sexual pattern does not work in the same way.

This all adds up to the prediction that if high androgen levels do indeed lead to a male-like differentiation of the brain (specifically of the hypothalamus), no matter what the genetic or gonadal sex, and that if low androgen levels do indeed lead to a female-like differentiation of the brain, no matter what the genetic or gonadal sex, then oestrogen priming of adults should lead to no feedback of LH in those with male-like differentiated hypothalami (whatever the sex) and to feedback of LH in those with female-like differentiated hypothalami (whatever the sex). And this was indeed the finding of Dörner in rats.

One other finding, which might or might not be relevant, was that animals exposed to high androgen levels during hypothalamus differentiation tended to be significantly shorter lived than animals not so exposed (Dörner 1976; Dörner and Hinz 1975). (See figure 5.17.)

We turn next to Dörner's ideas and work on humans. (See especially Dörner 1976, chapter 5.) His position is directly analogous to that which he believes he has verified for rats: the human hypothalamus is the organ directly responsible for adult sexual orientation, the direction that the hypothalamus will give is fixed at the time of the differentiation of

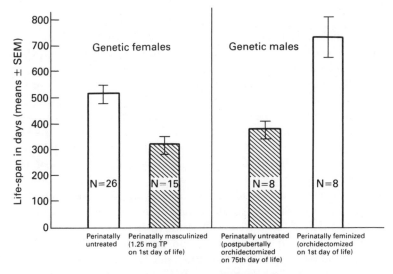

FIGURE 5.17   Androgen-dependent brain differentiation and life span
(TP = testosterone propionate)
(Dörner 1976: 171)

the hypothalamus (fourth to fifth month of fetal life), and the difference in direction of male or female adult sexual orientation is a direct function of relative androgen levels to which the fetus is exposed (exogenously or endogenously) at that time. In other words, a male fetus exposed at age four or five months to normal (that is, average) high levels of androgen will, as an adult, have a male sexual orientation — he will be a heterosexual attracted towards females; while a male fetus exposed at the same age to low levels of androgen will, as an adult, have a female sexual orientation — he will be a homosexual attracted towards males. A female fetus exposed at age four or five months to normal (that is, average) low levels of androgen will, as an adult, have a female sexual orientation — she will be a heterosexual attracted towards males; while a female fetus exposed at the same age to high levels of androgen will, as an adult, have a male sexual orientation — she will be a homosexual attracted towards females. Dörner (1976) does add that he thinks the average woman may be more bisexual than the average male, partly because the female fetus will normally be exposed to some androgen and partly because oestrogen can have a masculinizing effect on the brain. 'Consequently, it is conceivable that specific postnatal psychosocial factors may be able to affect the development of bi- or even homosexuality in females much better than in males' (Dörner 1976: 206).

What evidence can Dörner give for his position, other than the analogy from rats to humans? Dörner himself gives no direct evidence of hormonal balances in fetuses or in the fluids surrounding fetuses and of their possible effects, although he knows of and refers to the work of Money. He does, however, adduce a number of pieces of indirect evidence. First, there is good evidence that the human hypothalamus does differentiate sexually at the posited time (fourth to fifth month of fetal life). Also at this time it is known that testosterone (androgen) can affect the hypothalamus, and at this time male fetuses have significantly higher levels of testosterone than do female fetuses — indeed, the highest values occur at eleven to seventeen or eighteen weeks of fetal age, and then there is a decline to relatively low values at the time of birth (Reyes et al. 1974).

Second, there is some evidence that sleep patterns are a function of the same mechanisms which regulate sexual behaviour. Male rats with female differentiated hypothalami show the same sleep patterns as normal female rats (Branchey 1973). Interestingly and perhaps significantly, the deep sleep arousal patterns of male homosexuals have been found to be more similar to those of female heterosexuals than to those of male heterosexuals. This would be compatible with, and perhaps even point to, low testosterone levels of male homosexuals at the critical time of hypothalamus differentiation (Wilson et al. 1972).

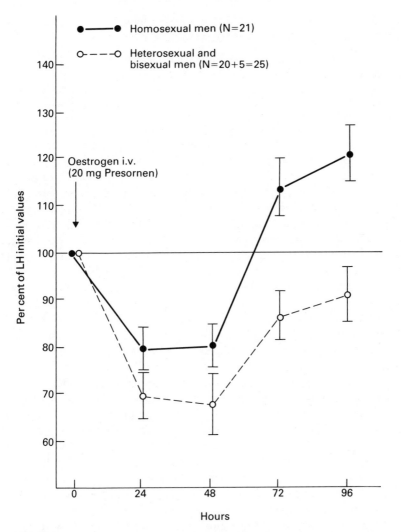

Serum LH response to an intravenous oestrogen injection expressed as per cent of the mean initial LH values in homosexual and hetero- or bisexual men (means ± SEM).

FIGURE 5.18   Effects of steroid injections on men
(Dörner 1976: 204)

Third and most importantly, male homosexuals as opposed to male heterosexuals show a positive oestrogen feedback effect. When twenty-one homosexual males were injected with oestrogen, following an initial LH drop there was a significant rise in LH levels above what there had been initially. This is a pattern which has been found in women also.

Twenty heterosexual men (and five bisexual men), however, showed no such LH rise after an oestrogen injection. (See figure 5.18.)

In view of these findings the evocability of a delayed positive estrogen feedback effect in the majority of intact, i.e. endogenously androgen-primed homosexual men in contrast to intact, i.e. endogenously androgen-primed heterosexual men suggests that male homosexuals possess in fact, at least in part, a predominantly female-differentiated brain. (Dörner 1976: 205)

Dörner also reports that lesbians (whose sexual orientation he believes to be a function of high androgen level at the time of hypothalamus differentiation) are more like heterosexual men than heterosexual women, in that they *fail* to show a feedback response (Dörner et al. 1975). Also, he cites the observation mentioned in an earlier chapter, namely that lesbians have a tendency to look older than their age and to be somewhat bigger than average females (Griffiths et al. 1974). This, Dörner believes, might be evidence in support of his position, given the fact that female rats with androgenized brains were found to have significantly increased body weights when adult and highly significantly decreased life spans.

Dörner has a number of suggestions as to how androgen imbalances might occur. In males, it is human chorionic gonadotrophin (HCG) produced by the fetal part of the placenta which stimulates the fetal testes into producing androgen. Less than usual HCG in males and more than usual in females could therefore bring about atypical brain differentiation; as also could too much oestrogen in females, given oestrogen's androgen-like effect on the developing hypothalamus. Again, imbalances might be caused by malfunctioning fetal gonads, or conversely the hypothalamus might be unable to respond properly to sex hormones. Stress or 'genetic defects' might be crucial here (Dörner 1976; Dörner et al. 1980; 1983a, b). Also, Dörner mentions the possibility that maternal sex hormonal levels might affect the differentiation of the fetal brain. Naturally enough he mentions the findings by Money that women who had been treated with androgenic progestogens during pregnancy had a tendency, if they gave birth to daughters, to give birth to tomboys. There is a fairly wide spectrum of animal evidence which supports similar conclusions (rats, Dörner 1969; rhesus monkeys, Eaton et al. 1973; sows, Hinz et al. 1974; ewes, Short 1974).

This concludes Dörner's case and my own exposition. We have now considered the main claims made about possible hormonal influences on human psychosexual development and orientation. Let us turn at once to critical philosophical discussion.

5.6 Hormones and development

With respect to studies on adult hormonal levels, I have little to add here
to what has been said already in passing. Many if not most of the studies
suffer from grave methodological defects. What does seem to emerge
from the studies is that if there be hormonal differences between adult
heterosexuals and adult homosexuals, they are not that great. This is not
to deny absolutely that such differences do exist or even that they might
be causally significant. However, the disinterested outside observer might
be forgiven for drawing a distinction between what is logically possible
and what is reasonably possible. Also, as in the psychoanalytic case, one
needs some argument that hormonal differences, if they exist, cause
homosexuality rather than follow from it. Homosexual life styles might
alter levels — as pointed out, stress affects hormonal concentrations and
many homosexuals live under stress. It could even be that it is
heterosexuals with odd hormonal levels — a function of trying to relate
to the opposite sex!

I turn at once, therefore, towards the work of those who have studied
possible influences of hormonal differences on the developing brain,
Money and Dörner. This, and related work, has been (and still is) the
object of stringent, impassioned criticism — from within and without the
biological community. Dörner has even been the subject of a public
letter of censure from an official sex society (Siguish et al. 1982; Dörner
1983). I suspect, however, that although much of the critics' charge is well
made, in certain fundamental respects their onslaught is off target.
Hoping to show this point later, I begin with a strictly methodological
analysis of the hormonal work. Value questions will be deferred until
after this has been given.

Today, Money's position is that adult sexual orientation in particular,
and more generally gender identity and role at all ages, is a function of
both hormones and environmental influences. There are three main
methodological comments I want to make. First, the numbers that Money
and his fellow workers are studying are really rather small. Admittedly,
relatively speaking the numbers of hermaphrodites studied is quite large
(certainly relative to what others have done), but still absolutely the
numbers are not great. For instance, in the study of fetally androgenized
girls, there were only twenty-five subjects, ten artificially androgenized
and fifteen naturally androgenized (Money and Ehrhardt 1972). Since
these early studies, ongoing numbers of relevant children have been
identified and brought into the analyses. But one supposes that always
the absolute figures must be few, if only because by the nature of the

research one is dealing directly with rather rare cases.

Moreover, as critics have been ready to point out, one knows that there are oddities in many of the studied cases, which could well affect development, especially including the development of sexual orientation. The subjects frequently come to notice because they have ambiguous genitalia — they are physically and physiologically hermaphroditic, requiring surgery to place them firmly in one anatomical sex or the other. As one disbeliever scathingly writes: 'The investigators . . . have never considered as relevant the effect on a girl child's emotional and psychic life of having a penis and scrotum for the first year or three and a half or even seven and a half or more years of their lives . . . nor the effects of *then* having them removed' (Bleier 1984: 99).

This is a serious charge. My second comment is also serious, but presumably one which time will (at least partially) allay. The problem with most of the studies is that they are generally exclusively on children or adolescents. The evidence on adult sexual orientation — on *long-term* adult sexual orientation — is necessarily rather sparse. And, of course, as one increases the numbers in the studies, the chances are very much that one is adding to the lower age ranks rather than the upper. Certainly, there are some very suggestive hints and apparently some harder evidence is starting to come in — but still we seem to be in need of more time before really solid judgements can be made.

For instance, much has been made by Money and others of a pair of identical (genetically male) twins, one of whom accidentally lost his penis through a bungled circumcision (Money and Schwartz 1978). This child was brought up as a girl and apparently developed a secure female gender identity. Supposedly, therefore, the environment can overrule all other factors. But a great deal of ambiguity (and perhaps downright obfuscation) surrounds this person's sexual orientation, now she has passed puberty (Diamond 1982). Time alone can give full answers in this and like cases. Indeed, as we have seen, over the crucial question of prenatally androgenized girls, Money himself seems to have had a very significant change of mind about their probable (or not improbable) direction of adult sexual orientation. Who dare say that ten more years will not provide even more crucial information?

My third point is that even if one grants that Money and his fellows have made positive progress in establishing the causes of gender identity and (in particular) adult sexual orientation, there are still questions about how widely their findings can be generalized. Suppose we grant that fetal androgenization of girls may lead to an increased chance of adult lesbian orientation. It is quite clear that there are far more lesbians than those who fall into the special categories studied by Money and others: girls who were known to have been super-androgenized, either through the mother being known to have taken male hormones or through possession of certain special kinds of genes. What about the vast majority of lesbians (and conversely, male homosexuals for that matter)? Are we supposed to assume that unbeknown to them, to their mothers and to us, their prenatal hormones got out of balance — or should we rely solely on other causal factors, like the environment? Money's studies do not really tell us.

The three points just given obviously show that Money and his fellows have presented a far from definitive case — and, to be fair, I doubt that he or anyone would want to claim otherwise. Is there anything else positive which can be said in support of the kinds of conclusion to which he seems to be heading? There are indeed some findings, which, for fairly obvious reasons, tempt researchers sympathetic to Money's approach. If you think that prenatal hormones do make a difference to adult sexual orientation, then it is hard not to home in on all of the reports about the atypical childhoods of many homosexuals — sissy boys and tomboy girls. Given that high-androgen girls tend to tomboyism and that low-androgen/high-oestrogen boys tend not to have aggressive natures and so forth, there is an almost overwhelming urge to generalize, arguing that for various unspecified reasons those children who do grow into a homosexual orientation are precisely those who had atypical prenatal hormonal levels.

Always cautious, the Second Kinsey researchers nevertheless hint that their sympathies could lie in this direction: 'our findings are not inconsistent with what one would expect to find if, indeed, there were a biological basis for sexual preference' (Bell et al. 1981: 216, in italics in original). This is hardly an enthusiastic endorsement, but it is about as positive as they get about any causal hypothesis. And it certainly stands out against the scorn which is usually shown towards Money and his fellows. Dare we here go as far as the Kinsey researchers? I suspect that we may — so long as it is remembered that the discussion is explicitly confined to the level of methodology. But it would be wise to keep all of our reservations firmly in mind, before we make even the most cautious of positive statements. No one could (or rather should) make general claims about direct causal links between fetal hormonal levels and adult sexual orientation — on the basis of Money's work, that is. There are far too many gaps, questions, and potentially disruptive factors.

And even if a link were firmer, its exact nature has not been articulated. For instance, do the hormones produce a child of a certain type, who is then automatically on the road to adult orientation? Or do the hormones programme a type, who then possibly, but only possibly, reacts in such a way as to produce a child on the road to adult homosexual orientation? Suppose that there were something in the suggestion that male homosexuals are physically slighter than heterosexuals, and suppose also that this is a difference going back to childhood (R. B. Evans 1972).[1] A hormonally produced slight child might not be particularly sissy-like in a society which did not have a heavy emphasis on body contact sports, and thus might not acquire a self-image which would lead to adult homosexuality. But things would be otherwise for such a boy born (say) in the state of Texas (Ross 1980).

One thing is certain. Even if there be a hormonal factor in the aetiology of homosexuality, work like Money's does not carry us very far forward in teasing out the precise details. What Money's work does show is that naive links between the hormones and sexuality are almost certainly wrong. There is a lot more to gender identity and sexual orientation than the effects of bodily fluids, however vital.

5.7 Of rats and men (and women)

Dörner's claims are stronger than Money's. He allows indeed that the environment may play some role in the attitudes and behaviour of men and women; but, essentially, he thinks that whether one is homo or heterosexual is a function of the kind of hypothalamus one has, and this in turn is a function of androgen (or possibly oestrogen) levels in the fourth and fifth months of fetal life. There are two sets of (methodological) questions that ought to be asked about Dörner's work. First, what relevance if any does his work on rats have for an understanding of human homosexuality and its causes? Second, what is the strength of the evidence that Dörner brings forward in his direct discussion of human sexual orientation?

The work on rats is obviously intended as an analogy, as a model, for human attitudes and behaviour. Speaking generally for a moment, what we have, therefore, is a comparison between two things, each with a set of properties, some of which are shared and some of which are not (one needs both of these to have an analogy). What one is trying to do is argue from the properties that one knows the one object has to a property that one hopes the other object has. If the case is strong, one can hope to prove the plausibility of the inferred property (analogy as justification). But, however tenuous, the analogy can be a source of insight or new ideas (analogy as heuristic). One's judgement about the strength of the analogy is influenced by the things one knows that the objects have in common, and one is assuming that these elements are enough to allow one to discount the things that one knows the objects do not have in common (Ruse 1986). Of course, since one can always expand the list of things in common, the really crucial things in an analogy are *relevant* similarities and dissimilarities (Salmon 1973). Obviously, what is relevant might vary according to one's end and be a matter of debate.

Specifically referring now to Dörner and hormones, the most obvious comment about his analogy is that rats are not humans, nor even primates. Moreover, there are fairly substantial relevant differences between rats and humans, or more generally between rats and primates (Birke 1981; Meyer-Bahlburg 1984b). For instance, female rats given early doses of androgens lose their normal fertility cycle in a fairly drastic fashion (Herbert 1978: 486). Rhesus monkeys so treated, on the other hand, continue to menstruate and ovulate in the normal way. This seems to suggest that the rat brain may be more sensitive to early doses of sex hormones than the primate brain. And another finding perhaps points in the same direction. Normal adult male monkeys castrated and given oestrogen surges show an LH feedback response. Normal adult male rats similarly treated show no such surge. This again suggests that the brains of rats are more fixed by early hormonal experiences than are the brains of primates (Hodges and Hearn 1978).

Dörner's case would have been more impressive had his animal experiments been based substantially on animals such as monkeys which are much closer to humans than are rats, and which therefore have fewer relevant dissimilarities. Indeed, one would surely be foolish to conclude that Dörner's case for humans could be definitively or even very plausibly established by his work and findings on rats. Moreover, in this context it is worth noting also that most of Dörner's experiments involve rats that have been castrated and primed with androgen to elicit sexual responses, by the time they are adults. This is certainly not usually the case for adult human homosexuals. Additionally, one should note that this castration and androgen priming, although an experimental technique to bring the animals to readiness when required, had side-effects. Androgenized female rats so treated showed far more male behaviour than did untreated rats (Dörner 1976: 164).

Dörner's rat work is bound to be more heuristic than justificatory. But is it merely of value as a source of ideas? There are surely some hormonal similarities between rats and primates, rats and humans even, which are relevant to Dörner's ends. Most significantly, whether or not this all ends in full-blown homosexuality, there is no doubt that in primates as well as in rats, altering androgen levels at the time of hypothalamus differentiation can and does alter behaviour. Moreover, the alteration is either towards or away from behaviour usually exhibited by males or females, and the alteration is a function of the relative degree of the androgen level in or around the organism. Quite apart from Money's findings on humans, experiments strongly suggest that prenatal androgenization of female rhesus monkeys significantly switches their behaviour towards that shown by males, particularly in such areas as sexual play (Goy et al. 1977).

In other words, if one is concerned with future sexual behaviour and gender role, hormone levels at the time of hypothalamus differentiation do seem important in mammals generally: rats and primates have this fact in common.[2] That Dörner has been able to manipulate his rats, not merely to show some cross-gender characteristics but to full homosexuality (as far as they are physiologically capable), is surely therefore of some justificatory value for claims he would make about other animals, including humans. As justification, it is weak. His position would be far stronger were his subject animals primates like rhesus monkeys, rather than rats. But it is positive evidence nevertheless.

However, at this point there is an objection that many critics will be raising (Birke 1986). Dörner talks quite confidently throughout of rat 'homosexuality', 'heterosexuality', and 'bisexuality'. But, in the eyes of these critics, this is precisely to beg the most crucial point: to fall into the pathetic fallacy in its most blatant form. Even if one thinks that in some circumstances rats can throw some light on humans, in this particular case they certainly cannot, simply because it is quite meaningless to talk of the behaviour that Dörner produces in his rats in such human terms as homo or heterosexuality. An adult male homosexual who is fellating another male is hardly analogous to one of Dörner's genetically male, hormonally manipulated rats who is showing lordosis. Apart from anything else, what has to be conceded (and what has certainly been conceded by me) is that human homosexuality centres primarily on feelings, desires, and fantasies, with behaviour somewhat secondary. But all of Dörner's judgements about rats are in terms of behaviour.

Again, much of Dörner's work rests on judgements about what constitutes 'male' as opposed to 'female' behaviour. This is suspect enough in the case of rats. In the case of humans it is downright ludicrous. If one man is having anal intercourse with another, who is showing what kind of behaviour? Is either of them any more 'female' in their behaviour than a male having heterosexual intercourse? Heterosexual men and women have anal intercourse, but on average such episodes must be far fewer than those involving vaginal intercourse. Hence, neither of the men engaged in anal intercourse can really be said to be demonstrating female behaviour (Silverstein and White 1977). In short, all of Dörner's work on rats and his analogies from rats to humans are conceptually confused and should be discarded.

This is a strong argument, which many critics think applies not merely to Dörner and his rats but to all animal models which might be used at a point like this. My response will be made in the light of this broader critique, represented by the specific attack on Dörner. There are three reasons why the argument fails to convince.

First, there is the question of attitudes and desires as compared to behaviour. I agree that in judgements of human homosexuality it is probably the former which is primary whereas in Dörner's rat work the latter is not merely primary but (as far as we are concerned) all there is. However, attitudes and desires and behaviour are not entirely separate. It would be rather odd to say that somebody wanted to do something, if in the absence of constraints he/she never did it (Hudson 1970). Conversely, if someone did something, even though they were perfectly free not to do it, then it would be rather odd to say that they did not want to do it. In other words, desires and behaviour normally go together unless there is some good reason to part them.

This being so, the fact that we can judge rats only by their behaviour seems somewhat less troublesome than the critic's argument implies. Assuming that one can properly speak of 'rat desires', and I do not see why we cannot think of them as existing at least in some rudimentary way — after all, we would speak of rats 'wanting' food and shelter — we can then go on to say that if rats show certain sexual behaviour, this is grounds for saying that they have certain sexual attitudes (and that the attitudes and desires in turn cause the behaviour). Rats, after all, have no social conventions about sex to observe or avoid or fear. Hence, since we cannot directly ask rats what they are wanting or desiring, it seems both sensible and proper to check on attitudes and dispositions by observation of behaviour.

I do not want to imply that rats have full-blown fantasies or anything like that; but we can take behaviour as indicative of rudimentary attitudes or dispositions or something of this nature. And this being so, in this respect comparing rats and humans no longer seems so heinous. The human ability to conceptualize and fantasize, in sex as in other matters, is a major difference between humans and rats, and a major reason why I for one would not take rat studies as sole support for a thesis about human sexuality. But logically the attempt to compare human and rat sexual orientation — desires and behaviours — seems not doomed to failure a priori.

As the second part of the response to the critic, let us take up the general objection about talking about 'male' and 'female' behaviour, and relatedly, talking about rats showing 'heterosexual' or 'homosexual' behaviour. (Obviously at this point we link up with and continue our incomplete discussion from the analysis of suggested psychoanalytic aetiologies of homosexuality.) Other than by ruling the attempt impossible by definition, I cannot see why one should not isolate certain elements of behaviour, nor why one should not label them as being 'male' and 'female' or at least typically male and female. Leading researchers on sexual behaviour in rhesus monkeys have put the point well in the following way:

If, for example, prenatal androgen induced new and bizarre types of behaviour not usually found in rhesus males or females, or if it introduced distortions in behaviour patterns usually displayed in the same way by all rhesus, then the effects would have to be characterized as abnormalities. In such a circumstance, the studies might be useful as curiosities or as animal psychiatric models. This is not the manner in which the prenatal androgens work, however, and although we have studied intensively over the past decade as many as 30 different kinds of behavioral responses, we have never found behavior that was modified in the hermaphrodite that did not normally differ in its expression in normal males and normal females. In short, the action of prenatal androgen is limited to those behavioral patterns that are normally sexually dimorphic. (Goy et al. 1977: 149−50)

For this reason, they feel justified in talking of male hermaphrodite monkeys as showing 'female' behaviour, and vice versa.

Similarly, Dörner may speak of his male rats as showing female behaviour, and vice versa. If, as seems to be the case, it is females that normally show the lordosis response, then when males do so they are showing a female response, and the same principle holds for females when they mount other animals. Note that it is not necessary for some behaviour to be virtually exclusively the province of males (or females) to be labelled 'male' (or 'female') behaviour. Like the sex hormones, what counts is that the behaviour be generally typical of that sex − it confirms its status, of course, if the behaviour has a clear biological function appropriate to the sex which performs it (like mounting and lordosis, both of which obviously aid getting the penis into the vagina).

But can one then go on to define heterosexual and homosexual behaviour in terms of male and female sexual behaviour − a homosexual animal being one which shows sexual behaviour more normally associated with the sex other than that to which it belongs? I really do not see why one should not. After all, what is homosexual behaviour if it is not this? It may seem a little strange to talk of a rat being homosexual or showing homosexual behaviour, but it is not thereby wrong.

Anticipating later discussion somewhat, I suspect that at the root of objections like this just being considered is not really a burning urge of linguistic purity, that is, an abhorrence of defining behaviour in a conceptually incorrect manner. Rather, what lies behind objections like this is a (perfectly justifiable) moral concern. There is a fear that if one labels certain behaviour 'male' or 'female', or what is perhaps even worse, 'masculine' or 'feminine', one is making certain value judgements — usually judgements that male is better than female, and also probably that what is normal in the sense of 'average' is what is normal in the sense of 'to be preferred'. Thus male homosexuals are to be despised because they show (inferior) female behaviour, and all homosexuals are to be despised because all show inappropriate sexual behaviour. (For expression of fears like this see Silverstein and White 1977; Sisley and Harris 1977; Martin and Lyon 1972; Birke 1981, 1986; Harding 1986.)

One would have to be insensitive and ignorant to deny that these sorts of connections are made in many people's minds. However, one can still sort out a conceptual or linguistic point from the common usage — and this point is important. One does not necessarily make a value judgement if one labels certain behaviour 'male' or 'female', meaning by this that it is more typical of one sex than the other. For instance, growing numbers of men are single parents raising small children. Necessarily, they do many things more typical of females than of males in our society. They would not pretend that they always like doing these things (nor I suspect do most women like doing them either). But I doubt they feel morally demeaned by their gender-role changes — if anything, they probably feel rather superior through having transcended petty sexual stereotyping!

But still there is a third part to the critic's objection to comparing rats and humans. Let us grant, it may be argued, that we can talk of homosexuality in rats and primates in the ways characterized above. This still does not mean that we can push the comparison to humans. The whole point about rats and monkeys, even, is that males and females have different distinctive sexual behaviours. For instance, rats, as we have seen, show mounting and lordosis in males and females respectively. For this — and only this — reason, we can make some sense of labelling certain behaviour 'male' and 'female', 'homosexual' and 'heterosexual'. However, as pointed out, in humans we do not get this rigidity of behaviour. Males and females, homo and heterosexuals, show much sexual diversity and flexibility, and much behaviour is neither distinctively 'male' nor 'female'. Who is to say that either of the participants in male anal intercourse is showing 'female' behaviour?

There is obvious force in this objection. If nothing else, it surely points to the fact that in understanding human homosexuality, particularly its varieties, we must allow for some 'cultural' factors, factors which are essentially or totally absent in animal sexual behaviour (factors the like of which, moreover, undoubtedly enter into all facets of human behaviour, but which are minimally present in animals). How human homosexuals relate to each other is surely much a matter of learning, imitation, and so forth. On the other hand, with this much granted, I wonder if the objection has full force. The fact undoubtedly is that, for all their variety, human homosexuals are like animal homosexuals in that they are relating sexually to members of their own sex, rather than to members of the opposite sex — and that they are doing this freely, not out of compulsion or for want of alternatives. It is this which is at the crux of two men having intercourse — they are relating to each other sexually. Precisely how they do it is very much a secondary matter.

This all being so, then I really do not see that the situation is essentially different from the animal case, or that the possibility of a meaningful analogy is barred, or even that one cannot properly speak of human homosexuals showing cross-gender sexual behaviour. After all, it is normally women, not men, who relate sexually to men; and it is normally men, not women, who relate sexually to women. To those who counter immediately that history and anthropology show that homosexuality is not less common than heterosexuality, let me reply that when homosexual behaviour is accepted and practised by all as part of a culture, it is generally associated with the unavailability of heterosexual contacts. A typical occurrence is heterosexuals behaving homosexually in prison, or homosexuality amongst young men, when kept separate from girls (Weinrich 1976; Dover 1978).

In conclusion: Dörner's rat—human analogies are not strong support for his position. But, in his quest for the causes of human homosexual orientation, Dörner's use of rat models is not conceptually inappropriate. What we need, having established the legitimacy of using animal models, is some good studies on animals close to us — like chimpanzees.

5.8 The evidence from humans

Let us turn now to Dörner's evidence for his case based directly on humans. Until recently, there would have been little to say at this point, other than that (as with rats) the case is undoubtedly suggestive but nowhere like definitive. We might well grant that something rather important happens to the human hypothalamus around the time that Dörner suggests that it does, but this in itself is hardly to justify all the conclusions about the fixity of adult sexual orientation that Dörner wants to draw (nor, obviously, does Dörner himself think that it does). The item about sleep patterns and their differences between homo and heterosexuals is interesting, but as it stands it is not much more than an idea. Only nine homosexuals were studied (Wilson et al. 1972). The same also holds for the speculations about the possible life spans of homosexuals as opposed to heterosexuals. Dörner offers no firm data here, nor, as far as I can make out, has anyone done an empirical study on this question.

This brings us down to Dörner's claim about the difference in responses between male homosexuals and male heterosexuals to an injection of oestrogen — homosexuals and only homosexuals showing an LH feedback response. If this work is valid, then truly we do have an important clue towards a general explanation of homosexuality, of male homosexuality at least. There is theory backing the findings, and that theory points to the importance of fetal hormonal levels. But there are questions or reservations. At the general level, even if the experiment holds universally (that is, all homosexuals show feedback responses), we still have a clue rather than hard justification. There is no absolute proof that male homosexuals did have reduced prenatal androgen levels and that these are the cause of their homosexuality. Apart from anything else, there is some evidence that one can get LH feedback responses with careful manipulation even in 'heterosexual' primates (Karsch et al. 1973; Hodges and Hearn 1978). One really would like to see the causal chain (in humans) followed through in more detail, from fetal life to adult orientation.

Then at the more specific level, referring to Dörner's own work, its empirical findings are hardly that wide ranging, for all the implications otherwise. We learn that some of Dörner's homosexual subjects were drawn from a VD clinic (Dörner et al. 1975). Were they typical? And what about a person under stress — does he show a different response to someone not under stress? Also, one would like to know a little more about why Dörner's bisexual subjects gave results like heterosexuals and not homosexuals. Does this mean that bisexuality is in some sense a superficial sexual orientation? And obviously, one would like to know about women. It is true that Dörner reports on some such comparable findings for women, where lesbians are more like heterosexual men than heterosexual women in that they fail to show a feedback response (Dörner 1976). But then one discovers that only four cases were involved, the women in question were transsexuals not ordinary lesbians, and that in one of the four cases a normal (that is, typically female) feedback response obtained. Need more be said?

I said just above that 'until recently' this would have been all that could be said on the matter. Fortunately, not only philosophers feel the imperatives of methodological inadequacies. So also do scientists. In particular, a group of American sexologists have now exactly replicated Dörner's work. They too injected homosexuals and heterosexuals with oestrogen. They too got LH feedback response in and only in homosexuals. They too were able to show that this is more akin to a 'female' response than to a 'male' response. They too tied their findings in with the effects of hormones on fetal brains:

The ability of increased estrogen to enhance the release of LH positive feedback is thought to reflect the adult consequences of hormonemediated sexual differentiation. Such an LH response pattern, typically seen in females, presumably reflects the 'female' differentiation of the brain; the typical absence of this response in males presumably reflects 'male' differentiation. (Gladue et al. 1984: 1496)

Going beyond Dörner, the Americans took care to avoid bias in choice of subjects. Likewise, they made sure that stress would not be a disruptive factor, and that drug use would not distort findings. Methodologically they were much more sensitive. At least some of the worries one has with Dörner's work are, therefore, answered. Yet, despite all of this — or perhaps because of all of this — the answers they obtained were unambiguous. Male homosexuals really do have a response pattern closer to female heterosexuals than do male heterosexuals. (As can be seen from figure 5.19, homosexual males do not have a response identical to women. They are about half-way there.)

The argument is not over yet. Apart from the general reservations noted above (about the overall link between such findings and the final conclusion about the aetiology of sexual orientation), the American study is itself hardly definitive. One negative note in particular is that the numbers of subjects were depressingly close to the usual low levels. For this reason, if for none other, one should be wary of sweeping claims about confirmation. Indeed, the Americans themselves are cagey: 'even though a developmental relation between neuroendocrine response and sexual orientation is not certain, our findings are not inconsistent with such an interpretation' (p. 1498). Nevertheless, when this is said, Dörner can surely (and properly) feel that the studies of humans are starting to add weight to the conclusions he would draw from his animal models. Bringing this methodological discussion to an end, therefore, we can perhaps say that although the road ahead may be long and hard, the first fumbling steps may now have been taken. No one could (or should) say that the hormones tell all. They may tell something.

5.9 Is there inevitable bias?

Even with the new findings from America, this is little more than a

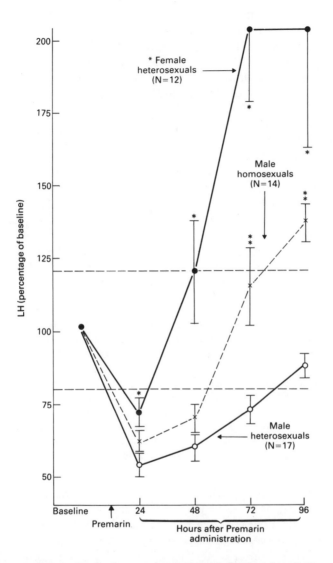

Values are means ± standard errors (vertical bars). Dashed lines indicate the 95 per cent confidence interval for baseline values for all groups. Group comparisons: (*) female heterosexuals significantly different from male heterosexuals and homosexuals at all times (p < 0.05, Newman-Keuls multiple comparison test) and (**) male homosexuals significantly different from male heterosexuals at 72 and 96 hours (p < 0.05, SNK). All groups show a decrease from baseline at 24 hours.

FIGURE 5.19   *Changes in LH in response to a single injection of Premarin, an oestrogen*
(Gladue et al. 1984: 1496)

cautious appreciation of the results of Money, Dörner and the like workers. Nor is it meant to be. However, it has surely been achieved without any desperate special pleading. Hormonal studies leave much to be desired. They may, nevertheless, have some genuine insights.

Or so one might think. Yet, as remarked at the beginning of the chapter, work like that of Money and Dörner reaps savage criticism, on a par with that which is levelled against Freud at his worst. (Often, it is the same critics in both cases.) Why should this be so? Usually, at least in large part, the criticisms are methodological, akin to (if not identical to) criticisms already brought in the earlier parts of this chapter. But this hardly explains the fury, and may even be (if my arguments are well made) a case of overkill. Other reasons for the dislike must be sought — and they are not hard to find. Methodology worries the critics only incidentally. The real objection to hormonal studies is a question of values — a charge of bias.

Listen to the words of one of the most articulate of feminist writers, Lynda Birke. In a stimulating article on hormones and lesbianism (but which she clearly intends to be generalizable to all human homosexuality), she writes:

Within the hormone literature . . . the implication is that Lesbians suffer from abnormal levels of sex hormones: either they have too much of the so-called 'male' hormones (androgens) or too little of the so-called 'female' hormones (oestrogens).

Lesbianism is commonly referred to as a 'condition', as a 'sexual dysfunction', as an 'abnormality', and similar pejorative terms. By contrast, heterosexuality is considered so normal as not to require explanation. In much of scientific literature on homosexuality, to be heterosexual is to be healthy, natural; while to be a Lesbian is to be sick and 'unnatural'. But is there, in fact, any evidence to suggest that Lesbian behaviour is 'unnatural'? (Birke 1979: 2; see also Birke 1981)

With some justification Birke is concerned about these attitudes she finds. Not only is it unpleasant to be labelled 'sick' or 'deviant', particularly when this labelling is based on 'scientific' judgements which are themselves perverted by researchers' initial personal prejudices; but also pseudo-conclusions of this nature lead straight to proposals for 'curing' or eliminating homosexuality. In short, under a bogus cloak of scientific legitimacy, naked fears and hatreds are given respectability and brought forward as a programme of social action.

There are two questions which need separating out here. First, are hormonal studies on homosexuality truly filled with value judgements against homosexuality? Second, is this a necessary state of affairs? Is there something actually in the hormonal approach which is inherently anti-homosexual? Note that in asking this second question, I am not asking whether (ultimately) we must judge homosexual attitudes/behaviour unfortunate — candidates for cure. The question is whether hormonal studies in themselves prove this.

Taking the first question first, even if one doubts whether subtle biases pervade all of the hormonal work on homosexuality, there can be no doubt whatsoever that very unsubtle value judgements glare out from some of the hormonal studies on homosexuality. As it happens, although at one point Money referred to homosexuality as a 'behavioural disorder' and contrasted it with 'normal and healthy cognitional eroticism' (Money 1961: 1397), in recent years he has been much more guarded in his language. Dörner, however, is another matter. In his language, in his theorizing, and in his suggestions for future action, he shows explicitly and unequivocally that he considers homosexuality a serious sickness brought about by accidents (like genetic mutation), that he considers his work to confirm this position, and that he believes action should be taken to eliminate homosexuality: action, that is, inspired by his scientific conclusions.

Hamburger (1953) after having received 465 letters from transsexuals wrote: 'The many personal letters from almost 500 deeply unhappy persons have an over-whelming impression. One tragic existence is unfolded after another. They cry for help and understanding. It is depressing to realize how little can be done to come to their aid. One feels it is a duty to appeal to the medical profession and to the responsible legislature: — do your utmost to ease the existence of these fellow men who are deprived of a harmonious and happy life through no fault of their own.' Since I have received similar letters from transsexuals and homosexuals, I can only agree to this statement. (Dörner 1976: 229)

Dörner's position is unambiguous. But this now brings up the second question. Granting that at least some of the hormonal work on homo-sexuality shows a bias against homosexuality (possibly, although not necessarily, homosexuals as well), is it the case that any hormonal study of homosexuality contains such a bias (in the sense of value judgement), even though it may be nothing like as explicit as Dörner's?

Not necessarily! At this point, I will skate around specific questions to do with health and sickness, for they will get explicit treatment later (chapter 9). Here, I will concentrate on the general value issues. Let us grant the hormonal case as strongly as we can, assuming that the difference between a homosexual and a heterosexual orientation is a function of a difference in hormonal levels, either pre- or postnatally. In what sense is this claim, in itself, putting down homosexuality and homosexuals? The most obvious reply is that such a case rests on the assumption that homosexual hormonal levels are different, and that moreover, they are 'abnormal'. But although certainly the argument is that they are different, what implications does this have about abnormality (if this is meant to imply undesirability)? There is no basis in biology for this conclusion. The fact that one has two members of a species with biological differences, even with hormonal differences, says nothing about whether one is better than or preferable to the other. From a biological point of view, in fact, diversity can be valuable to all involved. For instance, if a predator preys on a particular species and has first to learn to recognize its prey, then diversity in the prey could be of adaptive camouflage value, because with diversity the predator would be confused. Nor can one argue that the point is that homosexuality is a minority preference, and it is in its being a minority that the abnormality lies. Again biologically speaking, being a minority can be of great value — in the predator—prey situation, being very rare would be of greatest value of all, for then the predator would never recognize one as a potential victim (Sheppard 1975; Maynard Smith 1975).

At this point it may be objected that deliberately I seem to be avoiding the main issues. Dörner argues that the abnormality of homosexuality lies first in the fact that it is due to something irregular like a mutation or inadvertent human intervention, and secondly in the fact that it makes its bearer (and perhaps other people) unhappy. But neither of these points make the case against hormonal theories. Mutations as such are not bad — after all, we ourselves are the end of a long line of mutations from apes. Nor are human interventions in themselves bad — human interventions in the form of insulin injections keep diabetics alive, and indeed were one to carry out Dörner's programme what would this involve but human intervention?

As far as happiness and unhappiness are concerned, I concede that it may be true that homosexuals are less happy than heterosexuals — although then again this fact may not be true. This is a matter we shall have to discuss later. But whether or not homosexuals are happier or unhappier than heterosexuals — and whether or not this has any relevance to the matter of sickness and health — one thing is certain: we cannot drag these facts out of hormonal theories about homosexuality. Matters to do with happiness and so forth have to be imposed on the theory. If I or my fetus have more or less testosterone than usual, this tells us nothing about my state of mind — or whether it be desirable that I should have such a state of mind. This is additional information which must be added.

Again, to continue the line of argument, hormonal theories in themselves hardly prescribe or proscribe strategies for action. Dörner advocates the manipulation of prenatal hormonal levels to prevent adult homosexual orientation, but there is nothing in his theory to say that one *ought* to do this. The moral directive comes only from the theory *together* with beliefs about the undesirability of homosexuality and the need, if possible, to eliminate it. After all, one could just as easily use Dörner's theory as the basis of an action plan to prevent adult heterosexual orientation. One could argue that one ought to eliminate heterosexuality and that the way to do this is through the manipulation of prenatal hormone levels. I should add that if one does accept Dörner's theory, one consequence rather favourable to homosexuals does present itself, even to those who think homosexuality undesirable. Many today who dislike homosexuality argue that homosexuals ought not to be allowed to teach in schools, because they might contaminate young, developing minds. But if homosexuality is a function of prenatal hormonal levels, then such contamination is no longer a real possibility. Hence, legislation of this nature against homosexuals is quite unnecessary.

I conclude, therefore, that in themselves hormonal studies and explanations of human homosexuality have no necessary and inevitable biases against homosexuality or homosexuals. Whilst it is true that some studies, Dörner's particularly, do in fact show a bias against homosexuality, this is something which could in principle be eliminated. Suggestions for changing potential homosexuals could certainly be detached from the theory. Hormonal levels could be talked about in terms of differences from average instead of 'abnormalities'. One could, I suppose, even drop the talk about certain behaviour being distinctively 'male' or 'female', but as I have argued earlier, I do not see such use of terms as biased in itself against homosexuals. After all, a penis is a male organ and a vagina is a female organ, and that is that. In principle, I simply see no reason why such an ascription of gender should not similarly be applied to behaviour and desires.

One can understand fully why so many people — especially those with a homosexual orientation themselves — react so violently against the hormonal studies. Yet if the argument of this section is well founded, then, as I have said, much of the critical attack is off target. The real problem is not with methodology but with values. Admittedly, the methodology leaves much to be desired — but if one concentrates on it to the exclusion of nigh all else, given that one can do something about the values, one might miss something of real worth.

6

The Sociobiology of Homosexuality

We come to the third of our kinds of way of explaining homosexuality — the newcomer to the field. Explanations of this kind try to relate sexual orientation and activity to our evolutionary origins. In particular (since to the best of my knowledge everyone who has written positively on the subject has subscribed to the dominant evolutionary paradigm), these explanations try to understand homosexuality in a Darwinian mode — as, in some sense, a function of adaptation brought about by natural selection, in response to life's struggles for existence and (more importantly) reproduction. Because these explanations look upon homosexuality as being, in some way, a *social* phenomenon — homosexuality involves (if only in thought) the interaction between people — they fall within that sphere of the evolutionary field known today as *sociobiology*: 'the systematic study of the biological basis of all social behaviour' (E. O. Wilson 1975: 2).

Now, at once, we are plunged into controversy. There are few topics which have been more violently debated (and condemned) than sociobiology, particularly in its presumed application to humankind (Caplan 1978; Ruse 1985). It is almost unique in that it has brought down the scorn and ire of people of the left — one of whose more articulate spokesmen has recently written a whole book referring to his target as 'pop sociobiology' (Kitcher 1985) — and people of the right. Roger Scruton (1986) sneers that, having dealt with animals, 'a small leap of the imagination (or rather, the leap of a small imagination) takes us to the human world' (pp. 184—5).

I shall eschew the temptation to engage in general debate and shall confine myself to three brief introductory comments. Following this, we can turn to the pertinent arguments of the sociobiologists — exposition and analysis. (A good introduction to modern evolutionary thought is Ayala and Valentine 1979. In this book I shall stay away from all of the juicy philosophical questions about Darwinism per se. I have discussed them at length — at *great* length — elsewhere (for example, Ruse 1973, 1982b, 1986). Here, I assume without proof that natural selection was *the* key evolutionary mechanism and that, consequently, the organic world is to be understood as highly adapted.)

6.1 Why sociobiology of homosexuality?

My first point is that we cannot deny the fact of our simian origins. *Homo sapiens* is just as much a product of the forces of evolution as is any other organism, living or dead. We evolved away from other animals (specifically the chimpanzee line) a mere six million years ago — compare that with the three and a half billion plus years since life has been on this planet (Pilbeam 1984). Moreover, everything which we know of human evolution suggests that natural selection — the differential reproduction of organisms — played a major causal role in shaping our nature: physical, mental and behavioural. Putting the matter bluntly, those of our possible ancestors who had the sorts of features that have been passed down to us — bipedalism, large brains, manual dexterity, sociality, and so forth — tended to survive and reproduce. And those of our possible ancestors who did not have these sorts of features did not (Isaac 1980, 1983).

I am not now saying that evolutionary biology is all, and that it suffices for a full understanding of humankind. Obviously, at a minimum, we humans have to some extent escaped our biology. We live in a world of culture — of language, of science, of the arts, of customs and habits, of religion, and more. Change in these areas is far different from (and far more rapid than) anything in biology. What I am saying is that evolution was important for a very long time, and that we should be wary of a confident assumption that its effects have now been totally negated, or made redundant. Most particularly, we should be wary of critics, whatever their political persuasion, who confidently tell us that the extension of Darwinism to the social world is bound to be flawed or inadequate (for example, Lewontin et al. 1984). Marxists and conservatives tend to share pre-Darwinian convictions about the uniqueness of humankind. Thomas

Henry Huxley's old opponent, the Bishop of Oxford, may be dead, but his spirit is very much alive.

My second point, following on the first, is that although in their first flush of enthusiasm those much-criticized Darwinians, the (human) sociobiologists, undoubtedly said a lot of silly and extreme, unjustifiable things about human nature, now there has been a buckling down to the task at hand — the demonstration that, in the understanding of human thought and action, it is necessary to consider (as one factor) the way(s) in which we are directed towards the maximization of reproductive achievements. We now find serious scholars who are trying to show how language and science and religion and the arts and customs fit within a framework of biology. No one wants to deny or ignore the imperatives of culture, but the aim is to show that biological adaptation still has its place in human society.

I would not pretend that this serious (and unglamorous) study of humankind has, as yet, paid major dividends. But some promising results are starting to come in. For instance, if one studies human societies, one finds a dazzling array of marriage practices. Some peoples prescribe cousin marriage; others proscribe it. Some insist on monogamy; others allow (and even encourage) polygyny (one man, multiple wives); yet others, a very few, allow polyandry (one wife, multiple husbands). Some peoples demand dowries (payment to the husband); other peoples demand bride wealth (payment to the bride's family). And so the litany goes on. Yet it is starting to become clear that beneath all of this variety lies order — an order imposed by biology (Betzig et al. 1987). For instance, why is polygyny relatively common and yet polyandry so rare? The answer probably lies in the different biological natures of males and females. Only in certain very special circumstances, such as in Tibet where males must band tightly together to scratch out a living, will it be in males' reproductive interests to share a wife. Normally, especially if the wife can do most of the work, things go the other way (Durham 1987.)

I come to my third point. Why homosexuality? Why should human sociobiologists presume to write on, and theorize about, people with same-sex orientations and activities? One may or may not agree that homosexuality is something meriting medical attention. Yet one can surely understand how psychoanalysts have become involved with the topic, and the same goes for endocrinologists. But sociobiologists are quite another matter. Homosexuality seems beyond their field. The nasty suspicion lurks that beneath the skin of the human sociobiologist lies the heart and soul of the bigot. There is less interest in understanding human nature than in doing a job on some of the more persecuted minorities of our species. Here, there really is cause for moral concern.

For the moment, I shall simply point out that this concern is surely premature. There is an obvious reason why human sociobiologists have been so fascinated by the phenomenon of homosexuality (Ruse 1981a). Their theory, the background against which they work, is that human nature is directed towards reproduction. For the Darwinian, what counts in the long run is how well you replicate your kind — to this end all things are subsumed, be they physical characteristics, mental attributes, or social activities. Yet homosexual activity does not produce offspring. That the sociobiologist is concerned is hardly a mark of prejudice. It would be a mark of bad science were there no such concern. Hence, the sociobiology of homosexuality.

So much by way of preliminary. Let us turn now to the various sociobiological hypotheses which have been propounded.

6.2 The case presented

As always, the main concern is with homosexual orientation, but the understanding is that this leads to homosexual activity. I know of three suggestions which have been proposed, with more or less conviction, to explain such an orientation. There is also a hypothesis about the major difference between male homosexuals and lesbians, namely with respect to their sexual activities. I take these several proposals in turn.

The first suggestion centres on the well-known biological phenomenon of *balanced superior heterozygote fitness* (Dobzhansky et al. 1977). The unit of heredity, that which is passed on from generation to generation, the gene, is located on the chromosomes, a set of which exists in every cell of the body. Since the chromosomes come in pairs (except in irregular cases), each and every gene has a mate on the complementary chromosome. If the two gene forms (*alleles*) are identical, the plant or animal bearing them is a *homozygote* (with respect to that position or *locus*); otherwise, a *heterozygote*. The paired alleles ultimately express themselves in the physical body (the *phenotype*), for the unit of heredity is also the unit of function. Hence, indirectly, genes have an adaptive or inadaptive value. Sometimes, one particular homozygote (say A_1A_1) has a more beneficial effect on an organism's chances in the struggle than any other homozygote (say A_2A_2) or heterozygote (A_1A_2). In this case, the 'fitter' type (A_1A_1) soon becomes the norm, and all other alleles vanish. Sometimes, however, a heterozygote is fitter than either homozygote. One can then show, mathematically, that a 'balanced' situation will ensue, with both alleles, A_1 and A_2 being held in the population.

What is significant from our perspective is that, given such superior heterozygote fitness with the consequent balance, in each generation there will be a certain proportion of each and every kind of homozygote. And this follows even if some particular homozygote is totally unfit, never having any offspring at all. The best attested case of this phenomenon in humans is that centring on sickle cell anaemia. Possession of one sickling allele (heterozygously) gives a natural immunity to malaria, a highly adaptive feature in various parts of the world. Possession of two sickling alleles (homozygously) produces severe anaemia and death in childhood. The disease persists, because the threat of malaria is so strong (Ruse 1982b).

All you have to do is substitute homosexual orientation for sickle cell anaemia, and you have your first explanation (Hutchinson 1959; E. O. Wilson 1978). Biological unfitness does not necessarily equal death. Reproduction is what counts. If Superman has a zero sperm count, he is unfit. One starts with the assumption that the homosexual (of either sex) fails to reproduce, and is therefore unfit. One then hypothesizes that such an orientation is a direct function of some allele (say H) possessed homozygously (HH). The other homozygote (hh) is thought to reproduce at an average rate. The heterozygote (Hh) is presumed to be a super reproducer akin to the heterozygote with a natural immunity against malaria. Homosexuality will necessarily appear in each and every subsequent generation. Strictly speaking, of course, such an orientation is not really itself an adaptation. But it is linked to adaptive value in that (some of) the siblings of the homosexual are highly adaptive.

The next hypothesis centres on one of the triumphs of sociobiology, the mechanism of *kin selection*. Given our understanding of the role of the genes, one can reformulate the central Darwinian force of natural selection in terms of a form of gene selection. What counts, biologically, is propagation of one's genes — or, putting things more carefully, propagation of *copies* of one's genes. But as soon as you see this, you realize at once that it does not really matter where the copies come from, so long as they are faithful. In particular, since close relatives share copies of the same genes, inasmuch as one's close relatives reproduce, one reproduces oneself — reproduction by proxy, as it were (Dawkins 1976).

Unless one is an identical twin, one is more closely related to oneself than to anyone else. Hence, normally, it still pays to do one's own reproduction. But exceptions do occur. In the hymenoptera (ants, bees, wasps), for instance, kin selection has produced features which direct some females to care for their siblings, because thereby the females produce more copies of their own genes than if they reproduced themselves. (The reason behind all of this is that, because of an unusual reproductive system, female hymenoptera are more closely related to sisters than to daughters. Females have a full chromosome set, half from each parent. Males, however, have only mothers and hence only a half chromosome set. Hence, sisters get identical chromosomes from their father, and with more shared genes from mother, the sister—sister links are atypically close: Maynard Smith 1978.)

Famously, the working females of the hymenoptera are sterile. They do not need the distractions of their own fertility, and so (presumably) natural selection has done away with it. Here, obviously, we have another model for human homosexuality — with the lack of human reproduction again constituting a de facto sterility. Homosexuals are to be looked upon as if they were human worker ants, aiding the reproduction of close relatives (in theory, there is no need to stick strictly with siblings). Their sexual orientation frees them from the maladaptive sidetrack of trying to have and raise their own families (E. O. Wilson 1978; Weinrich 1976).

Of course, humans are not ants, and we do not have the distinctive reproductive system of the hymenoptera. Reasons must, therefore, be suggested as to why some humans might take the homosexual route. Two answers are usually given, not necessarily exclusively. First, one looks for reasons why the homosexual (or rather, person-who-is-to-develop-into-a-homosexual) would be a less than efficient personal reproducer. One expects the future homosexual to have been, potentially, a rather poor quality heterosexual. Second, one looks for reasons why the homosexual would be good at aiding close relatives. One looks for abilities in the homosexual that suggest he/she could turn society towards the reproductive ends of his/her family.

Given the basic sociobiological perspective on male/female differences, I suspect that this hypothesis might also be extended to explain why there seems to be so many more male than female homosexuals. Essentially, males (to the human sociobiologist) are seen as somewhat like high-risk investors (Symons 1979). Given their underlying physiology, males can have lots of (virtually limitless numbers of) offspring. But selection gives all males the sex drive to go out and copulate. Hence, there will be competition, and for every male who hits the reproductive jackpot, there must be others who go offspring-less. Females, to the contrary, are like low-risk investors. They are almost bound to have some offspring, but the absolute number for any one female is small. An easy extension of the kin selection hypothesis given above is that males stand at far greater (reproductive) risk, if anything goes wrong — anything, that is, that makes them less than efficient competitors in the heterosexual stakes. They thus have more pressure to switch to the homosexual alternative — and this they do. (I speak here, as sociobiologists are wont to speak, as though everything were a matter of conscious choice. I shall address this point shortly.)

The third hypothesis is not so very far from the kin selection hypothesis. What evolutionists now realize is that even within the family there can be biological conflicts — what is adaptive for one family member is not necessarily adaptive for another family member. (Why? Because, although relatives share genes, they also have genes they do not share. If my biological task is to propagate my set of genes, and your biological task is to propagate your set of genes, so long as they are not identical, there is room for conflict.) Given that there are these different biological interests, the way is opened for one family member to (try to) bring another family member's actions round to its own end. Specifically, since parents tend to be bigger and stronger than children, sociobiologists have argued that *parental manipulation* might be a significant causal factor in the affairs of humans (Trivers 1974).

How might this cause homosexuality? The answer comes readily (Ruse 1984b). Suppose a parent has a number of offspring. The genes have been passed on to the next generation. They have yet to be passed on to the generation succeeding that one. From the parent's viewpoint, it matters not whether one child does all of the reproducing, or all of the children do some of the reproducing — so long as the numbers (of genes in the succeeding generation) are not decreased. And if the number of genes can be increased, so much the better. If, by various actions, the parent can suppress the reproductive activities of one child, thereby releasing that child's efforts to help its siblings to yet greater reproduction, then so be it — that is, if the parent's reproductive chances are thus improved.

A simple example will make this point plain: suppose that a parent has four children, each potentially having two children. But if one of the parent's children is turned towards a homosexual helper role, the other three children will each have three children. Biological features aimed at achieving such an end would be favoured by selection. In this parental manipulation case, as in the kin selection case, one looks for evidence that the homosexual is in fact aiding close kin in some way. The difference in the two cases is that in kin selection the homosexual's sexual orientation is serving his/her own ends, whereas in parental manipulation the orientation is serving the ends of others.

Here, then, we have three suggestions. No doubt other options might be proposed. But let me conclude this review with a brief word on the different sexual practices of male homosexuals and lesbians. Male homosexuals are, by heterosexual standards at least, incredibly promiscuous. Female homosexuals, to the contrary, are much closer to the heterosexual norm. Donald Symons (1979) hypothesizes that this difference is a direct function of our biology. Since females get pregnant, it is in their biological interests to be very choosy about those with whom they copulate. They are going to have to put a lot of effort into having the baby. Since males do not get pregnant, it is in their biological interests to be promiscuous, or at least relatively so. Biologically, speaking, any offspring they father is an evolutionary plus. Normally, we get a compromise — the amount of heterosexual copulation must be the same for males as for females. But, in the homosexual case, the constraints are lifted, and males and females can follow their natural dispositions. 'Sexual relations among homosexuals are not constrained by the necessity to compromise male and female desires and dispositions, hence the sexual relations of lesbians should differ profoundly from the sexual relations of homosexual men' (p. 286). And differ they do, in the predicted way. Males, as we know, frequently have literally hundreds of partners. Females stay close to the heterosexual norm. In both cases, the ultimate causal factors lie back in the mists of evolutionary time.

6.3 Internal problems

As always with human sociobiology, there is a broad range of relevant issues of philosophical significance and interest. Continuing to restrict the discussion carefully to the direct topic of homosexuality, I shall look first at matters which are, in a sense, internal to the theorizing. Then I shall turn to the major question about any such work, namely its relation to the outside world.

A general complaint about human sociobiology, one which for obvious reasons applies particularly to its treatment of homosexuality, is that at heart it is conceptually confused or impoverished (Allen et al. 1977; Lewontin 1977; Weeks 1985). Quite apart from matters of evidence, there is something deeply flawed about the very attempt to understand human nature as a function of the genes, as selected in life's battles for survival and reproduction. As Scruton (1986) says, in exasperation, 'the theory [that is, human sociobiology] cannot really make contact with what is most puzzling in human behaviour' (p. 186). At best, it tells us about animals, and humans as animals. It cannot tell us about humans qua humans.

There are various ways in which this worry is expressed. Let me pick out and comment on three. First, there is the objection which is the biological flipside to the complaint of the social constructivist. Supposedly, one is postulating a quite unacceptable isomorphism between genes and behaviour. Illicitly, one is picking out certain human features, like homosexuality, giving them a real existence, and then trying to tie them in to the genes. One is reifying, in a quite unacceptable way. Homosexuality is being considered a 'thing', an identifiable part of human nature like eye colour, above culture, and preserved in splendid, eternal isolation. Unfortunately: 'We do not know if there are importantly different types of homosexuality and heterosexuality or whether some of the former are more similar to some of the latter than they are to other kinds of homosexuality' (Kitcher 1985: 249).

This is an important objection and, no doubt, in great part true. But I shall deal with it quickly, for the central thrust has been considered already and shown not really to bite as deeply as one might fear. The sociobiologist must acknowledge and appreciate it. He/she need not despair before it.[1] Homosexuality as it presents itself in our society is a phenomenon unique to our society. It is not the same as the homosexuality of Ancient Greece, for instance. Thus, simply to think that one can set up an isomorphism between one or more genes and those features and activities which we today label 'homosexual' is both naive and doomed to failure. Such an effort assumes bad biology, bad psychology, and bad history. Yet, having said this much, there are threads linking homosexuals. Culture may be crucial for homosexual identity. It is a lot less obvious that it is crucial for homosexual orientation. There is good reason to think that this is a transcultural phenomenon, and as such (at least) plausibly a candidate for a biological explanation (Whitam 1983).

Of course, it may transpire that homosexual orientation still cannot be linked to the genes in any meaningful way. You can conceptualize eye colour as an independent characteristic, linking it fairly directly with the genes, thinking about whether one colour is more adaptive than another. Apparently, the chin resists any such straightforward biological analysis in its own right, being merely a byproduct of genes controlling other adaptive features (Lewontin 1977). Perhaps homosexuality falls in the same category — from a biological perspective, it really has to be seen as an epiphenomenon on the intersection of other features. But this is something which can be discovered only after the evolutionist has tried to link physical features (including behavioural and attitudinal features) with our underlying biology. The mere fact of trying to link homosexual orientation to biology is not, in itself, misdirected. In principle, doing just this is doing no more than is done by any evolutionary biologist.

The second worry about the internal coherence of human sociobiology rests on the intentional language invariably used in its descriptions and explanations. We are always hearing about people 'choosing' to take this or that reproductive strategy or, what is worse, we are told that our genes 'choose' to do this or that. We learn of our attitudes or behaviours being 'directed' towards certain ends, that people 'compete' with each other, and that even within the family (especially within the family) there is a 'conflict' of 'interests'.

If such language is metaphorical it is meaningless, and if it is literal it is false (Sahlins 1976). Take, for instance the notion of parental manipulation. Are we truly supposed to believe that parents 'manipulate' their children into a homosexual role, having first done a quick actuarial calculation as to their own prospective reproductive advantages? Given that all the psychoanalysts in New York seem incapable of turning the average homosexual into a heterosexual, the instinctive powers supposed of parents are truly remarkable. Of course, this is ludicrous, just as much as it is to suppose that a young man, having broken his leg rather badly, then (in line with kin selection) 'decides' to forgo the stresses of heterosexuality for the lusher pastures of homosexuality and the helping of close relatives.

Again, the critic has a good point; but again, it is not definitive. There is no doubt that sociobiologists do use their language loosely, and fail frequently to acknowledge that they are speaking in metaphors — for metaphorical language is what they surely use when they speak of the mechanisms for producing homosexuals. There is no literal manipulation, nor is it supposed that actual relationships are calculated and acted upon. Indeed, it is frequently stressed by sociobiologists that, from a biological viewpoint, we achieve our ends more effectively when we are in some ignorance about nature's intentions (Trivers 1971).

Yet, more positively, let us recognize that, in using the language of intention or purpose or design, sociobiologists are doing no more than is done by any Darwinian evolutionist (Ruse 1981c). They are dealing with adaptations (or maladaptations), trying to see what ends they serve in the struggle to reproduce. The language of conscious purpose comes naturally here, and can be defended on the basis of its heuristic worth, if for no other reason. If one thinks of nature consciously trying to further its biological ends, and that natural selection 'designs' features to aid in this task, one can follow through pertinent causal chains, working out the exact nature and function of crucial adaptations. That we are here dealing with humans, their thought processes and their actions, is in a way irrelevant. We could as readily be dealing with (say) the protrusions on the back of an extinct reptile. The aim is primarily that of finding out what people are up to, without so much worrying about what people think they are up to.

But this leads straight to the third worry. Humans are not blind robots like ants. We are rational thinking beings. Remember Scruton's (1986) fear is that the sociobiology of sexuality, including human homosexuality, is bound to miss the main point: 'the social behaviour of human beings is mediated and transformed by a conception of itself. It may be rooted in instinct, but it is not reducible to instinct, not only because it exemplifies learning, but also because it involves rational response' (p. 187). This is a complaint frequently expressed about sociobiology, and comes right back to much that has been said (and will be said) about homosexuality. When, say, two lesbians interact, although there may well be physical sex, there may also be much more — there may be strong emotion, commitment, the whole range of communication between two rational agents. It is the difference between merely fucking and making love. And this difference is one to which human sociobiology, by its very approach, is blind. Like the behaviourists, the sociobiologists may (or may not) be able to tell us some wonderful things about what people do. Because (like behaviourism) it has a deliberately restricted ontology, it cannot tell us what people are.

For a third time, I admit to force in this charge, and for a third time I remain essentially untroubled. I shall have more to say later about human rationality, but I would admit (as I have admitted already in earlier chapters) that copulating humans — heterosexual or homosexual — are usually more than rutting dogs. But apart from harbouring some severe questions about the critics' conception of human rationality — whether it is quite the ethereal, beyond-biology phenomenon that people like Scruton pretend it is (Murphy 1982) — I cannot see that we have now a major threat to the sociobiology of homosexuality. The point is that we are dealing essentially with an orientation — an inclination, a feeling, an appetite — rather than what people decide to do with it. I am not saying that there is no connection between attitude and action, or that the latter is unimportant to the sociobiologist. Obviously there is a connection and action is important — although I am inclined to think that reason has a lesser role than Scruton implies. The point is that we do have orientations and they do lead to action, whatever the link, and the bottom line for the sociobiologist is the former.

Once we see we are dealing with an orientation, the sociobiological programme becomes again feasible. In type, an orientation seems no different from hunger — or, more precisely, from a love of Chinese food rather than Italian food. A causal explanation is appropriate. It is no threat to rationality to say that someone has a lifelong love of Chinese food because they grew up in a Chinese neighbourhood. Neither is it a threat to rationality to say that someone has a homosexual orientation because of their genes or because their childhood biology primed them to respond to certain clues rather than others. It is really no threat to rationality to say that parents instinctively do things which affect their children. Surely, no one would want to say that everything which we do is consciously premeditated — especially when it comes to our children?

Of course, you may argue that sociobiology fails to offer adequate causal explanations of the homosexual orientation. This is another question. What matters now is that, on grounds of denial of rationality, as with other internal criticisms, sociobiology is not doomed to failure a priori.

6.4 Unfalsifiable, false or plausible?

So much for questions to do with internal conceptual adequacy. We come now to that major philosophical question focusing on the relationship between the sociobiological hypotheses about homosexuality and the external world. Is the sociobiology of homosexuality falsifiable, or is it pseudo-science? If it is falsifiable, is it false? Or is it (at least) plausible?

There is no shortage of voices prepared to claim that human sociobiology, taken as a general enterprise, fails the falsifiability test (Allen et al. 1977). Nor is there silence on the particular case of homosexuality: 'We find . . . evolutionary theories of human sexual orientation to be unsupported by even the most rudimentary data. Moreover it is hard to see how some of these theories could ever be subjected to proper scientific testing; in our judgement, they cannot even be considered valid scientific hypotheses' (Futuyma and Risch 1984; see also MacCulloch 1980; Hoult 1984; Ricketts 1984).

Now, as I have hinted already, falsifiability per se is not quite the magic wand that people sometimes imply. When you have a developed successful theory, you expect to find new areas being pushed out from it — areas which, on their own, probably look a bit thin and not altogether in touch with the facts. Nevertheless, they merit being treated gently, if only because they can draw on the credit of the general theory. If you knock down any bright idea as soon as it appears, especially because you cannot think of a possible test, you are probably going to run out of new ideas — quickly. This warning surely applies to human sociobiology especially, since it is a part of well-established and genuine scientific theory, the Darwinian theory of evolution (Ruse 1985). Moreover, it is a part of a theory which, as we have seen, applies to our own species.

Tolerance is demanded. This does not mean that you can ignore counter-evidence or need not strive to find positive evidence. It does mean that you must keep things in perspective. As it happens, however, in the case of homosexuality, for all that the critics say or imply otherwise, there is a growing body of pertinent findings. Whatever else might be said, with respect to homosexuality the ideas of the sociobiologists are certainly not inherently unfalsifiable. Beginning at the beginning, the most obvious point of test arises over the general presumption that homosexuals do in fact have fewer offspring than heterosexuals, and that their orientation is consequently something standing in need of (biological) explanation. If this is not true, if the possibility (suggested by Kitcher 1985) that 'homosexuals might have a greater propensity for sex than heterosexuals and that social pressure might channel their sexual energy into heterosexual behaviour' (p. 251) is true, then the sociobiological models are (at best) irrelevant, and (at worst) false. Kin selection, for instance, simply cannot be working as the sociobiologists suggest.

The possibility of test is there. As with Freudianism, the actuality of the tests leaves something to be desired. Nevertheless, in the Second Kinsey study (Bell and Weinberg 1978) there is a discussion of marriage patterns which seems relevant. Starting with men, the researchers found that there was in their subject groups a very significant difference between the proportions of heterosexuals who married and homosexuals who married, with the former much more likely to make such a commitment than the latter. Furthermore, comparing just those who had been married, although many homosexuals had had children (over 50 per cent if one combines whites and blacks), homosexuals had significantly fewer children than heterosexuals. In the case of women, the researchers reported similar, although a little less striking, findings. Certainly, comparing just those who had been married, as with males, homosexuals had significantly fewer children than heterosexuals. (See tables 6.1 and 6.2.)

The obvious inference is that people with a homosexual orientation have fewer children than those with a heterosexual orientation — although, even in its own terms, a conclusion like this is hardly definitive. There are all sorts of questions which come up about children born out of wedlock, and so forth. And then we have the usual (already expressed) worries about the representative nature of the Kinsey study. I confess that, particularly in the case of females, I wonder how readily you should generalize from San Francisco lesbians to (say) women in the Pleistoscene, or even to women in preliterate societies today. It could be that, in such societies, women had/have considerably less choice about their repro- duction, whatever their orientation. A family expecting a handsome payment of bride-wealth may not be overly sensitive to a daughter's lesbian urges. (As pointed out earlier, however, this could all be connected to the relative infrequency of lesbianism. So might be the fact that, even in San Francisco, lesbians seem more like their heterosexual sisters than male homosexuals are like their heterosexual brothers.)

TABLE 6.1 Responses to the question, 'Have you ever been married?'

	WHM % (N=575)	BHM % (N=111)	WHTM % (N=284)	BHTM % (N=53)	WHF % (N=229)	BHF % (N=64)	WHTF % (N=101)	BHTF % (N=39)	Pilot Study % (N=458)
0: No	80	87	26	49	65	53	27	31	83
1: Yes	20	13	74	51	35	47	73	69	17

WHM: White homosexual male
BHM: Black homosexual male
WHTM: White heterosexual male
BHTM: Black heterosexual male
WHF: White homosexual female
BHF: Black homosexual female
WHTF: White heterosexual female
BHTF: Black heterosexual female
Pilot study represents white homosexual male in Chicago
Source: Bell and Weinberg 1978: 374.

TABLE 6.2 *Responses to the question, 'How many children have you had/did you have in this [first] marriage?'*

	WHM % (N=116)	BHM % (N=14)	WHTM % (N=210)	BHTM % (N=26)	WHF % (N=80)	BHF % (N=30)	WHTF % (N=74)	BHTF % (N=27)	*Pilot Study* % (N=80)
0: None	50	29	34	27	50	27	31	26	30
1: One	25	50	22	31	29	40	19	33	25
2: Two	15	21	26	27	6	13	15	22	26
3: Three	5	0	10	15	6	3	26	4	15
4–6: Four or more	5	0	8	0	9	17	9	15	4

WHM: White homosexual males
BHM: Black homosexual males
WHTM: White heterosexual males
BHTM: Black heterosexual males
WHF: White homosexual females
BHF: Black homosexual females
WHTF: White heterosexual females
BHTF: Black heterosexual females
Pilot study represents white homosexual male in Chicago
Source: Bell and Weinberg 1978: 391

Complete or incomplete, biased or unbiased though the information may be, we can surely say this much: with respect to individual reproductive achievements, the ideas of the sociobiologists do seem testable. If one wanted, following on the Kinsey study one could make more detailed, more direct, and more comprehensive surveys. At the moment, providing 'straws in the wind' is probably about the best conclusion we can or should draw.

What about the testing of and evidence for the individual hypotheses, giving a sociobiological basis to homosexual orientation? As far as balanced superior heterozygote fitness is concerned, far from being unfalsifiable, in the crude form it is almost certainly false. There is evidence that male homosexuality does run in families (Rainer 1976; Pillard and Weinrich 1986); yet, if homosexual orientation is a simple function of the homozygous possession of a certain allele, then everyone with such a pair should be similarly homosexually oriented. In particular, you should never find identical twins (who necessarily have identical sets of genes) with different sexual orientations. But, although there are some reports that identical twins do tend to share orientations, and some of these reports are better than others (Heston and Shields 1968), there are some very strong and very careful findings of identical twins, one of whom is heterosexual, and one of whom is homosexual (Rainer et al. 1960; Green 1974). Sexual orientation, therefore, simply cannot be a straight function of the genes. The persistence of homosexuality must be due to more than mere heterozygote balance.

The other hypotheses, kin selection and parental manipulation, differ from the heterozygote balance hypothesis in that they do not necessarily posit special genes separating homosexuals from heterosexuals. At least in theory, everyone could be the same genetically (in this respect). It is just that homosexual orientation (and any behaviour causing it) lies potentially in us all, waiting to be triggered by the right environmental factors. Hence, even if we knew all about the genes, the hypotheses would probably not be tested. We must therefore search for other ways in which we can get at the hypotheses. Presumably, these will be ways which look at the natures and behaviours of people, hoping to find differences appropriate to different orientations.

Let us start with kin selection. If this mechanism is important, we would expect to find that homosexuals had something in their childhood which might have made them less than efficient (heterosexual) reproducers, and had talents for and successes at bringing society's goods to the benefit of their own families. Again (somewhat depressingly) it has to be confessed that there are no systematic studies. However, one researcher, after a comprehensive literature search, does claim that there are pointers towards the operation of such selection (Weinrich 1976).

On the one hand, there are comments (usually in the writings of anthropologists) suggesting that (especially male) children grow into homosexuality after childhood traumas of various kinds. For instance, amongst the Araucans of South America, at one point all ritualized homosexuals 'were men who had taken up the role of women, who took "the passive role" in homosexual relations, and who were chosen for the role in childhood, due to their families' mannerisms or certain physical deformities' (Weinrich 1976: 170). Amongst the Nuer, a 'woman who marries another woman is usually barren' (p. 171). Amongst the Toradjas, male homosexual life style and males doing women's work occurred 'primarily because of cowardice or some harrowing experience' (p. 171). And generally, ritualized homosexual roles seem 'to be attractive to individuals who have undergone some trauma, regardless of whether this involves a change of sex' (p. 173), although there certainly are exceptions.

Conversely, again drawing heavily on the anthropological literature, we find that people taking on a homosexual role frequently have a major status in society, and are thus able to bring benefits to their near kin. In many societies, homosexuals are considered to have certain special magical or religious powers, and act as priests or 'shamans'. Thus, amongst the West Inoits, 'advice always followed' (Reclus 1896); the Araucans, 'advice required for every important decision' (Metraux 1942); the Cheyenne, 'goes to war; matchmaker; supervises scalps and scalp ceremonies' (Hoebel 1960); the Illinois, 'required for all important decisions' (Shea 1903); the Navaho, 'wealthy; leaders; matchmakers; unusual opportunity for material advancement' (Hill 1935); the Sioux, 'extraordinary privileges' (Catlin 1926); the Sea Dyaks, 'rich; person of great consequence, often chief' (Roth 1896; see also Weinrich 1976: 203–5). In other words, homosexuals do and achieve just what one would expect were the sociobiological hypothesis true.

I need hardly say, however, that at best such reports as these are suggestive rather than persuasive — let alone definitive. A host of questions flood in. What of the special talents homosexuals are supposed to have? There are some reports that (in our society) homosexuals persistently do better on IQ tests than heterosexuals — but there is a staggering distance from this claim (even if true) to the demonstration that homosexuals are skilled at bending society to their own ends (Weinrich 1978). What of the traumas which are supposed to have befallen homosexuals in our own society? There are reports that transsexuals frequently had rough childhoods and that they 'showed an above-average incidence of certain physical defects' (Weinrich 1976: 189). But, as we know, you should be very wary of making quick connections between the (comparatively rare) transsexual and the (comparatively common) homosexual. And, quite apart from the unanswered questions, other factors do not seem really promising. Suppose, as seems quite possible, future homosexuals truly do tend to show atypical gender behaviour when children. In what sense would this be a handicap to heterosexuality when adult? Moreover, how do you account for the fact that the atypical behaviour comes quite without obvious cause?

Then again, what do we do with the near truism that in our own society, homosexuals apparently do not gain high status, at least not as a function of their homosexuality? If anything, the reverse is the case. As always with a human sociobiological hypothesis, you could claim that the forces which held in the past (and which still hold in preliterate societies) no longer obtain in our own post-industrial revolution culture. But then, you have got to explain why homosexuality is such a persistent phenomenon for us today. Is it just a maladaptive legacy of the past?

There are more questions than solutions — many more. This is not to say that the kin selection hypothesis is wrong, or inapplicable. But it is to say that it is hardly more than a clever idea. To take it further, we need some detailed (quantified) studies on people with homosexual orientations, checking out family backgrounds, and counting the children of close kin. Also, some pertinent animal studies might help (Weinrich 1982). (See chapter 8.) And, of course, one needs to find some way of distinguishing the effects of kin selection from those of parental manipulation. I will say almost nothing here about the latter mechanism and its applicability. All that I have said about kin selection applies equally to it. There are intriguing anthropological reports about parental involvement in the development of children who are later to assume (influential) homosexual roles. For instance, in the case of the Sea Dyaks, in order to take on the cross-gender role of a *manang bali*, 'one's father must pay a series of increasing fees to initiate the grown son into the role, and all three investigators [of the phenomenon] agreed that the *manang bali* are invariably rich (often chiefs) as a result of their fees for shamanizing' (Weinrich 1976, p. 169; see also Roth 1896). Similarly, in societies where a high bride-price is demanded, parents will sometimes shift sons towards a female role, thus changing an economic liability into an asset. But here, as before, we have (at best) suggestive ideas, rather than solidly backed theory.

This brings us finally to the claim that male/female homosexual activity differences lie in our basic biology as men and women (Symons 1979). Male homosexuals are promiscuous, because they are men. Female homosexuals are not promiscuous, because they are not men. We are dealing here with an indirect claim; yet it is hard to deny there is some truth in it. In our society, men and women do behave differently, with males being (at least potentially) more promiscuous. The same holds true of many other societies. It is surely the case that male/female homosexual differences are in some sense a reflection of societal norms (or would-be norms), and (most particularly) that the great activity of male homosexuals stems from the absence of the braking effect of female reticence.

But whether male/female differences taken generally are grounded in biology is quite another matter. It could be that the differences are much more a function of environmental causes, particularly of the differential treatment of children by parents. In these pertinent gender distinguishing respects, it could well be that parents treat their future homosexual offspring no differently from the ways in which they treat their future heterosexual offspring. Hence, the homosexual male/female differences are no less cultural than are heterosexual male/female differences. As it happens, my own opinion (one which I have discussed at length elsewhere) hesitates before extreme cultural environmentalism (or social constructivism). I suspect that there probably is some link between male/female attitudinal differences and evolutionary biology. Given their respective reproductive physiologies and capacities, there really are good reasons why men and women should have different feelings about sex (Ruse 1981b, 1984b).

Yet just as these things are not all culture, so I doubt they are all biology. Since the 1950s, and the coming of cultural innovations like cheap efficient contraception, there has been no small shift in women's attitudes towards casual sexual encounters. Men and women are not the same. They are not all that different. Concluding this discussion, then, I see nothing particularly unfalsifiable about Symons' hypothesis. I myself suspect that it may well have a large measure of truth. But it does rest on theory which is highly controversial, where (to use an overly familiar but still appropriate metaphor) the final verdict has surely not yet been delivered.

6.5   Conclusion

The sociobiology of homosexuality is plainly scientific. Those who argue otherwise are simply being unfair — or have an odd idea about the true nature of science. Those, like myself, who think that evolution really matters and that Darwin held the key, are virtually bound to look seriously at the hypotheses. *But* that is a long way from belief. There are some interesting ideas and some suggestive facts. There is nothing which compels conviction. Of course, these are early days, and (as I have myself argued) tolerance is needed. Given what we have seen of other approaches, this is the least we can offer. Now, it is the turn of the sociobiologists to deliver on their promises. The task is not impossible. It is barely started.

7

Reductionism and Determinism: Twin Threats?

This is a transitional chapter which looks back to the various causal explanations that have now been presented, but prepares to move on. I look forward to the value questions which are to be raised, but am not yet quite ready to tackle them. First, I must address some important questions which always hover above discussions of the type in which we are engaged.

7.1 How should research proceed?

We have considered now three approaches purporting to tell us something of the causes of homosexual orientations. We have, I trust, found much of philosophical interest. No one of them compels assent. The adaptationists are almost certainly wrong, but Freud may be right on the phenomenal level — some family dynamics may fit patterns he identified, but he could well have confused cause and effect. Hormonal theorists have found important clues — and more — but their work is not yet finished. And the work of the sociobiologists is barely started. Summing up, thus far our conclusion is — *must* be — that about so significant a fact as human sexual orientation, we know depressingly little. Tantalizingly, there are a few tears in the veil, through which apparently we can catch glimpses of the truth. But no one has, as yet, ripped the coverings in two — and drawn them apart.

Where do we go from here? Philosophers are notoriously bad forecasters of the actual future course of science. I still have colleagues 'proving' that a molecular biology can never exist, because it is conceptually impossible. However, we can and must ask about the way that the future course of homosexual research *should* proceed. You might start the next round of inquiry with the fact that, already, we have three basic (causal) approaches to homosexual orientation, not to mention variations within individual approaches. Surely, some resolution or shaking down is necessary here? All three approaches — psychoanalytic, hormonal, sociobiological — cannot be equally true or promising. Certainly, they cannot be equally true or promising if you take seriously what the various practitioners have to say about each other! Some displacement of one or more approach is going to be necessary, not to say inevitable. This suggests that we might get a process that happens frequently in science — something about which philosophers have written extensively — where one branch of (often older) science is *reduced* to another branch of (often newer) science (Suppe 1972). Before the full story of sexual orientation is revealed, there is in the cards a 'reduction' of one or more approach to one or more other approach.

But who is to be reduced to whom? The disinterested bystander — whose disinterest might be starting to give way to fear — will point out that reduction frequently (if not always) involves explanation of the larger in terms of the smaller: compounds in terms of molecules, societies in terms of individuals, major evolutionary events in terms of selection and single genes. This suggests that the reductive future of research on homosexual orientation will end only when everything is explained, at least in terms of hormonal fluids, and more probably down at the level of steroid molecules, possibly as they are linked to the DNA and to the filtering effects of selection, as it operates 'selfishly' for the benefit of the individual human (who may or may not be the person with the homosexual orientation).

This, in the eyes of many commentators, is a pretty dismal prospect (Lewontin et al. 1984; Bleier 1984; Birke 1986; Harding 1986). Reductionism is rarely an unqualifiedly good thing, and in the case of something like the inquiry into the origins of human sexual orientation, it is far from a good thing. Thus, there will be — indeed, there already is — a general critique and rejection of virtually all work which has been done on putative causes of homosexual orientation. Furthermore, this critique is extended to the realms into which such work might be thought to be heading. Quite apart from particular problems lurking in specific suggestions, the overall reductionistic bent is dangerous and to be opposed.

Digging down into the detailed reasons behind this objection, I do at times wonder how seriously we are supposed to mount an opposition. I find it difficult to sympathize overly with the charge that reductionism (that is, the approval of reduction) is all a capitalist plot. Even if there be any truth in this, we are a long way from showing that (say) an evolutionary account of human sexual orientation will fill the coffers of the filthy rich (Birke 1986, p. 74). I am also unenthused by the complaint that reductionism is all part and parcel of an androcentric bias in modern science, bound up particularly with an undue drive for rigour and value free objectivity (Harding 1986). Whilst I would agree that much in science is less rigorous and value free than practitioners think, and much is indeed biased against women, to deny rigour and objectivity per se seems to set you on the road towards some horrendous circularities. And I can only stand speechless before the related grumble that the very inquiry into origins, particularly evolutionary origins, shows pro-male prejudice (p. 104). Anyone who thinks the writings of Elaine Morgan show pro-male prejudice is reading them through different spectacles from mine.

There is another aspect to the objection to reductionism, however, which deserves a more detailed and serious response. Suppose you push your inquiry through to the point where you have shown that everything to do with human sexual orientation is just a dance to the tune of the molecules. Surely, you must thereby have lost something — something which (Roger Scruton would say) is essential to the understanding of the human spirit. Given the ultimate in reduction, humankind would be no more than a set of *determined* robots, jerking to the movement of blind forces. Free will, rationality, morality, and everything else we hold dear, would be gone. Or, worse, the way would be opened for evil people to use us for their own ends. Even if you deny that modern science is all an anti-feminist, capitalist plot, you ought surely to be concerned at this point. Even if you think (as I do) that we are merely modified monkeys, you ought to be shuddering at such a castrated view of humankind.

Hence, the twin worries of reductionism and determinism, although frequently surrounded by appallingly bad arguments, do raise questions of genuine concern. They cannot and should not be ignored in a philosophical inquiry into the nature of homosexuality. I shall now take them in turn, recognizing that, although separate, they are interconnected.

7.2   Ontological reductionism

Almost every writer has his/her particular slant on the issue of reduction. As a preliminary, therefore, I shall adopt an explicit, three point dissection of the notion. Following the well-known evolutionist, Francisco Ayala, I shall distinguish *ontological reductionism, methodological reductionism*, and *epistemological* (or, as I would call it, *theory*) *reductionism*. We may not cover everything with this trichotomy, but we shall miss little important. First, we have ontological reductionism:

From the *ontological* point of view the question of reduction is whether physiochemical entities and processes underlie all living phenomena. Substantive vitalists claimed that living processes are, at least in part, the effect of a non-material principle or entity, which was variously called 'vital force', 'entelechy', '*elan vital*', 'soul', 'radial energy', or the like. (Ayala 1974: viii)

I take it, referring this discussion exclusively to work on the aetiology of sexual orientation, that just about everybody we have discussed is an ontological reductionist. This was not so much proved, as taken as a precondition of doing science. No one wanted to refer to or use other-worldly forces or powers or substances in their explanations. I take it also that no one we need respect finds this kind of reductionism in any way offensive. Although, today, we reject things like entelechies as a pre-condition for doing science, the decision is not irrational or bigoted in some way. Reference to vital forces really seems to throw no new light (for instance, from the viewpoint of prediction) on living things.

It is true that there are, even now, some evolutionists who skirt close to vitalism in their yearning to put direction, a teleological end point, into the evolutionary process (Rose 1982). But this is less a function of reality than a consequence of their own metaphysical urges to give meaning to life. Truly, evolution is going nowhere — and rather slowly at that. More interesting, perhaps, are those who subscribe to some kind of Cartesian mind/brain dualism, thinking that mental processes inhere in an immaterial mental substance of their own (Churchland 1984). Today, I suspect that most people (including most researchers on sexual orientation) are hard-line reductionists, subscribing to some kind of mind/brain 'identity' theory, thinking the mental a manifestation of the material. Yet there are (and have been) respectable exceptions. Karl Popper is a dualist (Eccles and Popper 1977), and in the past Freud was probably one, after a fashion (Grünbaum 1985). Presumably people like this do think that human beings are more than simply the sum and effects of molecules in motion — which I assume is the stand of the hard-line ontological reductionism.

But even these neo-Cartesians are 'soft-line' ontological reductionists, for in the material world, they affirm that the laws of physics and chemistry rule supreme. To be honest, the decision between hard-line and soft-line ontological reductionism probably rests more on philo-sophical commitment than scientific adequacy. Whatever the true mind/brain relationship, no one denies that (in principle) parental attitudes, hormones or gene products can affect the mind and our thinking; or that the brain is important, is made of molecules, and works according to the rules of physics and chemistry. This kind of reductionism, therefore, is essentially shared by everybody and (as I have said) I cannot see that it is in any sense objectionable.

7.3   Methodological reductionism

The second kind of reductionism embodies the urge to explain the bigger in terms of the smaller.

What I have called above the *methodological* domain encompasses questions concerning the strategy of research or the acquisition of knowledge. In the study of life phenomena, should we always seek explanations by investigating the underlying processes at lower levels of complexity, and ultimately at the level of atoms and molecules? or must we seek understanding from the study of higher as well as lower levels of organization? (Ayala 1974: vii)

Here we do start to steer into controversial waters. Two general comments first. On the one hand, methodological reductionism has been a powerful successful drive in science, at least since the sixteenth century — for instance, it produced the explanation of the classical gas laws in terms of the kinetic theory of gases. On the other hand, methodological reductionism is almost certainly not the only signpost to the doing of good science. In the geological theory of plate tectonics, for instance, all sorts of local and often relatively simple effects are explained in terms of monstrous plates, which have been moving slowly around the shell of the earth for aeons. There is not much by way of methodological reductionism here — but there is good geology (Ruse 1981d).

What about work on sexual orientation? Not all the theorizing at the moment is particularly reductionist (in the sense being discussed). The cognitive developmental and social learning theories are hardly so, and I cannot see that Freud's work is desperately so, although certainly if the libido concept worked, we would be edging a little this way. But what of the future? At one level, it strikes me as an empirical question as to whether a methodological reductionistic approach will become dominant. It is true that some of the types of explanation we have considered exemplify a methodologically reductionistic trend. But they certainly have no a priori hold on our affections. If sociobiology, for instance, fails to deliver on any of its promises, then it will fade away. If, conversely, cognitive developmental theory starts to yield good quality predictions, then it will flourish. From what we have seen at the moment, the person who proposed relating all of his/her explanations down to the molecules would be a fool.

But the complaint will go out that, by my own admission, methodological reductionism is already producing bad science. Those approaches which are methodologically inclined to reductionism are making just the sorts of errors that this philosophy always breeds. Take the suggestion that homosexual orientation is a function of atypical hormonal levels in fetal life. Thanks to reductionism, all sorts of factors are ignored, like possible effects of life style on hormonal levels and patterns. Any response 'might be altered, for example, by time of day, people with different life-styles having different hormonal peaks and troughs. It might be affected by stress, diet, alcohol consumption and so on' (Birke 1986: 69). But these very real possibilities are brushed aside.

Quite frankly, if this were true, then Money and Dörner had better find work in other fields. But, surely, the objection is not to methodological reductionism in itself. Rather it is to the way in which it is being used in the caricature of genuine science just given. I entirely fail to see why giving a causal role to the hormones means that you will necessarily ignore possibly conflicting factors like alcohol. Indeed, the opposite would seem to be the case. Pick out the hormones, and then see if you can control for and ferret out other factors. And, as it happens, the above charge is really most unfair. In their recent study of feedback responses, Gladue and associates (1984) explicitly acknowledged the possible effects on hormonal levels of drug use and stress, and took them into account.

There is a final worry about methodological reductionism. This is, perhaps, the most profound. In the rush to explain the big in terms of the small, the complex in terms of the simple, do we not run the risk of dropping something from our understanding? Are we not, necessarily, ignoring complexity and organization? A molecule on its own is a molecule on its own. It is not a molecule functioning in a brain cell.

Individual units, be they cells or organisms, cannot be assumed to have priority over the group of which they are part if they are seen as simultaneously being both. That may be how, ideally, we should look at any biological unit: but as soon as we begin to study it in any way . . . then we abstract the unit from its context. By so doing, it becomes in practice impossible to see the unit as part of a larger totality. (Birke 1986: 64)

Again this worry is misplaced, as I have shown already in my discussion of a related argument by the psychoanalytic adaptationist revisionists. As it happens, even in that super-reductionistic science, physics, we get attention to order — the different effects, for instance, of the same resistors in series or in parallel. In the sexual orientation case, no one could be more sensitive to order than the endocrinologist or socio-biologist. If the hormones do not hit the hypothalamus at a precise time, then they will not have adult effects. A gill of androgen in fetal life is worth a gallon after birth. The whole point of today's hormonal theorizing is that hormones alone are meaningless. They only make sense when put in temporal context.

And the same holds true of the genes. Take the heterozygote fitness case. Taken out of context, there is no such thing as a gene for homosexuality. One dose of the gene heterozygously makes you a super-heterosexual! It is only when you have the gene twice over, homozygously, that you are (supposedly) a homosexual. I am certainly not saying that every researcher on sexual orientation has been as sensitive to the critics' objections as they should be. But methodological reductionism does not in itself make for bad science — generally, or in the quest for causes of homosexual orientation.

7.4 Epistemological reductionism

This brings us now to epistemological or theory reduction: the fitting together of one theory with another.

Epistemologically, the general question of reduction is whether the theories and experimental laws formulated in one field of science can be shown to be special cases of theories and laws formulated in some other branch of science. If such is the case, the former branch of science is said to have been reduced to the latter. (Ayala 1974: ix)

Spelling things out in a little more detail, there seem to be three basic options describing the relation (or potential relation) between two theories. First, they might not compete at all, being essentially about different subjects. Second, one theory might move in to replace the other — shoving its rival entirely to one side. Third, we might get reduction, with one theory being the deductive consequence of the other (Hull 1974). Some philosophers (notably Thomas Kuhn 1970) have argued that there can be no genuine theory reduction; but this stand is altogether too extreme. There have been genuine cases of reduction in the physical sciences, and probably in the biological sciences also (Ruse 1973, 1976). (See also Rosenberg 1985.)

I shall say little here about different suggestions *within* some basic approach — *intra*-approach putative causal explanations of homosexual orientation. I take it that within a level or type there is sometimes little conflict at all, for one is basically talking about different things — or looking at differently applied consequences of the same theory. One thinks, for instance, of the different ways in which the same hypothesis might be applied to male and female homosexuals. I take it also that there is sometimes outright conflict within an approach, with one idea aiming to replace another — adaptationism and classical Freudianism, for instance. I have said just about all one can say on these matters. That particular takeover bid flops. Often, one suspects, accommodation is necessary and desirable. One approach gives one bit of the story. Another approach gives another bit. Of course, at the moment we usually have insufficient information to make a full judgement. Is kin selection to be preferred to parental manipulation? Who knows — even if sociobiology has a role to play?

I shall therefore turn to the more stimulating question of *inter*-approach relationships. I assume that the different fields are, more or less, talking about the same thing. So the questions arise. Does sociobiology bid to replace Freud, or merely to reduce him to the genes? Have the hormones a place in this battle? Or will the psychoanalytic theorists surprise us all (especially the endocrinologists and sociobiologists) by making all other approaches redundant, outdated, or mere minor consequences of Oedipal strivings? What of replacement? What of reduction?

In a way, asking these questions is no less premature than asking questions about intra-approach relationships. We simply do not yet have enough firm knowledge to make definitive judgements. Who would dare to say where sociobiology will really end up in the final assessment? But already, partisans are making judgements and telling us what will or will not happen. (See, for instance, Ross et al. 1978.) Therefore, recognizing that virtually everything is hypothetical, I shall explore possible inter-approach relationships. My hunch is that the situation may be more interesting than philosophers or sexologists usually allow. In discussions of this nature, the element of rivalry enters early. Either a theory is to be replaced by another, or it is to be shown a mere consequence of the other. I suspect, however, that the rivalry comes too soon. Here, in the case of sexual orientation, we might have less competition and more cooperation.

A theory reduction has a deductive inference at its heart (E. Nagel 1961). Let us start the inquiry by looking at the hormonal/genetic barrier (or gap or interface). In a sense, this seems by far the most hopeful place to seek connections, deductive or otherwise. Indeed, if one held to some of the sociobiological hypotheses, it is hard to see how one could avoid being tempted into embracing some kind of hormonal hypothesis as well. The balanced superior heterozygote fitness hypothesis (in its crude form) supposes that some people will grow up to be homosexual, regardless really of what their parents or the postnatal environment does to them. Conversely, some siblings, without any special postnatal input, will grow up to be super reproducers. It is difficult to see how this could happen unless the genes produce something which affects the growing child (pre- or postnatally), and it is equally difficult to see how this could happen unless the hormones are somewhere involved.

Similarly, the hormones fit fairly readily into the parental manipulation hypothesis. Suppose it is in a parent's reproductive interests to rear a child as an altruistic non-reproducer. It has been emphasized that this does not have to come through a conscious decision. Perhaps the mother, on realizing she is pregnant, gets very tense at the thought of an extra mouth to feed. Tension and stress in humans are known to alter hormonal levels, those of androgen specifically (Meyer-Bahlburg 1977), and so homosexuality in the child could come about as a result. The idea here presumably is that the mother carries genes which can affect hormone production, and the triggering of these genes is in turn a function of psychological state.

Similar remarks on the meshing of genes and hormones apply to other sociobiological hypotheses. What about matters considered from the perspective of hormonal hypotheses? It is certainly not necessary to invoke a particular sociobiological hypothesis to explain (say) some specific instance of the high or low prenatal androgen levels needed in Dörner's hypothesis. It could conceivably be due to some chance factor, like something the pregnant mother eats or drinks. On the other hand, there is no barrier stopping the invocation of sociobiological hypotheses to explain how certain hormonal levels get triggered. If one postulates (say) genes producing high or low testosterone levels in the pregnant mother, these could be under the control of selection, as in the parental manipulation hypothesis. Furthermore, it is difficult indeed to see how the genes could fail to get involved when one is working out the full details of a hypothesis like Dörner's, which supposes that prenatal hormonal levels can and do systematically affect development of the brain (the hypothalamus) in such a way that, when one is faced with a post-pubertal increase in sex hormones, one will exhibit and act out a certain kind of sexual orientation. The genes are not only the units of heredity — the things which are passed on from one generation to the next — they are also the units of development and of function, for they control the way one develops and in some ultimate way one's functioning.

In fact, Dörner himself has already started to speculate on ways in which genes and hormones might interact. He proposes the model sketched in figure 7.1. About this he writes as follows:

During the differentiation period, an effector E (for example, testosterone) activates the regulatory protein RD1 produced by the regulatory gene RGD1 and/or inactivates the regulatory protein RD2. Consequently, in the presence of the effector E during the differentiation phase, the specific regulatory gene RGF1 for the entire functional phase may be irreversibly activated, that is, organized or imprinted so as to result in the production of specific RNA and the regulatory protein RF1, which is primarily inactive. During the functional period, this regulatory protein RF1 then reacts as binding site to the same (or similar) effector E. Hence, specific structural genes (e.g. SGF1a and SGF1b) are now reversibly activated leading to the production of specific enzymes (1a and 1b . . .).

In the absence of the effector E during the differentiation period, the primarily active regulatory protein RD2 produced by the regulatory gene RGD2 is not inactivated and, thus, may irreversibly activate (organize or imprint) the regulatory gene RGF2 for the entire functional phase, resulting in the production of the primarily inactive regulatory protein RF2. During the functional period, this regulatory protein RF2 then reacts as an alternative regulating site to the same (or similar) effector E. Hence, other specific structural genes (SGF2a and SGF2b . . .) are now reversibly activated, leading to the production of other specific enzymes (2a and 2b . . .).

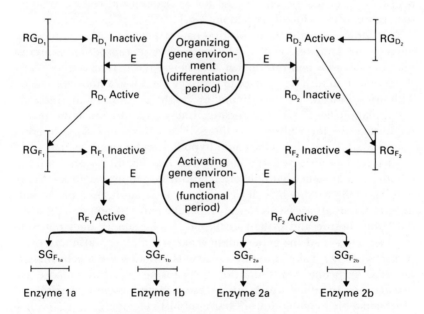

FIGURE 7.1 Possible interactions between genetic material and gene environment
(Dörner 1977: 236)

Consequently, the following correlations may be assumed at the molecular level: the higher the concentration of the effector E (for example, testosterone) during the critical differentiation period, the higher is the transcribeability of RGF1 and, hence, of SGF1b and/or the lower is the transcribeability of RGF2 and, hence, of SGF2a and SGF2b during the functional phase and vice versa. (Dörner 1977: 235)

I see no reason why some or all of the genes in Dörner's model should not be under the control of selection — indeed, given their crucial role in the human reproductive process, one would surely expect at least most to be carefully monitored by selective forces. And here there would be full room for sociobiological hypotheses. In short, in every respect I see hormonal and sociobiological explanations fitting together.

Leaving for the moment the question of what this 'fitting together' involves, and assuming that the other endocrinal hypotheses (such as they are) also would mesh smoothly with sociobiology (or could be made to mesh), let us go on to introduce and consider psychoanalytic hypotheses: here broadly including under 'psychoanalytic' both strict psychoanalytic and alternative cultural hypotheses. Some of the socio-biological hypotheses positively beckon some of the psychoanalytic approaches: there is no question of the sociobiology having to be restricted in order to make a case for environmental causes. Without such causes, the sociobiology will not work.

Take for example the sociobiological parental manipulation hypotheses. Suppose, for some reason, that it be in the parental reproductive interest that a child be a non-reproducer and hence the parent is genetically programmed to turn (or attempt to turn) the child into a non-reproducer. Although, indeed, the 'manipulation' might be hormonal, since the manipulation need not be conscious, one can readily imagine that it might take the form posited by the psychoanalysts as a cause of adult homosexual orientation. One could hypothesize, for instance, that a boy is born into an already large family, and that for this reason he is an additional and somewhat deleterious drain on family resources, to say nothing of the trouble he will cause when, as an adult, he wants to start his own family. It is easy to conceive that the parents' genes might make the father hostile and distant to the boy — he simply does not want another son — and the genes might make the mother warm and over-protective of her 'baby'. But this scenario is just what the psychoanalysts describe as prime conditions for the causing of adult homosexual orientation. In other words, in a case like this sociobiological and psychoanalytic hypotheses work harmoniously together.

Similarly, one can imagine kin selection and a psychoanalytic hypothesis being fitted together. Suppose that after a childhood accident or illness it would be in a (male) individual's best reproductive interests to be homosexual. This could easily occur through the child's state triggering responses in parents — a mother feeling sympathy and a father growing rather distant towards a delicate child to whom he could not respond. Hence, again we have the classic triangle and homosexuality ensues. Note, I am not saying that it is true that the triangle turns one into a homosexual. I am assuming this for the sake of argument. Neither am I denying that there are fathers sufficiently sensitive to respond to delicate children. I am trying to set up a pattern of how things might occur. If anyone doubts that many fathers do respond positively to 'macho' attitudes in their sons, they should go to a children's ice hockey game some time.

Looking at matters the other way, I suspect that many psychoanalytic theorists would be appalled to think that their theory has anything to do with biology, whether it be at the level of hormones or of genes. This was one of the main reasons why the adaptationists were stirred to action. They felt Freud left too much (that is, something) to biology. But certainly in the case of sociobiology, there seems no reason why (given their stress on environment) there should be any trouble fitting the approaches together. If it be objected (say by the phobic theorist) that the homosexual is an unhappy, tormented being, I can only say that it is a very naive view of evolutionary biology to think nature puts human happiness above the achievement of its own ends (E. O. Wilson 1975).

We have not yet considered the relationship, or possible relationship, between the psychoanalytic approach and the endocrinal approach. I see no reason why there should not be some accommodation. Obviously, if one argues that prenatal hormonal levels completely determine adult sexual orientation, then there is no more to be said. But if one takes a position like the later Money (for example, Money and Schwartz 1978), then hormones and family environment fit together neatly. Prenatal hormones set a certain pattern, certain potentialities, and perhaps even certain dispositions. But these all need to be reinforced or possibly discouraged during early growth (particularly very early growth) in order to produce the final adult orientation and behaviour. Conversely, one might argue that the family environment only has the effects that it does given particular hormonal levels, either pre- or postnatally.

Finally, one can certainly imagine hypotheses from all three approaches — psychoanalytic, endocrinal, and sociobiological — being involved in a total causal, explanatory picture of human homosexuality. For instance, one might have a basic background of sociobiological parental manipulation. How this manipulation takes effect could in some cases be due to prenatal stress and alteration of androgen levels (hormonal), and in other cases be due to distant fathers and overprotective mothers (psychoanalytic) which in turn leads to stress or lack of stress and thus to alteration of androgen/oestrogen levels (hormonal), as one comes into adolescence (figure 7.2). Or perhaps an even more complex pattern could hold against a background of parental manipulation (sociobiological). This manipulation could act first through prenatal stress, which could alter androgen levels (hormonal). When the child is born, because of the hormonal factors, we could have a rather effeminate boy or a tomboyish girl. But this in itself might not be enough to produce a homosexual. Only if the parents respond in the appropriate way to such a child (in the male case, hostile father and protective mother), might we get a homosexual produced (environmental-psychoanalytic) (figure 7.3). Add to this social learning at the time of adolescence to set the pattern of adult sexuality — very promiscuous, not at all coupled, attracted to people of a certain physique, and so forth.

This picture is not quite such an outlandish possibility as it seems at first sight. Suppose that stress really does alter prenatal androgen levels, and that if a woman already has too many children she gets tense, and thus produces an effeminate boy or a tomboyish girl (Ward 1972). Now obviously, lots of things cause stress, and a pregnant woman under stress is not necessarily a person whose reproductive strategy would favour the birth and development of a non-reproductive altruist, even though such a woman may be in such a position more than usually, thus causing selection for the requisite genes. Indeed a woman under stress may be a person who desperately needs and desires a reproducer and this is the

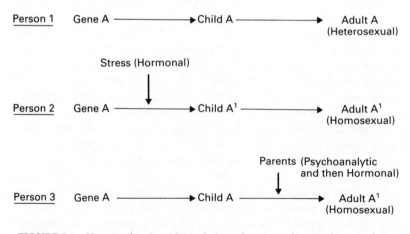

FIGURE 7.2   Hormonal and psychoanalytic explanations of parental manipulation

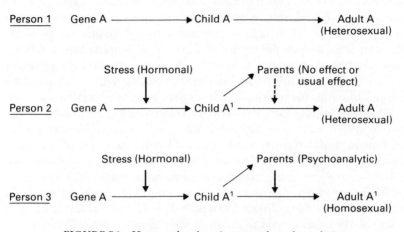

FIGURE 7.3   *Hormonal and environmental-psychoanalytic*
explanations of parental manipulation

cause of her stress. Suppose she is an older woman who has long been barren or (thinking of the kinds of infertility story in the Old Testament) has no son. (See Horner 1978.)

We have therefore the possibility of two kinds of woman (call them types A and B). Both types are under stress and have produced effeminate sons or tomboyish daughters, but type A's reproductive strategy needs a homosexual adult offspring and type B's needs a heterosexual adult. Obviously, therefore, it would be in a type B woman's reproductive interests if she could prevent her child from developing into a homosexual — and the same probably goes for her spouse's interests (we can assume monogamy to make the picture simpler, although the assumption is not essential). At this point, let us hypothesize that the environmental (psychoanalytic) level comes into play. If the parents do not need a reproducer (type A mother), then they respond to their child in such a way as to direct him/her or reinforce him/her into his/her adult homosexuality. This response is a response to the kind of child they have produced. However, nature has a failsafe mechanism. If the parents need a reproducer (type B mother), then despite the child's nature they can so alter or rear him/her as to produce not a homosexual, but rather a heterosexual.

Filling out the details of the picture and, for simplicity, concentrating just on father and son, suppose that normally a father cares for his son and aids in bringing him up in a male role. But suppose also that an effeminate son turns off his affections and thus he (the father) is distant and cold — the son gets more attention from the mother and grows up homosexual. Conversely, suppose that if the father needs a reproductive son — say the boy is the father's only son — then the father will persist in his attentions, despite the boy's effeminacy. And suppose finally this will be enough to steer the boy towards adult heterosexuality. Here then we get the two types of adult son: homosexual and heterosexual. (All of this supposition puts me in mind of Mr Jaggers in *Great Expectations*.)

This little fantasy story should all be taken with a grain of salt — many would say a mountain of salt! — but it does show that a full causal picture of human homosexuality could need reference to explanations at all levels: psychoanalytic-environmental, hormonal, and sociobiological.[1] Parents have different reproductive strategies (sociobiological level). Mothers get tense because they are pregnant, thus affecting the development of their offspring's hypothalami (hormonal level). Parents, particularly fathers, react in different ways towards their offspring, thus causing differences in psychosexual development (psychoanalytic level).

Enough has been said. My point is simply that piecing together the full picture of homosexual orientation and behaviour — male and female — can involve more than one hypothesis at any particular level, and can (and possibly will) require ideas and suggestions from all three of the approaches that we have considered. In concluding this discussion, let me pick up the question of the exact nature of the relationship which might be expected to obtain between the various levels (approaches) in a total picture of homosexual orientation. As intimated, I suspect we will have neither a replacement, nor a reduction, in the sense of one theory being deduced from another. Rather, what we will have are two (or more) theories being fitted together, *each filling out gaps indicated by the other*. Take, for one last illustrative time, the parental manipulation hypothesis. If one were to lay it out diagrammatically, it would have a structure somewhat along the lines shown in figure 7.4. But as can be readily seen, although the sociobiolgial argument gives a place for parental manipulation, it does not specify at all what form this 'manipulation' must take — whether it will involve hormones, or stress, or hostile parents, or over-protective parents, or several of these, or what. There is certainly no question of deducing the manipulation from the genetics in the sociobiological explanation. Rather, hormonal and/or psychoanalytic theories must be invoked in their own right to fill gaps left by the sociobiology. Looking at matters in the other direction, one can say that the sociobiological hypothesis helps to put the hormonal and/or psychoanalytic theories into a broader context. And obviously hormonal and psychoanalytic theories are independent. If one demands low prenatal androgen levels and a hostile father to make a male

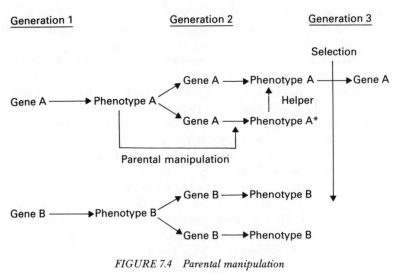

FIGURE 7.4   Parental manipulation
(Ruse 1979a: 188)

homosexual, there is no question of deducing the father from the androgen and vice versa. Both elements are essential, irreducible parts of the total explanation.

In short, there is a place for more than one level or type of explanation in the quest to understand homosexual orientation and behaviour (Ruse 1985). A full explanation of both origins and present causes could, and most probably would, involve different strands from different levels or approaches, working and meshing harmoniously together. Appeal to explanation of one approach or type does not exclude appeal to explanation of another type, nor does it make explanations of other types redundant deductive consequences — quite the contrary, in fact. Certainly, until we are a little more sure of our specific hypotheses, a tolerance for all points of view seems indicated. We may indeed not be aiming for a deductive reduction; but, like workers in other areas, we may find the coming together of different approaches yields dividends which far outweigh the insult to pride felt from having to share one's field and problems with strangers.

7.5   From frying pan to fire?

My conclusion thus far is that although the issue of reductionism raises questions of concern and interest to the student of homosexual orientation, it is not quite the bogeyman that it is sometimes portrayed as being. But still the worries will persist. Failure to condemn reductionism of all kinds leaves open the way for the second terror which destroys absolutely the possibility of non-prejudicial, soundly based, scientific understanding. After war comes plague; after reductionism comes determinism. 'Reductionism's hierarchy of levels and associated causes carries with it an implied biological determinism' (Birke 1986: 65). If you accept that we are no more than molecules, or at least no more than things obeying the laws of molecules, and especially if you think that the molecules work their effects up through the genes and the hormones, controlled and sifted by natural selection, then humans seem to be little more than blind robots. We are what we are and we do what we do, without choice or reason. We are puppets on the end of the DNA: 'we had best resign ourselves to the fact that the more unsavoury aspects of human behaviour, like wars, racism, and class struggle, are inevitable results of evolutionary adaptations based in our genes' (Bleier 1984: 15).

And more than that, even. To the determinist, being heterosexual or homosexual is something thrust upon one, quite beyond our control: 'it is . . . often assumed that homosexuality is itself biologically based, representing some kind of disorder of biological determination' (Birke 1986: 21). From there, it is only too easy to move to claims about sickness and the need for cure or elimination. We may have no choice about our sexuality, but (apparently) we have a choice about whether we will let homosexuality be — and the answer is usually negative.

This is a legitimate worry. Is it well founded? As with reductionism, I suggest that light will be thrown on matters if we separate out various meanings. Once again I propose a three part division, distinguishing *causal determinism, genetic* (or *biological*) *determinism*, and (what I shall call) *puppet determinism*. There may well be more meanings, but again we shall cover all the points we need to cover (Ruse 1987).

7.6 Causal determinism

'Causal determinism' implies that the world runs according to unbroken regularities, 'laws', where everything is part of a network. Nothing happens randomly or by chance. Everything is an effect of something else, a cause. Of course, modern physics has demanded revision of nineteenth-century views about laws and causation, but I assume that quantum indeterminacy can be fitted into causal determinism, as it is being construed. It implies also that humans are part of the causal nexus, and that however you construe the mind, it is subject to the laws of cause and effect. If the mind is material, then this follows at once. And if the mind has a substance unto itself, then there are causal laws operating in that domain also.

Given this notion of determinism, one ready conclusion follows. All of the explanations we have considered in this book presuppose causal determinism, and, insofar as they are well made, they underline and support such determinism. This is obvious in the cases of endocrinology and sociobiology. But it is true also of explanations within the first approach, those stressing the effects of the environment. Whatever Freud's position may have been on the mind/body problem, about causality he was emphatic: 'the intellect and the mind are objects for scientific research in exactly the same way as any non-human beings'. At the end of his life, he asked, somewhat plaintively: 'Psychology, too, is a natural science. What else can it be?' (Again, see Grünbaum 1985 for references and discussion.) Freud (1955b) recognized that we are often in ignorance about causes, so things do not appear to us as inevitable as they might. But that is another matter.

However, as with the first kind of reductionism, when all of this is said, who is concerned? So long as you do not think that sexual orientation is an act of God or the devil — an intervention from without the causal chain — providing a causal backing in no way demeans the homosexual or makes such an individual less of a person. Of course, you may disagree with all of the approaches being discussed, opting instead for something like an extreme social constructivism. Yet here also causality is presupposed. If you label me 'queer' or 'sick', my status is as much an effect as it would be were I a product of my mother's dominance.

The worry, I suppose, is that causal determinism excludes free will and moral capacity. If we are part of the causal network, then we do what we do because of our causes. An omniscient being could forecast exactly what we will be doing in twenty-five minutes time. Thus we can hardly decide between right and wrong, good and evil, because we are predetermined machines. Of course, this is a problem which affects us all, and not just homosexuals. But the arguments we have covered do serve to reinforce our pre-programmed natures. The omniscient being could say who you will be in bed with tonight, even though you yourself may not know (Harry 1984).

I cannot hope here to do full justice to this worry — one which has been discussed endlessly by philosophers for the past two and a half thousand years, since Aristotle first made us aware of the depth of the problem (Hudson 1970; Dennett 1984). I will say this, however. Simply lifting the causal chain does little to restore moral capacity. Take an unambiguous case of doing good: Mother Teresa bathing the brow of a dying man, in Calcutta. Why does she do this? I would say, from her love of God, from her training, because of her personality, and more. If you argue that all of these factors exist, and then, just at the point at which she is about to lift up the damp cloth, the causal chain is broken and 'free will' (whatever that is) enters in, her actions seem less like those of a saint and more like those of a crazy woman. Nothing in her past was connected to, makes predictable, or makes understandable, her actions in the present. She might as easily have picked up an axe and struck the man down (Ruse 1986).

There is a position to which I (like many other philosophers) am drawn. This suggests that Mother Teresa's very reasons function as causes, and that thus her morality stems from the fact that she is part of the causal network, rather than despite it (Davidson 1963). I will say no more about this position here (known as 'compatibilism' or 'soft determinism'). The point is that causal determinism is presupposed by *any* scientific understanding, and seems not as much a threat to moral integrity as first impressions might imply. And this applies to the case of homosexuality.

7.7 Biological determinism

Next we have genetic or biological determinism, which the critics invariably tell us is a major flaw in any hormonal or sociobiological approach to homosexual orientation. This kind of determinism incorporates the assumption that, ultimately, everything is a causal function of — exclusively a causal function of — biological factors. Specifically, in our case: 'Biologists argue that in two kinds of studies of biological sex differences, evolutionary studies and neuroendocrinological studies, the results of research intersect in such a way as to make a powerful case for biologically determined sex roles' (Harding 1986: 92−3). And from here to prejudice, repression, and elimination is one easy step: 'If our definitions of gender, sexual preference, or whatever, are seen to have *biological* roots, then they are likely to be seen as more natural, and by implication more desirable or unchangeable' (Bleier 1984: 73, her italics).

Of course, biological determinism, as just portrayed, is bad science — it is truly dreadful science. It is, moreover, truly dreadful biological science. No biologist worth his/her salt thinks that biological factors alone uniquely determine the organism, in physical nature, in behaviour, or in attitudes. It is always stressed that the finished organism is a product of its biology, in conjunction with its environment. Nor can you simply say of the finished organism: 'Here's the effect of one gene/hormone, here's the effect of another.' In ontogeny, there is an integration, as the parts become a whole. The English biologist, Patrick Bateson (1986), has aptly likened the whole process to the baking of a cake. The genes are the recipe. What you end with is a lot more than the recipe or the raw products.

However, having said this much, let us not swing too far the other way. It still makes sense to identify parts of the recipe or particular products, and to trace their effects on the cake. You certainly do not want your cake to end up tasting 'eggy'; but, you can follow through the effects of the eggs: what happens if you do not add them at the right temperature (a heavy, stodgy mess), how they are affected by too low or too high an oven temperature (dry or burned), and so forth. Likewise with biological factors. Sometimes the critics sound as if what they object to is not so much biological determinism, but biology period: 'is it not more plausible to argue that a more robust conception of evolutionary biology would understand it as part of a seamless weaving of our culture's dominant social projects?' (Harding 1986: 103). A more moderate and balanced position recognizes that you can start to sort out the effects of various biological factors, given various environmental conditions, as (similarly) you can start to sort out the effects of various environmental conditions, given various biological factors. It does make sense to say: 'Given biological factors θ (as opposed to Φ), and given conditions A (as opposed to B), we get end product a (as opposed to b).' And so forth.

Referring now specifically to the biological explanations of homosexual orientation — and I am not now talking about whether they are true, but where they stand on biological determinism — no one would want to pretend that every researcher has always been as pure as the driven snow. But neither in theory nor in practice does a simplistic charge of illicit biological determinism stick. Take Money's work, for instance. He is almost neurotically careful to emphasize that (as best we know) there is more to sexual orientation than the hormones — such as the effect of parental attitudes, societal expectations and customs, peer pressure, and so forth. Similarly, in the case of sociobiology, the closest we get to a deterministic position is the heterozygote fitness case — and we know that that, in its crude form, is false! (It should be noted, however, that one does sometimes get a behaviour, linked to one or a few identifiable genes, that is expressed in virtually any environment. Lesch-Nyhan syndrome, involving compulsive self-mutilation, is one such case: Hilton et al. 1973.)

As far as kin selection and parental manipulation are concerned, their very essence is that there is more to adult patterns than simple genetic effects. As we saw, these mechanisms work even when (in crucial respects) we are all genetically identical. Things start to happen only when the environment gets involved. Why manipulate (or 'manipulate') your child into a homosexual role, unless there is good reason? And the good reason comes down to societal pressures and needs and so forth. Here, again, we go beyond naked biological determinism — so obviously so, in fact, that one starts to suspect that the root of much of the obsession with the perils of biological determinism lies less in the poor worth of the work of biologists than in the extra-scientific objectives of the critics. If one is committed to a radical reconstruction of society according to some grand metaphysical plan, biological determinism is a good stick with which to beat the opposition.

7.8 Puppet determinism

I come now to the third and final kind of determinism, which I have (somewhat inelegantly) labelled 'puppet determinism'. This is the determinism which supposes that we are just blind robots, driven by external or internal forces, going about life in an ant-like fashion, without control or reason. We are at the mercy of our emotions, dangling on the end of strings. Putting things dramatically, the philosopher Dan Dennett (1984) has wondered if we are just like the wasp *Sphex*.

When the time comes for egg laying, the wasp Sphex builds a burrow for the purpose and seeks out a cricket which she stings in such a way as to paralyze but not kill it. She drags the cricket into the burrow, lays her eggs alongside, closes the burrow, then flies away, never to return. . . . To the human mind, such an elaborately organized and seemingly purposeful routine conveys a convincing flavour of logic and thoughtfulness — until more details are examined. . . . If the cricket is moved a few inches away while the wasp is inside making her preliminary inspection, the wasp, on emerging from the burrow, will bring the cricket back to the threshold, but not inside, and will then repeat the preparatory procedure of entering the burrow to see that everything is all right. . . . The wasp never thinks of pulling the cricket straight in. On one occasion this procedure was repeated forty times, always with the same result. (p. 32)

Speaking generally, like Dennett, I very much doubt that we are *Sphex*-like. Evolution has led us down different paths — else, why the big brains? But I will here confine myself to the specific issue of homosexuality. Does anything in the various proposals considered in earlier chapters circumscribe human freedom, pushing homosexuals to the degraded status of clockwork dolls, unreasoning insects, blindly driven by uncontrolled and uncontrollable forces? To answer this question, it will be useful to refer again to the various different notions encompassed when we talk of (homo)sexuality.

First, there is *biological sex*, broadly construed. This starts with chromosomal differences (XX as opposed to XY) and goes on to anatomical differences, with the genital female (usually) being XX and the genital male (usually) being XY. I take it that, at the initial level at least, there is no question of freedom or choice. We are what we are, and that is that. Presumably, now or in the near future, our parents could do something about the sex of their offspring, but were we aborted or prevented from conception, we would hardly be us. And if it proved possible to fiddle around with the prenatal hormones to the extent of genital change, it would hardly be (or ever could be) our decision. It is true that, in adulthood, there is today some option about biological sex. You cannot change the chromosome structure, but you can do something about the anatomy — more easily for males (wanting to change to females), than conversely. Nothing we have discussed threatens this new found freedom of the transsexual.

From biological sex, we move on to *gender*, primarily that of *identity*, but (for fullness) including *role*. The emphasis here is on one's sense of being a male or a female, and then on the extent to which one fits the male or female role, be the latter biologically, socially, or otherwise determined. Some of our approaches deal more explicitly with the question of identity than do others — the psychoanalytic/learning theorists, for instance, think directly about one's sense of maleness/femaleness. But the presumption of all is that gender identity is something more or less thrust upon one, in the early years of life (if it waits even that long). Money (1961), in the past, has certainly argued that gender identity is exclusively a function of social factors — so parents could make decisions. He now questions this stand. What is still clear is that we do not choose our own identity, and that it is something largely fixed for life.

Nor, I might add, does this seem such a bad thing. At least one radical thinker sees the very notion of gender identity (male or female) as part of a male chauvinist plot. Sandra Harding (1986) speaks of 'the elimination of gender that is apparently required if even the affirmative action goals for women in science are to succeed' (p. 127). I confess, given biological sex, I am not sure (even conceptually) what a genderless society would be like. What we can say, empirically, is that people never seem to be genderless. What they may be is radically confused about their gender identity. Also, speaking empirically, the really unhappy people seem to be those who are confused about gender identity, or whose gender identity does not match biological sex. These findings are reported by researchers who emphasize that people with homosexual orientations can (and regularly do) lead happy, fulfilled lives (Stoller 1968; Green 1974).

Gender role applies to the way you behave, whether it is in a fashion considered appropriate in society for males or for females. I take it that a transvestite is crossing gender roles, even though he/she might be heterosexual in orientation. At a more general level, the exact connection between gender role and sexual orientation is complex. We have seen some empirical evidence linking atypical childhood gender role and adult homosexual orientation. The problem here, however, is that of freedom. I shall simply state flatly that I cannot see that any of our causal theories impinge on one's freedom with respect to gender role. If I as a male have a yen to put on a bra and panties, then however caused — incomplete resolution of Oedipal strivings, social learning, high levels of hormones, an uncommon combination of genes — I can decide whether or not to go out and make my purchases. The explanations of homosexuality do not, in this respect, intensify the threat of puppet determinism.

There are some obvious queries. But they will be covered as we now raise the final items on the sexual spectrum: *sexual orientation, identity*, and *behaviour*. Put against these notions, what do our various causal hypotheses imply about freedom and determinism? As far as sexual orientation is concerned, just about all of the causal theories suggest that this is something found rather than chosen. One is straight or gay by destiny, and not by choice. If Freud is right, then (not necessarily with intention on their part) your parents make you a homosexual, without any say by you. Similarly, with the hormones; and even in the case of something like kin selection, there is no implication that the future homosexual consciously chooses such a future orientation. It is something which comes about through the forces of nature.

But none of this seems terribly troublesome or controversial. As we saw earlier, even the social constructivists seem prepared to allow that sexual orientation is a given rather than an option. It is what we (or others) do with it that counts. The only ones who dispute this (as far as I can make out) are certain radical feminist lesbians (such as Martin and Lyon 1972). They argue — or, at least, imply — that sexual orientation is a matter of political choice. Women *ought* to be attracted to women to show one's identity with universal sisterhood. Since this proposal seems never to be proposed by males, heterosexual or homosexual, I suspect that we may here be touching on a difference between males and females. Both empirical survey and (some) theory suggests that male orientation may be more polarized than female orientation. If one is bisexual in orientation, but locked early into a heterosexual role by society, then breaking out and identifying with a supportive lesbian group may well seem like a choice in orientation.

In the terms we are using, even for women it is probably better to think of such a move as a choice of homosexual identity or activity.[2] Certainly, speaking now generally, nothing that has been said by any of our putative causal theories denies one the freedom to choose whether or not one will identify with homosexuality, whether privately to oneself, or publicly as one 'comes out of the closet'. Analogously, nothing has been said to deny a person, male or female, the freedom to engage carnally or not with another of one's own biological sex. My mother may have made me a homosexual, but whether I go to bed with another man is my choice not hers. I may have lesbian urges because of my prenatal hormonal levels, but cunnilingus with another woman is my option — and mine (and hers) alone. There is nothing of the puppet determinist about the human homosexual, and nothing in our causal theories suggests or necessitates otherwise.

Of course, sometimes choice is circumscribed. If I am caught fellating someone in a public lavatory, I might be labelled a 'homosexual' whether I like it or not. The same goes for activity, at least in a passive role. If I am being forcibly sodomized in jail, I have little freedom. But these determining factors come from outside. They are not a dictating consequence of any of the theories about homosexuality. Yet, perhaps, this confidence about freedom and control is too quick. Surely there has to be some connection between orientation and action, with identity following somewhere down the line? This is especially so in the case of sociobiology. Why would kin selection bother to give us a homosexual orientation, if we were never going to use it — even if we use our orientation only negatively, in the sense of not going through the heterosexual motions? In other cases also, although there might not be the same functional connection, we do surely expect homosexual activity, at the very least — which means that we are puppets after all.

This is an objection which needs careful response, if only because of the crucial bearing a proper answer has for the inquiry into values on which we are about to embark (in the next chapter). Parenthetically, I would point out that the problem is not really one that is deeply exacerbated by causal speculations. Sociobiology notwithstanding, the real issue is the link between homosexual orientation, which is a kind of hunger or emotion or desire — and a given — and homosexual action. (Or, at a minimum, heterosexual non-action.) Is there a place for genuine freedom here, or not? It really matters not how the orientation was caused.

Relying on the best of contemporary philosophical discussion, joining a tradition which goes back to Plato, I would suggest that true freedom rests on a distinction to be drawn between first- and second-order desires (Frankfurt 1970; Ruse 1987). First-order desires are like (although not necessarily exclusively confined to) animal urges and emotions — the wanting of food and warmth and sleep and sex. Second-order desires are more akin to long-range goals — like political power or spiritual purity or marital happiness. Freedom consists in being able to bring one's first-order desires to bear on the achievement of one's second-order desires. The person who can do this is 'in control'. The person who cannot do this is 'out of control'. The person who has no second-order desires at all is a wanton or aimless or amoral.

Now, judged in this light, I see no reason why the person with a homosexual orientation should not be free. I meet somebody. I fall in love with him/her. I plan a long-term relationship, and I bring all of my abilities to bear on its successful end. I meet another person on the beach. I am desperately attracted and want to have sex. I remember all of the warnings about AIDS, and so, sadly but firmly, I turn away from such a casual encounter. Of course, the person with a homosexual orientation is likely to have some different ends (some different second-order desires) from the person with a heterosexual orientation. For this reason, all other things being equal, one does expect more homosexual activity from the person with a homosexual orientation. But the same freedom is there. Moreover, I can think of nothing in our putative aetiologies to suggest that the homosexual is, per se, any less in control than the heterosexual. If I have homosexual urges because of (say) social learning or the hormones, some of my ends may be different (from the heterosexual). But my control is not necessarily any the less (or the more).

However, having said this much, one or two complicating factors must be added. First, let us not pretend that any of us are always in control, all of the time. We are all given to lapses — if such they be. We all have a choice about whether to masturbate; but I defy the average male (at least) never to masturbate. And, of course, we all do things without fully thinking — either without clearly formulated second-order desires or while thinking that our plans are other than they will be. Referring back to gender role, perhaps the atypical actions of future homosexuals fall under the first alternative. And referring back to parental manipulation, perhaps the actions of parents fall under the second alternative. I deny that homosexuals are less in control than heterosexuals; but, like everybody, no homosexual will be in control all of the time.

Second, let us not forget that plans and goals are set by society, as much as by personal emotions and wishes. It is not implausible to assume that many homosexuals, even in matters of sex, will share the same goals as heterosexuals. But, since society is essentially heterosexual, these goals will be a lot easier for heterosexuals to attain than for homosexuals. At points like these, homosexuals may well be less in control than heterosexuals. Note that I am not saying that homosexuals should have the same goals as heterosexuals (in every respect). But frequently they do, and at points like these I imagine that they are often less free.

Third, I see no reason why males and females should have the same intensities of the same emotions, or even the same goals — whether these be societally or biologically caused (Hinde 1984). I suspect, in fact, that sociobiology suggests that males may have less ability to control their brute animal (sexual) passions (Symons 1979). I am *not* saying that all males are rapists, or that those who are should be forgiven for so being. Neither am I saying that women have no deep emotions. However, I do suspect that it is less easy for male homosexuals to avoid promiscuity than it is for the rest of humankind — given the strength of their emotions (that is, typical male emotions) and those of their partners (likewise, typical male emotions). It is not that they are particularly weak-willed or (especially given the threat of AIDS) have different goals from heterosexuals. But males are not females.

Like the other varieties of determinism, puppet determinism raises important and interesting issues. We have seen nothing in our discussion to suggest that a causal understanding of homosexual orientation implies that a sizeable minority of the human population is driven blindly, acting in a mad frenzy, at the mercy of uncontrollable lusts.

7.9 Conclusion

Freud, like his fellow-Jewish predecessor Spinoza, argued that genuine freedom lies in self-knowledge. When and only when we know what motivates us do we have a true hope of self-control. I doubt that things are always quite this simple, although I wish they were. However, both at the personal level and at the societal level, I am sure that ignorance is no real alternative. We have far to go before we will properly understand the (probably) many causes of homosexual orientation. What we can say is that neither of the twin threats, reductionism and determinism, vitiate the work which has been thus far produced. We see through a glass darkly, and this must temper our analysis of normative questions. Yet we do now know that, in facing the tasks which lie before us, we do not leave behind us work which, by its very nature, is irredeemably flawed and corrupt. It may not be as good as its enthusiasts claim. It is certainly not as bad as its critics protest.

8

Is Homosexuality Bad Sexuality?

Is homosexuality, inclination and behaviour, an acceptable way for a human being to feel and act, or is it pernicious? Undoubtedly, although there will be less unanimity on this matter today than there would have been (say) a hundred years ago, for a good many people the answer will seem obvious — that homosexuality is aesthetically revolting and morally gross; that in all its aspects it is wrong, and that this is a conclusion not merely confirmed by modern thought but underlined by the whole western religious/philosophical tradition.

Whether or not this is really the case is the topic of this chapter. A matter which (today) is usually entwined with questions about the moral worth of homosexuality, namely the health status of the homosexual, will get a separate discussion in the next chapter.

8.1 Greek homosexuality

The major formative influences on western civilization, particularly in the areas of morality and behaviour, were those of the Ancient Greeks and of the Jews. Very roughly speaking, from the Greeks we inherit the attempt to see and live in the world guided by our physical senses and our reason, and from the Jews we inherit the attempt to see and live in the world guided by our faith and our religious sense. I suspect that if most people were questioned, they would be inclined to argue that over the matter of homosexuality, Greek and Jewish thought come into conflict, and that it is the Jewish tradition which triumphs. The Greeks, so the story would go, accepted and even promoted homosexual relations. Furthermore, this attitude is to be found in the greatest of their philosophers, most especially Plato. The Jews, however, both those of the Old and New Testaments, uniformly and unambiguously condemned all forms of homosexuality. It merited the punishment of man and of God. And it is this latter position which has prevailed ever since, thanks to the rise of Christianity, a religion which has such deep roots in Judaism.

But is this story true? Let us turn to the sources, beginning first with the Greeks. As is so often the case, popular opinion has a very inadequate grasp of the whole (Dover 1973, 1978; Verstraete 1977; Ungaretti 1982). It is indeed true that by the time of 'classical Greece' (from 480 BC, the date of the rejection of Persian colonial aspirations, to the coming of the Romans, 146 BC) — a time which firmly includes the life span of the philosopher Plato (428—347 BC) — overt homosexuality was a well-established tradition and acceptable part of the Greek life style. But the sexuality of classical Greece was apparently not simply an unrestrained free-for-all, with any two or more people doing whatsoever they liked, to whomsoever they liked. Specifically, the homosexuality one hears about was very much an upper-class phenomenon, strongly associated with the enforced segregation of the sexes, and highly stylized, with emotions rather than actions playing a major role. The central focus was a bond which would be formed between a somewhat older and a somewhat younger man (ideally, a 25-year-old paired with a 15-year-old). It seems to have been rare indeed (and certainly not proper) for two men of exactly the same age to have fallen in love and to have had any kind of physical relationship. Moreover, after marriage the need for (and acceptability of) homosexual relations fell away rapidly. (It is assumed that an analogous story can be told about women, although we know far less about lesbianism. It seems, for some unknown reason, to have been a taboo subject for the male writers. However, see figure 8.1.)

The constraint about ages was accompanied also by a constraint about emotions. The older man (the *erastes* or lover) was expected to feel strong sexual emotion for the younger man or boy (the *eromenos* or loved one), admiring his beauty, wanting to get physically close to him, and being prepared to court him with gifts and favours. The boy, however, was not expected to feel the same kind of sexual attraction in response, but rather to admire his older lover, looking upon him as an ideal or model, and wanting to make him happy. This convention about love and ages helped dictate the nature of the physical sexual relations. Officially at least, sodomy was definitely taboo, not to mention things like fellatio. Being sodomized was considered far too degrading — indeed, someone who indulged too freely in this in his youth, certainly someone who rented his body for such favours, stood in grave danger of losing various

FIGURE 8.1   One woman stimulates another
(detail from Greek vase, Dover 1978)

powers as a citizen. Hence, the usual method of intercourse between upper-class lovers was somewhat limited, in a stylized manner. The erastes, the older, would push his penis between the thighs of the eromenos, the younger, and bring himself to ejaculation this way, 'intercrurally'. (See figure 8.2.) The boy was not supposed to ejaculate in return — indeed, he was supposed to find the whole business rather asexual, and to remain unaroused throughout. No doubt there was frequently a gap between the ideal and the actual.

Against this background we can understand Plato's position of homosexuality. As is well known, Plato was the student and follower of Socrates, who was put to death on a charge of corrupting the youth, because he filled the heads of young aristocrats with all sorts of radical ideas. Reputedly, Socrates had a strong heterosexual appetite (all of his appetites were strong) and he was married, although supposedly his wife was somewhat of a shrew. Plato, tradition has it, was unmarried and

FIGURE 8.2   A man and boy prepare for intercrural copulation
(detail from Greek vase, Dover 1978)

fairly exclusively homosexual in orientation. Be this as it may, Socrates and his (exclusively male) companions lived, thought, and behaved very much in the homosexual milieu described above as being the norm for upper-class Athenians. In Plato's early writings (which report, fairly authentically, on actual Socratic discussions or dialogues), we get repeated, unselfconscious references to the sexual pangs that an older man would feel for a boy or younger man, and the liaisons that would spring up between them. The following translation of a passage from the *Charmides* (an early dialogue) needs no further comment:

Then I just didn't know what to do, and all the confidence that I'd previously felt, in the belief that I'd find it easy to talk to him, was knocked out of me. When Kritias told him that I was the man who knew the cure [for headache], and he looked me in the eye — oh, what a look! and made as if to ask me, and everyone in the wrestling-school crowded close all round us, that was the moment when I saw inside his cloak, and I was on fire, absolutely beside myself . . . All the same, when he asked me if I knew the cure for his head, I did somehow manage to answer that I knew it. (Dover 1978: 155)

However, with this much said, matters start to get a little more complicated. Although there is much talk of sexual desire, which seems even to be cherished, both Socrates and Plato unambiguously reject and condemn all taking of homosexual attraction to the point of intercourse and orgasm. According to Xenophon, Kritias and Socrates fell out over this very point, because Kritias wanted to copulate with his lover Euthydemos and Socrates thought he ought not. And in the greatest of all of Plato's works, the *Republic* (which, although it uses the historical Socrates as a mouthpiece, probably more truly represents Plato's own ideas), Socrates, in describing the nature of the ideal state, endorses homosexual attractions and liaisons and yet strictly prohibits the taking of them to the physical climax.

Why were Socrates and Plato so strongly against physical homosexual relations? There is an obvious reason, which had nothing to do with homosexuality per se. Both Socrates and Plato were reflecting an important attitude of their society and class, namely a great respect for self-constraint and control. Emotions were seen as things which took control of one, and the man who could withstand them gained stature in his and his colleagues' eyes. This applies to any kind of emotion, including homosexual impulses. Yet given that there was this condemn-ation of the fulfilment of homosexual feelings, were not Socrates and Plato somewhat inconsistent in apparently accepting the feelings them-selves? Making the distinction between homosexual orientation (even if only partial) and homosexual behaviour, for consistency should not Socrates and Plato at least have regretted homosexual inclinations rather than accepting them? The answer to this question probably lies in the fact that Plato (and Socrates also) saw them as inevitable, rather like the feelings of hunger and thirst. They are thrust upon you, so no moral opprobrium can be attached to them. Morality enters in only at the point of action.

Indeed, for Plato, so obvious and inevitable were homosexual urges, and so crucial was their control, he gave both parts a central place in his metaphysics. As is well known, Plato argued that there is a world of ultimate reality, the unchanging eternal world of the Forms, which are (among other things) the universals, like the Form of Bed, or Horse, or Happiness. The highest Form is that of the Good, which in some sense both illuminates the other Forms and is the source of their being. The ultimate in human philosophical achievement is to gaze upon the Form of the Good, which we are to do in some way through our rational or intuitive faculty. (See the *Republic* and Cross and Woozley 1964.) But we cannot just do this as soon as we feel so inclined. It requires long years of rigorous training; and a key part of this route of achievement involves homosexual attraction. We start by gazing upon and being overwhelmed by beautiful boys. From this we can go on to contemplate beautiful souls and pursuits (like the fascination of the quest for knowledge). As we do so, we start to realize that it is not the particular beautiful thing which attracts us, but the element in which they all participate, the Form of Beauty or the Good. So, finally, having restrained ourselves in the physical (genital) realm, we come to be rewarded by what is almost literally a philosophical orgasm. As in the physical world, at the moment of climax we get a real sense of oneness with everything. (See the *Symposium* 211 c—e.)

For the mature Plato, therefore, control is essential. To read Plato's early and middle writings as providing a licence for homosexual inclination and behaviour is not to read them properly. Homosexual attraction is accepted and even venerated, but consummation is condemned. The man who lets his passions thus govern his reason is an object of pity. This, however, is not quite all that there is to Plato's treatment of homosexuality. Towards the end of his life he developed his ideas yet further, and indeed he arrived at a position by a line of argument that was profoundly to influence subsequent thinking on the matter of homosexuality. Simply and categorically Plato condemned homosexual behaviour because it is 'unnatural'. It is not done by the animals. No more should it be done by us.

Anyone who, in conformity with nature, proposes to re-establish the law as it was before Laios, declaring that it was right not to join with men and boys in sexual intercourse as with females, adducing as evidence the nature of animals and pointing out that [among them] male does not touch male for sexual purposes, since that is not natural, he could, I think, make a very strong case. (Plato, *Laws*, 836c—e, trans. Dover 1978: 166)

The opposition to homosexual acts becomes absolute. And, although the third of the great Greek philosophers, Aristotle, said little on the topic of homosexuality, what little he did say could be taken as underlining this point. Under the classification of pleasures which do not come about naturally, and under the sub-classification of things which are found pleasurable by those with bad natures ('disease-like or as a result of habituation'), Aristotle includes pulling out one's hair, eating earth, and 'the disposition of sexual intercourse for males' (Aristotle, *Nichomachean Ethics*, 1148b 15—19a 20, trans. Dover 1978: 168). Probably, given all we know of his society, Aristotle here was more concerned with (condemning) the passive role in sodomy. But, be this as it may, there was no challenge to the finality of Plato.

8.2   The Judaeo/Christian tradition

Let us turn now to Judaism and its breakaway offspring, Christianity. Here, on the surface at least, popular opinion does seem closer to the truth. The primary source of information about the positions of the Jews and the early Christians is obviously the Bible, Old and New Testaments. In the Old Testament, there are two main sources of information about the position taken by God and his chosen people on the subject of homosexuality: the story of Sodom and Gomorrah, and various scattered dictates about homosexual practices. Both sources apparently tell the same tale: homosexual behaviour is abhorrent in the eyes of the Lord and therefore morally barred to humankind. As it happens, the Sodom and Gomorrah story about the citizens of Sodom, who wanted to have homosexual intercourse with two of God's angels, has been the subject of much Biblical reinterpretation. Most pertinently, it has been argued that the homosexual theme of the Sodom and Gomorrah story is a later interpolation (Bailey 1955). But the 'holiness Code' of Leviticus is unambiguous.

Thou shalt not lie with mankind, as with womankind: it is abomination. (Leviticus xviii.22)

If a man also lie with mankind, as he lieth with a woman, both of them have committed an abomination: they shall surely be put to death; their blood shall be upon them. (Leviticus xx.13)

In the New Testament, one likewise finds passages which categorically prohibit homosexual behaviour. As is usual on matters of sex, it was not the founder himself who pronounced on these matters, but his chief proselytizer, Paul.

the men, leaving the natural use of the woman, burned in their lust one toward another, men with men working unseemliness, and receiving in themselves that recompense of their error which was due. (Romans i.27)

Be not deceived: neither fornicators, nor idolaters, nor adulterers, nor effeminate, nor abusers of themselves with men, nor thieves, nor covetous, nor drunkards, nor revilers, nor extortioners, shall inherit the kingdom of God. (I Corinthians vi.9–10) law is not made for a righteous man, but for the lawless and unruly . . . for abusers of themselves with men . . . (I Timothy i.9 – 10)

Nor is lesbian behaviour neglected.

God gave them up unto vile passions: for their women changed the natural use into that which is against nature . . . (Romans i.26)

Of course, as you might imagine, there has been no shortage of voices prepared to argue that these passages do not really mean what they say. We are told that the condemnations are really against homosexual prostitution, and the like (Horner 1978). If so, one can only wish that God had chosen a less ambiguous scribe than Paul. What is clear, however, is that (much like the Greeks) both the Old and the New Testament authors are really concerned with *behaviour*. Attitudes and orientation go unmentioned and uncondemned.

Turning now to the great Christian philosophers, not unexpectedly we find that they too take a negative view of homosexual activity. Fairly typical was St Augustine (354 – 430), whose philosophical thought was a subtle blend of Neo-Platonism and Christianity. He saw homosexual acts as a failure to love either God or one's neighbour, writing that:

. . . those shameful acts against nature, such as were committed in Sodom, ought everywhere and always to be detested and punished. If all nations were to do such things, they would be held guilty of the same crime by the law of God, which has not so made men that they should use one another in this way. (Augustine, *Confessions*, III, viii (15), trans. Bailey 1955: 83)

Indeed, Augustine went so far as to say that in order to avoid homosexual advances one is permitted to commit acts which in other circumstances would be considered sins, like lying.

But the most detailed philosophical discussion of homosexuality by a Christian thinker is to be found in the writings of the thirteenth-century theologian St Thomas Aquinas (1968). Aquinas's treatment of homosexuality, as of most moral issues, depends crucially on the notion of 'natural law'. Essentially, he saw the whole world as created and regulated according to divine reason, which gives rise to eternal law ('This rational guidance of created things on the part of God . . . we can call the Eternal law'). Then, in turn, Aquinas thought that humans, inasmuch as we ourselves can control our destinies, have an obligation to fit with this eternal law. 'This participation in the Eternal law by rational creatures is called the Natural law' (Aquinas, *Summa Theologiae*, 1a 2ae, quae. 91, art. 1). Coming to sexuality, Aquinas (who was much influenced by Aristotle) did not ask the straightforward causal question, 'How do things work?', but rather the teleological question, 'What are things for? What end do they serve?' And the answer he gave is that sex exists for the procreation and raising of children. This is why God made us sexual beings, and this therefore is the end towards which we must strive if we are not to violate natural law, that area of the eternal law where we ourselves must make a contribution.

The consequence of Aquinas's position, as he thought, is that all sex outside marriage is wrong because it is a violation of natural law. Thus, quite apart from homosexuality's prohibition on Biblical grounds, for Aquinas it is necessarily barred as being against natural law: as being in conflict with 'right reason' (Aquinas 1968, p. 245). Homosexual encounters do not lead to children, therefore they must be wrong. But there is rather more than this. All lust is immoral, but some acts are doubly to be condemned, because 'they are in conflict with the natural pattern of sexuality for the benefit of the species' (p. 245). These are termed 'unnatural vices' ('vitiae contra naturum'). There are four kinds of such vices: masturbation, bestiality, homosexuality, and sex acts where 'the natural style of intercourse is not observed, as regards the proper organ or according to other rather beastly and monstrous techniques' (p. 245). Unnatural vices are the worst kinds of sins of lust (worse even than incest), and they are ordered according to the object being abused. Hence in the depths of depravity comes bestiality, then homosexuality, then 'lechery which does not observe the due mode of intercourse', and at the top of a sorry lot comes masturbation.

And in quite unchanged form, this is the official Catholic position unto this day: 'To choose someone of the same sex for one's sexual activity is to annul the rich symbolism and meaning, not to mention the goals of the creator's sexual design' (letter from Cardinal Ratzinger of the Sacred Congregation for the Doctrine of the Faith, to Catholic bishops: reported in *The Times*, 31 October 1986).[1]

8.3   Modern ethical philosophies

Let us turn now to the modern era, the time after the scientific revolution. There are two major, secular moral philosophies, those of the German thinker, Immanuel Kant (1949, 1959), and of the (primarily) British utilitarians. Both groups thought their views threw light on the status of homosexual behaviour (again, feelings get short shrift). Let us take them in turn.

Kant thought humans are subject to an overriding and necessary moral law, a supreme directive, the 'categorical imperative'. It is this law which tells us what we ought to do; wherein lies our duty. There are various ways in which Kant formulated his maxim (Körner 1955 gives a readable introduction). At one point he suggested that the key lies in the need to be able to *universalize* our actions: never do anything which you would not want to say that anybody and everybody should be able to do in a similar situation. Wanton cruelty is therefore wrong because one would not want to give people licence to do it to oneself. Another formulation of the categorical imperative is that one should always treat people as ends and not as means. In other words, one ought not simply use people for one's own benefit or for the benefit of others. People must be treated as subjective worthy beings in their own right.

As Kant (1963) himself recognized, at a quite general level sex and the categorical imperative have a rather uneasy relationship. The starting point to sex is the sheer desire of a person for the body of another. One wants to feel the skin, to smell the hair, to see the eyes — one wants to bring one's own genitals into contact with those of the other, and to reach orgasm. This gets dangerously close to treating the other as a means to the fulfilment of one's own sexual desire — as an object, rather than as an end. And this, according to the categorical imperative, is immoral. To escape from this dilemma, and one surely must if the end of the human race is not to be advocated on moral grounds, one must go on to treat the object of one's sexual advances as an end. One does this by broadening one's feelings, so that the personhood of the object of one's desire is brought within one's attraction, and by giving oneself reciprocally — by yielding oneself, body and soul, one shows respect for the other as an end, and not just as a means.

But what about a sincere commitment between two people of the same sex, the sort of homosexual equivalent of heterosexual marriage? At this point Kant invokes the notion of a *crimina carnis*, an abuse of one's sexuality. There are two kinds. First, there are acts which are contrary to sound reason, *crimina carnis secundum naturam*. These are immoral acts which go against the moral code imposed upon us as humans, and include such things as adultery. Second, there are acts contrary to our animal nature, *crimina carnis contra naturam*. These include masturbation, sex with animals, and homosexuality. They are the lowest and most disgusting sort of vice, worse in a sense even than suicide, and they are practices that we hesitate to mention. In fact, Kant found himself in something of a dilemma: mention the vices and you draw people's attention to them; fail to mention them and you do not warn people of them.

On balance, though, because they involve so great a violation of the categorical imperative, something must be said:

A second *crimen carnis contra naturam* is intercourse between *sexus homogenii*, in which the object of sexual impulse is a human being but there is homogeneity instead of heterogeneity of sex, as when a woman satisfies her desire on a woman, or a man on a man. This practice too is contrary to the ends of humanity; for the end of humanity in respect of sexuality is to preserve the species without debasing the person; but in this instance the species is not being preserved (as it can be by a *crimen carnis secundum naturam*), but the person is set aside, the self is degraded below the level of the animals, and humanity is dishonoured. (Kant 1963: 170)

Contrasting with Kantian ethics is that of the utilitarians, the most prominent of whom were Jeremy Bentham and the two Mills, James (father) and John Stuart (son). For them, the key to ethical theory is happiness: 'The creed which accepts as the foundation of morals utility or the greatest happiness principle holds that actions are right in proportion as they tend to promote happiness; wrong as they tend to produce the reverse of happiness' (Mill 1910: 6). Of course, there is a lot more to the theory than this, particularly revolving around what one might mean by 'happiness' and 'pleasure'. To the more intellectually robust Bentham, 'quantity of pleasure being equal, pushpin is as good as poetry' (Bentham 1834). To the more sensitive (and greater) John Stuart Mill, 'better to be Socrates dissatisfied than a fool satisfied' (Mill 1910: 9). But the important point is that to evaluate a moral action, one simply judges its consequences in terms of happiness (or pleasure) and unhappiness. And one action is better than another, and consequently that which one ought to do or approve, if it leads to greater happiness and to less unhappiness than the other.

Like Kant, Bentham applied his ethical theory to homosexual behaviour. Yet although they were writing at the same time, and although Bentham's language is frequently uncomplimentary, they might as well have been in different worlds. Bentham thinks homosexual interactions as acceptable morally as Kant finds them pernicious. Such interactions give pleasure to the people engaged in them, and so by the greatest happiness principle they ought to be valued. 'As to any primary mischief, it is evident that [a homosexual interaction] produces no pain in anyone. On the contrary it produces pleasure . . .' (Bentham 1978: 390). Bentham is not advocating homosexual behaviour for everyone, only for those who want to so indulge. Then, there will be no harm. Nor is there any real problem stemming from the possibility that homosexual practices might incline or influence others into similar behaviour. People who indulge homosexual appetites seem to enjoy themselves; so at most one is inclining others to enjoyable practices.

What of the claim that homosexual behaviour runs one down physically, thus as it were reducing one's long-term pleasure in life? Bentham's conclusion is that there is no evidence to this effect. In any case, being in line with medical opinion of the time, and accepting that masturbation is physically debilitating, Bentham pointed out the injustice of trying to eliminate homosexuality through the law, when one did (and obviously could) do nothing about self-abuse. What of the claim that homosexuality is a threat to the keeping of population numbers up to an acceptable level? (Bentham had no doubts that a sizeable population is a good thing.) Again Bentham saw no danger on this score. Men's sexual appetites and capabilities far exceed those of females, particularly in the sense that a man can fertilize many more times than a fertilized female can give birth. Hence, for homosexuality to be a threat to population numbers 'the nature of the human composition must receive a total change' (Bentham 1978: 396). Indeed, suggested Bentham rather tongue in cheek, with more homosexuality we should need fewer (heterosexual) prostitutes. These women, who rarely give birth, would therefore be freed for child-bearing purposes.

What about the idea that homosexuality amongst men deprives women of sex and marriage? Here, Bentham shows that what he is concerned to defend is the right of anyone to have homosexual relations, including those people chiefly of a heterosexual bent.

Were the prevalence of this taste to rise to ever so great a height the most considerable part of the motives to marriage would remain entire. In the first place, the desire of having children, in the next place the desire of forming alliances between families, thirdly the convenience of having a domestic companion whose company will continue to be agreeable throughout life, fourthly the convenience of gratifying the appetite in question at any time when the want occurs and without the expense and trouble of concealing it or the danger of a discovery. (p. 400)

I take it that Bentham's concern with the right of heterosexuals to indulge homosexuality was (in part) a function of the fact that he was dealing with a society much like the Ancient Greeks', where upper-class young men were segregated from members of the opposite sex.

Bentham does incidentally make brief acknowledgement of the fact of lesbianism, but although noting that 'where women contrive to procure themselves the sensation by means of women, the ordinary course of nature is as much departed from as when the like abomination is practised by men with men' (p. 100), he says nothing at all about its moral status. Presumably, he considered lesbian behaviour as no more immoral than male homosexual behaviour. It should be noted that Bentham's failure to discuss lesbianism in detail was not sexist bias. In writing on male homosexuality he was trying to show that it did not merit the very severe legal penalties to which it was then subject. There were no such laws against lesbianism in England at the time that he was writing.

Bentham never published his ideas — perhaps out of prudence. We never therefore got public debate and opposition between the great ethical philosophers. But, with respect to homosexual activity, the difference is about as great as one could get. And this being so, we have reached a good point to stop and take stock.[2]

8.4   Is homosexual behaviour biologically unnatural?

I take it that the switch we have now encountered, from the focus (in previous chapters) on sexual orientation to the present concern with homosexual activity, is understandable and relatively uncontroversial. Homosexual orientation is something thrust upon you. You have no choice or freedom in the matter. Consequently, in this respect you are not a moral agent. Homosexual behaviour, however, is a question of choice. Here you do have the power to make decisions, to act rationally. Here, therefore, it is appropriate to make value judgements.

Turning now to discussion, as a philosopher I shall not presume to judge the purely religious input to the question of the moral status of homosexual behaviour. I shall use my exposition primarily to ferret out religious themes which sneak into ostensibly philosophical theses, and conversely. Indeed, with respect to homosexual activity it seems to me as an outsider that the religious position is thoroughly ambiguous. On the one hand, however much reinterpretation you may do, the Biblical prohibitions really are explicit. On the other hand, does the Christian truly have to take as literal everything in Leviticus or in the epistles of St Paul? You simply cannot make a reasonable decision about the moral status of homosexual activity, without some philosophical input — a conclusion which is supported by the fact that there are as many different stands on the homosexual question as there are religious denominations. (Batchelor 1980 carries an excellent survey of the various (American) church positions on homosexuality.)

We turn to philosophy, and as always we turn back to Plato, for it was he who introduced the argument which has had the greatest influence on western thought about the worth of homosexuality. Plato stated categorically that homosexuality (the behaviour at least) is wrong because it is unnatural — it is not something done by the animals. 'Our citizens should not be inferior to birds and many species of animals . . .' (Plato, *Laws*, 840de, tr. Dover 1978: 166). And this is an argument which repeats itself through history. There are some things which ought not to be done because they go against nature in some way, and homosexual acts must be included. Our bodies are 'designed' for proper functioning, and the genitalia specifically are designed for heterosexual relations, which are themselves the beginning step on the way to reproduction and thence to the creation of new humans. A penis in a vagina is doing what it was intended to do; a penis in an anus is not; and this is all there is to the matter. We learn this fact directly from the non-human world where, uncorrupted by perverted lusts, animals behave in their proper fashion, that is to say where they behave heterosexually. Homosexuality is unnatural, because it goes against our biology. Therefore it is immoral. Christian philosophers like Aquinas (1968) sing the theme; Kant (1963) finds homosexuality worse than suicide because of this; and there are loud echoes of it today. Undoubtedly the average (heterosexual!) woman or man would condemn homosexuality because it 'goes against nature'.

At least, now, we can see fully why so many radical thinkers were so hostile to biology, especially to a biology being applied to the understanding of homosexuality. It is biology which is the strongest plank in the barrier against the permissibility of same-gender sex. But should *we* condemn homosexual behaviour as immoral because it is unnatural, in the sense of being against biology? Should we say that animals do not behave homosexually; therefore humans should not behave homosexually? Is it true that genitals were 'designed' for heterosexual ends and that all other uses are a wicked corruption? We must try to answer these questions for ourselves, and to this end a number of points must be raised.

First, it is simply not true, if by 'unnatural' one means 'not performed by animals' or even 'not commonly performed by animals', that homosexuality is unnatural. We know that in species after species, right through the animal kingdom, students of animal behaviour report unambiguous evidence of homosexual attachments and behaviour — in insects, fish, birds, and lower and higher mammals (reviewed in Weinrich 1982). Of course, you can always maintain that animal homosexual behaviour is not really homosexual behaviour. But granting that talk of animal homosexuality is not a conceptual confusion — and I have said all I have to say on that topic in the context of Dörner's rats — there are the kinds of behaviour and bonds occurring in nature that fully fit the description. There is evidence of anal penetration of one male by another and emission of semen (Denniston 1980), and one cannot go further than that. Whatever the moral implications of homosexuality and naturalness may be, it is false that homosexuality is immoral because it does not exist amongst animals. It has taken people a long time to realize how universal animal homosexual behaviour really is, or perhaps we should say that it has taken a long time for those knowledgeable about animal homosexuality (such as farmers and naturalists) to pass on their knowledge to those interested in the possibility of animal homosexuality (such as philosophers and theologians). But it does exist nevertheless, and we cannot pretend otherwise.

A second point is that, if by 'unnatural' we mean 'going against our biology' — and this is the sense of 'unnatural' we are considering in this section — then if there is any truth at all in the sociobiological hypotheses, much human homosexuality (no doubt like much animal homosexuality) has a solid biological basis. It is something maintained by natural selection. To say, for example, that vaginas were designed for penises and that anuses were not so designed is simply not relevant. If, as a consequence of putting his penis in another man's anus, or allowing his own anus to be so used, a man better replicates his genes than if he were to devote his attention to seeking out vaginas, then biologically speaking this is perfectly proper or natural. Admittedly, anuses are also for defecating; but then, penises are also for urinating. There is a popular joke amongst gay men: 'If God had meant us to be homosexuals, then he would have given us all anuses.'

A third point against the thesis that homosexuality is biologically unnatural is that humans are not mere animals. This remains true even after Darwin. Humans have a social and cultural realm to a degree virtually inconceivable, by comparison with animals (Boyd and Richerson 1985). I see, therefore, no reason why things as important to our social and general life as our sexual emotions and attachments should be judged by animal standards. I do not condemn the male walrus for being polygamous; but neither do I suggest that therefore humans have the universal right to be polygamous (Barash 1977). Why should the male walrus be a standard for me? Or why should the (supposedly) heterosexual birds be a standard?

I think, in fact, that one can take this argument a little further. One sociobiological claim which does seem reasonably uncontentious is that humans, because they need so much parental care, have evolved sexual habits somewhat different from the rest of the animal world. In particular, unlike most mammals the male human must get involved in child rearing (Hrdy 1981). One way in which the female keeps the male in attendance is by being continuously sexually receptive. This means that much human sexual intercourse — the heterosexual variety — does not have the direct biological end of reproduction, in the sense of insemination. Hence, the whole set of arguments that any kind of sex that could not potentially lead to conception is unnatural is simply based on bad biology. Even if humans were physiologically like monkeys or rats in their reproductive mechanisms (and we have seen that in some respects they certainly are not), still at the non-cultural biological level humans differ essentially from monkeys and rats (Meyer-Bahlburg 1984b). What is natural for others is not necessarily natural for us, nor do all human organs have simple, obvious uses.

A fourth and perhaps related point is that, even if it turns out that some kinds of sexual behaviour have nothing to do with straight biology, even if it turns out that the homosexual is doing him/herself a biological disservice and perhaps even his/her race or species a similar disservice, this does not as such imply that anything sexual, including homosexual, is immoral. What moral obligation has the individual got to reproduce (Ruse 1984b)? What moral obligation has the individual got to help his/her species reproduce?[3] It might be argued that any behaviour which is so disruptive of society that society itself fails to reproduce is immoral; but this is a contingent claim and one must justify it (Gray 1978). One has to show first that any such behaviour is in fact so disruptive of society, and secondly either that society's reproduction is a morally good thing, or that the disruption in itself causes so much trouble as to be a bad thing.

But, in reply, first of all it is obvious that homosexual activity today is not so disruptive of society as to prevent overall reproduction. Second, the moral importance of society's reproduction is not that obvious. We may have an obligation to future generations not so to pollute our planet that life for them becomes depressingly difficult, but do we have an obligation to produce future generations? I confess that I see no straightforward reasons to suggest that we do. Of course, if people want society to continue, then that is reason enough, and I think most people do want the human race to continue. But if enough of us felt otherwise, then why should their wish be wrong? (I am not saying that it would be moral to destroy all living people.) Third, even if homosexual activity were reducing population numbers, it would hardly be that disruptive of heterosexuals. No one is arguing that heterosexuals must be castrated, merely that those who do not want to reproduce need not.

The morality of homosexuality, therefore, must be judged on grounds other than those of biological naturalness. If what is natural is judged by what occurs in the animal world, then homosexuality is not unnatural. If what is natural is what it is biologically advantageous to do, then homosexuality is not obviously unnatural. And even if one agreed that naturalness for humans could be defined in terms of biological advantage, and even if one also agreed (which I do not) that homosexuality is unnatural, then it still would not necessarily be immoral. Its wrongness would have to be judged on other grounds. I am not denying that there is any concept of naturalness which is appropriate for humans; nor am I denying that violations of this concept might be, or be considered, bad things. When you have an argument with the ongoing appeal that the one we are now considering obviously has, it would be rash to pretend that there is nothing to it. Indeed, I shall be suggesting shortly that there may well be something to a notion of naturalness which is connected to value — although where this will leave homosexual behaviour is another matter. What I am saying is that one cannot tease out the moral status of human homosexual behaviour on grounds of *biological* naturalness. (This whole argument about biological unnaturalness strikes me as being a conceptual sibling of many of the arguments for evolutionary ethics; and with about as much validity. See Flew 1967; Ruse 1986.)

Obviously, one might try to resurrect the argument by appealing to additional premises. One possible way in which one could keep defending the thesis that homosexuality is immoral because it is biologically unnatural is along the lines suggested by Aquinas, where that which is biologically natural is seen as the rationale of boundaries that God wants us to respect. But apart from the fact that we still have the problem of explicating what is biologically natural for humans, we have also got to prove that it is God's will that we stay within bounds. Of course, Aquinas thinks he can do this and sets about the task with much subtlety and brilliance. But here, clearly, we move again from the philosophical to the theological. I can respect the Catholic doctrine of natural law, but it is not my job to believe it, defend it, or attack it. The fact remains that, on its own, the argument that homosexuality is biologically unnatural and hence immoral, fails. And with it goes much of the mainstay of the traditional critique of homosexual activity.

8.5   Homosexuality and the modern philosophers

We come to the present. Some radical thinkers would have us jettison all established moral principles, relying merely on intuitions and feelings. Thus, Jeffrey Weeks writes:

If we endorse the radical approach that no erotic act has any intrinsic meaning this suggests that, though they may not be the conclusive factors, subjective feelings, intentions and meanings are vital elements in deciding on the merits of an activity. The decisive factor is an awareness of context, of the situation in which choices are made. (Weeks 1985: 219)

But this leaves you quite powerless. Both Adolf Hitler and Mother Teresa were aware in their different ways; yet we must evaluate their actions differently. Throwing out moral principles sacrifices integrity on the altar of subjectivity.

We would do better to stay with the great ethical theories of the modern era, Kantianism and utilitarianism. We have seen how Kant and the major utilitarian thinker Jeremy Bentham reached almost diametrically opposed positions on the morality of homosexual behaviour. Given that both thinkers explicitly and (I think) genuinely referred to their ethical foundations to justify their conclusions, one may conclude that this is all there is to the matter. I am not sure, however, that this is quite so. I suspect that the Kantian position is, if anything, somewhat more conservative than the utilitarian position, or at least some versions of the position, but I remain unconvinced that (as moral philosophies) they lead to totally different conclusions on the question of homosexual behaviour. On neither scheme will the Greek admiration for personal restraint be entirely lost.

Speaking of sexuality generally, Kant (1963) argued that the danger in any erotic encounter lies in the using of one's partner simply as an end to one's own (orgasmic) ends. Only through marriage can one achieve sex without violation of the categorical imperative. Here, one enters into an agreement to let another have complete rights over oneself, in return for equal rights over that person.

if I yield myself completely to another and obtain the person of the other in return, I win myself back; I have given myself up as the property of another, but in turn I take that other as my property, and so win myself back again in winning the person whose property I have become. (p. 167)

I get myself back as an end and treat my partner as an end in some way, because I have given myself absolutely to another who has given him/herself absolutely to me.

Now, putting matters this way, legal questions about marriage aside, I simply cannot see that a homosexual relationship is any less a potentially full, moral encounter than is a heterosexual relationship. There is no reason why homosexuals should reach out in a loving and giving relationship any less than do heterosexuals. At this level, whatever Kant himself says to the contrary, homosexuality is quite compatible with the categorical imperative — it is a good, even. Kant himself, as we saw, speaks of the self being 'degraded' and of humanity being 'dishonoured', and I am sure that he thought that in homosexual acts people — including oneself — were being used as means rather than ends. Again, he spoke of 'the species not being preserved' and, considering the categorical imperative as a demand that actions be universalizable, no doubt, he thought that if we were all homosexual then humankind would come to a rapid halt. But if you remove the biology-as-unnatural-therefore-immoral element, then nothing remains to Kant's objections. We are no longer degraded by being lower than the animals, and even if we were different — breaking from the 'naturalness' of animals — then so what? Humans uniquely cook their meat. Does this debase us? And, in any case, preservation of the species is not an ultimate, either in biology or morality. Of course, I would like the human species to continue. Kant would like the species to continue. But these desires do not stem from the categorical imperative.

I expect there will be those Kantians who try a different tack, arguing on empirical grounds that full, loving homosexual relationships are impossible. The empirical information of the first chapter, and the causal discussions of the succeeding chapters (especially the critique of the phobic theorists) is my backing against this, and if more is needed, it will be found in the discussion of health and disease in the next chapter.[4] I am not, of course, arguing that homosexuality is a good above heterosexuality, and ought therefore to be practised by heterosexuals. For the sake of argument, at this point, I am prepared even to accept a conservative claim that, perhaps if there are no children, a homosexual relationship will be less fulfilled than a heterosexual relationship. My point simply is that for those whose inclinations tend to homosexuality, and who can and would enter into full relationships that way, it is a good on Kantian grounds. It is certainly morally superior to the alternatives, which are either that homosexuals enter into heterosexual relationships or that they suffer an imposed celibacy. (I shall leave until the final chapter all of the somewhat convoluted arguments about 'setting an example'. Here, I shall assume that two homosexuals, living in a loving relationship, do not cause a collapse in the wellbeing of all of the heterosexuals around them.)

Nevertheless, all of this talk of intense, one-to-one relationships, does rather raise the question of casual sexual encounters. These, heterosexual as well as homosexual, are far more difficult to justify within a Kantian framework (despite what some modern interpreters have implied to the contrary: Elliston 1975). It is true that, however casual an encounter, one can give one's body reciprocally to one's partner; but one is caught in a situation where people are treating each other as objects to such an extent that I doubt that this giving fully compensates. Obviously, this is a matter of degrees: not all casual sex is as impersonal as fellatio with a stranger through a hole in the wall in a public lavatory. But generally speaking, in a transient sexual encounter one seems not to be involved with the other person as a person. If nothing else, the case can surely be made that in casual sex one is sexually desensitizing oneself, so the full-blown sexual relationship — precious precisely because it is unique — is made that much more difficult. Hence, I suspect that the promiscuous lifestyles of so many male homosexuals transgress the categorical imperative. (I will take as given all of the qualifications one must now make in this era of AIDS. Even if 'safe sex' is, or becomes, possible, the Kantian has trouble with promiscuity — although, I confess that the thought of several hundred men, in an abandoned warehouse, clad in nothing but gym-shoes, engaging in group masturbation, strikes me as more ludicrous than positively evil. I assume that if one is knowingly engaging in any sex that might infect others, this is wrong to the Kantian — or to any other moral theorist, for that matter. Whether running a risk for oneself is immoral is a nice point. Kant would have thought it is. Since none of us is Robinson Crusoe, I would myself probably argue likewise, if not for the same reasons.)

Turning to the utilitarian position, Bentham (1978) is surely right in concluding that, judged by the criterion of pleasure, there is nothing immoral in homosexuality per se. If people who indulge in such activities get pleasure from the activities, then so be it. It may be objected that homosexuals on average are less happy than heterosexuals. However, even if this objection were true (and we shall be turning to this matter in the next chapter), it would hardly be all that relevant. The point is whether people of homosexual inclination get more pleasure from homosexual activities than they would from enforced heterosexual activities, and there is no question about the answer to this. They are happier in freely chosen homosexual activity than they would be in compulsory heterosexuality. Nor is it plausible that the discomfort caused to heterosexuals by homosexuals' practices alters the overall calculus of pleasure. Letting homosexuals behave after their inclinations increases the total pleasure. Therefore homosexual activity is not a moral evil. It is a positively good thing, in fact. (As noted above, in the final chapters I shall discuss in detail the whole question of the homosexual and society at large.)

I suspect that the Benthamite version of the greatest happiness principle most probably extends to an endorsement of fairly casual sexual affairs as well as long-term, deep, loving relationships. If people get pleasure from casual sex acts at whatever level, then they are acceptable. 'Push-pin is as good as poetry.' The only qualifications would come from the above mentioned dangers of disease. However, in this context of casual sex one really ought to mention the views of John Stuart Mill (1910) and his distinction between qualities of pleasures. Mill certainly does not want to rule out sex entirely. He himself was for years deeply in love with Harriet Taylor, finally marrying her. But his position, borne out by his own relationship with Mrs Taylor, is that a sexual relationship must be part of an overall relationship: a union demanding intellect and emotions, if it is to achieve true happiness and be morally worthwhile. I see nothing in any of this which would bar a homosexual relationship from reaching just such a desirable state as a heterosexual relationship. However, I really cannot imagine that Mill would rate casual encounters very high on the happiness scale. Quite apart from the pleasure-destroying risks that such encounters carry, he would surely think that the efforts expounded on them could be better employed elsewhere. For Mill, physical pleasures are far outweighed by pleasures which involve the intellect or meaningful interaction between people: 'Human beings have faculties more elevated than the animal appetites, and when once made conscious of them, do not regard anything as happiness which does not include their gratification' (1910: 7). Undoubtedly, this eliminates casual encounters as objects of moral desirability — certainly casual encounters which do not go beyond the level of physical animal sex.

My conclusions, therefore, are that once you strike out fallacious arguments about biological naturalness, and bring forward modern realizations of the possibilities for homosexuals of meaningful relationships, the Kantian and utilitarian positions come very much closer together. Certainly, at a minimum, there is moral worth in the close-coupled relationships of the Second Kinsey study, and probably more. Yet, Benthamite utilitarianism excepted, there simply has to be concern at total sexual promiscuity. To radicals, this may sound like retreat. But moral philosophies, if they are to have any bite, have to draw the line somewhere — and I believe they draw the line here.

I have no wish, myself, to hide behind the great names of the past. I have elsewhere argued for the central worth of both Kantian and (Millian) utilitarian moral philosophies (Ruse 1986). I see no reason now to back off from what I take to be their consequences qua homosexual behaviour. Homosexuality within a loving relationship is a morally good thing. Casual promiscuity threatens us all, heterosexual and homosexual. One qualification must be added, however, It is a great deal easier to avoid wrongdoing, if you are not tempted. Thinking now especially of the average heterosexual male, to sleep with 1003 women would truly demand the charm and dedication of Don Giovanni, not to mention the assistance of Leporello. For the average homosexual male, the opportunities are readily available and the numbers easily passed (qualifications about AIDS, and so forth, taken as read). Also — whether the reasons be biological or cultural — the actual harm done in 1003 homosexual encounters might be much, much less than the harm done in 1003 heterosexual encounters (Symons 1979). I defy anyone to have 1003 heterosexual encounters without an extraordinary amount of cheating and lying — even if you do not end by killing a Commandatore. For these and like reasons, I think the moral philosopher — Kantian or utilitarian — should be very wary of rushing in and, although allowing the ideal of a homosexual relationship, denying the reality as it affects many (if not most) homosexual males. (Since lesbians apparently are far less promiscuous than male homosexuals, these qualifying words hardly apply to them.)

8.6   Sexual perversion

In theory, this should conclude our discussion at this point. Once you have strained out religious elements, once you have dropped outmoded scientific claims, once you have sorted through the proper relationship between 'is' and 'ought', once you have discovered a little bit about what homosexuals are really like rather than what you think they might be like, moral conclusions start to fall fairly readily into place. Yet there is something about homosexual activity — and, indeed, the whole overt homosexual life style — that other people find disturbing and threatening; something which drives people to conclude that, for all of the fancy arguments of the philosophers, homosexual activity is a wrong: a moral evil. (The feeling is particularly strong of males, by males — an asymmetry to which I shall return.)

What is it about homosexuality — what is it about male homosexuality in particular — that brings forth such negative judgements? One thing, above all else, comes across. Listen to the eminent theologian Karl Barth (1980): '[Homosexuality] is the physical, psychological and social sickness, the phenomenon of perversion, decadence and decay, which can emerge when man refuses to admit the validity of the divine command in the sense in which we are now considering it' (p. 49). Forget about the sickness part of the complaint. God does not condemn the diabetic. What troubles Barth and his God — what troubles virtually all of those who hate homosexuality — is that they see it as a *perversion*. It is the epitome of wrongdoing, and therefore must be censored in the strongest possible way.

Obviously, from our perspective, we have seen a paradox. Homosexual behaviour seems not so very morally pernicious; yet, through the notion of perversion, this is precisely how it appears to many people — in our society, at least. How can we resolve it? Fortunately, some help is at hand, for the notion of perversion has been much discussed by analytic philosophers in recent years.[5] Typical in many respects, certainly in that which ties in best with our previous discussion, is an analysis by Sara Ruddick (1975). Trying to capture the concept, she turns to traditional arguments, claiming that what people have been arguing about down through the ages is less a moral question and more one of perversity. She suggests that the natural end of sex is reproduction: that all and only acts which tend to lead to reproduction are natural, and that all unnatural acts are perverted.

The ground for classifying sexual acts as either natural or unnatural is that the former type serve or could serve the evolutionary and biological function of sexuality — namely, reproduction. 'Natural' sexual desire has as its 'object' living persons of the opposite sex, and in particular their postpubertal genitals. The 'aim' of natural sexual desire — that is, the act that 'naturally' completes it — is genital intercourse. Perverse sex acts are deviations . . . (p. 91)

Clearly, on her criterion, Ruddick finds homosexual acts perverse. However, unlike many, Ruddick sees nothing morally inferior about perverted sex acts. Indeed she goes so far as to say that, all other things being equal, 'perverted sex acts are preferable to natural ones if the latter are less pleasurable or less complete' (p. 96).

As Ruddick's proposal stands, it obviously will not do. Apart from the difficulties with the notion of 'biological naturalness', how do you deal with non-obviously sexual perversions? I should say that a man who spreads his sheets with faeces before he hops into bed is perverse. Yet Ruddick's analysis tells us nothing of it. Conversely, are we supposed to believe that such non-reproductive sex as using a condom is perverse? And, in any case, although I agree that homosexuality per se is not immoral, Ruddick — in what one critic has called the 'over-intellectualized-approach' typical of philosophers (Goldman 1977) — surely misses what is most central to the notion of perversion: the very strong emotional reaction that perverse acts raise in us. To most people, to say 'perverted sex acts are preferable to natural ones' is virtually a contradiction in terms. Perversion *is* a value concept. (Weeks 1985 is quite right in connecting judgements of perversion with political commitments — the latter are value notions also.)

So, how does one do better? Naturalness keeps coming up. Perhaps the time has come to make it work for us, rather than against us. And indeed, this is a reasonable move, for people like Ruddick are surely right in thinking naturalness important. The pervert who spreads faeces all over his bedsheets is unnatural. And, because he is unnatural, he is a pervert. Yet a biological definition will not do. Perhaps the time has come to make a break. We are human beings: that means we live in a cultural realm, unlike animals who are fundamentally trapped down at the level of pure biology. What I argue, therefore, is that naturalness ought to be defined in terms of culture and not simple biology. What is unnatural, and what is consequently in some important sense perverse, is what goes against or breaks with our culture. It is what violates the ends or aims that human beings think are important or worth striving for. This may include reproduction, but extends to all the things we hold dear, the things that make us happy and make life worth living generally. And this is why perversity is indeed a value laden term, because a perversion puts itself against human norms and values. (In invoking culture to define perversion, I am with Gray 1978, and Margolis 1975, although I doubt they would agree with all that I would claim.)

We have to go a little bit further than just referring to culture to define perversion, however. Stealing or murder go against western culture's rules, but one would not want to say that the thief qua thief or the murderer qua murderer was a pervert. It is true indeed that some who break society's moral rules are perverts, but I suspect that the breaking of the rules and the perversity are not quite logically identical, even though they may coincide. Reginald Halliday Christie used to get a sexual thrill from murdering women while having intercourse with them (Kennedy 1960). He was a pervert. But his perversity lay not in the murder per se but in his sexual propensities. Conversely, not all perversities violate moral rules, at least not in a straightforward way. A person who eats 10 kg of chocolates per day, and then vomits them up, is close to perversion — even though there may not be much immoral about the action. Had Christie confined his activities to copulating with (suitably hollowed) cabbages, tearing them to shreds at the point of orgasm, he would still have been a pervert, although his actions would not have been immoral.

This is the key to perversions: what I like to call the 'Ugh! factor'. A perversion involves a breaking not of a moral rule, but more of an aesthetic rule. We find perversions disgusting, revolting. But why is this? I would suggest the following reason. A perversion involves going against one of culture's values or ends or things considered desirable, and other members of society cannot understand why one would want to go against the value. People cannot empathize with the pervert or understand why he/she has done what he/she has (Stoller 1975). One may not approve of what the murderer has done, but at least one can understand the action. We have all felt hate for others, even wishing that people were dead. Very few of us have felt the urge to strangle our partner during copulation, or think we or anyone else could enjoy it.

Put matters this way: in the *Republic* (11. 359—60), Plato tells the story of Gyges who found a magic ring which would make him invisible at will. Hence, he had full power to do and get whatever he wanted. Gyges in fact killed the king, and seduced the queen, and set himself up in power. We may not approve: we can understand. Were Gyges to have stolen 10 kg of chocolates per day, or copulated with cabbages, we simply would not have understood. Nor would we have understood had he wanted to strangle the queen during intercourse. (By understand here, I do not mean 'understand causally'; I mean 'feel an empathy with a fellow human being'. Of course, causal understanding may lead to empathy.) My point, therefore, is that a perversion is something which goes against the very things we hold worthwhile: that we could not imagine wanting to do, even if we could.

Note that a perversion does not necessarily involve doing something that one does not want to do. I may not want to become a celibate monk, but such a monk is not therefore a pervert. I can understand a monk's feelings well enough to empathize. I simply cannot so empathize with a child molester. Note also that although a perversion is not immoral because it is a perversion, often its perversity lies in that which makes it immoral. We find it so alien to use a person as Christie used his victims that we think his actions perverse. This explains why many perversions are not merely aesthetically revolting but also morally pernicious.

We have come back to the original Platonic position — but with crucial shifts. Unnaturalness is connected to culture, not biology. (As a Darwinian, though, I would never deny that the former comes from and is moulded by the latter. That is why many perversions do involve biologically unsavoury acts — like eating faeces.) And the values involved are not so much moral as aesthetic. So what about homosexuality? Are homosexual acts perverse acts, and is the inclination to such acts a perverse inclination? Acknowledging that I am trying to offer a descriptive rather than prescriptive analysis, I do not think there is any straightforward answer to these questions. But I look upon this as a strength of my analysis, not a weakness! I think the question of the perversity of homosexuality is to a great extent an empirical matter.

How do people feel about homosexual behaviour? Can they in some sense relate to it, whether or not they want to do it themselves and whether or not they have homosexual inclinations? The answer surely is that some people can — homosexuals themselves and some heterosexuals. Many others, like Karl Barth, cannot — they find it totally alien and disgusting. Hence, I suggest that for some people in our society homosexuality is not a perversion and for some it is. Some other societies have seen homosexuality totally as a perversion. Some other societies have not seen it as a perversion at all (Churchill 1967; Bullough 1976; Blackwood 1985).

What I am arguing, therefore, is that, faced with divided opinion in our society about the perverted nature of homosexuality (inclination and behaviour), neither side is absolutely right and neither side is absolutely wrong. There is a crucial element of subjectivity at work here, as with liking or disliking spinach. Perversion, especially as it applies to homosexuality, is a relative concept. But this does not mean that people's minds on the subject cannot be changed, or that one has no obligation to change people's minds. If one agrees that homosexuality is not immoral, then surely one ought to persuade people not to regard homosexuals and their habits with loathing. Certainly, one ought to persuade people not to confuse their disgust at a perversion with moral indignation. This does not mean that one should try to turn everyone or anyone into a homosexual; but, given that feelings of loathing are hurtful to people in a society, if there is no good reason for the feelings (that is, if they do not reinforce moral norms), then they are simply divisive, and one should try to end them. And not simply for the sake of those despised. Homophobics are not paradigmatically happy people (De Cecco 1984).

8.7 Conclusion

This brings this part of the discussion to an end. If you need further argument to convince you of the truth of what I have been saying, let me remind you of the curious phenomenon of lesbianism and the law. Morally, I defy you to find any difference between a male homosexual act and a lesbian act. Yet western law, as enforcer of morals, has always been more strict against the former than against the latter. It has not been from the reluctance of the (almost invariably) male legislators to judge female morality — the laws against adultery usually fall more heavily on women than on men. The answer lies in the fact that the average male heterosexual can regard lesbianism without strong counter-emotions.

He finds it erotic, even. Thus, he does not stand in danger of confusing disgust at perversion with moral outrage. (See chapter 10.)

For men, it is otherwise. Many people have strongly negative feelings about male homosexuality. What I suggest is that they mistake the nature of their emotions. In their disgust, they make moral judgements whereas (at most) they should admit to aesthetic judgements. This is not to say that people cannot back up their feelings with moral arguments. But if these latter can be dismissed — and I have given my opinion on this — then we should work on our feelings. Not to do so is morally wrong. Indeed, it is important that this chapter end with this point resonating in your mind. Heterosexuals are only too ready to make moral judgements about homosexuals. Unrestrained homophobia is a far worse sin than two or twenty homosexuals grappling together.

9

Homosexuality as Sickness: The Arguments

Thanks to the work of the sexologists, many people no longer look upon homosexual activity as a moral lapse, as a vile sin. It is often thought rather to be the consequence of an unfortunate affliction: homosexual orientation. The homosexual is sick or diseased, no less than is the woman with a broken leg or the man with lungs rotted by TB. For this reason, homosexuals ought to be objects of compassion, not condemnation: although this is not to preclude the fact that, like the man with TB, they might require special treatment.

Undoubtedly this sickness model, if I can so term it, has played a powerful role in the removing of some of the most oppressive laws against homosexuals and their orientation. Nevertheless, as can be imagined, many homosexuals do not view it very favourably. Somewhat naturally, homosexuals do not want to be grouped automatically with people who have measles or various kinds of mental problems like manic depression. Rather, what they argue is that homosexuality is an alternative sexual orientation (leading perhaps to an alternative kind of life style), and that falling under or choosing this alternative has all the moral and health implications of being a woman rather than being a man or of being black rather than being white, namely nil.

We have a problem here, obviously, and it is one which divides the medical profession. The American Psychiatric Association de-listed homosexual orientation as a mental disorder in 1974, by a postal vote of 5854 to 3810 (Bayer 1981). However, in the International Classification of Diseases (9th edition, 1980) homosexuality is still a disease. Unfortunately, this does not seem to be the sort of problem which will simply go away with the discovery or application of a little more science. Although scientific theories and ideas are obviously relevant and important, what is really at stake is more of a philosophical question: under what circumstances and to what degree are we prepared to speak of something as 'diseased'? What do we mean when we speak of someone as being 'healthy' or as being 'sick' or 'ill'? Only when we have got some answers to these questions can we then hope to arrive at answers about the specific case of homosexuality. Fortunately we do not have to attempt our task unaided. In recent years, philosophers and fellow workers have been inquiring deeply into questions about 'health' and 'disease', and we can therefore draw on their findings (Caplan et al. 1981).

9.1   Health and disease: two models

There is a disagreement between those who believe that the notions of health and disease refer simply to natural phenomena, without any presuppositions about values like desirability, and those who believe that health and disease notions are indeed value laden. Let us start by looking at the position of the former set of thinkers and then turn to that of the latter set. For the moment, discussion is restricted entirely to the physical/physiological level. (The discussion centres initially solely on the concepts of 'health' and 'disease'. The concept of 'illness' is derivative from these other concepts. The term 'sickness' is not really analysed by anyone, but I find it convenient to use the term in an informal sense to cover the whole area of ill health.)

The most articulate spokesman for the value free (or non-normative or *naturalist*) position is Christopher Boorse (1975, 1977). 'On our view disease judgments are value-neutral . . . their recognition is a matter of natural science, not evaluative decision' (Boorse 1977: 543). Boorse's analysis is in its central core fairly simple, for essentially he follows a well-established straightforward medical tradition in seeing health and disease as opposite sides of virtually the same coin. Health is the absence of disease. Disease is what one has when one is not healthy. (The use of 'disease' here follows standard medical practice by including all sorts of phenomena which in lay language would not normally be considered diseases, like broken legs, gun-shot wounds, and drowning.) In order to break from the circle of health defined in terms of disease and vice versa, Boorse homes in on the notion of normality. The normal is the natural, that is to say, the healthy. Approvingly, Boorse refers both to ancient and to modern writers who have seized on this idea.

There is a definite standard of normality inherent in the structure and effective functioning of each species or organism . . . Human beings are to be considered normal if they possess the full number of . . . capacities natural to the human race, and if these . . . are so balanced and inter-related that they function together effectively and harmoniously. (Boorse 1977: 554, quoting King 1945: 4941)

In other words, to be healthy is to fit the average or full standards of a functioning member of one's species, in our case of *Homo sapiens*. Functioning here means survival and reproduction: 'A *normal function* of a part or process within members of the reference class is a statistically typical contribution by it to their individual survival and reproduction' (p. 555, his italics). To be diseased is to fall below one's species' standards, and diseases are what brings this about.

But what about values, something of which Boorse's analysis of health and disease apparently says nothing? Surely most people would want to associate health with feeling good, that is to say, with something we desire and hold desirable? Conversely, we associate disease with feeling bad, that is with something we do not desire and do not (certainly ought not) wish on others. To deal with this fact, Boorse introduces a distinction between 'disease' and 'illness'. Normally or often we consider a person with a disease to be ill. A person with the disease cancer is generally considered to be fairly ill, even though the degree of illness would vary with the degree of cancer — a person with an advanced case of lung cancer would be considered far sicker than a person with a minor case of skin cancer. However, we do separate out the two notions of disease and illness. A person with athlete's foot, for instance, would be considered to have a disease, but would not generally be considered ill. Consequently, in Boorse's view, it is the notion of illness alone that can and should bear the value judgements. To say that someone has a disease is simply to describe a state of affairs. To say that someone is ill is to say that they are in a disease state that is not desirable.

Let us turn now to the other major position on the notions of health and disease. Here it is argued that the concept of disease, as well as that of illness, contains within it value notions. The difference between the two lies not in the fact that only the latter has value connotations, but in that only the latter has a directly, apparent, troublesome nature. H. Tristram Engelhardt Jr. writes that:

We identify illnesses by virtue of our experience of them as physically or psychologically disagreeable, distasteful, unpleasant, deforming — by virtue of some form of suffering or pathos due to the malfunctioning of our bodies or our minds. We identify disease states as constellations of observables related through a disease explanation of a state of being ill. (Engelhardt 1976: 259; see also Margolis 1976)

In other words, although the *normative* theorists agree with Boorse that disease involves functioning, or rather malfunctioning, of the body or person, they disagree in how they feel it should be regarded. For them, a disease is a bad thing. It follows therefore that they believe that one ought to eliminate diseases, wherever possible. A disease is something which detracts from the good life, which reduces the functioning of the person in a whole and happy way. It goes without saying that this claim acknowledges that a person may be unhappy and yet functioning in a proper way and thus not sick. A disease/illness goes beyond something simply imposed from outside like war or poverty; it involves a breakdown of the individual in some sense. (See also Merskey 1986.)

We have therefore two positions on disease and illness. The *naturalist* position sees disease as a non-value laden concept, defined in terms of biological goals of survival and reproduction. Illness therefore carries the value notions: it is an illness which makes one unhappy and which one therefore wants to get rid of. The *normativists* argue, to the contrary, that disease is a value concept, being defined in terms of functioning as a human person, which involves reference to the value notion of a good life. Illness is disease of which one is physically aware.

My own sympathies lie with the normativists. After the last chapter, you might perhaps expect this, for the naturalists are akin to those who (supposedly) appeal only to biology, whereas the normativists explicitly bring in feelings and values, including those of our culture, right at the beginning. And there are other problems with the naturalist position (which we shall encounter later). Yet, perhaps even more than in previous chapters, I want to stand back and to try not to let my own opinions intrude very much. I want to let the reader have the opportunity to judge for him/herself, both about the correct analyses of health, disease, and illness, and about the relevance of these analyses to judgements about the status of homosexual orientation and behaviour. Consequently, when I turn to homosexuality, its facts, and its explanatory models, I shall be judging and evaluating with reference both to the naturalist and the normativist positions. I think it can be shown that there are different conclusions to be drawn about the status of homosexuality depending on the position one takes on the naturalist/normativist question. In other words, I would hypothesize that in part the differences over the health/ disease/illness status of homosexuality might be a function of acceptance of different sickness models. Were we simply to work with what I think is right, we would miss the point.

9.2 Are mental disease and illness possible?

So much for health and sickness at the general level. Before turning to homosexuality, there is another matter that must be raised and discussed briefly. Up to this point, the discussion deliberately has been concerned almost exclusively with physiological health, disease, and illness. The focus has been on things which affect the physical body, like syphilis, cancer, castration, and sickle cell anaemia. But when we turn to homosexuality, we enter the mental realm, and (associated with this) the behavioural realm. It is true that our explanatory models for homosexuality posit physical causes — genes, hormones, dominant mothers, and so forth (and this in itself, suggesting no absolute break between the physical and the mental, goes a long way towards supporting the conclusion I am about to endorse) — but the essence of homosexuality, unlike say cancer, is that it exists in the psychic/behavioural realm. Hence, if homosexuality is a disease or illness it must be what is generally called a 'mental disease' or 'mental illness'. But in recent years a number of eloquent thinkers, including psychiatrists (who should know!), have argued that the whole area of mental disease and illness is a chimera: at best a fiction, at worst an immoral hoax. In other words, if we are even to ask whether or not homosexuality is a disease or illness, we must first establish the possibility of mental sickness. (For useful discussions, see Macklin 1972, 1973; Klerman 1977.)

The most forceful proponent of the mental-illness-as-myth thesis has been Thomas S. Szasz (1961, for example). At times Szasz writes as though some sort of logical or conceptual error were involved in speaking of 'mental illness', because it simply does not make sense to classify psychological problems in the categories of disease and illness. Szasz seems to see a rigid distinction between the physical and the mental, and he believes that as a matter of logic only the physical can fall ill or be diseased — these are concepts which can apply only to the physical. Any mental phenomena, which may or may not be accompanied by physical phenomena (although proponents of 'mental illness' think they always are), must be considered in other categories — 'problems in human living', and so forth (Szasz 1961: 115).

Along with this logical point, however, Szasz brings out a pragmatic argument. The concept of mental illness is not only logically absurd, but also leads to an (ultimately) bad course of social action. What happens is that, instead of treating cases of psychosocial, ethical, or legal deviation as events where a person ought to be taught personal responsibility, we attempt to 'cure' the deviants, filling them full of tranquilizers and the like (Szasz 1961: 115). Instead of the honest treatment (and its beneficial effects) owed to full human beings, deviants and transgressors get pity and medical treatment. (Shades of *One Flew Over the Cuckoo's Nest?*)

Even the most liberal of us must feel some empathy with Szasz's outcry. There are few things more irritating than the social worker (professional or amateur) who refuses to treat one's actions at face value, insisting instead on delving into the psychological roots. ('Why are you so tense? What are you hiding?'). However, taken generally, his conclusion is much too strong. One can readily and properly extend the notions of disease and illness to the mental realm, irrespective of whether or not there are corresponding physical factors, causal or otherwise. And the possibility of such extension is unaffected by the fact that such concepts were first formulated in the sphere of the physiological. As Margolis (1980) points out, using an example of the philosopher John Wisdom, everyone knows what Christ (or Jimmy Carter for that matter) meant when he spoke of committing adultery in one's heart. The original, literal meaning has been extended. Similarly in the case of disease and illness: mental illness is an extension on physical illness, but this does not mean that it is therefore logically absurd.

Of course, this in itself does not mean that the extension from physical to mental illness is a useful or very sensible extension. I could extend the term 'adultery' to cover the eating of strawberries, but it would be highly misleading to do so, to say the least. An extension of a term implies that the new area has something in common with the old — something distinctively in common. Although adultery and strawberry eating both involve an enjoyable gratification of the senses, there is really not that much distinctively in common — certainly not enough to exclude other sensual pleasures. The question therefore is whether there are mental phenomena (including behaviour) which get close enough to physiological disease and illness to merit 'disease/illness' labels in their own right.

And the answer is that there clearly are. For instance, under Boorse's naturalist analysis, disease involves failure to function at the survival/ reproduction level, and illness is disease that one does not want. Suppose one has someone with a mental state (some extreme form of schizophrenia) that leads to self mutilation, possibly leading to self castration. This obviously fits the naturalist criterion for a disease, for it clearly runs counter to survival and reproduction (Boorse 1976). Moreover, this condition is surely not anything anyone wants, at least, not in their periods of lucidity. (I presume that when people are in the grip of mental illness, because they might not be able to judge for themselves, one can legitimately appeal to what a disinterested rational observer would want.)

The normativists' definition of 'disease' and 'illness' can likewise be extended to the mental realm. Certainly, mental beliefs or states and corresponding behaviour can lead to a malfunctioning state, in the sense that the person involved can no longer enjoy or experience the worthwhile life — and obviously one can be aware of this fact. Manic depression, for the normativist, is both a disease and an illness. This does not necessarily mean that anyone who is in a different or minority mental state is therefore diseased or ill, or conversely that anyone who is happy with their situation cannot be judged mentally ill. Agreeing with Boorse, we have to invoke the notion of what a rational, fully aware person would want, notwithstanding the recognition that such people may simply want or desire different things.

Enough has now been said at the theoretical level about health, disease, and illness. Let us turn to homosexuality, most specifically homosexual orientation. How are we to relate our theoretical discussion to what is known or suspected about homosexuals, either at the empirical or explanatory level, in order to answer specific questions about health/disease/illness? There are two, not necessarily incompatible, approaches open to us. On the one hand, we might try the empirical or near empirical approach. Our models or analyses of health and ill health — naturalist and normativist — require answers to questions about reproduction, sense of wellbeing, and the like. We can try to answer these questions by asking people, and thus see what sorts of result our models generate. On the other hand, we might try relating our models to the phenomenon of homosexuality indirectly, through the putative explanatory causal hypotheses which were presented in the first chapters of this book. These hypotheses predict or suggest certain claims about the nature of homosexuality (particularly homosexual orientation), and these claims in turn answer questions which are asked by the health/sickness models. I will take the approaches in turn.

9.3 The Second Kinsey study

To follow the empirical approach, judging the health/sickness status of homosexuality in the light of our models, we need specific answers to a number of specific questions. Initially, I shall stay close to work which, as a general policy, treats people's self-reports at face value. In particular, I shall look at results reported by the Second Kinsey study, the Bell and Weinberg (1978) report. Despite all of the qualifications one must make, this is the most comprehensive study we have at the moment. However, we shall find that self-reports do not tell an entirely straightforward story. Following this, therefore, I shall turn to work which attempts,

more obliquely, to assess the mental state of homosexuals as opposed to
heterosexuals, through the use of psychological questionnaires designed
to ferret out particular aspects of people's psyche.

The naturalist model demands answers about survival and reproduction. On the basis of these, one can judge health and disease.
Unfortunately, the Bell and Weinberg report gives no direct information
on either survival or reproduction. In fact, I have been able to find
nothing at all directly on the survival chances of homosexuals as opposed
to heterosexuals. A major problem obviously is that dead people tend
not to answer questionnaires. Clutching at straws, one can say that there
is some evidence that people who never marry tend to live shorter lives
than people who do marry (Michalos 1980—2). Moreover, as ages rise,
the percentage of unmarried people who are homosexual rises (Kinsey et
al. 1948, 1953). Putting these facts together, one might infer that
homosexuals on average live shorter lives than do heterosexuals.
However, there are probably too many unknown factors being dismissed
as irrelevant for one to have much confidence in this conclusion. Perhaps
the unmarried heterosexuals, who probably will not have very adequate
sex lives, are dissatisfied disgruntled people, with very short life spans,
whereas the homosexuals do rather better than average. Truly one
cannot set too much store by the kinds of inference one can draw from
the inadequate data that we possess.

Although there are no direct answers about reproduction, we have
seen that perhaps the Bell and Weinberg report can yield some limited
information on this matter. Summarizing data given before, one can say
that (on the basis of the study) the chances of getting married if one is a
homosexual are very much less than if one is a heterosexual, and even if
one does get married, one tends to have fewer children (See tables 6.1 and
6.2, pp. 143—4.) For instance, around 25 per cent of homosexuals marry, as
opposed to 75 per cent who do not marry. The figures are about reversed
for heterosexuals. And for those homosexuals who do marry, the numbers
of children produced are significantly smaller than those for married
heterosexuals, and the rates of heterosexual intercourse significantly
lower. Therefore, recognizing that there are still gaps which have to be
filled with unproven assumptions — not the least of which centre on the
putative representative nature of the Bell and Weinberg respondents —
the evidence does point towards reduced reproduction as a causal
consequence of homosexual orientation.

In order to apply our models of health and sickness, the second kind of
question we want answered is: how do people feel about themselves?
Generally speaking, is one happy as a homosexual? Would one be
happier were one a heterosexual? The Bell and Weinberg findings give

some pertinent information, although they do not point unambiguously in one direction. Let us take first the question about how homosexuals feel about being homosexual. Are they happy with their orientation? Or would they wish (have they wished) to change? The answers are mixed, although on balance they strongly support the claim that most homosexuals are reasonably satisfied with their sexual orientation. The pertinent figures on sexual-orientation regret are given in table 9.1. Amongst those who did feel a sense of regret, societal rejection was the main cause (about 50 per cent), followed by the inability to have children (about 25 per cent). In their conclusions on these findings, the authors point out that they find far more satisfied homosexuals than do surveys restricted to people in treatment, and they suggest that such surveys suffer from the fallacy of biased statistics. Many homosexuals in treatment are there precisely because they cannot handle their sexual orientation.

Next, let us look at happiness perceptions ('psychological adjustment'). When people were asked how they felt, the Kinsey researchers found that most people were pretty satisfied with their lot, and that there was not indeed a great deal of difference between homosexuals and heterosexuals. The pertinent findings are given in table 9.2. Using their typology (presented by me in chapter 1), one interesting finding was that 'although the Asexuals and the Dysfunctionals were less happy than the heterosexual men, the Close-Coupleds tended to report even more happiness than those in the heterosexual group' (Bell and Weinberg 1978: 199).

One other set of questions asked by the researchers perhaps helps us to edge a little closer to finding out how people really feel about themselves.

TABLE 9.1   *Acceptance of homosexuality*

	WHM % (N=575)	BHM % (N=111)	WHF % (N=229)	BHF % (N=64)	Pilot Study % (N=458)
Amount of regret					
0: None	49	59	64	73	45
1: Very little	24	21	20	17	24
2: Some	21	18	14	9	20
3: A great deal	6	3	2	0	10

WHM: White homosexual males
BHM: Black homosexual males
WHF: White homosexual females
BHF: Black homosexual females
Source: Bell and Weinberg 1978: 337

TABLE 9.2 Responses to the question, 'Taking things altogether, how would you say you are feeling these days? Very happy, pretty happy, not too happy or very unhappy?'

	WHM % (N=575)	BHM % (N=111)	WHTM % (N=284)	BHTM % (N=53)	WHF % (N=229)	BHF %(N=63)	WHTF % (N=101)	BHTF % (N=39)
0: Very unhappy	3	2	1	0	2	3	1	3
1: Not too happy	14	18	11	4	16	22	10	10
2: Pretty happy	55	61	67	53	57	59	57	61
3: Very happy	28	19	20	43	25	16	32	26

Source: Bell and Weinberg 1978: 432

This was to do with suicide — about whether people had actually attempted it or thought seriously about it. The topic of suicide is certainly not a perfect gauge of mental happiness. People who have been suicidal at one point do not always remain so. But information on the subject would seem to tell us something about how people feel about themselves, how stable they are, how they adjust to life, how happy they are, and how content they are with their lot.

The Second Kinsey researchers found sharp differences between homosexuals and heterosexuals, particularly homosexual and heterosexual men. Homosexuals are far more likely than are heterosexuals to have attempted or seriously considered suicide. Summarizing the results from a number of questions, Bell and Weinberg found that about 20 per cent of homosexual males attempt suicide and another 20 per cent think seriously about it. Although the ratios are closer for women, this is at least a three to one imbalance for homosexuals compared with heterosexuals. Not all of the suicide attempts or thoughts are related to homosexuality, but something of the order of a half are. This means about one homosexual in five is troubled by homosexuality to the extent of trying or seriously thinking about suicide. Undoubtedly, much of this is a function of the pressures society brings to bear on homosexuals. Nevertheless, according to the self-reports of the subjects, about half of these would-be suicides are having severe personal internal problems over their homosexuality — these problems are not simply a function of societal disapproval. One interesting fact is that suicide attempts tend to be the province of the young, for both homosexuals and heterosexuals. Whatever inferences one might draw about disease and illness may well be more applicable to younger people than to older people.

So, what conclusions might we want to draw from these various facts and figures? It would be wrong to say that all ʰomosexuals are unhappy, tormented people. Indeed some homosexuals, particularly close coupleds and functionals, are very positive about their homosexuality, apparently being at least as satisfied if not happier than comparable heterosexuals. On the other hand, there are homosexuals who have trouble accepting their sexual orientation, and there are homosexuals (the Second Kinsey study suggests much the same group) who are not very happy. Moreover, many homosexuals have gone through crises of one kind or another which have driven them to serious thoughts of, or even attempts at, suicide. One simply cannot deny this fact, or that we are looking at a minority of the order of 10−20 per cent. Admittedly, this affected minority might reflect a transitory phase of development, say pre-25, which is then followed by a happier maturity.

9.4 Implications of the study

How then do these empirical findings fit in with our models of health, disease, and illness? Taking first the naturalist position promulgated by Boorse, and concentrating on the negative notions (disease and illness), we have seen nothing directly about how homosexuality affects survival prospects. Only if we link attempted suicide with successful suicide can we suggest that homosexuality may in some respects reduce survival chances. However, we have got reasonably strong evidence that being a homosexual reduces reproduction, and this clearly seems to be a function of homosexuality itself, rather than something else. Hence, on one prong of Boorse's criterion, homosexuality must be judged a disease. I realize, incidentally, that the figures show that some homosexuals apparently reproduce very efficiently. My point is that, *on average*, it seems that homosexuality reduces reproductive efficiency. In this sense I claim (in the present context) that it is a disease for all, just as lung cancer is a disease for all, even though some with lung cancer live as long as some without.

Illness is another matter. Some homosexuals, indeed most homosexuals, cannot be judged ill by Boorse's criterion. They are at least as satisfied with their lot, specifically with their sexual orientation, as are heterosexuals. Nevertheless, we have to allow that by the naturalist criterion, a minority of homosexuals are ill, and that this illness must be laid at the feet of their homosexuality. There are, for instance, some who would really like to be heterosexual, to marry, and to have children, and because of their orientation they cannot and this makes them unhappy. These people are ill, as perhaps are others who at various times in their lives are driven to the brink because of their sexual orientation. Certainly people who try to kill themselves because of their homosexuality have a disease which is 'serious enough to be incapacitating' (Boorse 1975: 61).

The normativist conclusion overlaps in part with the naturalist conclusion, but not entirely. Those homosexuals that the naturalist would judge to be *both* diseased and ill (because of their homosexuality) would probably be judged both diseased and ill (because of their homosexuality) by the normativist. Certainly, these are people who are not much enjoying life because of their sexual orientation, and this all seems to fit the normativists' criteria for disease and illness. However, the normativist parts company with the naturalist's claim that, judgements of illness apart, homosexuality generally is a disease. For the naturalist, homosexuality is a disease because it reduces biological fitness. For the normativist, whether loss of biological fitness is a disease is a contingent matter, dependent upon whether such loss makes the loser in any way regretful or unhappy. And apparently, since many homosexuals are happy in their homosexuality, the normativist would have no reason to judge them diseased (or ill).

One can put matters this way. The naturalist would say of the integrated happy homosexual that he/she had a disease but was not thereby ill. (See Boorse 1975.) The normativist would deny both disease and illness. Already, therefore, we start to see confirmation of what is a major theme of this whole discussion of health and sickness in the context of homosexuality, namely that the different conclusions that people draw are in part a direct function of the different models of health/disease/illness that people hold. We are going to get yet more results as the discussion goes on. The reader might care therefore to refer ahead to table 9.4, p. 232, in which I have attempted to draw up a matrix giving all my results, showing at one glance where the various differences lie.

In concluding this section, a number of points of clarification and qualification seem appropriate. First, even if one does judge (some) homosexuals diseased/ill on the basis of the direct empirical data, this does not imply that they are diseased/ill all of their lives. If anything, the data seems to imply that homosexuality-as-disease/illness is more of a young person's problem, perhaps giving the lie to the popular notion about the tragedy of the aging homosexual — a sentiment which Bell and Weinberg (1978) endorse. Whether spontaneously or through human intervention, the possibility that homosexuality-as-disease/illness will vanish is certainly not barred. Second, if one talks in terms of 'cure' at this point, and the argument does seem to imply that such talk is appropriate for some, one should note that such cure does not necessarily entail changing a person's sexual orientation (even if this be at all possible). The way to dissolve homosexuality-as-disease/illness may be to come to accept one's sexual orientation, and to appreciate and cherish it for its own values and virtues.

Third, and finally, related to this last point, total cure might well (undoubtedly would) involve the heterosexual majority as well. If the majority stop thinking of homosexuality as a handicap and as something unpleasant, and if they stop hating homosexuals, then if nothing else we shall get a rise in the self-image of presently troubled homosexuals. This is not to deny that the evidence does seem to be that there is more to the problem than societal attitudes. For instance, some homosexuals dislike their homosexuality because they want to be heterosexual, get married and have children. Admittedly society endorses the having of children, but the happiness of child rearing transcends societal approval.

9.5   Psychological tests

Psychologists have all kinds of questionnaires and tests designed to probe into people's minds, with the aim of discovering how people really feel — their attitudes, their likes and dislikes, their fears, their hopes, and so forth. Using these tests, a great deal of effort has been expended on the homosexual/heterosexual interface. On the one hand, it has been asked whether through the tests one can distinguish between homosexuals and heterosexuals. On the other hand, it has been asked whether the tests show significant differences between the mental characteristics of homosexuals and of heterosexuals. Both of these endeavours seem potentially pertinent to our inquiry. It is true that if one found that one could distinguish sexual orientation on the basis of eye colour, this would imply little about mental health; but more realistically one might find that the distinguishing marks really are informative about states of mind. Conversely: 'If a group cannot be reliably differentiated using these tests, then designating such a group as differentially more disturbed is a dubious enterprise' (Gonsiorek 1977: 17; see also Gonsiorek 1982).

Taking first the question of whether one can distinguish homosexuals from heterosexuals, we find that work has centred on the so-called 'Minnesota Multiphasic Personality Inventory' (MMPI), a test which attempts to assess people's personalities by asking a great number (550) of questions about oneself, to be answered in a true/false manner (Hathaway and McKinley 1942; Dahlstrom and Welsh 1960; Graham 1978). The hope is that in answering so many questions, some of which are fairly direct and some of which are less so, personality patterns will emerge. One therefore goes beyond one simple question with one simple answer — 'I am happy: true or false?' — which can so easily be faked or answered incorrectly. As one answers one question after another, almost despite oneself the truth emerges. 'Sometimes I get so excited I find it hard to sleep'; 'My memory seems to be alright'; 'I do not always tell the truth'; 'At times I am all full of energy'; 'Once in a while I laugh at a dirty joke'; 'I have a good appetite'; and so on 544 more times! There are no 'right' or 'wrong' answers — rather, the test is empirical in that one's responses are judged against replies common to certain groups of definitely known types.

There is a scale on the MMPI designed to pick out male homosexuals (that is, there is a subset of questions which is supposedly answered in a distinctive way by male homosexuals). This scale, the *Mf* scale, and a scale developed later, the *HSX* scale, have been administered to many groups of people with known or suspected orientations, in order to check their validities. (See figure 9.1.) The results have been mixed, to say the least. Burton (1947) used the *Mf* scale to try to distinguish (from a prison population) thirty-four homosexuals, twenty rapists, and eighty-seven non-homosexual non-rapists. He found some differences, but not sufficiently strong or consistent to allow prediction at an individual level. All group means were within normal limits and not that far apart. Panton (1960) felt he could generally distinguish homosexuals from heterosexuals, although not individually, using the *HSX* scale (which he developed). Friberg (1967), on the other hand, could not separate hospitalized patients using the *HSX* scale, although he could separate hospitalized homosexuals from non-hospitalized heterosexuals. Pierce (1973) found differences on the *HSX* scale in incarcerated active homosexuals between those non-homosexually active before imprisonment and those homosexually active before imprisonment. Cubitt and Gendreau (1972) found no significant *HSX* mean differences between homosexuals and heterosexuals in prison, although they felt that the *Mf* scale yielded differences.

And so the story goes on. Some researchers can find some differences on some scale. Others cannot. It is perhaps true to say that looking at all the studies overall, the consensus is that if anything one does get some (repeatable) differences between heterosexuals and homosexuals, on the *Mf* scale at least. But are the MMPI studies of any real value to us? Unfortunately, the answer is probably not. Even if one agreed that the studies do show that one can pick out homosexuals (especially male homosexuals), as in the case of dominant-mother studies, there is a terrible problem of biased statistics. The numbers involved are small, they are drawn from all sorts of atypical groups like prisoners and psychiatric patients, and there is independent evidence that other factors can intrude and distort the findings — for instance, intelligent people score higher on the *Mf* scale than unintelligent people. ('Intelligent' here means people who score high on IQ tests.)

However, from our perspective what really makes the results of the tests of little worth is that the scales are not that informative on how people feel about themselves, as figure 9.1 readily shows. Is one happier if one likes *Alice in Wonderland*, or not? And what about 'I would like to be a journalist'? A positive answer on this scores towards homosexuality. Are journalists an unhappy breed of people? Or what about 'I daydream very little'? If, as anticipated, homosexuals answer negatively, does this mean that they are more or less happy than the rest of us? Admittedly one or two questions bear on state of mind. Homosexuals are supposed to answer 'false' to 'My feelings are not easily hurt.' But generally, one has to conclude that even if the tests worked perfectly, one could not then go

True

I think I would like the work of a librarian.
I used to like drop-the-handkerchief.
I have often wished I were a girl. (Or if you
    are a girl) I have never been sorry that I
    am a girl.
I like poetry.
I would like to be a florist.
I would like to be a nurse.
I like collecting flowers or growing house
    plants.
I like to cook.
I used to keep a diary.
If I were a reporter I would very much like
    to report news of the theater.
I would like to be a journalist.
If I were an artist I would like to draw
    flowers.
I like "Alice in Wonderland" by Lewis Car-
    roll.

False

I like mechanics magazines.
My feelings are not easily hurt.
I do not have a great fear of snakes.
I daydream very little.
I have never had any breaking out on my
    skin that has worried me.
I like science.
I believe there is a Devil and a Hell in after-
    life.
I am entirely self-confident.
There never was a time in my life when I
    liked to play with dolls.

FIGURE 9.1   *Statements taken from the* Mf *scale of the MMPI.*
The first block supposedly tends to evoke a 'True' response from homosexuals, and
the second block a 'False' response. (This is the scale referred to in chapter 2,
designed to detect cross-gender dispositions in adult homosexuals)
(Dahlstrom and Welsh 1960: 65)

on to claim that homosexuals are less happy or satisfied with their lives
than heterosexuals.

Let us move forward to the area of investigation which may seem a
little more hopeful in our quest to assess the happiness of homosexuals
vis à vis heterosexuals. Given people known to be homosexual and
people known to be heterosexual, can personality questionnaires and
other tests find differences between them, or at least find that homosexuals
are very similar to small sub-groups of heterosexuals and not to others?

And do these results, if positive, reflect adversely on the mental states of homosexuals? There are a great many studies of this nature, and I am sure it will come as no surprise to the reader to learn that the results are not entirely consistent. Some researchers have found differences between heterosexuals and homosexuals which do seem to show that homosexuals are less happy and generally stable than heterosexuals; other researchers have found precisely the opposite; and yet others have found no real differences at all.

Most prominently, there are studies using the MMPI. Manosevitz (1971) found differences between male heterosexuals and homosexuals over a number of scales, *F, K, D, Pd, Mf, Pa, Pt, Sc* and *Si*, with the homosexuals scoring higher. (See table 9.3 for interpretation of these symbols.) This seemingly paints a rather gloomy picture of homosexuals, but since the measures for the homosexuals were all within the normal range, Manosevitz felt able to conclude only that homosexuals may be atypical, not that they are downright pathological. Doidge and Holtzman (1960), however, were able to find significantly high scores for and only for predominant homosexuals on *F, Hs, D, Hy, Pd, Mf, Pa, Pt, Sc* and *Si*. They did indeed feel able to conclude that male homosexuals are seriously disturbed, unhappy human beings. But then it turns out that their subjects were an atypical group of air force trainees, so one wonders what that result is worth — especially since other workers administering the MMPI test have found no differences between hetero and homosexuals (Gonsiorek 1977).

Going on beyond the MMPI studies we find that work in the same vein leads to similar conflicting results and is hampered by similar methodological difficulties and flaws. And then, as if all of this were not enough to muddy waters, we have studies by Siegelman (1972a, 1979) suggesting that homosexuals may in some respects be better balanced than heterosexuals. Lesbians were found to be less neurotic and less depressed than heterosexual women; also they were more goal directed and self accepting. Homosexual males turned out to be somewhat more neurotic than heterosexuals, but less depressed. Male homosexuals were more goal directed and self-respecting than male heterosexuals. Furthermore, Siegelman has found independently that his results hold for English homosexuals (male and female) as well as American homosexuals.

I could report on many more studies, but there is little need or point. Those studies which argue for the greatest differences between homosexuals and heterosexuals, particularly with respect to happiness, are those very studies most probably rendered relatively unreliable because of methodological inadequacies (such as Doidge and Holtzman 1960; Cattell and Morony 1962). Perhaps one sees a slight tendency towards

TABLE 9.3   Interpretive inferences for standard MMPI scales

Scale name	Scale abbreviation	Interpretation of high scores	Interpretation of low scores
—	F	May indicate invalid profile; severe pathology; moody; restless; dissatisfied	Socially conforming; free of disabling psychopathology; may be 'faking good'
—	K	May indicate invalid profile; defensive; inhibited; intolerant; lacks insight	May indicate invalid profile; exaggerates problems; self-critical; dissatisfied; conforming; lacks insight; cynical
Hypochondriasis	Hs	Excessive bodily concern; somatic symptoms; narcissistic; pessimistic; demanding; critical; long-standing problems	Free of somatic preoccupation; optimistic; sensitive; insightful
Depression	D	Depressed; pessimistic; irritable; dissatisfied; lacks self-confidence; introverted; overcontrolled	Free of psychological turmoil; optimistic; energetic; competitive; impulsive; undercontrolled; exhibitionistic
Hysteria	Hy	Physical symptoms of functional origin; lacks insight; self-centered; socially involved; demands attention and affection	Constricted; conventional; narrow interests; limited social participation; untrusting; hard to get to know; realistic
Psychopathic deviate	Pd	Asocial or antisocial; rebellious; impulsive; poor judgment; immature; creates good first impression; superficial relationships; aggressive; free of psychological turmoil	Conventional; conforming; accepts authority; low drive level; concerned about status and security; persistent; moralistic
Masculinity-femininity	Mf	Male: aesthetic interests; insecure in masculine role; creative; good judgment; sensitive; passive; dependent; good self-control	Male: overemphasizes strength and physical prowess; adventurous; narrow interests; inflexible; contented; lacks insight
Paranoia	Pa	May exhibit frankly psychotic behaviour; suspicious; sensitive; resentful; projects; rationalizes; moralistic; rigid	May have frankly psychotic symptoms; evasive; defensive; guarded; secretive; withdrawn

Psychasthenia	*Pt*	Anxious; worried; difficulties in concentrating; ruminative; obsessive; compulsive; insecure; lacks self-confidence; organized; persistent; problems in decision making	Free of disabling fears and anxieties; self-confident; responsible; adaptable; values success and status
Schizophrenia	*Sc*	May have thinking disturbance; withdrawn; self-doubts; feels alienated and unaccepted; vague goals	Friendly, sensitive, trustful; avoids deep emotional involvement; conventional; unimaginative
Social introversion	*Si*	Socially introverted; shy; sensitive; overcontrolled; conforming; problems in decision making	Socially extroverted; friendly; active; competitive; impulsive; self-indulgent

Source: Graham 1978: 316–17

neurotic tendencies in homosexuals, but that is about all. And some studies indeed contradict this trend. It really does not seem that one can justifiably conclude that there are great differences in the overall sense of wellbeing of heterosexuals and homosexuals. This is not to say that all homosexuals are well-balanced and happy. The studies surely show that some are not. But on average, compared to heterosexuals, homosexuals do not differ too greatly.

Correlating the empirical conclusions of this section with our models of health/disease/illness, the answers therefore seem not too much different from those derived in the last section. Although some people may be (almost certainly are) unwell because of their homosexual orientation, there are no firm grounds for saying that all homosexuals are unwell — the evidence supports the contrary position. Unfortunately, as always, we must not forget that over all our conclusions hangs the storm cloud of possible biases in sampling. Every one of our researchers had to get his/her subjects from somewhere, and those sources — college campuses, prisons, psychiatrists' couches, homosexual organizations — are simply not always typical of the overall population.

9.6 Psychoanalytic theory

The time has come to swing away from empirical surveys. Can we throw more light on the health/sickness status of homosexuality by going at the problem indirectly, as it were? Do our putative causal explanations of homosexual orientation yield predictions or conclusions germane to our study? Let us begin with psychoanalytic theory, in its various forms and revisions and reactions.

We start with the classical Freudian account of the genesis of homosexual orientation depending (as it does) on our bisexual nature and the various ways in which a heterosexual outcome might not be achieved. Although Freud was without doubt the key influential figure in moving homosexuality from the sphere of morality to that of medicine, perhaps somewhat paradoxically one does sometimes see it argued that orthodox Freudianism does not, and more importantly, cannot see homosexuals as diseased, or as ill, or as any such thing. (That is, it does not and cannot see homosexuals as sick because of their homosexuality per se — they might be sick for other reasons.) Remember that Freud himself at one point said that 'homosexuality cannot be classified as an illness' (Jones 1955: 3, 208). The reason offered is that homosexuals are seen, not as people with things wrong with them as such, but rather as people in a state of arrested development. They are not so much people who are diseased or ill, as people who are immature.

However, immaturity, does not a priori rule out a judgement of disease or illness. In the physiological realm, which is our paradigm for such judgements, we call people diseased or ill because of immaturity in the adult. The girl with Turner's Syndrome, for instance, is considered diseased and ill precisely because her body will not mature sexually without artificial administration of female hormones (Levitan and Montagu 1977). Analogously, there is no reason in principle why, homosexuality being an immaturity, it should not be a mental illness. Hence, the possibility of disease/illness judgements in the Freudian context cannot be ruled out by fiat.

This being so, let us now turn to our sickness models, beginning with Boorse's naturalism. Almost certainly, judging by the Freudian model alone, homosexuality must be seen as a disease when considered in the light of naturalist criteria (Boorse 1976). Strictly speaking, Freudianism seems to say nothing at all about survival; but, whilst it certainly does not prove that homosexuals will have reduced reproduction, it does rather presuppose the fact. The Freudian naturalist would surely judge homosexuality to be a disease. But would it also be an illness? Here the answer is less straightforward. The crux of the matter is whether being a homosexual makes one less happy or more dissatisfied in some respect. If it does, then having concluded already that homosexuality is a disease, one can go on to say that it is also an illness — otherwise not. Plunging straight to a conclusion, let me say that although there is no a priori reason why homosexuality should not be judged an illness, as a matter of contingent fact (in terms of orthodox Freudianism) I rather doubt it is.

To the contrary, in fact. Although a Freudian may see homosexuals as immature in some aspects, the analogy with physiologically immature adults breaks down in crucial respects at this point. The physiologically immature adult will be unhappy (and thus judged ill) simply because he/she cannot achieve any kind of sexuality. The typical girl with Turner's Syndrome would just love to have babies (Money and Ehrhardt 1972). But this sense of futile incompleteness does not necessarily occur at all in the case of homosexuals. The homosexual has adult sexuality — it is simply that it is directed to his/her own sex, rather than to a member of the opposite sex. But in itself, the sexuality might be quite enjoyable and satisfying. The homosexual could be quite satisfied with his/her sexual orientation, even preferring the thought of it to heterosexual orientation. Of course, no one is denying that some people might be unhappy with their particular mix of male and female drives, and thus the Freudian would judge them 'ill'. Nor is it to deny that the process of being made a homosexual — in the case of males with strong mother and cold and distant father — might be unpleasant. Conversely, though, the process might be quite an enjoyable experience — mother's love might compensate for all.

How would the normativist judge the homosexual, when seen through the lens of orthodox Freudianism? The major difference from Boorse is that the normativist would not claim that homosexuality is always a disease. The normativist views disease as involving a failure to achieve a fully functioning, integrated and worthwhile life. If this definition deliberately divorces itself from reproduction for reproduction's sake, and it certainly seems that it does, then there is no necessity always to label the homosexual as diseased. For the normativist, the well-balanced homosexual (which Freudianism seems to allow) can be as healthy as anyone else. And obviously, in his/her case there is no question of illness either, since illness presupposes disease. This is not to deny that some homosexual people will be troubled about their sexuality, and that the normativist, like the naturalist, would in these cases be prepared to use terms like 'disease' and 'illness'.

Going beyond Freud, we come to the adaptationists with their denial of bisexuality. As we know, it is they who have really pushed the sickness/unhappiness theme. For the adaptationist, homosexuality is a function of fears, of dread, and of being unable to respond properly to other human beings. Any supposed happiness is something of an illusion, a surface layer of emotion covering deep and irrational fears. There is bound to be self-delusion and fragility about the most contented of homosexuals. And in the case of pseudo-homosexuality (that notion which the adaptationists invoke to explain homosexual flashes in predominantly heterosexual lives), fear and unhappiness seem almost impossible to avoid. In this case a person who is heterosexual — by definition constantly and overtly so — and who is under stress in the first place suddenly falls victim to homosexual fantasies and dreams and the like. None of this is exactly calculated to make one feel particularly good. Rather, the mood is going to be one of increased fear, insecurity, and self loathing. (See the side comments in Bieber et al. 1962, or any of the papers by Ovesey, for instance 1965.)

In the light of these facts, on both the naturalists' and the normativists' accounts, homosexuality cannot fail to strike loud notes on the disease and the illness scales. For the naturalist, homosexuality will be a disease, for there is nothing in the adaptationist account to suggest that homosexuals will reproduce at the rate of heterosexuals. Indeed, with all the fear supposedly involved, one would definitely expect that homosexuals would *not* reproduce at a heterosexual rate. No man willingly will put his most prized organ in a situation where it is liable to be bitten off, nor will a woman willingly allow herself to be mutilated and ripped by the unfeeling weapon males use to threaten and dominate females. Further, not only will we have reduced reproduction (and thus a disease), the naturalist will have to judge many or all homosexuals to be ill — certainly more than one would expect were the Freudian account true. Every homosexual will be walking under threat of mental disorder, enough probably to attach some sort of 'illness' label.

On the normativist's account homosexuality (given the adaptationist/ phobic model) would often, if not always, be both a disease and an illness. Indeed, in the phobic-adaptationist case, unlike the Freudian case, the normativist might have to judge even apparently happy homosexuals diseased. Margolis states:

A diseased state, on any plausible theory whatsoever, is a morbid or abnormal state of some sort, a state defective or deranged with respect to some condition of healthy functioning *or* suitably related to such a state even if there is no complainant. (1976: 243)

Certainly the phobic-adaptationist seems to make·the assumption that what we would all want to do, if we had free choice, is function heterosexually — this is our basic nature. In this sense, therefore, perhaps we should judge all homosexuals diseased. As far as illness is concerned, homosexuals are certainly going to be aware of their disease (which is the condition for illness), but perhaps they would not always be aware of their disease as a disease or their illness as an illness. They could delude themselves. Fortunately, however, since we are talking of genuine disease and illness — something which transcends societal prejudice — realistic talk of 'cure' is appropriate. And since we are all essentially of one sex or the other, cure for the homosexual means changing to a heterosexual.

Finally, in dealing with the adaptationist theory, we have pseudo-homosexuality. This is (philosophically) interesting. It is certainly not something very pleasant and on the normativist account seems to hold little difficulty. It is both a disease and an illness. On the account of the Boorsian naturalist things are a little less straightforward. One's inclination is to say that it is both disease and illness, but is this so? Given the fact that by definition pseudohomosexuality can occur only against a background of heterosexuality, does the phenomenon really reduce survival and reproduction all that much? I imagine that in a lot of cases the answer is simply that it does not. In which case, one might want to argue that pseudohomosexuality is neither disease nor illness. Perhaps it is more like grief: something rather unpleasant which happens to one at certain times, but not really a disease or illness.

Very briefly, what of other suggestions about environmental causes of homosexual orientation? Where do they direct us over the status of homosexuality? Almost by definition, however you ring the changes, transsexuals will never be particularly healthy — they are bound to be surrounded by problems, at least before their operations. With respect to true homosexuality, some social learning theorists lean towards sickness assessments, whereas others do not. (For instance, West 1967 hints that there is sickness, whereas Churchill 1967 suggests that there is not.) But I am not sure that their theories as such imply very much about homosexuality from a disease/illness perspective, wherever you come down on the naturalist/normativist scale. If anything, probably the presumption is that homosexuals will not necessarily be distressed by their orientation. The whole point of the learning theory approach is that human beings start as blank books waiting to be written in. It is not claimed that one kind of writing is better or happier than any other. And the same probably goes for cognitive development theory — for all that Kohlberg (1966) speaks of 'psychopathology'. Post-Freudians really start to move away from inevitable sickness judgements.

9.7   Hormonal theories of homosexuality

There were two ways in which hormones might be linked with sexual orientation: pre- and postnatally. On the one hand, it might be argued that homosexual orientation is a function of unusual or atypical hormonal levels, particularly sex hormonal levels, either in the developing foetus, or in the environment to which it is exposed. On the other hand, it might be argued that homosexuality is a function of unusual or atypical (sex) hormonal levels in the adult. We need hardly linger over this latter question: atypical adult hormonal levels are so hard to detect — if they exist at all — that there is little reason to think they could make much significant input to the health/sickness discussion. What then of the foetal theory? We know that the main proponent of the thesis that adult sexual orientation is a direct product of sex hormonal levels before birth, the German endocrinologist Gunther Dörner, strongly believes that homosexuality is a disease and that homosexuals are ill. In the context of homosexuality he uses terms like 'pathogenesis' and 'disturbance', and he suggests ways in which he thinks the births of people with homosexual orientations might be avoided. Yet Dörner's opinion is an opinion. I have already had some strong things to say at a general level about (or, rather, against) Dörner's normative views in my earlier discussion of his work. Briefly now, therefore, given our formal analysis of health/disease/ illness, is there reason to think that his scientific views contribute meaningfully to specific judgements about health and sickness?

Turning first to Boorse's naturalist analysis of ill health, we find ourselves at once thrust into paradox. There is nothing in Dörner's work to alter our empirical conclusion that homosexuals would have low reproductive potential (and actuality). In this respect, homosexuality would qualify as a disease. However, there is another key notion within Boorse's concept of a disease, namely survival. He sees a disease as something which endangers '*survival* and reproduction' (Boorse 1977: 555: my italics). But here's the rub: Dörner suggests that, possibly as a result of their unusual prenatal hormonal levels, male homosexuals may well be more long-lived than male heterosexuals (Dörner 1976, chapter 5). Now, assuming that this is true, and in this chapter for the sake of argument we can assume the truth of our explanatory models, this means that in one crucial respect male homosexuals are suffering from no disease. If anything, they are healthier than heterosexuals! Females do not generate this paradox, because Dörner suggests that if anything lesbians have a shorter life span than heterosexuals. Lesbianism, I am afraid, remains a disease.

If nothing else, it seems clear that Boorse must tidy up his position. (One hopes, given evolutionary theory, that he will put reproduction before survival — even though this would put homosexuality back in the disease column.) What now about illness? Fairly obviously, there are no automatic implications at all that homosexuality will have to be judged an illness, or rather — as I pointed out before — there are no such implications when one takes into account Dörner's theorizing. Whether homosexuals are happy or unhappy with their homosexuality, a matter of crucial importance in the assessment of an illness, is not something we can learn directly, as a matter of necessity, from Dörner's work. The only information which is even tangentially relevant is the speculation about possible difference in life spans between hetero and homosexuals. Generally speaking, I think most people want longer rather than shorter lives. Hence, if the speculation were to prove true, it might influence people's feelings about their homosexuality (or heterosexuality for that matter). But there is no saying how much it would influence people, if at all. The immediate consequences of being homo or heterosexual might well far outweigh other matters.

Turning from the naturalist position to that of the normativists on the health/disease/illness question, little more needs to be said, for all of the pertinent points have now been covered. The normativist does not get caught in the tangles Boorse does, because of his gluing together of survival and reproduction, so there are no inherent problems about applying or withholding judgements. For the normativists, to talk of disease and illness we must show that there is something bad or unpleasant happening to a person's body or mind. Now this may or may not be true of someone because of their homosexuality — we have in fact seen empirical evidence to suggest that it does happen to some people sometimes, and does not happen to the same or other people at other times. The point is whether there is anything peculiar to Dörner's theorizing to suggest that the homosexual will have symptoms of disease or illness. And the answer is that, as we have seen, there is nothing with direct implications.

Hence, summing up, I continue to maintain that one must separate out Dörner's value opinions from his theory's implications. Specifically, he certainly does not prove that all homosexuals are going to be depressed and ill. Neither naturalist nor normativist will want to argue this.

9.8   The sociobiological hypotheses

The reader must have anticipated that if there is any truth at all to the sociobiological explanatory hypotheses for homosexual orientation, then questions of disease and illness become very interesting indeed, and the conclusions one should draw might be quite different from anything one could have expected initially. Let us run through the models, seeing what light they throw on the health/disease/illness analyses of the naturalists and the normativists.

First, there is the *balanced superior heterozygote fitness* model (Hutchinson

1959, E. O. Wilson 1975). In this explanation, the homosexual is seen as the biologically unfit homozygote, balanced out (that is, kept in the population) by the biologically superfit heterozygote sibling. The implication (or rather the initial assumption) definitely is that the homosexual him/herself is a less efficient reproducer than the normal (that is, homozygote) heterosexual. No assumptions are made or implications drawn about how long homosexuals will live or about how healthy they will be. It is certainly the case that in the sickle cell anaemia situation, analogous in being also a function of balanced heterozygote fitness, the sickle cell anaemic fails in reproduction because he/she fails in survival. But an individual can be physically healthy and strong and biologically unfit (that is, a poor reproducer) — the mule, for instance.

It is highly probable that, at this point, the naturalist would want to label homosexuality a disease. The homosexual does not reproduce as well as the heterosexual. On the other hand, Boorse's own analysis runs into trouble with balanced heterozygote fitness models (Engelhardt 1976). The homozygote homosexual is just as typical or normal a species member (with respect to reproduction) as are his/her heterosexual siblings, in the sense that they are all part of the 'species design': that is, they are all kept in the population by the forces of natural selection. The homozygote homosexual is not some reproductive freak being eliminated rapidly by the driving force behind evolution. In other words, given the way in which Boorse has defined 'disease', there are no sound grounds for labelling homosexuality (seen as a function of balanced heterozygote fitness) as a disease. And this though one feels sure that Boorse's inclination would be so to label it. (If there is no such inclination, then how does one tackle sickle cell anaemia?)

Of course, even if homosexuality were counted a disease by Boorse, it would not follow that it was also an illness, as he understands the latter concept. As things stand, since homosexuality is not a disease, Boorse cannot count it an illness, but even if he could there is really nothing in the balanced heterozygote fitness model to suggest that he should. There is no implication that homosexuals will not live full and satisfying lives. To get such a negative conclusion one needs some additional assumptions about ability (or inclination) to reproduce being something which leads to happiness, and inability to reproduce being something which leads to unhappiness, and so forth. But these are assumptions, and not to be derived straight from the sociobiological model.

The normativists have less trouble than does Boorse with balanced heterozygote fitness models. In the specific case of homosexuality kept in populations through this mechanism, there is no especial reason to believe that homosexuality is either disease or illness (no especial reason, that is, by virtue of the causal model). Homosexuals may or may not be happy and satisfied with their lot, and their feelings may or may not be intrinsic to themselves; but the fact that they are homosexual because they carry two genes homozygously is not relevant to the normativists' assessment of disease and illness.

The second sociobiological model is the one centring on *kin selection* (Weinrich 1976, 1987; E. O. Wilson 1978). In this case the homosexual is reproducing vicariously, that is, by aiding close relatives in their reproduction. Kin selection does not usually operate, so one expects to find special factors at work making it the most efficient or successful reproductive strategy. Two factors in particular might be expected, either together or apart: first, one might expect some reason why an individual him/herself would not do his/her own reproducing; second, one might expect some reason why an individual him/herself would be rather good at helping relatives to reproduce.

Now, as usual starting with the naturalist's analysis of disease and illness, I think with justifiable reason he/she would seize on the first of these factors possibly causing kin selection. Perhaps nothing very directly is being said about survival, but the implication surely is that the person at the centre of the kin selection is going to be (or has the potential to be) a rather poor direct reproducer, and hence such a person will be diseased at the very least. Indeed, one might rather expect such a person to be ill also, because the sorts of things which might make them potentially a poor reproducer could be very unpleasant — like childhood accidents or diseases such as TB or smallpox. And this expectation is certainly not an unfair extrapolation from the sociobiological position, because its most enthusiastic backer himself suggests that homosexual orientation might be triggered by just such a childhood trauma, or indeed general substandard health when one is young (Weinrich 1976).

But a number of comments are in order. First, the model of kin selection is rather supposed to have been operating at its fullest and most efficient in preliterate societies: that is, societies without the benefits of modern medicine and health care. Hence, homosexuals in our society might be just as healthy as heterosexuals, even though they would not have been so in preliterate societies where their various ailments could not have been completely cured. Second, any disease or illness of the homosexual is not a function of his/her homosexuality as such. Indeed, quite the reverse: the kin selection model supposes that the homosexuality is an adaptive manoeuvre to help a person become a better reproducer than he/she would otherwise be. The homosexuality stops the person vainly or inefficiently following heterosexual pursuits, and thus frees him/her to concentrate on aiding the reproduction of close relatives. In other words, from the sociobiological perspective alone the sexual orientation of the homosexual is not more a disease or illness than is the coagulating of the blood a disease or illness of the person with a cut in the skin. Third, it would not be at all impossible for the kin selection model to apply even though there is nothing physically wrong at all, at any time, with the homosexual. If an individual had qualities which would make him/her a superb relative-helper, say high intelligence, then this itself could trigger homosexuality (perhaps indirectly through the reactions of adults to children with high intelligence). In other words, although the homosexual might have peculiar attributes, these might not at all be things one would look upon as handicaps. With the model working this way, the naturalist could speak neither of illness nor disease — nor, presumably, would he/she want to.

Turning to the normativists' analysis of health/illness/disease, we find that many if not all of the pertinent points have been covered in our discussion of the naturalist's position. It is certainly true that the kin selection model suggests that in the backgrounds of some homosexuals, particularly in their childhoods, may lie some bad diseases and illnesses (in the senses that the normativists would understand them). However, the implications are not that homosexuality per se is either disease or illness, and obviously the kinds of qualifying point discussed in the context of the naturalist hold here also. In particular, in modern society with sophisticated medical techniques and comprehensive health care, it could quite well be that, in all senses of the words, adult homosexuals are as healthy and free from disease as heterosexuals.

Finally, we have *parental manipulation* (Alexander 1974; Trivers 1974). This model causes trouble for Boorse's naturalist analysis similar to problems encountered before. On the one hand, the manipulated child's personal reproduction is depressed and this is not compensated for by kin selection. For this reason, according to Boorse, one ought to be thinking in terms of disease. On the other hand, the mechanism of parental manipulation is preserved in the species by natural selection, so for this reason the homosexuality of the manipulated child is no disease. Who is to say what is 'statistically typical' in a species where parental manipulation is operating? The manipulated child is just as typical as anyone else, in the crucial sense of being a function of natural selection.

If we assume for the naturalist that (viewed in the light of this model) homosexuality is a disease, is it then also an illness? Obviously there is no direct implication that the parentally manipulated homosexual will be unhappy or dissatisfied with his/her lot. I am not sure either that there is any implication that being manipulated would be all that unpleasant. It might perhaps involve a hostile unloving father, but then again relations with parents might be very close as one is directed away from a heterosexual role. However, one point should be noted. In the parental manipulation case, it is not in the child's reproductive interests to be a homosexual. One has parental and child reproductive strategies in conflict. This could mean that at the phenotypic behavioural level there is conflict between parent(s) and child, and possibly the child's sexual orientation ends up somewhere between the extremes of hetero-sexuality and homosexuality. Perhaps some of these middle people belong to that subclass who are torn by their homosexuality, even to the extent that we would classify them as ill.

Essentially, the normativist position is the same as that of the naturalist, although there is not the same conceptual confusion over whether or not we are faced with a disease. And, with this, we can end this review of the sociobiological models.

9.9   The AIDS factor

Not long ago, this chapter could have been finished here. As promised, I offer a matrix (table 9.4) which lays out the various empirical and causal claims about homosexual orientation and inclinations compared against the different models of health/disease/illness. As we now know, the different conclusions drawn by different people depend crucially on their inputs. I have already made clear my own views, preferring a normativist to a naturalist analysis and having little sympathy for the Freudian revisionists. Hence, both empirically and causally I incline away from judgements about the sickness of people with a homosexual orientation. This is not to deny that there are sick homosexuals, and that this sickness can be in part or entirely a function of their orientation. There are such people and it would be wrong to deny their existence. However, they are a minority, their sickness may well be a transient condition, and inasmuch as one can talk of 'cure' in such cases as these, perhaps Freud was right all along. Try to change people's attitudes, both those of homosexuals and those of society at large: the attempt to shift orientation is probably doomed anyway.

Yet there is one piece — a major piece — of unfinished business. What of the AIDS factor? Today, in the west at least, there is a growing number of male homosexuals who are dead or dying from AIDS, and a great many more who are infected. Moreover, the evidence is unambiguous that this is a function of the male gay life style. You get the HTLV-III virus from intimate sexual contact, and that is precisely what male homosexuals have — lots of it. Surely, therefore (so one can imagine the

TABLE 9.4   *Matrix comparing models of disease/illness against putative facts about homosexuality, empirical and causal*

	Naturalism		Normativism	
	Disease	*Illness*	*Disease*	*Illness*
Empirical				
Second Kinsey study	All (homo-sexuals are diseased)	Few	Few	Few
Environmental				
Classical Freudian	All	Few	Few	Few
Phobic: Homosexuality	All	All	All	All
Pseudohomosexuality	None	None	All	All
Transsexual work and theories	All[d]	All	All	All
Social learning theory	All	Few	Few	Few
Cognitive development theory	All	Few	Few	Few
Endocrinal				
Male				
Survival	None	None	Few	Few
Reproduction	All	Few	Few	Few
Female				
Survival	All	Few	Few	Few
Reproduction	All	Few	Few	Few
Sociobiological				
Balanced heterozygote fitness	None (All)[a]	None (Few)[a]	Few	Few
Kin selection	Some→ All[b]	Few →Many[b]	Few →Many	Few →Many
Parental manipulation	None (All)[a]	None (Many?)[c]	Some	Some

a   I suspect that this is the result that the normativist really wants
b   But disease/illness is not the result of homosexuality, which is in fact a 'cure'!
c   Presumably the answer really wanted depends on how happy/unhappy parental manipulation makes you
d   The reference in this line is to transsexuals.

argument going), conclusions must be revised. Unfortunate though it may be to have to say this, in present circumstances a homosexual orientation (in males) is indeed a sickness, and we should redouble efforts to find a cure. And in this context, let us be unambiguous. 'Cure' means change of orientation, or, if need be (through detection and abortion) elimination.

No doubt, many people, especially homosexuals, will now cry that prejudice is again rearing its ugly head. AIDS, they may say, is just a pretext for the resurgence of barely latent homophobia. Is it not enough that a terrible disease strikes down even the most healthy? Leave quasi-medical prejudices firmly in the past — where they belong. I am afraid, however, that while this response is understandable, it is less rational than emotional. AIDS is a terribly serious problem and not to raise such questions as these is irresponsible. Problems do not vanish by ignoring them. For this reason, I shall not remain silent. The way to tackle the issue, I suspect, is in a graduated fashion.

Let us start with the central fact of male homosexual promiscuity. In the last chapter, I discussed the moral aspects of this phenomenon, and suggested that, at least judged by the very greatest ethical systems, it was not obvious that it escapes moral censure. But whether promiscuous sex is a harmless hobby is one thing. That it is soul-destroying to the point of sickness is quite another. And the evidence we have, from such sources as the Second Kinsey survey, is that it is not the latter. The truth indeed seems to be that the promiscuous homosexual can find happiness — not as much as the close coupled homosexual, perhaps, but enough to satisfy any normal mortal. And, this being so, we can surely grant that promiscuity per se is not a disease/illness.

What next of the male homosexual whose promiscuity has led to AIDS? (Consider now those actually with AIDS, but take the point to apply in modified fashion to all those infected.) We are talking now — as we can still just about do — of people who got AIDS *without* knowing that their promiscuity would lead to AIDS. Yet, however obtained, we are obviously dealing with people who are sick. They have a disease. They are ill. This is true by all criteria. (For convenience, I am assuming that AIDS is a disease and not just the effects.) Nevertheless, although the homosexual orientation led to sickness, I am loath to say that the homosexual orientation is itself a sickness. The situation is closely analogous to being a Jew in Nazi Germany. Being Jewish was certainly 'bad for your health', but Jews were hardly uniformly unwell — even though it is interesting, and surely pertinent, how their oppressors so often presented Jews as 'sick' or 'diseased' (as, of course, they did homosexuals). The crucial point surely is that for the Jew/homosexual the threat comes from without, and we can well imagine circumstances — normal circumstances — where the Jew/homosexual functions perfectly, in a quite unexceptional way. Jews and homosexuals are not responsible for their predicament, although it so happens that what they are or have done has led them to their predicament. (Of course, even if this argument had gone through, it would have had no implications about lesbianism, since lesbians tend not to be promiscuous, and have not been struck by AIDS.)

Now, let us press the case to the limit. We have spoken of the homosexual with AIDS. What of the uninfected male homosexual? Given the dangers, now knowing the consequences of promiscuous sex, is he diseased or ill? Paradoxically, given that someone who today has AIDS is not to be labelled 'sick' by virtue of having been promiscuous, there is no straight answer to this question. If such a homosexual simply cuts out promiscuous sex — and, as many have shown, this is not impossible — then obviously there is no question of illness. But what if such a person goes on frequenting the homosexual baths, and the like, searching out casual carnal encounters? The answer depends on the extent to which he is in control of himself. Consider, analogously, smoking. The person who smokes but who could stop is just plain stupid. The person who would love to stop but cannot is an object of pity. He/she is weak-willed and (at least) verging on the point of sickness. (If you do not feel as I do about smoking, substitute alcohol abuse.)

In like fashion, granting what was argued earlier — that free will and self-control are real phenomena — I would argue that the male homosexual who is deliberately promiscuous is not sick. He is unbelievably stupid and (much more so than the smoker) morally irresponsible, given the danger with which he threatens others. But he is not ill. In contrast, the homosexual who wants desperately to stay away from the baths and bars, but who finds himself irresistibly drawn into dangerous forms of transient sex — hating himself and racked with fear — is close to, if not over the edge of, mental illness. Conceptually, the situation seems no different from being an alcoholic (Black 1986). Conceptually, also, the situation in principle for the heterosexual is absolutely no different. The heterosexual who deliberately puts him/herself at risk is either stupid or sick.

Of course, my treatment of this issue does make 'sickness' somewhat of a societal phenomenon, akin to 'perversion'; but (in opting for normativism rather than naturalism) I have implicitly admitted that already. Illness is not an all or nothing phenomenon: the medical anthropologist Stephen Kellert (1976) gives an example of a South American tribe that considers a person ill *unless* they have a certain disfiguring skin condition (dyschromatic spirochetosis). Were there no such thing as AIDS, self-control with respect to promiscuity would have no health connotations. But there is, and it does. (I should qualify this point by recalling that AIDS is not the only sexually transmitted disease.)

What of cure (or 'cure')? This question points us towards the next, final chapter, for (given the dangers of promiscuity) the issues of societal involvement start to arise. Here, let me simply say that, since the problem starts with the will, it probably ends with the will. I am not sanguine about plans to change human nature through surgery or pharmacology or the like. But since we are now moving right from the realm of philosophy to that of medicine, this is a good place for me to pause. Homosexuality and health concepts have had an uneasy relationship for many years now. I am not sure that this relationship is yet resolved.[1]

10

Homosexuals and Society

In the summer of 1986, the Supreme Court of the United States of America refused to overturn a Georgia state law which makes sodomy an offence. In that state, anal intercourse between men is illegal — even if practised by adults, alone, in total privacy, of their own free will. If you are caught, you are liable to a fine and/or imprisonment of up to twenty years. Needless to say, heterosexual intercourse is not thus penalized.

This discrimination sets the scene for the final topic of this book, the remaining major philosophical question about homosexual orientation and activity: what, if anything, should be the attitude and relationship of society as a whole, with its power to pass laws and to inflict punishment, towards those of its members who are sexually active with people of their own biological sex? May society, indeed must society, with all the forces that it has at its disposal, attempt to prevent any kind of homosexual activity and inclination towards such activity? Or is it the case that society may or must tolerate all varieties of sexual behaviour, whether they be hetero- or homosexual? Is it the case that, as a recent Prime Minister of Canada (Pierre Trudeau) is on record as saying: 'The state has no place in the nation's bedroom'? (Trudeau uttered his aphorism in an interview on 22 December 1967, when he was Minister of Justice.)

Our inquiry is philosophical: it is not simply an exercise in legal journalism. We are asking what society *ought* to do about its homosexual minority, and not primarily about what it actually does do. At this point, we have therefore to make an investigation into values; an ethical inquiry, in short. But even though we may (surely will) conclude that our earlier analyses are highly relevant to our present concerns, the study here cannot simply be a rerun of the earlier discussions of homosexuality and its moral status in relation to the individual: the relationship between individuals and their group is not just personal morality writ large. Suppose one thought that masturbation leads to grave personal harm — headaches, sunken chests, clammy hands, and so forth. If one were also a utilitarian, presumably one would think that masturbation is wrong, because the transitory pleasures are far outweighed by the subsequent discomfort. However, as a utilitarian one might feel equally that any attempt to legislate against the practice would be wrong, for the obvious reasons of the difficulty of enforcing such legislation. One would have to increase the police force significantly, to say nothing of the need to build and staff vast new jails to house convicted masturbators! (A similar point can be made if one subscribes to other moral theories.)

It is necessary, therefore, to go back to our various theories of values and see how they propose to handle the peculiar problems posed by the relationship between the individual and the state. We must discover the individual's rights and obligations, and learn the state's powers and limitations. But before we do this, we might turn first to the briefest of reviews of the current legal situation. Although it is not my task to provide a handbook to the actual state of affairs between homosexuals and their societies, the current state of the law will certainly give us some useful ideas about where other people think the lines should be drawn, and this in turn can help to structure our discussion. (In writing the following section I have been much aided by Bailey 1955; Fairburn 1974; Knutson 1980; Crane 1982; Boggan et al. 1983.)

10.1 Homosexuality and the law

To the best of my knowledge, no one has tried directly to legislate on homosexual inclinations, whatever their morality. As in the case of masturbation, the attempt would be impossible. This is not to say that there have been no indirect attempts to influence people's thinking and lusts, for instance through the regulation or outright prohibition of pornography, and through attempts to ban associations where homosexual information might be transmitted and homosexual inclinations encouraged (Solomon 1980). But in a way, these efforts have been tangential to the main focus of concern: homosexual activity. Here, as is so usual in matters of sex, it is important to make a distinction between English-speaking peoples and others. In Western Europe, particularly in those states whose laws were founded on the Code Napoleon, the law tends to tolerance of minority sexual preferences (Grey 1974). In France, Italy, Belgium, and Spain, for instance, homosexual activity between consulting adults in private is legal, or at least, not illegal, and has been for nearly two centuries. Similarly, the countries of Northern Europe, Germany, Holland, Denmark, Scandinavia, take a fairly or extremely liberal attitude towards homosexual activity. Holland, for instance, has long been virtually a mecca for homosexuals (Magee 1978).

In Britain and in countries based on or influenced by British law and customs, particularly in North America, the situation is rather different. Although it is true that things have changed very drastically in the past twenty years or so, there is still much legislation which falls more heavily on homosexuals than heterosexuals, the rights and liberties of homosexuals are not fully protected, and the power of the law is in fact more strictly enforced against those with the minority sexual orientation. At least, to be precise what one should say is that things are more strict against male homosexuals than against male heterosexuals. Lesbianism falls beyond the law's concerns, as it has tended to do elsewhere in the west, except in Austria which has a history of prosecuting female homosexuals (Leiser 1979). At the end of chapter 8, I explained why, in this respect, there are such different attitudes towards the sexes. Like males, however, lesbians tend to get no protection under the law, with respect (say) to employment security.

In the Middle Ages in England, although one authority suggested burying alive as the penalty for sodomy, the same as for those 'who have dealings with Jews or Jewesses' (Bailey 1955: 145), the traditional punishment was burning at the stake. But apparently by the later Middle Ages the penalty was rarely applied, and so, beginning in 1533, the law was reformed (that is, the method of execution was made less cruel) and evidently brought into greater use. Even in 1828 it was reaffirmed that anal intercourse was to be regarded as a capital offence: '9 GEO. IV. c. 31 S 15: . . . That every Person convicted of the abominable Crime of Buggery committed either with Mankind or with any Animal, shall suffer death as a Felon' (quoted by Bailey 1955: 150). It was indeed not until 1861 that the threat of the death penalty was lifted from sodomites, although a maximum of life imprisonment was the replacement (with a minimum of ten years). During this time, however, other forms of homosexual contact like fellatio and mutual masturbation were not subject to penalty. This changed in 1885, thanks to the efforts of one Mr Labouchere MP, who saw to it that all male homosexual activity, in public or in private, was made illegal.

This was the virtually unchanged situation in England and Wales right down through the 1950s. At that time the government decided that perhaps a fresh look was in order. The government of the day therefore set up a royally commissioned group, the Wolfenden Committee, to examine the proper attitude of the state towards its homosexuals (the committee looked also at the question of prostitution). And in 1957 the committee reported back to Parliament, recommending, with only one dissension, that homosexual activity in private between consenting adults should cease to be a matter for legal prohibition and prosecution (Wolfenden 1963: 48).

However, it was to be another ten years before the committee's recommendation was accepted and made law, and this is how things stand today. 'Notwithstanding any statutory or commonlaw provision . . . a homosexual act in private will not be an offence provided the parties consent thereto and have attained the age of 21 years' (Sexual Offences Act 1967; see Fairburn 1974). But note what the law does not do or permit: it is not as liberal towards homosexuals as it is towards heterosexuals. The privacy conditions are more stringent, in law and in fact. Unlike heterosexuals, homosexuals may not have group sex. Heterosexuals can start copulating with impunity at sixteen; homosexuals (in line with the Wolfenden report's suggestions) must wait until twenty-one. Indeed, if a man over twenty-one and a man under twenty-one (but over sixteen) are caught in a homosexual act, the former is liable for five years' and the latter for two years' imprisonment (Grey 1974: 144). And members of the Armed Forces and also sailors in the Merchant Navy are forbidden homosexual activity.

A similar story can be told of Scotland and Northern Ireland and, crossing the Atlantic, of Canada. Section 155 of the Canadian penal code states that: 'Everyone who commits buggery or bestiality is guilty of an indictable offence and is liable to imprisonment for fourteen years.' But then, thanks to legislation passed some years ago, it is allowed that these sections do not apply to acts committed in private between '(a) a husband and his wife, or (b) any two persons, each of whom is twenty-one years or more of age, both of whom consent to the commission of the act'. The burden is on the accused to show that the exception applies to him (J. C. Martin et al. 1974). Again we see a homosexual/heterosexual difference in the law as far as the age of permissible sexual behaviour is concerned. Heterosexuals are allowed to start copulating legally at sixteen, with some few exceptions.

In the US, to complete our brief survey, we find a complex and rapidly changing scene, often with major differences between what is actually legal or illegal, and what the police and other authorities think it their business to enforce, regulate, or prohibit. Although, because of its British origins, the law used to be extremely repressive of homosexuality, today from state to state one finds the widest of variations. In Illinois, for instance, homosexual acts are criminal only where minors or force is involved. Conversely, in Massachusetts one can in theory be jailed for up

to twenty years for homosexual activity, although obviously in practice
the law is widely ignored, both by homosexuals and the authorities. And
other states, particularly those in the South, have very repressive laws,
allowing penalties up to life imprisonment for buggery. In South
Carolina, for instance, the *minimum* penalty for conviction on such a
charge is five years (Boggan et al. 1983).

In other spheres also, in the US, homosexuals face barriers. They are
not permitted to join the Armed Forces, and if discovered when already
enlisted face dismissal with less than honourable discharges. Recent
Defence Department regulations are quite explicit: 'Homosexuality is
incompatible with military service.' Here as so often one must separate
the law and the rules from the reality. Many soldiers, sailors, and airmen
are homosexual — actively so. They do not get caught or prosecuted
because they are discreet or lucky, or because authorities turn a blind
eye. But the rules do exist, and every now and then some unfortunate
gets enmeshed in the net.

Concluding this survey, let me note that some really positive moves
have been made on behalf of homosexual rights. The United States Civil
Service Commission, for instance, has guidelines which forbid discrimin-
ation against homosexuals (United States Civil Service Commission FPM
Letter 731−3, *Federal Personnel Manual System* (3 July 1975); see also
Hedgpath 1980). Also the California Supreme Court has ruled against
employment discrimination by private firms (*Gay Law Students Ass'n* v.
Pacific Telephone and Telegraph, 156 Cal. Rptr. 14 (Calif., 31 May 1979)).
This is particularly significant because other courts often follow the
California lead. And in certain parts of the US, thanks to organization,
homosexuals — like other minority groups before them — have begun to
realize that an effective way to change society in a direction more
favourable to them lies through the ballot box.

Enough has been said at this point for our purposes. Given this quick
review, I suggest that three matters come to the fore. First, we must ask
whether the state may/must allow any homosexual activity at all, even
activity between consenting adults in private. Let us speak of this as
'minimal' homosexuality or homosexual activity. We ask, therefore,
whether minimal homosexual activity ought to be legal, or at least not
illegal. Second, since minimal activity is obviously nowhere like the
legal limit that homosexuals would like or that heterosexuals would like,
or that heterosexuals are legally permitted, we must ask whether a case
can be made for giving and guaranteeing homosexuals all the freedoms
and privileges of heterosexuals. Should homosexuals be allowed to have
group or casual sex if they wish? Should the legal age for homosexual
activity be as low as that for heterosexuals? Should homosexuals be

allowed (guaranteed the right) to join the military or the teaching profession? And so forth. Third, in light of trends today with respect to other minorities or traditionally deprived groups, should the state try to do something positive for homosexuals? For instance, should worthwhile employment opportunities have quotas reserved for homosexuals? Should homosexuals be aided by reverse discrimination, or (to use popular terminology) by 'affirmative action'?

These will be our three structuring questions, which obviously form a kind of progression. In order to answer them, we must turn next to our theories of value to see how in principle they would deal with the relationship between the individual and the state.

10.2   Value theories and the state

In our discussion of the individual morality of the active homosexual, we encountered three different approaches which seem still applicable/applied today. First, we had the Judaeo-Christian tradition. Second, we had Kant's theory, based on his categorical imperative. Third, we had utilitarianism in its different versions, centring on the greatest happiness principle. Because this is a philosophical rather than religious discussion, I was able to give the Judaeo-Christian position short shrift. However, when it comes to society at large, given the influence of religion, such a quick dismissal is not possible. Hence, let us look briefly at each of these approaches, or their modern successors, as they try to tackle individual— state relations. I shall leave evaluative comments to the end of the section, after the approaches have been presented.

I doubt that anyone has wanted (or today would want) to equate moral law exactly with legal law. Nevertheless, in the past many have clearly seen a close connection between sins (violations of moral laws) and crimes (violations of state laws). People have felt that inasmuch as possible the state law ought to uphold the moral law, legislating against sin, and in turn being supported by the moral law. Furthermore, in the west moral law has been seen in turn to be part and parcel of the Christian religion (Bailey 1955). This position (let me call it without prejudice the 'conservative' position) has been very ably defended and elaborated by an English judge, the late Lord (Patrick) Devlin (1959). Let us look briefly at the case he makes. (See also Hart 1963; Dworkin 1977a; Leiser 1979. One hundred years ago Stephen 1874 made much the same case as Devlin.)

Devlin starts with the premise that morality is necessary for society.

Without it, society would collapse. But how is morality to be enforced, and which morality is to be enforced?

A man who concedes that morality is necessary to society must support the use of those instruments without which morality cannot be maintained. The two instruments are those of teaching, which is doctrine, and of enforcement, which is the law. If morals could be taught simply on the basis that they are necessary to society, there would be no social need for religion; it could be left as a purely personal affair. But morality cannot be taught in that way. Loyalty is not taught in that way either. No society has yet solved the problem of how to teach morality without religion. So the law must base itself on Christian morals and to the limit of its ability enforce them, not simply because they are the morals of most of us, nor simply because they are the morals which are taught by the established Church — on these points the law recognizes the right to dissent — but for the compelling reason that without the help of Christian teaching the law will fail. (1959: 24—5)

How does Devlin try to justify himself, given that as he admits we have no reason to think that ours is a particularly Christian society, in the sense that everyone agrees that Christianity is true (although he obviously thinks that most of us accept Christian morals)? There seem to be two thrusts to Devlin's attempt at validating the connection of moral law with state law. On the one hand, Devlin points out that in fact today many of our legal prohibitions do have a moral justification and only a moral justification. Why else is euthanasia (for instance) illegal? Or duelling or sibling incest? On the other hand, Devlin appeals to more general principles. Basically he sees morality as an essential underpinning of society, he believes society to be a good thing, and thus he thinks society has the right to protect itself against those who would break the moral law.

Devlin does not argue for total conformity. He recognizes, as important moral principles, people's right to privacy and 'toleration of the maximum individual freedom that is consistent with the integrity of society' (p. 16). This means that the law need not and may not try to stop and punish every kind of moral transgression. Rather, it must hold itself in check for those practices that 'lie beyond the limits of tolerance' (pp. 16—17). But how is one to judge what is beyond tolerance, particularly in times of changing moral codes and in the absence of a universally accepted Christian religion? Here Devlin shows his background as a working lawyer. He appeals to the decency and sentiments of the average man: the man in the jurybox or 'the man on the Clapham omnibus' (p. 15). What is sufficiently immoral to be legislated against must not simply be that which most people do not like — principles of tolerance allow people to do much that others disapprove of — but rather that which truly brings up a feeling of moral outrage in reasonable people considering the matter dispassionately. What really counts is deep down disgust and moral revulsion. 'Not everything is to be tolerated. No society can do without intolerance, indignation, and disgust; they are the forces behind the moral law . . .' (p. 17).

We turn next to the second position on the individual and the state, that which originates with the ideas of Immanuel Kant. However, I shall not refer directly to the work of the eighteenth-century thinker himself. In recent years, Kant's ideas on the proper relation between the individual and the state have been taken and refurbished in a powerful new way by the American philosopher John Rawls, in his highly acclaimed and influential work, *A Theory of Justice* (1971). In order to enhance the contemporary relevance of my work, it is this neo-Kantian analysis I shall present and use. I do not think the historical purist will lose anything and we shall certainly gain by Rawls's knowledge of our own society. (There has been much written on Rawls. The interested reader might start with Barry 1973, and Wolff 1977.)

In his work, Rawls sets up what might best be described as a hypothetical position about the way a truly good, a truly 'just' state might be founded. According to Rawls, from this 'original position' it follows that justice, the way in which a state or society is to be run and affect its members, must be judged as an attempt to be fair. This means that in setting up the state the members should be directed to act in such a way as to be fair to all, simply because if they are fair then this will rebound as maximum benefit for themselves: a kind of enlightened self-interest. Rawls does not mean to be understood as claiming that the ideal state will necessarily give equal shares to all. Rather the fair state is one where, when the members are drawing up the rules, all should act as though they are in total ignorance about the position they themselves will find themselves in when they enter the state, whether rich or poor, clever or stupid, or whatever. This is to say that the state should be constituted so that no one gets a special advantage from the state, because there is no way of knowing that when one enters the state one will be that specially advantaged person.

In practical terms Rawls thinks that various principles follow from his original position, of which to us the crucial one is a principle about liberty: 'Each person is to have an equal right to the most extensive total system of equal basic liberties compatible with a similar system of liberty for all' (p. 302). This obviously does not mean that everybody has total freedom in every respect. I certainly do not have liberty to murder my neighbour, because clearly such an act causes the most severe curtailment of his/her liberty. The idea is that somehow in itself liberty or freedom is a good thing and we are to try to maximize it for all. Obviously, sometimes different people's wishes or desires come into conflict and we have to compromise or accommodate. What would not be fair, and therefore not just, would be to decide a priori that one person or set of people would be entitled to certain freedoms not open to others. Ceteris paribus, if one American can be allowed to run for president, all should be allowed to.

The basic liberties of citizens are, roughly speaking, political liberty (the right to vote and to be eligible for public office) together with freedom of speech and assembly; liberty of conscience and freedom of thought; freedom of the person along with the right to hold (personal) property; and freedom from arbitrary arrest and seizure as defined by the concept of the rule of law. These liberties are all required to be equal by the first principle, since citizens of a just society are to have the same basic rights. (p. 61)

It is easy to see why Rawls sees his position as a modern-day version of Kantianism. We have the clearest possible statement of a person deserving to be treated as an end and not as a means. The position and rights of the individual, right down to the lowest and poorest in society, is inviolable. One simply cannot let the group, or any of its members, gain at the expense of other members. Sometimes an individual's freedoms must be curtailed; but only because not so to do would seriously infringe on the freedoms of others.

Again, as with Devlin, leaving comment for the moment, I will rush on to present the third and final account of the proper relationship between the individual and the state. This is that due to the utilitarians, those philosophers who make overall pleasure or happiness paramount. Here, as with ethics and the individual, it is probably necessary (and certainly useful) to distinguish between a more classical, Benthamite approach to society and a more subtle (John Stuart) Millian approach.

To the Benthamite, the proper analysis of the relationship between a person and the state comes fairly readily. Liberty or freedom undoubtedly would be something valued as increasing pleasure or happiness; but it would be one of a number of such pleasures or happinesses. I cannot see that liberty would have a particularly exalted status — better perhaps to increase the standard of living than the freedom of the press (Barry 1973; Hart 1973). However, John Stuart Mill takes a somewhat different line, arguing in his famous essay *On Liberty* (first published in 1859; reprinted 1975) that from utilitarian premises one can draw conclusions that are very similar to those of Rawls, at least insofar as the importance and priority of liberty is concerned: 'The only part of the conduct of any one, for which he is amenable to society, is that which concerns others. In the part which merely concerns himself, his independence is, of right, absolute. Over himself, over his own body and mind, the individual is sovereign' (1975: 72—3).

How does Mill argue to this conclusion? Not, he tells us, by assuming that humans have an absolute right to liberty; rather because, although liberty may not apparently always lead to immediate happiness, as a general rule a policy promoting liberty does pay dividends of happiness. Consider eccentricities or deviations of behaviour. Mill argues that different things (that is, different attitudes and behaviours) make different people happy. Therefore, as a rule we ought to accept and tolerate strange attitudes and practices. If we do not, then it is quite possible that that which we ourselves like to do will be limited or banned by others — certainly many practices which we think acceptable and not harmful to others will be proscribed. And the overall result will be a general loss of happiness. Mill certainly does not want to say that any kind of behaviour is acceptable. That which is hurtful to others is barred. But only inasmuch as it is hurtful to others should behaviour be barred. That which concerns us alone is our business, and on utilitarian grounds we should have the liberty to act or refrain as we please. Liberty means precisely letting others do what they want to do because they want to do it, not because we approve.

These, then, are our three working positions: conservative, Kantian, and utilitarian. There are obvious points of overlap and difference. Most obviously, on the question of the importance of liberty, the neo-Kantian Rawls and the utilitarian John Stuart Mill really come down not that far apart, if at all. They both cherish liberty above many things, if not above almost all, even though obviously both recognize that in an individual case liberty may indeed lead to personal unhappiness or misfortune. It is the principle of the thing which counts. Here, we have a contrast between a Rawls/Mill approach to liberty and a more straightforward utilitarianism, which rates liberty of no more worth than anything else, and which might certainly think the calculus of pleasures tips in other directions. Also, for somewhat different reasons, we have a contrast with Devlin's conservative position. For Mill (and I think for Rawls also) there is a vital division between a public morality and a private morality. What a person does in private, insofar as it harms no one else, is his/her own affair — absolutely. Devlin categorically denies this distinction and consequent restriction of law.

You may argue that if a man's sins affect only himself it cannot be the concern of society. If he chooses to get drunk every night in the privacy of his own home, is any one except himself the worse for it? But suppose a quarter or a half of the population got drunk every night, what sort of society would it be? . . . I do not think one can talk sensibly of a public and private morality any more than one can of a public and private highway. Morality is a sphere in which there is a public interest and a private interest, often in conflict, and the problem is to reconcile the two. (1959: 14–16)

As has been true throughout this book, my concern is as much with giving you, the reader, the tools to make your own evaluations as with giving my own opinions. In the discussion which follows I shall use all three approaches — conservative, neo-Kantian, utilitarian — as background against which to draw conclusions. But you do know already that I sympathize with a philosophy drawing from (as I believe one can) the overlap between Kantianism and utilitarianism. And here, accordingly, I would endorse the public morality/private morality dichotomy. Yet I would not have you reject a position like Devlin's absolutely and uncritically. Apart from the fact that his arguments are stated elegantly and forcefully, he certainly captures a spirit many would endorse. Whatever the morality of a situation may be, Devlin's lawyer's criteria can tell us about the point at which we might reasonably hope to get laws changed — or be cross if they are not changed.

Enough of general theory. Let us see what light the various approaches to the proper relationship between the individual and the state throw on our three questions about homosexual rights.

10.3   Should homosexual behaviour be illegal?

My first question is the basic and minimal one: should homosexual activity, male or female, be totally banned by the state, or should the state permit private homosexual behaviour between consenting adults?

Beginning with the conservative position, historically we find that those who have wanted to bring together morals and the law have argued that homosexual activity of all kinds ought to be prohibited, precisely because it goes against Judaeo-Christian teachings. And obviously they have been successful in their endeavours. Indeed, the very terms used for anal intercourse show their origins in a philosophy which intertwines law and Judaeo-Christian morality. 'Sodomy' obviously comes from the name of the doomed city of the plain, and 'buggery' is a corruption of 'bougrerie', named after so-called 'Bulgarian' heretics who were guilty of a form of Manichean heresy, Albigensianism. They believed that physical things are evil, and thus refused to propagate the species, turning therefore to other sexual outlets. Hence banning buggery struck a twofold blow for morality: against unnatural vice and against heretical religion.

Coming up to the present, where would or should the conservative stand on minimal homosexual behaviour? If one thinks that Christian moral teaching should still be the basis of the law, and many people do still think this, then a case can be made for saying that all such behaviour should be illegal. Obviously, however, one's case would be predicated on one's interpretation of scripture. But what if one takes a stance like Devlin, arguing that the law must be backed by and reflect morality, even though Christian beliefs are not necessarily universally held, and thus cannot simply be appealed to as an absolute standard? In fact, Devlin's own thinking on the particular subject of homosexuality shows that matters are more complex than one might think at first sight, because he does not want to legislate against behaviour simply because (by Christian standards) it is immoral. Potentially illegal acts must raise 'intolerance, indignation, and disgust'. But, also, there is the possibility of change of mind.

Thus judged, Devlin himself felt able to co-sign a letter to *The Times*, on 11 May 1965, calling for the removal of legal barriers against minimal homosexual activity. Moral opinion (in Britain) had shifted to the point where there was real diversity. Certainly, people had started to grasp fully the futility of trying to legislate effectively against something which involves so many people and is a victimless crime — where there is no automatic appeal to the authorities. People could see that anti-homosexual laws must either be ignored or applied selectively and inefficiently — overusing police resources and generally downgrading the power of the law. If nothing else, the point had been reached where it would not be obvious to the average juryman that homosexuals should be punished by the law. Hence, on Devlin's own terms, the law should be dropped. Minimal homosexual behaviour ought to be allowed in Britain — as indeed it is now. And similarly it should be permitted for Canada and much of the US.

Nevertheless, we really ought to acknowledge a subjectivity or relativity in Devlin's approach — which, of course, is precisely what one would expect from someone who mixes disgust with morality (a point at which, given my earlier discussion of perversion, I myself would fault Devlin). Without the absolute standards of Christianity, we are thrown on public opinion in some crucial sense. Public opinion changes from time to time, and varies from place to place. We can still find societies, even today, even in the west, where the average man would find homosexual activity beyond toleration. Perhaps some of the southern states of the US are cases in point. Their laws are certainly still set solidly against any kind of homosexual activity. On Devlin's position, I doubt that legal prohibitions in those places should be changed. Presumably the prohibitions should apply only to males, since most people do not find lesbianism that disgusting. And of course, one is not barred from trying to change public opinion, nor need one fail to play on the contempt that all people feel towards the blackmailer who leeches on the homosexual forced to be secretive. But today I am sure many people in these places find even minimal behaviour intolerable — and that is enough for Devlin.

Going on now to the neo-Kantian, considering merely minimal homosexual activity, the conclusion seems obvious. 'Each person is to have an equal right to the most extensive total system of equal basic liberties compatible with a similar system of liberty for all' (Rawls 1971: 302). In this day and age, freedom to copulate with whomsoever you like is surely a 'basic freedom'. A conclusion that Rawls himself endorses, for, although he does not have an explicit discussion of sexual freedom, he remarks tangentially that the principles of justice do require the state to tolerate sexual relationships which some find 'degrading and shameful' (p. 331).

Yet let us not be overly confident. Can one bring a counter-argument, based on Rawlsian premises? The principle of liberty does not give one unrestricted liberty. It has to be compatible with a similar system of liberty for all. Rape, for example, would be ruled out because one's freedom to have intercourse with whomsoever one pleases conflicts with others' freedom not to have intercourse with whomsoever one does not please. Cannot an argument against minimal activity along these lines be created within the Rawlsian framework? Surely, there is some human activity which is so revolting that it has an inhibitory effect on the rest of us, or at least some of us? To take a personal example, I find some people's table manners — or rather lack of them — so disgusting that my stomach is turned, and I have difficulty eating alongside them. Certainly my pleasure in my food is destroyed absolutely. It would seem, therefore, that their liberty to eat is infringing on my liberty to eat (or rather, their liberty to eat in the way that they do is infringing on my liberty). Analogously, one might argue that the liberty of homosexuals could infringe on the liberty of heterosexuals or at least some heterosexuals. My enjoyment of sex might be destroyed, or at least severely lessened, by thoughts of what I might see as the homosexual's perverted travesty of sex.

The crucial question is whether the analogy between disgust at eating habits and disgust at homosexual activity really holds. I doubt it does. It might well be the case that many heterosexuals would be inhibited were homosexual activity going on in a bed next to them. Frankly, many heterosexuals would be inhibited were heterosexual activity going on in a bed next to them. The relevant point is that in the eating case I can and do put distance and barriers between myself and people with disgusting table manners, and that as a normal, healthy person I do not dwell obsessively on such people's habits as I eat and relish my own food. Thus, although such people can upset me to the point of inhibition, only very rarely do they in fact so upset me. Analogously, even though the sight and thought of homosexual activity might upset to the point of inhibition, there is absolutely no reason to think that minimal homosexual activity (that is, homosexual activity between consenting adults, in private, unadvertised) need or will in fact ever do so. Furthermore, it is surely possible to modify people's eating habits, so that however inhibitory they may presently be there is no question of having to stop these people from eating altogether for the sake of others. Homosexuality, however, seems distinctly resistant to change, so it would seem that the sex lives of some would have to be stopped entirely for the sake of others; or at least, the only kinds of sex lives that some find at all enjoyable would have to be stopped.

The neo-Kantian permits minimal homosexual activity. What of the utilitarian? First, there is the straightforward variety, the kind that someone like Bentham might endorse. There is no doubt that if people with a homosexual orientation are allowed to have homosexual encounters, without fear of persecution by the law or from blackmailers, they are going to be a lot happier than otherwise. This is not to say that practising homosexuals will be happier than or even necessarily as happy as practising heterosexuals; but they will undoubtedly be a lot happier than compulsorily non-practising homosexuals, or homosexuals practising by stealth despite the threat of the law (Bentham 1978). Of course, the utilitarian has to take into account the unhappiness that homosexual activity (by homosexuals) causes in many heterosexuals. However, despite this, for a number of reasons it does not seem that the utilitarian would in fact want to bar minimal homosexual activity.

First, it just does not seem that the unhappiness of heterosexuals about homosexuality in any way compares to the unhappiness of homosexuals being prevented from or being threatened about their sexual activity. The agonies of the persecuted or blackmailed homosexual require very much heterosexual pain to outbalance them. Second, I doubt that absolute laws against homosexuality are really going to do all that much good, in the sense of reducing heterosexuals' unhappiness. Experience shows that laws against homosexuality certainly do not wipe it out — they do not even wipe out most of it, even though it is forced to go underground. Hence, homophobic heterosexuals are still going to be unhappy. And in the meantime we are all — homo and heterosexual — going to have to tolerate a certain degree of unpleasantness as our personal lives are examined and checked by the keepers of the law. The thought that every time one uses a public lavatory one may be on the television screen at the local police station is not particularly edifying. Third, to a utilitarian the kind of punishment or treatment one could mete out to a convicted homosexual seems particularly inept. By all accounts, forcible medical treatment is worse than useless, and sending a homosexual to prison is akin to sending a drunkard to a brewery. Moreover, for males in prison, homosexual rape is an ever-present threat, and rape is rape whatever one's gender or sexual orientation.

On balance, therefore, the Benthamite agrees with Bentham. Minimal behaviour should be tolerated. Second, we have the more subtle version of utilitarianism. With both the Rawlsian and the classical utilitarian agreeing that minimal homosexual activity ought to be tolerated by the state, one would not expect that Mill's position would point to a very different conclusion: 'the sole end for which mankind are warranted, individually or collectively, in interfering with the liberty of action of any of their number, is self-protection . . . His own good, either physical or moral, is not a sufficient warrant' (Mill 1975: 72−3). Although Mill tempers his examples to his Victorian audience, it is hard to imagine that he would not advocate tolerance of minimal homosexuality. Certainly, if one ought to tolerate pork-eaters in a Muslim society − to use an example of Mill himself − we ought to tolerate homosexual activity between consenting adults.

Concluding this discussion, therefore, virtually everything points to the tolerance of minimal homosexual activity − a tolerance which should be acknowledged by law. This is not to say that one likes homosexual activity, or thinks it moral. It is to say that the state ought not take it upon itself to ban it. The primary dissensions from this conclusion would come from those who denounce homosexual activity in the name of morality, a morality which is presumably backed by religion, and which (because it is moral/religious) they think should be the law of the land. Not sharing such a moral/religious perspective, the philosopher can only ask that reasons be given why theologically derived dictates should be imposed on us all. And, as soon as an argument like Devlin's is produced, the place for tolerance is again opened. It is true that were a Devlin supporter put in complete control of a society which does not want to allow even minimal homosexual activity, he/she might hesitate before changing the laws. But the place for moral suasion is open, and in real life in such societies that is probably the best one can hope for anyway.

10.4   The matter of privacy

Let us move to more thorny and contentious issues. Suppose that we grant tolerance of minimal homosexual activity: at once our second question becomes pressing. Can a case be made for giving homosexuals full, equal rights with heterosexuals? Our brief survey of actual restrictions and rights of homosexuals highlighted three specific points of concern. First, the tendency seems to be towards a more restrictive notion of privacy for homosexuals than for heterosexuals. Can one justify this? Second, the legal age of consent has almost always been fixed at a higher level for homosexuals than for heterosexuals, even when minimal homosexual activity is permitted. Is this right or fair or just? Third, homosexuals frequently face dismissal, if their orientation is uncovered — in the civil service, in the military, as teachers, and so forth. Is this not a discrimination which should be ended? We can take these points in turn.

First, what of the public/private issue? For instance, should there be a restriction on the permissible number present during acts of homosexual intercourse? As we have seen by way of example, in Britain and in Canada no other people may be present during anal intercourse. This restriction applies, of course, if a group of people want to stand around and watch a man and a woman have anal intercourse; but I assume that in fact the law strikes more severely at homosexuals, particularly male homosexuals. Some gays, as part of their usual sex lives, like to engage in group activity — in private homes, in baths, and the like. Group heterosexual activity (involving penile—vaginal intercourse) is not similarly illegal, and even if it were it would not in fact be a restriction of the degree laid on male homosexuals, simply because fewer heterosexuals practise group sex. Moreover, supposing male homosexuals do not much care for group sex, they frequently enjoy casual sex — which involves meetings at places like gay baths or public lavatories (Bell and Weinberg 1978; Humphreys 1970). Even if consequent behaviour is kept from public eye, in law such behaviour is public. And homosexuals are thus open to harassment — which occurs. Hence, given the laws, we have discrimination de facto, if not de jure. Is this not unjust?

A Judaeo-Christian conservative would deny group or causal sex a place within the bounds of the law. Even if one allowed minimal homosexual activity, group or casual sex (heterosexual or homosexual) seems immoral by Jewish or Christian standards, and therefore ought to be barred by law. One might agree that a law against group or casual sex in private homes would be unenforceable, but one would surely try to stamp out more public meeting places, like steam baths. I simply do not know where a Devlin-like conservative would stand on the matter. It seems to me a matter decidable only by empirical investigation. My suspicion is that the average man would certainly find most group or casual homosexual activity (amongst males) really rather disgusting. Whether this would go beyond the limits of tolerance is a matter of debate. Perhaps again a line would be drawn between group or casual sex in private homes (allowed) and such sex on commercial premises (forbidden). I should think also that there would be an element of relativity from place to place. A homosexual steam bath that would go unnoticed in San Francisco would attract much hostile attention in other parts of North America — like Toronto, a city with a large homosexual population but still only emerging from a very repressive Protestant atmosphere. Devlin's position, however, does not bar someone from campaigning for change. His point is that it would be wrong to change laws until public opinion no longer looks upon the proposed liberties with absolute revulsion.

Turning to Rawls' position on this matter of privacy, matters are more clear cut. One ought to drop all privacy requirements that do not apply equally to heterosexuals. There are no overwhelming factors which would lead one to separate homosexuality and heterosexuality in the eyes of the law in this respect. No one is telling heterosexuals how to run or not run their sex lives. Homosexuals practising group sex certainly do not affect the liberty of people whose orientation is towards members of the opposite sex. Nor, analogously, does a homosexual's going down to a baths with the intention of having sex with strangers affect a heterosexual's liberty, even though these baths may in the eyes of the law not be 'private'. Of course, this is not to say that homosexuals should be allowed to have sex when, where, and how they like, without restriction. I would think it an infringement on the liberty of heterosexuals if they were unable to use a public lavatory without being surrounded by open scenes of fellatio. Nor should it mean that homosexual baths should be permitted in any and every residential neighbourhood — any more than super-markets should! But, if consistent with restrictions which apply to all, homo or heterosexual, it is hard to see how group or casual activity can fairly be barred.

Similar conclusions to that of the Rawlsian hold both for a traditional utilitarian position and for a position akin to that proposed by Mill in his *On Liberty*. Maximizing happiness points toward giving homosexuals the freedom of heterosexuals, and the same is true of Mill's principle of liberty. Even if it were the case that group and casual sex destroyed people's sensitivity in some way, the choice must be theirs. A person 'cannot rightfully be compelled to do or forbear because it will be better for him to do so, because it will make him happier, because, in the opinions of others, to do so would be wise, or even right' (Mill 1975: 73). And indeed, it is not difficult to think of happier situations than what we have now, where so much is at the whim of police forces and courts; where so much homosexual activity goes on in semi-legal or illegal circumstances, and hence where there are all the attendant ills like fear of exposure and blackmail (Crane 1982).

Summing up, our more philosophical approaches point towards a more generous interpretation of 'privacy' for homosexual conduct, whereas our more conservative approaches rather point in the opposite direction. But even in the latter cases — at least, so long as you do not take an absolutist stance on Biblical grounds — there is a place for argument and persuasion, trying to turn others to your own position. However, having said this, we should remember that argument can go both ways. There is no inevitability in a trend towards greater homosexual freedom. Moral conclusions, like those of the Kantian or the utilitarian, depend not only on moral principles but also on beliefs about matters of fact. And as the moral conclusions go, so also might go the opinion of the man on the street.

I hint, of course, at the threat of AIDS — intertwined, as it so very much is, with the anonymous casual sex of the male homosexual sub-culture (Black 1986). Given that the spread of this disease is tightly linked with the 'public' sex of the male homosexual, is this not in itself a definitive argument against changes in the law? Today, it may be said, our obligation is to make the de jure become the de facto. Neither Rawlsian nor utilitarian can allow any facility or practice which threatens the very lives of so many people, and it goes without saying that the conservative's intolerance level goes shooting right up.

I can offer no definitive — certainly, no easy — answer to this objection. Apart from anything else, I doubt the Kantian or the utilitarian is obligated simply to pay indefinitely the health care costs resulting from the freedom of the promiscuous homosexual. Nor, given the arguments of the last chapter, am I so sure that we are dealing with fully rational beings. Certainly, AIDS raises the paradox of having the liberty to end liberty (through death). One point, nevertheless, does seem relevant. AIDS, or rather the virus which causes it, is not something which spreads and infects quite at random. You fall ill only after you have (almost invariably) voluntarily performed various sex acts, like anal intercourse. (I exclude infection through polluted blood and the like.) In other words, a group of homosexuals heading for the gay baths may put themselves at risk. They do not put the whole city at risk. AIDS is not the bubonic plague. This being so, apart from the near futility of preventing people from having casual sex if they want to have it, apart from the added disease control you will have if you know where, when, and how people are having casual sex, to both Kantian and utilitarian there is still strong reason for letting people do as they will — at least, there is one strong reason less for not letting people do as they will. (See also Mohr 1987.)

10.5   The age of consent

We move next to the most tense issue of them all. One might think, if only out of expediency, no one would question publicly the need for some minimum legal age of consent, for any and all kinds of sexual activity, whatever it might be fixed at, and whether or not it be equal for hetero and homosexuals. One might also think that here, at least, expediency would coincide with conviction. This assumption is one that one cannot make. For instance, the Canadian Lesbian and Gay Rights Coalition — a representative body for Canadian homosexuals — has, as part of its specific programme of requests, the demand that all age of consent laws be abolished. ('Statement of Principles and Structure of the Canadian Lesbian and Gay Rights Coalition', Ottawa 1975, revised Halifax 1978, demand number 11.) Quite candidly, it is hard to see what cogent arguments could be given for such a demand. What we can truly say with confidence is that all the value approaches we have introduced would argue unequivocally for the need of a just society to enact and enforce age of consent laws, even though there may be debate about what the age should be.

In the case of the conservative, virtually no argument is needed to justify such laws. Even if the Christian moralist would allow adult homosexual (as well as heterosexual) activity, there is no licence for child sexual behaviour. David and Jonathan were not pre-adolescents; neither were Naomi and Ruth. Again, I am sure that Devlin's average man would find any such sexual activity well beyond the limits of tolerance. There would be no shortage of 'intolerance, indignation, and disgust' (Devlin 1959: 17). As far as Rawls is concerned, the way in which he deals with the position and rights of children is to argue that the state is to be set up as if all people were parents, or at least concerned about someone in the next generation. And, conversely, all children are supposed to have concerned parents. Putting matters this way, the principle of liberty unambiguously justifies laws protecting children from the sexual advances of adults. The freedom of an adult to seek sexual encounters where he/she wishes, clashes with the freedom or liberty of parents to protect their children from the potential harm of such encounters. Similarly, a utilitarian position demands age of consent laws. The transitory pleasure of the adult does not outweigh the potential damage to and lasting unhappiness of the child, not to mention the anguish of the parents. Moreover, Mill, who wants to put more responsibility on the individual than perhaps would a more traditional utilitarian, explicitly excepts children from the liberty to engage in acts which might cause them harm: 'Those who are still in a state to require being taken care of by others, must be protected against their own actions as well as against external injury' (Mill 1975: 73).

So, let us move on from the fact that there should be age of consent laws to our main question. Should these laws specify the same minimum ages for hetero and homosexual behaviour? More specifically, should the age of consent for minimal homosexual activity be fixed at about the age of sixteen, which seems to be the age at which the law in many or most countries or states in the west fix the lower limit for legal hetero-sexual activity (that is, activity going all the way to intercourse)? Prima facie, one might think that the answer should be 'yes'. If the conservative like Devlin is prepared to let some homosexual activity through the net, and similarly finds it tolerable that a girl of sixteen should be permitted to engage in heterosexual intercourse, why then should the boy (or girl) of sixteen who wants to engage homosexually be denied his/her pleasure? And the same goes for the partner, of whatever age. Similarly, the neo-Kantian seems directed to the same conclusion of equality. The slogan for Rawls's position is, after all, 'justice as fairness'. If one is going to work out a just system, then surely one ought to give homosexuals the same rights as heterosexuals, particularly since one is not banning homosexual activity entirely. Again, from any kind of utilitarian perspective, if late adolescents or young adults are to be allowed the total joys of heterosexual activity, why should the same freedom be denied those who prefer the total joys of homosexual activity?

However, we must be careful here not to be stampeded into a hasty conclusion. What Devlin's average man finds tolerable in one situation is not necessarily what he will find tolerable in another situation, even though there may be similarities between the two cases. Nor does justice as fairness always imply that the same laws must apply in exactly the same way to all people, children or adults — no one is going to say that there should be no laws against the blind driving; and perhaps there should be the same laws against the very old. Similarly the utilitarians, including Mill, are going to allow that happiness might demand different approaches: again, the case of the blind being barred from driving seems appropriate. What everyone is after is the bounds of toleration or fairness or equality; but only when the circumstances are the same. The question, therefore, is whether, even if we allow minimal homosexual activity, the circumstances are exactly the same in homo and heterosexual situations, specifically as they apply to age of consent laws. Let me try to construct a counter-argument which I suspect many would think valid against a position of equality: an argument which can certainly be based on conservative grounds, and probably on either Rawlsian or utilitarian grounds also. For the moment, I will put the argument forward without questioning the truth of the premises.

We start with the facts that most people are essentially heterosexual and that we simply do not know definitely what causes sexual orientation, or rather differences in orientation, and why it is that some people grow up either totally or partially homosexual. What we do know is that as they grow into sexuality at adolescence many people are confused or troubled about their sexuality, and it takes a number of years to resolve things fully. Many adolescent males, for example, mutually masturbate, even though as adults they are exclusively heterosexual. Now given these facts, particularly our ignorance, and given also that the evidence which we have is that (for whatever reason) the lives of homosexuals or bisexuals are on average less satisfying than those of heterosexuals, we ought to do everything we can to stop the turning of potential heterosexuals into homosexuals. And keeping high the minimum in age of consent laws is, precisely, one such thing. No one can say that the confused sixteen-year-old will not be preparing for a lifetime of troubled or less satisfactory sexual orientation if he/she can freely consort with and have physical relations with older people who are homosexual. Perhaps the effects will not be all that bad, but at present we cannot say definitively. Consequently, it would be irresponsible to take other than a very guarded position.

Furthermore, the argument would continue, one should not underestimate the problem here. The recent Kinsey evidence is that, amongst males at least, many homosexuals rather fancy young adolescents. Twenty-five per cent of the white male sample studied had had relations with boys at or under sixteen, *after* they themselves had reached the age of twenty-one (Bell and Weinberg 1978: 311, table 7). Hence, unless we have rigid prohibitive laws, proponents of this argument might claim, we are going to have a real problem caused by homosexuals forcing themselves on young people, causing unhappiness both now and in the future. Certainly, the stupid, irresponsible demands of the Canadian Lesbian and Gay Rights Coalition do nothing to allay this fear. The situation with heterosexuals is not as extreme, although no one denies the need for some pertinent age of consent laws. The argument would run that adult heterosexuals do not generally have a desperate yen for young adolescents, and even those episodes of adult—adolescent sexual interaction which do occur (primarily between men and girls) tend not to alter the young people's development of sexual orientation. Moreover, for various reasons, whether biological or social, girls are better at saying 'no' than boys, and so are less likely to fall into damaging relationships. Hence, so the argument would conclude, on virtually all grounds, one can see reasons for imposing different age of consent laws on homo and heterosexuals. Equality of treatment is justified only when the situations are equal, and in the cases of ages of consent the situations are not equal between hetero and homosexuals.

Obviously there are a number of assumptions being made on the route to this conclusion and we must examine some of them. Part of the problem is that, as is so often the case where crucial questions about homosexuality are concerned, the pertinent information is scanty or contradictory. From what we know, in certain respects the life of the homosexual is liable to be less satisfactory than that of the heterosexual. Certainly the San Francisco suicide figures incline us this way, not to mention the obvious fact that being a member of a despised and persecuted minority is in itself a drawback to happy living. There is also now the threat of AIDS. This is not to deny that many homosexuals are as happy as, if not happier than, comparable heterosexuals. (See chapters 1 and 9 for details.)

In the case of the assumption about the pressure on young people from older homosexuals, unfortunately, the Bell and Weinberg study is not as informative as one might wish. Although it is true that one quarter of the white homosexual males had had some sexual partners who were sixteen or younger when they themselves were at least twenty-one years old, what one does not learn is just how commonly these men had partners who were this young (except that the numbers were less than half the total partners), how many partners were actually younger than sixteen, to what extent seduction of the innocent was involved, whether there was significant possibility of deceit or misinformation in reporting the information, and so forth. Furthermore, the study obviously does not tell us what proportion of heterosexuals have a strong passion for young adolescents. However, there is cause for concern here.

But I think that the key issue in this context is the effect that the (homo)sexual attentions of older people do actually have on adolescents, even those of sixteen and up, coming out of adolescence. (The Bell and Weinberg data suggest that this is almost exclusively a question which concerns males.) Moreover, adults aside, we want to know the effects of homosexual behaviour between late adolescents themselves. I am afraid that the only conclusion that can be drawn from our discussions of early chapters is that we simply do not know absolutely. Homosexual activity in late adolescence with adults or with people of one's own age may confuse adult sexual orientation; it may not. Some of the social learning theory speculations suggest that there may be some effects; other theories, like the psychoanalytic theories, would rather deny this. (See chapters 2 and 4.) On average, the strong impression is that by sixteen things are pretty much fixed in major channels — but I doubt anyone would say that bisexuality could never come after fifteen. Nor could one truly deny that there are some, perhaps a small subgroup, whose orientation is more fluid than this. One study, one of very few, has suggested that such late adolescent homosexual activity certainly does not necessarily lead to adult ambiguity about sexual orientation, or even to an orientation which is anything but exclusively heterosexual in thought and deed. Unfortunately, however, the study is based essentially on only nine cases, and although the author is drawing on a much larger sample (200) he has to admit that he simply does not know how biased his conclusions are (Tindall 1978).

Because of all of this ignorance, therefore, perhaps a case can be made for fairly conservative age of consent laws for homosexual activity, on any of the value approaches we have considered: conservative, Rawlsian, or utilitarian. It does not follow, of course, that they have to be as conservative as often presently stipulated, namely an absolute minimum limit of twenty-one years. Perhaps one might think that a general age limit of eighteen years would be adequate — virtually everyone knows their sexual preferences by then, and habits are reasonably fixed. What would particularly worry a lot of people, irrespective of their theoretical value framework, is the possibility of significantly older people imposing their will on younger people. Whatever the effects of adolescent sexuality may be, somehow there is a feeling that if people of the same age are involved, in some sense the actions are less coerced than if an older person is implicated and directing the activity. For this reason, note that I am only saying that the law, if at all, should be directed towards the older and more responsible. That a boy of sixteen should be liable, even in theory, to two years in jail for homosexual activity is reprehensible — and self-defeating.

Of course, all of this discussion does not give a definitive answer to the crucial question of whether the age of consent laws for homosexual activity should be lowered to such a degree that they are identical to those imposed for heterosexual activity, or whether the heterosexual limits should be raised to those of the homosexual limit. Perhaps I can best end this discussion by referring again to the Wolfenden Report, whose authors obviously wrestled with this question, finally endorsing a 21-year limit, with ways of relaxing the full letter of the law where appropriate. What finally tipped the balance for the Committee was the extent to which opting for a homosexual life style really sets one apart, making one so different from others.

While there are some grounds for fixing the age as low as sixteen, it is obvious that however 'mature' a boy of that age may be as regards physical development or psycho-sexual make-up, and whatever analogies may be drawn from the law relating to offenses against young girls, a boy is incapable, at the age of sixteen, of forming a mature judgement about actions of a kind which might have the effect of setting him apart from the rest of society. (p. 52)

In fact, the Committee felt that even 18-year-olds are not that mature, given that they are often just leaving home and open to new pressures. I would think that today the worries about the vulnerability of 18-year-olds is less than the Committee feared. Teenagers in the 1980s are more sexually sophisticated than were their counterparts of the 1950s. (I speak with feeling, for I was a late adolescent in England just when the Committee was producing its report!) But I suspect that the Committee's point about homosexual activity setting one apart is still valid. Do not misunderstand me. I am not now arguing that the homosexual is worse than or inferior to the heterosexual; but I would say that he/she is different, in emotion and life style often. If adolescents are going to let their orientation guide them towards active homosexuality, then that is their choice. If they want to engage sexually with their age-mates, then I think that also should be their choice. What I do share with the Wolfenden Committee members is a feeling that the developing young person should be able to take his (or her) own path unpressured by older people, whose own motives for wanting to sleep with them are hardly that disinterested. Perhaps my worries are exaggerated. I await more information.[1]

10.6 Homosexuals and employment

Employment prospects and security are matters of no small concern to homosexuals. They tend to have no guarantees of job security should their sexual orientation become public knowledge, and even less guarantee that a prospective employer will consider them on their merits rather than on their minority sexual status (Hedgpath 1980; McCrary and Gutierrez 1980). Let me start the discussion by asking whether, under our various value approaches, one could justify general laws banning discrimination on grounds of sexual orientation, just as we often now have laws banning employment discrimination against other hitherto underprivileged groups like women and blacks. (I realize that 'homosexual', 'woman', and 'black' are not exclusive terms. For a moment, I will leave difficult cases on one side.)

I am not really sure where the conservative would stand on this issue. My suspicion is that if one appealed to the man in the street, the man who 'is not expected to reason about anything and [whose] judgement may be largely a matter of feeling' (Devlin 1959: 15), he would not care particularly about homosexual employment rights. Indeed, I would rather suspect that the average man would find it intolerable that anyone should be compelled to employ or work alongside a homosexual, against their will. I would go even further and hazard that many people — and I include women here too — feel little sympathy for existent laws prohibiting discrimination against women and blacks. My experience is that there is a fairly widespread feeling that one ought not force anyone to work with someone they do not wish to. I do not say that I find this a very moral situation — indeed, I would say that the law tends to be ahead of popular sentiment on this matter — but if we are to appeal to the man on the Clapham omnibus as our standard, then I doubt much justification can be found for insisting that we must have employment laws prohibiting discrimination on grounds of sexual orientation. I suspect also that the kind of believer who insisted that the law must reflect Judaeo-Christian morality would not respond sympathetically to anti-discrimination laws. After all, the Bible is hardly a textbook for female rights.

Turning to Rawls's neo-Kantianism, the story is quite otherwise. The Rawlsian concludes unambiguously that sexual orientation should not be grounds for discrimination, potential or actual. From the original position, if one does not know what sexual orientation one will have, one will undoubtedly want the guarantee of job opportunities and security if one is homosexual. One will want these guarantees, even though one is most probably going to be heterosexual oneself. This does not mean that anyone at any time can have any job. One certainly does not want someone with no medical training to become chief of surgery at a hospital. But it does surely mean that if the chief of surgery prefers to sleep with people of her own sex rather than with men, then since this has no effect on her skill with the scalpel, this is her business and nobody else's.

The utilitarian position is perhaps a little less easy to discern. One could argue that in some particular case, assuming one treats the happiness of each person as a single unit, the happiness of the hired homosexual is outweighed by the unhappiness of the homophobic co-workers. But this is clearly a very limited position. The unhappiness of the never-hired or later-fired homosexual (and trepidation of other homosexuals) surely equals the pleasure of the discriminating homophobic co-workers. Moreover, unless one is prepared to guarantee job opportunities and security despite irrelevant attributes, then not only is one losing the undoubted abilities of homosexuals but also one is preparing the way for prejudice against other kinds of people — women, blacks, Jews, Catholics, older people, stutterers, and so forth. And certainly, before very long, by any criterion one has a situation where total overall happiness is not being maximized. Hence, in the long run, the utilitarian (of any stripe) must defend the rights of homosexuals.

Suppose, ignoring now possible conservative opposition, we do grant that as a rule — that is, under normal circumstances — a person's sexual orientation ought to be held irrelevant to their job opportunities and security, and that this rule ought to be protected by law. What are 'normal circumstances'? Let us run through some possible exceptions to the general rule, recognizing that this list is not exhaustive but is certainly representative. The first possible exception that springs to mind, particularly given the recent past history of Great Britain, is some sort of sensitive state post, for instance in the higher echelons of the civil service or foreign service. Should these be closed to homosexuals? (On this matter see the valuable McCrary and Gutierrez 1980.)

I take it that we can dismiss the suggestion that homosexuals should be barred from such posts simply on the grounds that they and they alone generally have attached to their sexual orientation various incapacitating characteristics, like a propensity to drunkenness or lack of moral fibre (despite claims like Bergler 1956 and Socarides 1973). The major ground for claiming an exception at this point has to be that sensitive posts require people who cannot be blackmailed or otherwise pressured because of their personal lives — and that homosexuality does leave people open in this respect. And obviously, if this point about vulnerability to blackmail is well founded, no further argument is needed to convince the conservative that homosexuals should be excluded. Both Rawlsian and utilitarian would concur on this.

The only problem with this rather smug conclusion is that the argument leading to it is invalid. In fact, to the contrary, making an exception for these sorts of posts seems if anything liable to compound the very problem it is designed to avoid! The aim is to prevent the putting of people into sensitive posts where they could be blackmailed. But why could they be blackmailed? Because they would not want people to find out that they are homosexual — such a discovery, whether or not they had done wrong, would lead to loss of face and dismissal. However, if this is the case, surely what one should therefore do is remove the threat of dismissal and thus the main item in the blackmailer's power. If one is indeed allowed to hold sensitive posts whatever one's sexual orientation, then such an orientation's being discovered is no threat. In other words, it would seem that the very last thing one should do — whether one be a Rawlsian or a utilitarian — is make an exception to universal hiring of homosexuals for sensitive posts. Such a move simply exacerbates the problem it is meant to solve. (Perhaps on these grounds, one could even win some conservatives over to one's opinion: a nice dilemma for those conservatives who are intuitively opposed to job discrimination laws.)

As a second kind of case where exceptions might be claimed for laws against sexual discrimination, let us take up the question of the armed forces. What is at issue is not really whether homosexuals would meet minimum standards of physique or behaviour: no one, for instance, is arguing that an army should have to employ the stereotype of a male homosexual, with mincing gait and high affected voice. (Although there are interesting questions if systematic differences between homosexuals and heterosexuals were discovered.) The usually expressed worry starts with the fact that military personnel are frequently put for long periods of time in groups of the same sex, with no opportunities for sexual contacts with outsiders. It is therefore argued that permitting homosexuals in the military may lead to uncontrolled promiscuity within such groups of soldiers, airmen, and (most particularly) sailors. If nothing else, innocent heterosexuals will be under constant threat from homosexual comrades, and (what is worse) superior officers. A similar argument can no doubt be made for police forces like the RCMP (Mounties) which have a quasi-military structure and life style. In the words of sometime US Air Force Secretary Thomas Reed, the presence of homosexual soldiers in the military might 'corrupt the young recruits' (McCrary and Gutierrez 1980: 142).

To what extent do the premises of this argument hold true today, given the extent to which women are being integrated into the armed forces and given also the extent to which in peacetime, the usual state of the armed forces, the military have opportunity to mix with civilians of both sexes? Why is it that similar arguments were not thought to provide conclusive reasons against the integration of women? If homosexual sergeants provide such a threat to innocent young privates (of the same sex), why is it that heterosexual sergeants did not provide a similar threat to innocent young privates (of the opposite sex)? No doubt the heterosexual situation does pose problems. One accepts them, inasmuch as one must, because the principles of justice — Rawlsian or utilitarian — demand such tolerance. And one tries to minimize them by enacting fairly strict rules. For instance, to stop undue influence, one bars sexual fraternization between officers and other ranks. To stop uncontrolled, visible promiscuity, one certainly does not permit sexual intercourse in the dormitories. And so forth.

I see no reason why the homosexual situation should be essentially different. The principles of justice demand that homosexuals be allowed to join the military. On a military base where all men (or women) must use a communal shower room, however, one should not permit homosexuals to engage in any sexual activity they like. There seems to me no reason why they should not be expected to conduct their sex lives with the control and circumspection demanded of heterosexuals. (See Williams and Weinberg 1971 for more on this topic.)

Let me conclude this discussion of employment prospects for homosexuals by considering one final class of possible exceptions to the rule of general hiring, the class which some might consider the most sensitive of all: schoolteachers. I shall not really attempt to answer matters from the conservative position, that is, one akin to Devlin's. I do not know what the average man thinks on these matters. My suspicion is that, generally, openly homosexual schoolteachers would get little sympathy and much hostility. On the other hand, I doubt most people would want the authorities to go on a deliberate witch-hunt, smoking out all real and apparent homosexuals. What counts is what the children are doing during the week, not what the teachers are doing at the weekend. (I say this despite the fact that the well-known moral philosopher David Gauthier argued, in a letter to the (Toronto) *Globe & Mail*, Summer 1978, that homosexuals ought not to be allowed to teach.)

What of neo-Kantianism and utilitarianism? As far as teachers of the pre-pubescent are concerned, on the basis of either of these theories I see no cogent reason for denying homosexuals equal opportunities for employment. No one has suggested with evidence that homosexuals (of either sex) are child molesters or in any other way unsuitable as teachers. Indeed, what empirical evidence we have seen points in precisely the opposite direction. (See, for example, the work of Freund 1974.) Of course, if one allows people who are acknowledged homosexuals to teach, then, even though they may not advertise the fact, children and parents will probably learn about their sexual orientation. But, with respect, so what? Children, even pre-pubescent children, learn about homosexuality — if not all the physical details, then at least about people of the same sex falling in love. And if they do not, then I see no reason why they should not. Unfortunately, the usual way such information is gleaned is through dirty jokes, sniggers, and outright prejudice, as often as not, from parents. It would seem that much could come from meeting and working with homosexuals (acknowledged homosexuals) from one's earliest years — that is, in the classroom. Not only would this be just to homosexuals now, it would lead to an even more just and happy society tomorrow. Of course, again no one is claiming that homosexuals should have licence denied heterosexuals, behaving in outlandish ways or flaunting their sexual activities and dispositions. What we are talking about is the right of average decent people to be schoolteachers, whether they be heterosexual or homosexual.

What about the teachers of adolescents and very young adults? As either Rawlsian or utilitarian, one can certainly think of positive reasons why homosexual teachers could make a valuable and special contribution to school life, understood in the broadest sense. As young people come into awareness and possession of their sexuality, many are troubled; and this applies particularly to those with homosexual yearnings, whether these be transistory or permanent. Having teachers who show by example that one can function as an integrated person, despite being homosexual (perhaps because of being homosexual), and who can help adolescents to understand themselves in a guilt-free way, can only lead to good, however defined. And obviously, having teachers who are known to be homosexual will continue the process of showing all children (and parents) that homosexuals are just people, and not filthy perverts and deserved objects of fun.

No doubt, even from Rawlsians and utilitarians, there will be objections, which perhaps will be felt even more keenly given the kind of discussion which has occurred already in this chapter. Will there not be a danger that homosexual teachers (particularly men) will attempt to seduce their charges? I suppose that the answer is that one certainly cannot guarantee that some will not, just as one can give no absolute guarantees about heterosexuals either. But the point at issue is whether or not to offer homosexuals jobs, not whether or not to put them above the law. One would think that they, no less than anyone else, would recognize the dangers, legal and social, and act to preserve their status and liberty. Indeed, it would seem that if this is in fact a problem, acknowledged homosexuals are less of a threat than covert homosexuals. A person, especially a man, who was known to be homosexual would take maximum pains not to let any breath of scandal, real or imaginary, taint him/her. And in addition to this, I am sure that there would be a monitoring — intentional or unintentional — by others to see that no untoward behaviour occurred. As things stand at the moment, there are possibilities of all kinds of abuse by tormented people, concealing their true sexual feelings.

People working in sensitive posts, the military, teachers — I do not pretend that my discussion so far has been exhaustive. However, having run through a list of possible exceptions to a rule barring sexual orientation as a criterion for employment qualifications — a list which includes some of the most-frequently cited possible exceptions — and having found no grounds for making any of the possibilities actual exceptions, I think we can conclude that the clause about sexual orientation ought to be virtually universal. And this conclusion holds whether one be a Rawlsian or a utilitarian. No doubt the conservative will take a more restrictive attitude. Here, obviously, is a place where the moral leader must work to redirect the gut feelings of the man in the street.

10.7 Does homosexuality merit affirmative action?

I come to the third and final question. Does the state have, or could the state have, an obligation to provide positive benefits, not given to all, for its homosexuals? Should there, for instance, be some sort of minimum quota system for homosexuals, a kind of reverse discrimination: so-called 'affirmative action'? If we grant that homosexuals should not be barred from job employment, should we not go even further and insist that they (or at least a certain percentage) be guaranteed job opportunities? And analogously, should homosexuals get special preferential treatment when it comes to other desirable offerings which the state has the power to regulate, like admission to medical school? (See Sher 1975; Dworkin 1977b; Jaggar 1977; Sher et al. 1979, for some general discussion on the issue.)

I must confess that (like many) I have difficulties with reverse discrimination arguments at the best of times. Particularly if one endorses any kind of Kantian or neo-Kantian foundation, then however worthy the end one might be striving for, one is running dangerously close to treating some people as means. The person not on the quota list and who just fails to get the coveted job or into medical school looks very much like a person whose own interests have been sacrificed for the sake of others. Perhaps a utilitarian appealing to general happiness can find a better foundation for reverse discrimination than can the Kantian; although how good a foundation is a little problematical. There are still difficulties with the unhappiness of those excluded, the adequacy of those on the quota who are included, and so forth.

This is all a very complex problem and I am loath to launch into a full-blown general discussion. However, such a discussion is surely not needed. When we consider the rights of homosexuals, it is clear that (viewed from all respects), even though the case for anti-discrimination laws may seem strong, the case for reverse discrimination laws does not — whatever the merits of the general case for such laws may be. The following reasons are pertinent.

First, there is a difficulty in defining 'homosexual' for the purposes of any minimum quotas. A quota for women, whether right or wrong, can be based on the reasonable assumption that the concept of 'womanhood' is fairly unambiguous. Despite the odd hermaphrodite, a woman is a woman is a woman. But what about homosexuals? Must one be at point 6 on the Kinsey scale to qualify? If not, what then would qualify one? Would passing homosexual experience in youth be enough, or the odd homosexual dream? Or what about the man married to an ardently Catholic wife, who has six children already, and who finds his sexual relief, not in a local brothel (since this does not exist) but in fellatio in public lavatories on his way home from work (Humphreys 1970)? And conversely, what about the person who lies, whether in word or deed? I fear that the whole question of definition would ruin the attempt to set a quota system.

Second, there is the problem for affirmative action caused by those who prefer not to have their sexual orientation exposed and discussed. Suppose a firm has ten employees, that the owner knows privately that two of these employees are homosexual, but that the employees prefer this knowledge not become public. Suppose also that one has a 10 per cent hiring quota, and that with a vacancy a known homosexual comes knocking at the door. Must the employer hire this homosexual, even though he/she is less qualified than other applicants, in order to preserve the privacy of the present employees? Either way, one has an unfortunate dilemma: one which would not occur with a quota for women, because sex is not something easily or desiredly concealed.

Third, a major reason often given to justify quota systems does not exist. In the case of ethnic minority groups and particularly blacks, it is argued that since they are more likely to be disadvantaged, facing adversity and low educational opportunities, even though their actual marks or qualifications may be less than those of comparable whites, their achievements are as high if not higher. Hence, one can justifiably discriminate in favour of such people — in fact, viewed in the broader context there is no discrimination at all here. But even if one accepts this line of argument, in the case of the homosexual it fails to apply. There is no evidence to suggest that homosexuals will be less well trained or qualified than heterosexuals. Indeed, if Weinrich's (1976) claims are well-made, homosexuals perform rather better over some of society's hurdles than do heterosexuals. Homosexuals certainly do not constitute a deprived group in the way that ethnic minorities do. If one is to justify affirmative action one has to appeal to such reasons as compensation to homosexuals for past wrongs done by heterosexuals. But this is a morally dubious line of argument at best. Why should a heterosexual today, who may never have hurt a homosexual, suffer for the sins of past hetero-sexuals? There is an unsavoury flavour of the scapegoat about the whole argument.

I conclude, therefore, that although justice requires us not to discrimin-ate against homosexuals, justice forbids us to discriminate in their favour. If, in employment, we treat homosexuals like normal people, then perhaps to our surprise we shall find that they are normal people. And this, it seems to me, is a good note on which to end the section, the chapter, and the book.

Notes

Chapter 1   Words and Facts

1   In the discussion here, and in the chapters following, I shall assume a fairly conventional view of scientific theories, wherein one has various low-grade factual generalizations (like Kepler's laws) which are explained by being seen as the consequences of upper-level causal claims (like Newton's laws of motion). See Hempel 1966 or Ruse 1973.
2   The problem is that no one knows how quickly AIDS will spread from today's infected group to the (primarily heterosexual) group as a whole. There is a major threat, as the preliminary analysis of May and Anderson (1987) shows. As Altman (1986) and Patton (1985) stress, there is every reason to think that male homosexuals will be better as a group at responding than heterosexuals. There is much less hypocrisy.

Chapter 2   The Freudian Analysis

1   Anticipating: the usual test given to distinguish masculinity from femininity is the Mf scale of the MMPI. See chapter 9 for explanation and details.
2   This claim must be qualified. Bieber and associates would revise classical Freudianism in radical ways belonging to the school to be discussed in the next chapter. But they are at one with Freud on the nature and effects of atypical family constellations.

Chapter 3   The Adaptational Analysis

1   As already mentioned, a matter which must be troubling some readers is the propriety of calling a characteristic 'male' or 'masculine', if one is then going

to argue that it is found in some females also. This is a fair comment which needs discussion. I shall, however, continue to defer discussion. When I consider hormonal explanations (chapter 5), the problem will be highlighted, intensified and considered.

2 Freund (1974) queries bisexuality on the empirical ground that few people get actually sexually aroused *both* by male and female pornography. But he admits that his results must be somewhat distorted, because in fact there are functioning bisexuals. In any case, against adaptationists, Freund et al. (1974a) found that homosexuals were not sexually upset by pictures of female genitals, whereas pictures of revolting skin diseases had an immediate effect. (See figures 3.3 and 3.4.)

Chapter 4 Freud: Extensions and Replacements

1 I presume the lack of long-term studies (of the kind Green 1985 is providing for boys) stems at least partially from the fact that, tomboyism being more socially acceptable than sissyism, girls tend not to end up in gender-dysfunction clinics.

2 Green and Stoller — perhaps the former more than the latter — both think hormonal factors, to be discussed in the next chapters, may play some causal roles in pushing people towards the other gender.

Chapter 5 Hormones and Homosexuality

1 Anyone who walks into a gay bar has to be struck by how trim so many of the men look. But it might reasonably be claimed that that is just what you would expect in a subculture given to extreme promiscuity, with the consequent pressure towards sexual attractiveness.

2 Deliberately, I use the term 'gender role' rather than 'sexual orientation' here, because the former seems to cover only the doing of certain (male- or female-like) things, unlike the latter which refers also (in humans at least) to attitudes. I shall discuss the worries one might have about the attitudes of rats (and other non-humans) shortly.

Chapter 7 Reductionism and Determinism: Twin Threats?

1 Not so much salt now as previously. There are some promising signs that a pattern such as that just sketched is not entirely fantasy. Most of the early accounts rather suggested that sissy sons are invariably homosexual men. But Green (1985) reports on some such sons who are now unambiguously heterosexual. Interestingly, some of these boys were subjected to behaviour modification.

2　This is certainly the position of Simone de Beauvoir (1953). Like her companion, Jean-Paul Sartre, she takes freedom to be paramount. She speaks of lesbianism as 'an attitude *chosen in a certain situation* — that is, at once motivated and freely adopted' (p. 424, her italics). She does nevertheless stress that adult females tend more to (erotic) bisexuality than males (p. 418).

Chapter 8　Is Homosexuality Bad Sexuality?

1　Boswell (1980), in what is recognized as the authoritative source on the history of the attitude of the Catholic church towards homosexuality in the first twelve centuries of its existence, shows that — despite the arguments of the philosophers — in thought and behaviour authorities were often tolerant of homosexuality in its various forms. I do think Boswell underestimates the subtlety and integrity of Aquinas's arguments — but, of course, as a fellow philosopher I am defending one of my own.

2　Since the eighteenth century, there has been comparatively little written on the topic of homosexuality by professional philosophers. One who does touch on the subject is the French existentialist, Jean-Paul Sartre; but he is mainly interested in using the refusal to accept homosexual identity as an example of bad faith ('*mauvais fois*'). See Sartre 1965; also 1947, 1962.

3　Already, here, with the emphasis on the group we are going beyond biology, but let it pass. Today's evolutionists emphasize that natural selection works for, and only for, the species. Anyone who says that the homosexual is letting down the side, biologically speaking, is twenty years out of date, biologically speaking.

4　An interesting Kantian-like suggestion from Scruton (1986) is that perhaps homosexual relationships fail to measure with heterosexual relationships because, being narcissus-like, they do not involve the same level of mystery (and consequent need to risk oneself) as is required when dealing with a person of the other gender. Perhaps paradoxically, given that I am more sympathetic to the significance of human biology than is Scruton, I would claim that any relationship with another requires such a self-transcending commitment.

5　The classic article in this field is by Thomas Nagel (1969). But I agree with his critics that he speaks less of the sexually perverse and more of the sexually complete or incomplete. I take it that the Freudian notion of 'perversion', encountered in chapter 2, is a technical term, with no immediate connection to the general sense being discussed here.

Chapter 9　Homosexuality as Sickness: The Arguments

1　Although I obviously have mixed feelings about social constructivism, the conclusions of this chapter should win approval from such a theorist. On the one hand, like the social constructivist, I am agreeing that illness is not some objective phenomenon 'out there'. It is — in part, at least — a cultural construction. On the other hand, I argue that there is no foundation, even on a cultural understanding, for an automatic labelling of the homosexual as 'sick'. Today, if one persists in so doing, then probably one has some (unsavoury) agenda. Of course, this is not necessarily to say that Foucault and others are right in seeing the homosexual-as-sick thesis merely as a tool in the hands of the members of the medical profession, wanting to have power over their fellow humans. Perhaps it was. I have yet to see the historical evidence.

Chapter 10   Homosexuals and Society

1   Weeks (1985: 229) reaches a conclusion diametrically opposed to mine, arguing that (if anything) the age of consent laws should be higher for girls than boys. I think he can reach such an end only by ignoring all of his own (sensible) warnings about the significance of a sense of sexual *identity*. I am gratified, however, to find him agreeing with me that justice does not necessarily imply that males and females must get exactly the same treatment under the law.

Bibliography

Aaronson, B. S. and Grumpelt, H. R. (1961). Homosexuality and some MMPI measures of masculinity—femininity. *Journal of Clinical Psychology*, 17, 245—7.

Abraham, K. (1927). The influence of oral erotism on character formation. In *Selected Papers*, London: Hogarth, 383—406.

——— (1954). Manifestations of the female castration complex. In *Selected Papers of Karl Abraham*, New York: Basic Books, 338—69. (First published 1920).

Acosta, Frank X. (1975). Etiology and treatment of homosexuality: a review. *Archives of Sexual Behaviour*, 4 (1), 9—29.

Alexander, R. D. (1974). The evolution of social behaviour. *Annual Review of Ecology and Systematics*, 5, 325—84.

——— (1979). *Darwinism and Human Affairs*. Seattle: University of Washington Press.

Allen, E., Alper, J., Beckwith, B., Beckwith, J., Chorover, S., Culver, D., Daniels, N., Dorfman, E., Duncan, M., Engelman, E., Fitten, R., Fuda, K., Gould, S., Gross, C., Hill, W., Hubbard, R., Hunt, J., Inouye, H., Judd, T., Kotelchuck, M., Lange, B., Leeds, A., Levins, R., Lewontin, R., Lieber, M., Livingstone, J., Loechler, E., Ludwig, B., Madansky, C., Merskey, M., Miller, L., Morales, R., Motheral, S., Muzal, K., Nestie, M., Ostrom, N., Pyeritz, R., Reingold, A., Rosenthal, M., Rosner, D., Schreier, H., Simon, M., Sternberg, P., Walicke, P., Warshaw, F., and Wilson, M. (1977). Sociobiology: a new biological determinism. In Sociobiology Study Group of Boston (ed.), *Biology as a Social Weapon*, Minneapolis: Burgess, 133—49.

Altman, D. (1986). *Aids and the New Puritanism*. London: Pluto.

Aquinas, St T. (1968). *Summa Theologiae, 43, Temperance* (2a, 2ae, 141—54). Trans. T. Gilby. London: Blackfriars.

Aronson, H. and Weintraub, W. (1968). Social background of the patient in classical psychoanalysis. *Journal of Nervous and Mental Disease*, 146, 91—7.

Ayala, F. J. (1974). Introduction. In F. J. Ayala and T. Dobzhansky (eds), *Studies in the Philosophy of Biology*, London: Macmillan, vii—xvi.

Ayala, F. J. and Valentine, J. W. (1979). *Evolving*. Menlo Park, Calif.: Benjamin/ Cummings.

Bailey, D. S. (1955). *Homosexuality and the Western Christian Tradition*. London: Longmans, Green and Co.

Bancroft, J. (1974a). *Deviant Sexual Behaviour: Modification and Assessment*. Oxford: Clarendon Press.

────── (1974b). Review of M. P. Feldman and M. J. McCulloch, *Homosexual Behaviour: Therapy and Assessment*. *Archives of Sexual Behavior*, 3, 389 – 90.

Bandura, A. (1969). Social-learning theory of identificatory processes. In D. A. Goslin (ed.), *Handbook of Socialization Theory and Research*, Chicago: Rand McNally, 213 – 62.

Barash, D. P. (1977). *Sociobiology and Behaviour*. New York: Elsevier.

Bardwick, J. M. (1971). *Psychology of Women*. New York: Harper and Row.

Barry, B. (1973). *The Liberal Theory of Justice: A Critical Examination of the Principal Doctrines in 'A Theory of Justice' by John Rawls*. Oxford: Oxford University Press.

Barth, K. (1980). Church dogmatics. In E. Batchelor (ed.), *Homosexuality and Ethics*, New York: Pilgrim, 48 – 51.

Batchelor, E. (1980). *Homosexuality and Ethics*. New York: Pilgrim.

Bateson, P. (1986). Sociobiology and human politics. In S. Rose and L. Appignanesi (eds), *Science and Beyond*, Oxford: Blackwell.

Bayer, R. (1981). *Homosexuality and American Psychiatry*. New York: Basic Books.

Bell, A. P. and Weinberg, S. (1978). *Homosexualities – A Study of Diversity among Men and Women*. New York: Simon & Schuster.

Bell, A. P., Weinberg, M. S. and Hammersmith, S. K. (1981). *Sexual Preference: Its Development in Men and Women*. Bloomington, Ind.: Indiana University Press.

Bene, E. (1965a). On the genesis of male homosexuality: an attempt at clarifying the role of the parents. *British Journal of Psychiatry*, 111, 803 – 13.

────── (1965b). On the genesis of female homosexuality. *British Journal of Psychiatry*, 111, 815 – 21.

Bentham, J. (1834). *Deontology*. Ed. J. Bowring. London: Longman, Rees, Orme, Browne, Greene, Longman.

────── (1978). Offences against one's self: paederasty. *Journal of Homosexuality*, 3 (4), 383 – 405; 1 (4), 91 – 107.

Bergler, E. (1956). *Homosexuality: Disease or Way of Life?* New York: Hill and Wang.

Betzig, L. L., Borgerhoff Mulder, M. and Turke, P. W. (1987). *Human Reproductive Behaviour*. Cambridge: Cambridge University Press.

Bieber, I. (1976). A discussion of 'Homosexuality: the ethical challenge'. *Journal of Consulting and Clinical Psychology*, 44 (2), 163 – 6.

Bieber, I., Dain, H. J., Dince, P. R., Drellich, M. G., Grand, H. G., Gundlach, R. H., Kremer, M. W., Rifkin, A. H., Wilbur, C. B., and Bieber, T. B. (1962). *Homosexuality: A Psychoanalytic Study of Male Homosexuals*. New York: Basic Books.

Birk, L. (1974). Group psychotherapy for men who are homosexual. *Journal of Sex and Marital Therapy*. 1, 29 – 52.

Birke, L. (1979). Hormonal determinism and lesbianism. Unpublished paper read at American Association for the Advancement of Science Annual Meeting, Houston, Texas.

———— (1981). Is homosexuality hormonally determined? *Journal of Homosexuality*, 6 (4), 35—49.

———— (1986). *Women, Feminism and Biology*. Brighton: Wheatsheaf.

Black, D. (1986). *The Plague Years*. London: Picador.

Blackwood, E. (1985). *Anthropology and Homosexual Behaviour*. New York: Haworth Press. (Originally in *Journal of Homosexuality*, 11 (3/4)), 1—217.

Bleier, R. (1984). *Science and Gender: A Critique of Biology and Its Theories on Women*. New York: Pergamon Press.

Boggan, E., Haft, M., Lister, C., Rupp, J. and Stoddard, T. (1983). *The Rights of Gay People*. New York: Bantam.

Boorse, C. (1975). On the distinction between disease and illness. *Philosophy and Public Affairs*, 5, 49—68.

———— (1976). What a theory of mental health should be. *Journal for the Theory of Social Behaviour*, 6, 61—84.

———— (1977). Health as a theoretical concept. *Philosophy of Science*, 44, 542—73.

Boswell, J. (1980). *Christianity, Social Tolerance, and Homosexuality*. Chicago: University of Chicago Press.

———— (1982). Revolutions, universals and sexual categories. *Salmagundi*, 58/59, 89—113.

Boyd, R. and Richerson, P. (1985). *Culture and the Evolutionary Process*. Chicago: University of Chicago Press.

Braaten, L. J., and Darling, C. D. (1965). Overt and covert homosexual problems among male college students. *Genetic Psychology Monographs*, 71, 269—310.

Branchey, L. (1973). Effects of sex hormones on sleep patterns of male rats gonadectomized in adulthood and in the neonatal period. *Physiological Behavior*, 11, 609—11.

Bridgman, P. W. (1959). *The Way Things Are*. Cambridge, Mass.: Harvard University Press.

Brooks-Gunn, J. and Matthews, W. S. (1979). *He and She: How Children Develop Their Sex-Role Identity*. Englewood Cliffs, NJ: Prentice-Hall.

Bullough, V. L. (1976). *Sexual Variance in Society and History*. New York: Wiley.

Burton, A. (1947). Use of the *Mf* scale of the MMPI as an aid in diagnosis of sexual inversion. *Journal of Psychology*, 24, 161—4.

Caplan, A. (ed.) (1978). *The Sociobiology Debate*. New York: Harper and Row.

Caplan, A., Engelhardt, H. T., McCartney, J. (eds) (1981). *Concepts of Health and Disease*. Reading, Mass.: Addison-Wesley.

Carrier, J. (1971). Participants in urban Mexican male homosexual encounters. *Archives of Sexual Behavior*, 1, 279—91.

———— (1986). Childhood cross-gender behaviour and adult homosexuality. *Archives of Sexual Behavior*, 15, 89—93.

Cass, V. C. (1984). Homosexual identity: a concept in need of definition. *Journal of Homosexuality*, 9 (2/3), 105—26.

Catlin, G. (1926). *North American Indians*. Edinburgh: Grant.

Cattell, R. B. and Morony, J. H. (1962). The use of the 16PF in distinguishing homosexuals, normals and general criminals. *Journal of Consulting Psychology*, 26, 531—40.

Causey, R. (1969). Polanyi on structure and reduction. *Synthese*, 20, 230—7.

Chapman, L. J. and Chapman, J. P. (1967). Genesis of popular but erroneous psychodiagnostic observations. *Journal of Abnormal Psychology*, 72, 193—204.

Chess, S., Thomas, A., Birch, H. G. and Hertzig, M. (1960). Implications of a longitudinal study of child development for child psychiatry. *American Journal of Psychiatry*, 117, 434—41.

Churchill, W. (1967). *Homosexual Behaviour Among Males; A Cross-Cultural and Cross-Species Investigation*. New York: Hawthorn Books.

Churchland, P. M. (1984). *Matter and Consciousness*. Cambridge, Mass.: MIT Press.

Cooper, J. (1974). Aetiology of homosexuality. In J. A. Loraine (ed.), *Understanding Homosexuality; Its Biological and Psychological Bases*, New York: American Elsevier, 1—23.

Crane, P. (1982). *Gays and the Law*. London: Pluto.

Cross, R. C. and Woozley, A. D. (1964). *Plato's Republic: A Philosophical Commentary*. London: Macmillan.

Cubitt, G. and Gendreau, P. (1972). Assessing the diagnostic utility of MMPI and 16PF indexes of homosexuality in prison samples. *Journal of Consulting and Clinical Psychology*, 39, 342.

Dahlstrom, W. and Welsh, G. (1960). *An MMPI Handbook*. Minneapolis: University of Minnesota Press.

Dahlstrom, W., Welsh, G. and Dahlstrom, L. (1973). *MMPI Handbook. Volume I.* (Revised edition). Minneapolis: University of Minnesota Press.

Darwin, C. (1859). *On the Origin of Species*. London: John Murray.

Davidson, D. (1963). Actions, reasons and causes. *Journal of Philosophy*, 60, 685—700.

Dawkins, R. (1976). *The Selfish Gene*. Oxford: Oxford University Press.

Dean, R. and Richardson, H. (1966). On MMPI high-point codes of homosexual versus heterosexual males. *Journal of Consulting Psychology*, 30, 558—60.

De Beauvoir, S. (1953). *The Second Sex*. New York: Knopf.

De Cecco, J. P. (ed.) (1984). *Homophobia: An Overview*. New York: Haworth Press. (Originally in *Journal of Homosexuality*, 10 (1/2), 1—198.)

De Cecco, J. P. and Shively, M. G. (1978). Children's development: social sex-role and hetero—homosexual orientation. In J. Oremland and E. Oremland (eds), *The Sexual and Gender Development of Young Children*, Cambridge: Ballinger.

—— (1984). From sexual identity to sexual relationships: a contextual shift. *Journal of Homosexuality*, 9 (2/3), 1—26.

Dennett, D. (1984). *Elbow Room*. Cambridge, Mass.: MIT Press.

Denniston, R. M. (1980). Ambisexuality in animals. In J. Marmor (ed.), *Homosexual Behaviour: A Modern Reappraisal*. New York: Basic Books.

Devlin, P. (1959). *The Enforcement of Morals*. Maccabaean Lecture in Jurisprudence of the British Academy, 1959. Oxford: Oxford University Press. Reprinted in P. Devlin, *The Enforcement of Morals*, Oxford: Oxford University Press, 1965.

Diamond, M. (1968). *Perspectives in Reproduction and Sexual Behaviour.* Bloomington, Indiana: Indiana University Press.

———— (1982). Sexual identity, monozygotic twins reared in discordant sex roles and a BBC follow-up. *Archives of Sexual Behavior*, 11, 181—6.

Dobzhansky, T., Ayala, F., Stebbins, G. and Valentine, J. (1977). *Evolution.* San Francisco: W. H. Freeman.

Doering, C. M., Doering, C. H., Kraemer, H. C., Brodie, K. H. and Hamburg, D. A. (1975). A cycle of plasma testosterone in the human male. *Journal of Clinical Endocrinology and Metabolism*, 40, 492—500.

Doidge, W. and Holtzman, W. (1960). Implications of homosexuality among air force trainees. *Journal of Consulting Psychology*, 24, 9—13.

Donne, J. (1975). *Devotions Upon Emergent Occasions.* Ed. A. Raspa. Montreal: McGill-Queen's University Press.

Dörner, G. (1969). Homo- and hypersexuality in rats with hypothalamic lesions. *Neuroendocrinology*, 4, 20—4.

———— (1970). The influence of sex hormones on the differentiation, maturation and function of hypothalamic sex and mating centres. In *Third International Congress on Hormonal Steroids. 7—12. 9. 1970*, Hamburg.

———— (1971). Paradoxical effects of estrogen on brain differentiation. *Neuroendocrinology*, 7, 146—55.

———— (1972). *Sexualhormonalhängige Gehindifferenzierung und Sexualitat.* Vienna: Fischer.

———— (1976). *Hormones and Brain Differentiation.* Amsterdam: Elsevier.

———— (1977). Sex-hormone-dependent brain differentiation and reproduction. In J. Money and H. Musaph (eds), *Handbook of Sexology.* New York: Elsevier.

———— (1983). Letter to the editor. *Archives of Sexual Behavior*, 12, 577—82.

Dörner, G. and Hinz, G. (1975). Androgen dependent brain differentiation and life-span. *Endokrinologie*, 65, 378—80.

Dörner, G. and Staudt, J. (1968). Structural changes in the preoptic anterior hypothalamic area of the male rat, following neonatal castration and androgen substitution. *Neuroendocrinology*, 3, 136—40.

Dörner, G., Rohde, W.. Stahl, F., Krell, L. and Masius, W. G. (1975). A neuroendocrine predisposition for homosexuality in men. *Archives of Sexual Behavior*, 4, 1—8.

Dörner, G., Geier, T., Ahrens, L., Krell, L., Münx, G., Sieler, H., Kittner, E. and Müller, H. (1980). Prenatal stress as a possible aetiogenetic factor of homosexuality in human males. *Endokrinologie*, 75, 365—8.

Dörner, G., Schenk, B., Schmiedel, B. and Ahrens, L. (1983a). Stressful events in prenatal life of bi- and homosexual men. *Experimental and Clinical Endocrinology*, 81, 83--7.

———— (1983b). On the LH response to oestrogen and LH-RH in transsexual men. *Experimental and Clinical Endocrinology*, 81, 257—67.

Dover, K. J. (1973). Classical Greek attitudes to sexual behaviour. *Arethusa*, 6, 59—73.

———— (1978). *Greek Homosexuality.* Cambridge, Mass.: Harvard University Press.

Durham, W. H. (1987). *Coevolution: Genes, Culture, and Human Diversity.* Stanford: Stanford University Press.

Dworkin, R. (1977a). Liberty and moralism. In *Taking Rights Seriously*, Cambridge, Mass.: Harvard University Press.

_____ (1977b). Why Bakke has no case. *New York Review of Books*, 24, 15.

Eaton, G. G., Goy, R. W. and Phoenix, C. M. (1973). Effects of testosterone treatment in adulthood on sexual behaviour of female pseudohermaphrodite rhesus monkeys. *Nature*, 242, 119–20.

Eccles, J. C. and Popper, K. R. (1977). *The Self and Its Brain.* New York: Springer-Verlag.

Ehrhardt, A. A. (1977). Prenatal androgenization and human psychosexual behaviour. In J. Money and H. Musaph (eds), *Handbook of Sexology*, New York: Elsevier, 245–57.

Ehrhardt, A. A. and Baker, S. W. (1974). Fetal androgens, human central nervous system differentiation, and behaviour sex differences. In R. C. Friedman, R. Richart, R. Vande Wiele (eds), *Sex Differences in Behaviour*, New York: Wiley.

Ehrhardt, A. A. and Meyer-Bahlburg, H. F. L. (1981). Effects of prenatal sex hormones on gender-related behaviour. *Science*, 211, 1312–18.

Elliston, F. (1975). In defense of promiscuity. In R. Baker and F. Elliston (eds), *Philosophy and Sex*, Buffalo: Prometheus, 222–46.

Engelhardt, H. T. (1976). Ideology and etiology. *Journal of Medicine and Philosophy*, 1, 256–68.

Evans, D. R. (1968). Masturbatory fantasy and sexual deviation. *Behavior Research and Therapy*, 6, 17–19.

Evans, R. B. (1969). Childhood parental relationships of homosexual men. *Journal of Consulting and Clinical Psychology*, 33, 129–35.

_____ (1972). Physical and biochemical characteristics of homosexual men. *Journal of Consulting and Clinical Psychology*, 39 (1), 140–7.

Eysenck, H. J. (1952). The effects of psychotherapy: an evaluation. *Journal of Consulting Psychology*, 16, 319–24.

_____ (1966). *The Effects of Psychotherapy.* New York: International Science.

Fairburn, N. H. (1974). Homosexuality and the law. In J. A. Loraine (ed.), *Understanding Homosexuality: Its Biological and Psychological Bases*, New York: American Elsevier, 159–64.

Fausto-Sterling, A. (1986). *Myths of Gender.* New York: Basic Books.

Feldman, M. P. and MacCulloch, M. J. (1971). *Homosexual Behaviour: Therapy and Assessment.* Oxford: Pergamon.

Fenichel, O. (1945). *The Psychoanalytic Theory of Neurosis.* New York: Norton.

Fisher, S. (1973). *The Female Orgasm: Psychology, Physiology, Fantasy.* New York: Basic Books.

Fisher, S. and Greenberg, R. P. (1977). *The Scientific Credibility of Freud's Theories and Therapy.* New York: Basic Books.

Flew, A. G. N. (1967). *Evolutionary Ethics.* London: Macmillan.

Foucault, M. (1978). *History of Sexuality.* New York: Pantheon, vol. 1.

Frankfurt, H. (1970). Freedom of the will and the concept of a person. *Journal of*

Philosophy, 68, 5—20.

Freud, S. (1932). Female sexuality. *International Journal of Psychoanalysis*, 13, 281—97.

―――― (1933). The psychology of women. In *New Introductory Lectures on Psychoanalysis*, New York: Norton, 153—85.

―――― (1953). *Three Essays on the Theory of Sexuality*. In J. Strachey (ed.), *Collected Works of Freud*, London: Hogarth, vol. 7, 125—243. (First published 1905).

―――― (1955a). Some neurotic mechanisms in jealousy, paranoia and homosexuality. In J. Strachey (ed.) (in collaboration with A. Freud), *The Standard Edition of the Complete Psychological Works of Sigmund Freud*, London: Hogarth, vol. 18, 221—32. (First published 1922).

―――― (1955b). The psychogenesis of a case of homosexuality in a woman. In J. Strachey (ed.) (in collaboration with A. Freud), *The Standard Edition of the Complete Psychological Works of Sigmund Freud*, London: Hogarth, vol. 18, 145—72. (First published 1920).

―――― (1958). Psychoanalytic notes on an autobiographical account of a case of paranoia (Dementia Paranoides). In J. Strachey (ed.) (in collaboration with A. Freud). *The Standard Edition of the Complete Psychological Works of Sigmund Freud*, London: Hogarth, vol. 12, 1—82. (First published 1911).

―――― (1959). Character and anal erotism. In J. Strachey (ed.) (in collaboration with A. Freud), *The Standard Edition of the Complete Psychological Works of Sigmund Freud*, London: Hogarth, vol. 9, 169—75. (First published 1908).

―――― (1961a). Female sexuality. In J. Strachey (ed.) (in collaboration with A. Freud), *The Standard Edition of the Complete Psychological Works of Sigmund Freud*, London: Hogarth, vol. 21, 221—43. (First published 1931).

―――― (1961b). Some psychological consequences of the anatomical distinction between the sexes. In J. Strachey (ed.), *The Standard Edition of the Complete Psychological Works of Sigmund Freud*, London: Hogarth, vol. 21, 173—96. (Originally in *International Journal of Psychoanalysis*, 8, 133—42. First published 1925).

―――― (1961c). The dissolution of the Oedipus Complex. In J. Strachey (ed.), *The Standard Edition of the Complete Psychological Works of Sigmund Freud*, London: Hogarth, vol. 19, 173—9. (First published 1924).

―――― (1961d). The ego and the id. In J. Strachey (ed.), *The Standard Edition of the Complete Psychological Works of Sigmund Freud*, London: Hogarth, vol. 19, 3—66. (First published 1923).

Freund, K. W. (1974). Male homosexuality: An analysis of the pattern. In J. A. Loraine (ed.), *Understanding Homosexuality: Its Biological and Psychological Bases*, New York: American Elsevier, 25—81.

Freund, K., Langevin, R., Chamberlayne, R., Deosoran, A. and Zajac, Y. (1974a). The phobic theory of male homosexuality. *Archives of General Psychiatry*, 31, 495—9.

Freund, K., Langevin, R., Zajac, Y., Steiner, B. and Zajac, A. (1974b). Parent—child relations in transsexual and non-transsexual homosexual males. *British Journal of Psychiatry*, 124, 22—3.

Freund, K., Nagler, E., Langevin, R., Zajac, A. and Steiner, B. (1974c). Measuring feminine gender identity in homosexual males. *Archives of Sexual Behavior*, 3, 249—60.

Friberg, R. (1967). Measures of homosexuality: cross validation of 2 MMP scales and implications for usage. *Journal of Consulting Psychology*, 31, 88—91.

Frieze, I. H., Parsons, J. E., Johnson, P. B., Ruble, D. N. and Zellman, G. L. (1978). *Women and Sex Roles: A Social Psychological Perspective*. New York: Norton.

Futuyma, D. and Risch, S. (1984). Sexual orientation. *Journal of Homosexuality*, 9 (2/3), 157—68.

Gagnon, J. H. and Simon, W. (1973). *Sexual Conduct: The Social Sources of Human Sexuality*. Chicago: Aldine.

Gardner, L. I. (1975). *Endocrine and Genetic Diseases of Childhood and Adolescence*. 2nd edn. Philadelphia: Saunders.

Gigi, J. L. (1970). The overt male homosexual: a primary description of a self-selected population. Unpublished doctoral dissertation. University of Oregon.

Gladue, B., Green, R. and Hellman, R. (1984). Neuroendocrine response to estrogen and sexual orientation. *Science*, 225, 1496—9.

Goldberg, P. A. and Milstein, J. T. (1965). Perceptual investigation of psycho-analytic theory concerning latent homosexuality in women. *Perceptual and Motor Skills*, 21, 645—6.

Goldman, A. H. (1977). Plain sex. *Philosophy and Public Affairs*, 6, 267—88.

Gonsiorek, J. (1977). Psychological adjustment and homosexuality. *Journal Supplement Abstract Service* (American Psychological Association), MS 1478.

_____ (1982). Homosexuality: The end of a mental illness. *American Behavioural Scientist*, 25, 4.

Goy, R. W., Wolf, J. E. and Eisele, S. G. (1977). Experimental female hermaphro-ditism in rhesus monkeys: anatomical and psychological characteristics. In J. Money and H. Musaph (eds), *Handbook of Sexology*, New York: Elsevier, 139—56.

Graham, J. R. (1978). The Minnesota Multiphasic Personality Inventory (MMPI). In B. Wolman (ed.), *Clinical Diagnosis of Mental Disorders: A Handbook*, New York: Plenum, 311—31.

Gray, R. (1978). Sex and sexual perversion. *Journal of Philosophy*, 75, 189—99.

Green, R. (1974). *Sexual Identity Conflict in Children and Adults*. New York: Basic Books.

_____ (1975). Sexual identity: research strategies. *Archives of Sexual Behavior*, 4, 337—52.

_____ (1976). One-hundred ten feminine and masculine boys: Behavioural contrasts and demographic similarities. *Archives of Sexual Behavior*, 5 (5), 425—46.

_____ (1985). Gender identity in childhood and later sexual orientation: follow-up of 78 males. *American Journal of Psychiatry*, 142, 339—41.

Greer, G. (1970). *The Female Eunuch*. London: MacGibbon and Kee.

Grellert, E. A., Newcomb, M. and Bentler, P. (1982). Childhood play activities of male and female homosexuals and heterosexuals. *Archives of Sexual Behavior*, 11, 451—78.

Grey, A. (1974). Homosexuality – some social and legal aspects. In J. A. Loraine (ed.), *Understanding Homosexuality: Its Biological and Psychological Bases*, New York: American Elsevier, 141–58.

Griffiths, P. D., Merry, J., Browning, M. C. K., Eisinger, A. J., Huntsman, R. G., Lord, E. J. A., Polani, P. E., Tanner, J. M. and Whitehouse, R. H. (1974). Homosexual women: An endocrine and psychological study. *Journal of Endocrinology*, 63, 549–56.

Grünbaum, A. (1985). *The Foundations of Psychoanalysis*. Berkeley: University of California Press.

Gundlach, R. H. and Riess, B. F. (1968). Self and sexual identity in the female: A study of female homosexuals. In B. F. Riess (ed.), *New Directions in Mental Health*, New York: Grune and Stratton.

Hamburger, C. (1953). Desire for change of sex. 465 letters. *Acta Endocrinologie (Kbh)*, 14, 361–75.

Harding, S. (1986). *The Science Question in Feminism*. Ithaca: Cornell University Press.

Harry, J. (1984). Sexual orientation as destiny. *Journal of Homosexuality*, 10 (3/4), 111–24.

Hart, H. L. A. (1963). *Law, Liberty and Morality*. Oxford: Oxford University Press.

―――― (1973). Rawls on liberty and its priority. *University of Chicago Law Review*, 40, 534–55.

Hart, J. and Richardson, D. (1981). *The Theory and Practice of Homosexuality*. London: Routledge and Kegan Paul.

Hathaway, S. R. and McKinley, J. C. (1942). *Minnesota Multiphasic Personality Inventory*. Minneapolis: University of Minnesota Press.

Hedgpath, J. M. (1980). Employment discrimination law and the rights of gay persons. *Journal of Homosexuality*, 5, 67–78.

Hempel, C. G. (1966). *Philosophy of Natural Science*. Englewood Cliffs, NJ: Prentice-Hall.

Herbert, J. (1978). Neuro-hormonal integration of sexual behaviour in female primates. In J. B. Hutchison (ed.), *Biological Determinants of Sexual Behaviour*, Chichester: Wiley, 467–91.

Hesse, M. (1980). *Revolutions and Reconstructions in the Philosophy of Science*. Brighton: Harvester.

Heston, L. L. and Shields, J., (1968). Homosexuality in twins: A family study and a registry study. *Archives of General Psychiatry*, 18 (2), 149–60.

Hill, W. W. (1935). The status of the hermaphrodite and transvestite in Navaho culture. *American Anthropologist*, 37, 273–9.

Hilton, B., Callahan, D., Harris, M., Condliffe, P. and Berkley, B. (1973). *Ethical Issues in Human Genetics*. New York: Plenum.

Hinde, R. (1984). Why do the sexes behave differently in close relationships? *Journal of Social and Personal Relationships*, 1, 471–501.

Hinz, G., Schlenker, G. and Dörner, G. (1974). Pranatale Behandlung von Schweinen mit Testosteronpropionat. *Endokrinologie*, 63, 161–5.

Hodges, J. K. and Hearn, J. P. (1978). A positive feedback effect of oestradiol on

LH release in the male marmoset monkey, *Callithrix jacchus. Journal of Reproduction and Fertility*, 52, 83—6.

Hoebel, E. A. (1960). *The Cheyennes: Indians of the Great Plains*. New York: Holt, Rinehart, and Winston.

Hogan, R. A., Fox, A. N. and Kitchner, J. H. (1977). Attitudes, opinions, and sexual development of 205 homosexual women. *Journal of Homosexuality*, 3 (2), 123—36.

Horner, T. (1978). *Jonathan Loved David*. Philadelphia: Westminster.

Hoult, T. F. (1984). Human sexuality in biological perspective: theoretical and methodological considerations. *Journal of Homosexuality*, 9 (2/3), 137—55.

Hrdy, S. (1981). *The Woman that Never Evolved*. Cambridge, Mass.: Harvard University Press.

Hudson, W. D. (1970). *Modern Moral Philosophy*. London: Macmillan.

Hull, D. L. (1974). *Philosophy of Biological Science*. Englewood Cliffs, NJ: Prentice-Hall.

Humphreys, L. (1970). *Tearoom Trade: Impersonal Sex in Public Places*. Chicago: Aldine.

Hutchinson, G. E. (1959). A speculative consideration of certain possible forms of sexual selection in man. *American Naturalist*, 93 (869), 81—91.

Institute of Medicine/National Academy of Sciences (1986). *Mobilizing Against AIDS: The Unfinished Story of a Virus*. Cambridge, Mass.: Harvard University Press.

Isaac, G. L. (1980). Casting the net wide: a review of archaeological evidence for early hominid land-use and ecological relations. In L.-K. Konigsson (ed.), *Current Argument on Early Man*, Oxford: Pergamon, 226—53.

———— (1983). Aspects of human evolution. In D. S. Bendall (ed.), *Evolution from Molecules to Men*, Cambridge: Cambridge University Press, 509—43.

Jaggar, A. (1977). Relaxing the limits on preferential hiring. *Social Theory and Practice*, 4, 231—5.

Janeway, E. (1974). On 'Female sexuality'. In J. Strouse (ed.), *Women and Analysis*, New York: Grossman, 57—70.

Jones, E. (1955). *The Life and Work of Sigmund Freud*. New York: Basic Books.

Kadushin, C. (1969). *Why People Go To Psychiatrists*. New York: Atherton.

Kagan, J. (1956). The child's perception of the parent. *Journal of Abnormal and Social Psychology*, 53, 257—8.

Kagan, J. and Lemkin, J. (1960). The child's differential perception of parental attributes. *Journal of Abnormal and Social Psychology*, 61, 440—7.

Kagan, J. and Moss, H. A. (1962). *Birth to Maturity: A Study in Psychological Development*. New York: Wiley.

Kant, I. (1949). *Critique of Practical Reason*. Trans. L. W. Beck. Chicago: Chicago University Press.

———— (1959). *Foundations of the Metaphysics of Morals*. Trans. L. W. Beck. Indianapolis: Bobbs-Merrill.

———— (1963). *Lectures on Ethics*. Trans. L. Infield. New York: Harper & Row.

Kardiner, A., Karush, A. and Ovesey, L. (1959a). A methodological study of

Freudian theory: I. Basic concepts. *Journal of Nervous and Mental Disease*, 129, 11—19.

───── (1959b). A methodological study of Freudian theory: II. The libido theory. *Journal of Nervous and Mental Disease*, 129, 133—43.

─────(1959c). A methodological study of Freudian theory: III. Narcissism, bisexuality and the dual instinct theory. *Journal of Nervous and Mental Disease*, 129, 207—21.

───── (1959d). A methodological study of Freudian theory: IV. The structural hypothesis, the problem of anxiety, and post-Freudian ego psychology. *Journal of Nervous and Mental Disease*, 129, 341—56.

Karsch, F. J., Dievschke, D. J. and Knobie, E. (1973). Sexual differentiation of pituitary function: apparent differences between primates and rodents. *Science*, 179, 484—6.

Kaye, H. E., Berl, S., Clare, J., Eleston, M., Gershwin, B. S., Gershwin, P., Kogan, L. S., Torda, C. and Wilbur, C. B. (1967). Homosexuality in women. *Archives of General Psychiatry*, 17, 626—34.

Kellert, S. R. (1976). A sociocultural concept of health and illness. *Journal of Medicine and Philosophy*, 1, 222—8.

Kennedy, L. (1960). *Ten Rillington Place*. London: Gollancz.

Kenyon, F. E. (1968). Physique and physical health of female homosexuals. *Journal of Neurology, Neurosurgery, and Psychiatry*, 31 (5), 487—9.

───── (1974). Female homosexuality — a review. In J. A. Loraine (ed.), *Understanding Homosexuality; Its Biological and Psychological Bases*. New York: American Elsevier, 83—119.

King, C. D. (1945). The meaning of normal. *Yale Journal of Biology and Medicine*, 17, 493—501.

Kinsey, A. C., Pomeroy, W. B. and Martin, C. E. (1948). *Sexual Behaviour in the Human Male*. Philadelphia: W. B. Saunders.

Kinsey, A. C., Pomeroy, W. B., Martin, C. E. and Gebhard, P. H. (1953). *Sexual Behaviour in the Human Female*. Philadelphia: W. B. Saunders.

Kitcher, P. (1983). *Abusing Science*. Cambridge, Mass.: MIT Press.

───── (1985). *Vaulting Ambition*. Cambridge, Mass.: MIT Press.

Klein, F. and Wolf, T. J. (eds) (1985). *Bisexualities: Theory and Research*. New York: Haworth Press. (Originally in *Journal of Homosexuality*, 11 (1/2), 1—255.)

Klein, M. (1932). *The Psychoanalysis of Children*, London: Hogarth Press.

Klerman, G. L. (1977). Mental illness, the medical model, and psychiatry. *Journal of Medicine and Philosophy*, 2, 220—43.

Kline, P. (1981). *Fact and Fantasy in Freudian Theory*. 2nd edn. London: Methuen.

Knapp, P. H. (1966). Libido: A latter-day look. *Journal of Nervous and Mental Disease*, 142, 395—417.

Knutson, D. C. (ed.) (1980). Homosexuality and the law. A special double issue of the *Journal of Homosexuality*, 5, 3—160.

Kohlberg, L. (1966). A cognitive-developmental analysis of children's sex-role concepts and attitudes. In E. Maccoby (ed.), *The Development of Sex Differences*, Stanford: Stanford University Press, 82—173.

_____ (1969). Stages and sequence: the cognitive-developmental approach to socialization. In D. A. Goslin (ed.), *Handbook of Socialization Theory and Research*, Chicago: Rand McNally, 374—480.

Körner, S. (1955). *Kant*. Harmondsworth, Middlesex: Penguin.

Kremer, M. W. and Rifkin, A. (1969). The early development of homosexuality: a study of adolescent lesbians. *American Journal of Psychiatry*, 126, 91—6.

Kuhn, T. (1970). *The Structure of Scientific Revolutions*. 2nd edn. Chicago: University of Chicago Press.

Lakoff, G. and Johnson, M. (1980). *Metaphors We Live By*. Chicago: University of Chicago Press.

Le Baron, R. (1972). *Hormones: A Delicate Balance*. New York: Pegasus.

Lebovits, P. S. (1972). Feminine behaviour in boys: aspects of its outcome. *American Journal of Psychiatry*, 128 (3), 1283—9, 103—9.

Leiser, B. M. (1979). *Liberty, Justice and Morals*. 2nd edn. New York: Macmillan.

Lester, D. (1975). *Unusual Sexual Behaviour: The Standard Deviations*. Springfield: Thomas.

Levin, R. B. (1966). An empirical test of the female castration complex. *Journal of Abnormal Psychology*, 71, 181—8.

Levitan, M. and Montagu, A. (1977). *Textbook of Human Genetics*. New York: Oxford University Press.

Lev-Ran, A. (1977). Sex reversal as related to clinical syndromes in human beings. In J. Money and H. Musaph (eds), *Handbook of Sexology*, New York: Elsevier, 157—76.

Lewontin, R. C. (1977). Sociobiology: a caricature of Darwinism. In F. Asquith and F. Suppe (eds), *PSA 1976*, East Lansing, Mich.: Philosophy of Science Association, vol. 2, 22—31.

Lewontin, R. C., Rose, S. and Kamin, L. J. (1984). *Not in Our Genes: Biology, Ideology, and Human Nature*. New York: Pantheon.

Loney, J. (1973). Family dynamics in homosexual women. *Archives of Sexual Behaviour*, 2, 343--50.

Loraine, J. A., Adamopoulos, D. A., Kirkham, K. E., Ismaie, A. A. A. and Dove, G. A. (1971). Patterns of hormone excretion in male and female homosexuals. *Nature*, 234, 552—5.

Loraine, J. A., Ismaie, A. A. A., Adamopoulos, D. A. and Dove, G. A. (1970). Endocrine function in male and female homosexuals. *British Medical Journal*, 4, 406—8.

MacCulloch, M. (1980). Biological aspects of homosexuality. *Journal of Medical Ethics*, 6, 133—8.

Macklin, R. (1972). Mental health and mental illness: Some problems of definition and concept formation. *Philosophy of Science*, 39, 341—65.

_____ (1973). The medical model in psychotherapy and psychoanalysis. *Comprehensive Psychiatry*, 14, 49—69.

Magee, B. (1978). *The Gays Among Us*. New York: Steing and Day.

Manosevitz, M. (1970). Early sexual behaviour in adult homosexual and heterosexual males. *Journal of Abnormal Psychology*, 76 (3), 396—402.

—— (1971). Item analysis of the MMPI *Mf* scale using homosexual and heterosexual males. *Journal of Consulting and Clinical Psychology*, 35, 395—9.

Margolis, J. (1975). The question of homosexuality. In R. Baker and F. Elliston
(eds), *Philosophy and Sex*, Buffalo: Prometheus, 288—302.

—— (1976). The concept of disease. *Journal of Medicine and Philosophy*, 1, 238—55.

—— (1980). The concept of mental illness: a philosophical examination. In
B. A. Brody and H. T. Engelhardt, Jr., (eds), *Mental Illness: Law and Public
Policy*, Dordrecht: Reidel, 3—23.

Marmor, J. (ed.) (1980). *Homosexual Behaviour: A Modern Reappraisal*. New York:
Basic Books.

Marotta, T. (1981). *The Politics of Homosexuality*. Boston: Houghton Mifflin.

Martin, D. and Lyon, P. (1972). *Lesbian/Woman*. New York: Bantam.

Martin, J. C., Mewett, A. W. and Cartwright, I. (1974). *Martin's Annual Criminal
Code*. Agincourt, Ont.: Canada Law Book.

Masters, W. H. and Johnson, V. E. (1966). *Human Sexual Response*. Boston: Little,
Brown, and Co.

—— (1979). *Homosexuality in Perspective*. Boston: Little, Brown, and Co.

May, R. M. and Anderson, R. M. (1987). Transmission dynamics of HIV infection.
Nature, 326, 137—42.

Maynard Smith, J. (1975). *The Theory of Evolution*. 3rd edn. Harmondsworth,
Middlesex: Penguin.

—— (1978). The evolution of behaviour. *Scientific American*, 239 (3), 176—93.

McCrary, J. and Gutierrez, L. (1980). The homosexual person in the military and
in national security employment. *Journal of Homosexuality*, 5, 115—46.

McGuire, R. J., Carlisle, J. M. and Young, B. G. (1965). Sexual deviations as
conditioned behaviour: a hypothesis. *Behavior Research and Therapy*, 2, 185—90.

McIntosh, M. (1968). The homosexual role. *Social Problems*, 16, 182—92.

McMullin, E. (1983). Values in science. In P. Asquith and T. Nickles (eds), *PSA
1982*, East Lansing, Mich.: Philosophy of Science Association, vol. 2, 3—28.

Medawar, P. B. (1975). Review of *The Victim is Always the Same* by I. S. Cooper.
New York Review of Books, 21 (21), 17.

Merskey, H. (1986). Variable meanings for the definition of disease. *Journal of
Medicine and Philosophy*, 11, 215—32.

Metraux, A. (1942). Le Shamanisme Araucan. *Revista del Instituto de Antropologia*,
2, 309—62.

Meyer-Bahlburg, F. L. (1977). Sex hormones and male homosexuality in
comparative perspective. *Archives of Sexual Behaviour*, 6 (4), 297—325.

—— (1979). Sex hormones and female homosexuality: A critical examination.
Archives of Sexual Behaviour, 8, 101—19.

—— (ed.) (1984a). *Gender Development: Social Influences and Prenatal Hormone
Effects*. Special issue of *Archives of Sexual Behavior*, 13, 391—502.

—— (1984b). Psychoendocrine research on sexual orientation. Current status
and future options. In G. J. De Vries, J. De Bruin, H. Uylings and M. Corner
(eds), *Progress in Brain Research*, Amsterdam: Elsevier, vol. 61, 375—98.

Michalos, A. (1980—2). *North American Social Report: A Comparative Study of the*

Quality of Life in Canada and the USA from 1964 to 1974. Dordrecht: Reidel.

Mill, J. S. (1910). *Utilitarianism.* London: Dent. (First published 1859).

———— (1975). *On Liberty.* Ed. D. Spitz. New York: Norton. (First published 1859).

Millet, K. (1970). *Sexual Politics.* Garden City: Doubleday.

Mitchell, J. (1972). *Woman's Estate.* New York: Pantheon.

———— (1974). On Freud and the distinction between the sexes. In J. Strouse (ed.), *Women and Analysis,* New York: Grossman, 27–36.

Moberly, E. (1982). Homosexuality: restating the conservative case. *Salmagundi,* 58/9, 281–99.

Mohr, R. D. (1987). Aids, gays and state coercion. *Bioethics,* 1, 35–50.

Money, J. (1961). Sex hormones and other variables in human eroticism. In W. C. Young (ed.), *Sex and Internal Secretions,* 3rd edn, Baltimore: Williams and Wilkins, 1383–1400.

———— (1977). Prenatal deandrogenization of human beings. In J. Money and H. Musaph (eds), *Handbook of Sexology,* New York: Elsevier, 259–68.

Money, J. and Ehrhardt, A. (1972). *Man and Woman: Boy and Girl: The Differentiation and Dimorphism of Gender Identity from Conception to Maturity.* Baltimore: Johns Hopkins University Press.

Money, J. and Mathews, D. (1982). Prenatal exposure to virilizing progestins: an adult follow-up study of twelve women. *Archives of Sexual Behavior,* 11, 73–83.

Money, J. and Ogunro, C. (1974). Behavioral sexology: ten cases of genetic male intersexuality with impaired prenatal and pubertal androgenization. *Archives of Sexual Behavior,* 3, 181–205.

Money, J. and Schwartz, M. (1978). Biosocial determinants of gender identity differentiation and development. In J. B. Hutchison (ed.), *Biological Determinants of Sexual Behaviour,* New York: Wiley, 765–84.

Money, J., Schwartz, M. and Lewis, V. G. (1984). Adult erotosexual status and fetal hormonal masculinization and demasculinization. *Psychoneuroendocrinology,* 9, 405–14.

Morgan, E. (1973). *The Descent of Woman.* New York: Bantam Books.

Murphy, J. G. (1982). *Evolution, Morality, and the Meaning of Life.* Totowa, NJ: Rowman and Littlefield.

Nagel, E. (1961). *The Structure of Science.* London: Routledge and Kegan Paul.

Nagel, T. (1969). Sexual perversion. *Journal of Philosophy,* 66, 1–17.

Oster, G. and Wilson, E. O. (1978). *Caste and Ecology in the Social Insects.* Princeton: Princeton University Press.

Ovesey, L. (1954). The homosexual conflict: an adaptational analysis. *Psychiatry,* 17, 243–50.

———— (1955a). Pseudohomosexuality, the paranoid mechanism, and paranoia: an adaptational revision of a classical Freudian theory. *Psychiatry,* 18, 163–73.

———— (1955b). The pseudohomosexual anxiety. *Psychiatry,* 18, 17–25.

———— (1956). Masculine aspirations in women: an adaptational analysis. *Psychiatry,* 19, 341–51.

———— (1965). Pseudohomosexuality and homosexuality in men: Psychodynamics as a guide to treatment. In J. Marmor (ed.), *Sexual Inversion: The Multiple Roots of Homosexuality*, New York: Basic Books, 211—33.

Ovesey, L. and Person, E. (1973). Gender identity and sexual psychopathology in men: a psychodynamic analysis of homosexuality, transsexualism, and transvestitism. *Journal of the American Academy of Psychoanalysts*, 1, 53—72.

Panton, J. R. (1960). A new MMPI scale for the identification of homosexuality. *Journal of Clinical Psychology*, 16, 17—21.

Pap, A. (1958). On the empirical interpretation of psychoanalytic concepts. In S. Hook (ed.), *Psychoanalysis, Scientific Method, and Philosophy*, New York: New York University Press, 283—97.

Parks, G. A., Korth-Schutz, S., Penny, R., Hilding, R. F., Dumars, K. W., Frasier, S. D. and New, M. I. (1974). Variation in pituitary-gonadal function in adolescent male homosexuals and heterosexuals. *Journal of Clinical Endocrinology and Metabolism*, 39 (4), 796—801.

Paton, W. (1918). *Greek Anthology*. Cambridge, Mass.: Harvard University Press.

Patton, C. (1985). *Sex and Germs: The Politics of AIDS*. Boston: South End Press.

Person, E. (1980). Sexuality as the mainstay of identity: psychoanalytic perspectives. *Signs*, 5, 605—30.

Pierce, D. M. (1973). Test and non-test correlates of active and situational homosexuality. *Psychiatry*, 10, 23—6.

Pilbeam, D. (1984). The descent of Hominoids and Hominids. *Scientific American*, 250/3, 84—97.

Pillard, R. C. and Weinrich, J. D. (1986). Evidence of familial nature of male homosexuality. *Archives of General Psychiatry*, 43, 808—12.

Pitcher, E. G. and Prelinger, E. (1963). *Children Tell Stories: An Analysis of Fantasy*. New York: International Universities.

Plato (1941). *The Republic*. Trans. F. M. Cornford. Oxford: Oxford University Press.

Plummer, K. (1981). *The Making of the Modern Homosexual*. London: Hutchinson.

Polanyi, M. (1968). Life's irreducible structure. *Science*, 160, 1308—12.

Pomeroy, W. B. (1975). The diagnosis and treatment of transvestites and transsexuals. *Journal of Sex and Marital Therapy*, 1, 215—24.

Popper, K. R. (1959). *The Logic of Scientific Discovery*. London: Hutchinson.

—— (1962). *Conjectures and Refutations*. London: Routledge and Kegan Paul.

Rado, S. (1940). A critical examination of the concept of bisexuality. *Psychosomatic Medicine*, 2, 459—67. (Reprinted in J. Marmor (ed.), *Sexual Inversion: The Multiple Roots of Homosexuality*, New York: Basic Books).

—— (1949). An adaptational view of sexual behaviour. In P. Hock and J. Zubin (eds), *Psychosexual development in Health and Disease*, New York: Grune and Stratton, 186—213.

Rainer, J. D. (1976). Genetics and homosexuality. In A. Kaplan (ed.), *Human Behaviour Genetics*, Springfield: Thomas, 301—16.

Rainer, J. D., Mesnikoff, A., Kolb, L. and Carr, A. (1960). Homosexuality and heterosexuality in identical twins. *Psychosomatic Medicine*, 22, 251—8.

Ramsay, R. W., Heringa, P. M. and Boorsma, I. (1974). A case study: homosexuality in the Netherlands. In J. A. Loraine (ed.), *Understanding Homosexuality: Its Biological and Psychological Bases*, New York: American Elsevier, 121—40.

Rawls, J. (1971). *A Theory of Justice.* Cambridge, Mass.: Belknap.

Reclus, E. (1896). *Primitive Folk: Studies in Comparative Ethnology.* London: Scott.

Repace, J. L. and Lowrey, A. H. (1980). Indoor air pollution, tobacco smoke, and public health. *Science,* 208, 464–72.

Reyes, F. I., Bonodtsky, R. S., Winter, J. S. D. and Faiman, C. (1974). Studies on human sexual development II. *Journal of Clinical Endocrinology,* 38, 612–17.

Richardson, D. (1981). Theoretical perspectives on homosexuality. In J. Hart and D. Richardson (eds), *The Theory and Practice of Homosexuality,* London: Routledge and Kegan Paul, 5–37.

———— (1984). The dilemma of essentiality in homosexual theory. *Journal of Homosexuality,* 9 (2/3), 79–90.

Ricketts, W. (1984). Biological research on homosexuality: Ansell's cow or Occam's Razor? *Journal of Homosexuality,* 9 (2/3), 65–93.

Rogers, L. and Walsh, J. (1982). Shortcomings of the psychomedical research of John Money and co-workers into sex differences in behaviour: Social and political implications. *Sex Roles,* 8 (3), 269–81.

Rose, S. (1982). *Towards a Liberatory Biology.* London: Allison and Busby.

Rosenberg, A. (1985). *The Structure of Biological Science.* Cambridge: Cambridge University Press.

Rosenthal, R. (1966). *Experimenter Effects in Behavioral Research.* New York: Appleton-Century-Crofts.

Ross, M. W. (1980). Retrospective distortion in homosexual research. *Archives of Sexual Behavior,* 9, 523–31.

Ross, M. W., Rogers, L. J. and McCulloch, H. (1978). Stigma, sex and society: a new look at gender differentiation and sexual variation. *Journal of Homosexuality,* 3 (4), 315–30.

Roth, H. L. (1896). *The Natives of Sarawak and British North Borneo.* London: Truelove and Hanson.

Ruddick, S. (1975). Better sex. In R. Baker and F. Elliston (eds), *Philosophy and Sex,* Buffalo: Prometheus, 83–104.

Ruse, M. (1973). *The Philosophy of Biology.* London: Hutchinson.

———— (1976). Reduction in genetics. In R. S. Cohen, C. Hooker, A. Michalos and J. Van Evra (eds), *PSA 1974,* Dordrecht: Reidel, 653–70.

———— (1979a). *Sociobiology: Sense or Nonsense?* Dordrecht: Reidel.

———— (1979b). *The Darwinian Revolution.* Chicago: University of Chicago Press.

———— (1981a). Are there gay genes? The sociobiology of homosexuality. *Journal of Homosexuality,* 6 (4), 5–34.

———— (1981b). *Is Science Sexist? And Other Problems in the Biomedical Sciences.* Dordrecht: Reidel.

———— (1981c). The last word on teleology, or optimality models vindicated. In his *Is Science Sexist? And Other Problems in the Biomedical Sciences,* Dordrecht: Reidel, 85–101.

———— (1981d). What kind of revolution occurred in geology? In P. Asquith and I. Hacking (eds), *PSA 1978,* East Lansing, Mich.: PSA, vol. 2, 240–73.

———— (1982a). Creation-science is not science. *Science, Technology and Human Values,* 40, 72–8.

———— (1982b). *Darwinism Defended: A Guide to the Evolution Controversies.* Reading,

Mass.: Addison-Wesley.

———— (1984a). A philosopher's day in court. In A. Montagu (ed.), *Science and Creationism*, New York: Oxford University Press, 311—42.

———— (1984b). The sociobiology of human sexuality. In D. M. Brock and A. Harward (eds), *The Culture of Biomedicine*, Newark: University of Delaware Press, vol. 1, 98—123.

———— (1985). *Sociobiology: Sense or Nonsense?* 2nd edn. Dordrecht: Reidel.

———— (1986). *Taking Darwin Seriously*. Oxford: Blackwell.

———— (1987). Darwin and determinism. *Zygon* 22.

Saghir, M. T. and Robins, E. (1973). *Male and Female Homosexuality: A Comprehensive Investigation*. Baltimore: Williams and Wilkins.

Sahlins, M. (1976). *The Use and Abuse of Biology*. Ann Arbor: University of Michigan Press.

Salmon, W. (1973). *Logic*. 2nd edn. Englewood Cliffs, NJ: Prentice-Hall.

Salzman, L. (1965). 'Latent' homosexuality. In J. Marmor (ed.), *Sexual Inversion: The Multiple Roots of Homosexuality*, New York: Basic Books, 234—47.

Sanders, R., Bain, J. and Langevin, R. (1984). Peripheral sex hormones, homosexuality, and gender identity. In R. Langevin (ed.), *Erotic Preference, Gender Identity, and Aggression in Men*, Hillsdale, NJ: Erlbaum, 227—47.

Sartre, J. -P. (1947). *The Age of Reason*. London: Hamish Hamilton.

———— (1962). *Saint Genet*. Paris: Gallimard.

———— (1965). *The Humanism of Existentialism*. In W. Baskin (ed.), *The Philosophy of Existentialism*, New York: Philosophical Library, 31—62.

Schmidt, G. (1984). Allies and persecutors: science and medicine in the homosexuality issue. *Journal of Homosexuality*, 10 (3/4), 127—40.

Schwartz, M. F. and Money, J. (1983). Dating, romance and sexuality in young adult androgenital females. *Neuroendocrinological Letters*, 5, 132.

Scruton, R. (1986). *Sexual Desire*. London: Weidenfeld.

Shea, J. G. (1903). *Discovery and Exploration of the Mississippi Valley with the Original Narratives of Marquette, Allouez, Membre and Anastase Doucy*. 2nd edn. Albany: McDonough.

Sheppard, P. M. (1975). *Natural Selection and Heredity*. 4th edn. London: Hutchinson.

Sher, G. (1975). Justifying reverse discrimination in employment. *Philosophy and Public Affairs*, 4, 159—70.

Sher, G., Simon, R. L. and Gahringer, R. E. (1979). Symposium on reverse discrimination. *Ethics* 90, 81—114.

Short, R. V. (1974). Sexual differentiation of the brain of the sheep. In M. Forest and J. Bertrand (eds), *Endocrinologie Sexuelle de La Periode Perinatale*, Paris: Inserm, 121—42.

Siegel, N. H. (1962). Characteristics of patients in psychoanalysis. *Journal of Nervous and Mental Disease*, 135, 155—8.

Siegelman, M. (1972a). Adjustment of homosexual and heterosexual women. *British Journal of Psychiatry*, 120, 477—81.

———— (1972b). Adjustment of male homosexuals and heterosexuals. *Archives of Sexual Behavior*, 2, 9—25.

———— (1973). Birth order and family size of homosexual men and women. *Journal of Consulting and Clinical Psychology*, 41, 164.

———— (1974a). Parental background of homosexual and heterosexual women. *British Journal of Psychiatry*, 124 (578): 14—21.

———— (1974b). Parental background of male homosexuals and heterosexuals. *Archives of Sexual Behavior*, 3, 3—18.

———— (1978). Psychological adjustment of homosexual and heterosexual men: a cross-national replication. *Archives of Sexual Behavior*, 7, 1—11.

———— (1979). Adjustment of homosexual and heterosexual women: a cross-national replication. *Archives of Sexual Behavior*, 8, 121—5.

Siguish, V., Schorsch, E., Dannecker, M. and Schmidt, G. (1982). Official statement by the German Society for Sex Research (Deutsche Gesellschaft für sexualforschung e. v.) on the research of Prof. Dr. Gunter Dörner on the subject of homosexuality. *Archives of Sexual Behavior*, 11 (5), 445—9.

Silverman, L. H., Klinger, H., Lustbader, L., Farrell, J. and Martin, A. D. (1972). The effects of subliminal drive stimulation on the speech of stutterers. *Journal of Nervous and Mental Disease*, 155, 14—21.

Silverman, L. H., Kwawer, J. S., Wolitzky, C. and Coron, M. (1973). An experimental study of aspects of the psychoanalytic theory of male homosexuality. *Journal of Abnormal Psychology*, 82, 178—88.

Silverstein, C. and White, E. (1977). *The Joy of Gay Sex*. New York: Simon and Schuster.

Sisley, E. L. and Harris, B. (1977). *The Joy of Lesbian Sex*. New York: Simon and Schuster.

Snortum, J. R., Gillespie, J. F., Marshall, J. E., McLaughin, J. P. and Mosberg, L. (1969). Family dynamics and homosexuality. *Psychological Reports*, 24, 763—70.

Socarides, C. (1968). *The Overt Homosexual*. New York: Jason Aronson.

———— (1973). Homosexuality: Findings derived from 15 years of clinical research. A Symposium: Should homosexuality be in the APA nomenclature? *American Journal of Psychiatry*, 130 (1973), 1212—13.

———— (1978). *Homosexuality*. New York: Jason Aronson.

Solomon, D. M. (1980). The emergence of associational rights for homosexual persons. *Journal of Homosexuality*, 5, 147—56.

Staudt, J. and Dörner, G. (1968). Untersuchungen über veranderungen der Zellkerne der Area praeoptic und des vorderen Anteils der Area hypothalamica anterior neonatal kastrierter mannlicher Ratte. *Zeitschrift für Mikroskopisch-Anatomische Forschung*, 79, 363—72.

Stephen, J. F. (1874). *Liberty, Equality, Fraternity*. 2nd edn. London: Smith Elgard.

Stoller, R. (1968). *Sex and Gender: On the Development of Masculinity and Femininity*. New York: Science House.

———— (1975). *Perversion: The Erotic Form of Hatred*. New York: Pantheon.

———— (1976). *Sex and Gender, Volume II: The Transsexual Experiment*. New York: Aronson.

Sulloway, F. (1979). *Freud: Biologist of the Mind*. New York: Basic Books.

Suppe, F. (1972). *The Structure of Scientific Theories*. Urbana: University of Illionois

Press.

Symons, D. (1979). *The Evolution of Human Sexuality*. New York: Oxford University Press.

Szasz, T. S. (1961). *The Myth of Mental Illness*. New York: Delta.

Thompson, C. (1963). Changing concepts of homosexuality in psychoanalysis. In H. M. Ruitenbeek (ed.), *The Problem of Homosexuality in Modern Society*, New York: Dutton.

Thompson, N. L., Jr., Schwartz, D. M., McCandless, B. R. and Edwards, D. A. (1973). Parent-child relationships and sexual identity in male and female homosexuals and heterosexuals. *Journal of Consulting and Clinical Psychology*, 41, 120−7.

Tindall, R. H. (1978). The male adolescent involved with a pederast becomes an adult. *Journal of Homosexuality*, 3 (4), 373−82.

Tripp, C. A. (1975). *The Homosexual Matrix*. New York: McGraw-Hill.

Trivers, R. L. (1971). The evolution of reciprocal altruism. *Quarterly Review of Biology*, 46, 35−57.

—— (1974). Parent-offspring conflict. *American Zoologist*, 14, 249−64.

Turner, C. D. and Bagnara, J. T. (1971). *General Endocrinology*. Philadelphia: Saunders.

Ungaretti, J. R. (1982). De-moralizing morality: where Dover's *Greek Homosexuality* leaves us. *Journal of Homosexuality*, 8 (1), 1−17.

Vance, E. B. and Wager, N. N. (1976). Written descriptions of orgasm: a study of sex differences. *Archives of Sexual Behavior*, 5, 87−98.

Verstraete, B. C. (1977). Homosexuality in ancient Greek and Roman civilization: a critical bibliography. *Journal of Homosexuality*, 3 (1), 79−89.

Ward, I. L. (1972). Prenatal stress feminizes and demasculinizes the behaviour of males. *Science*, 175, 82−4.

Weeks, J. (1977). *Coming Out: Homosexual Politics in Britain, from the Nineteenth Century to the Present*. London: Quartet.

—— (1981). *Sex, Politics and Society*. London: Longman.

—— (1985). *Sexuality and Its Discontents*. London: Routledge and Kegan Paul.

Weinrich, J. D. (1976). Human Reproductive Strategy. I Environmental Predictability and Reproductive Strategy; Effects of Social Class and Race. II Homosexuality and Non-Reproduction; Some Evolutionary Models. Unpublished PhD thesis, Harvard University.

—— (1978). Nonreproduction, homosexuality, transsexualism, and intelligence. A systematic literature search. *Journal of Homosexuality*, 3 (3), 275−89.

—— (1982). Is homosexuality biologically natural? In W. Paul, J. D. Weinrich, J. C. Gonsiorek and M. E. Hatvedt (eds), *Homosexuality: Social, Psychological, and Biological Issues*, Beverly Hills: Sage, 197−208.

—— (1987). A new sociobiological theory of homosexuality applicable to societies with universal marriage. *Ethology and Sociobiology*, 8, 37−48.

West, D. J. (1959−60). Parental figures in the genesis of male homosexuality. *International Journal of Social Psychiatry*, 64, 169−79.

—— (1967). *Homosexuality*. Harmondsworth: Penguin.

_____ (1977). *Homosexuality Re-Examined*. Minneapolis: University of Minnesota Press.

Whitam, F. (1977). Childhood indicators of male homosexuality. *Archives of Sexual Behavior*, 6, 89–96.

_____ (1983). Culturally invariable properties of male homosexuality: tentative conclusions from cross-cultural research. *Archives of Sexual Behavior*, 12, 207–26.

Whitam, F. and Zent, M. (1984). A cross-cultural assessment of early cross-gender behavior and familial factors in male homosexuality. *Archives of Sexual Behavior*, 13, 427–39.

Williams, C. J. amd Weinberg, M. S. (1971). *Homosexuals and the Military: A Study of Less than Honorable Discharge*. New York: Harper and Row.

Wilson, E. O. (1975). *Sociobiology: The New Synthesis*. Cambridge, Mass.: Harvard University Press.

Wilson, E. O. (1978). *On Human Nature*. Cambridge, Mass.: Harvard University Press.

Wilson, W. P., Zung, W. W. K. and Lee, J. C. M. (1972). Homosexual's sleep arousal patterns found different. *Psychiatric News*, 7, 14, 13.

Wolfenden, J. (1963). *The Wolfenden Report: Report of the Committee on Homosexual Offenses and Prostitution*. New York: Stein and Day.

Wolff, R. P. (1977). *Understanding Rawls*. Princeton: Princeton University Press.

Wollheim, R. and Hopkins, J. (1982). *Philosophical Essays on Freud*. Cambridge: Cambridge University Press.

Yalom, I., Green, R. and Fisk, N. (1973). Prenatal exposure to female hormones – effect on psychosexual development in boys. *Archives of General Psychiatry*, 28, 554–61.

Zuger, B. (1978). Effeminate behaviour present in boys from childhood: ten additional years to follow-up. *Comparative Psychiatry*, 19, 363–9.

Index